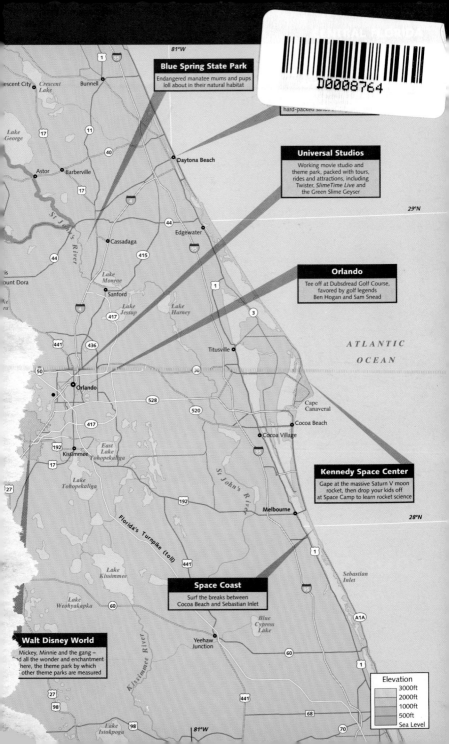

81°W

Blue Spring State Park
Endangered manatee mums and pups
loll about in their natural habitat

hard-packed sands

Universal Studios
Working movie studio and
theme park, packed with tours,
rides and attractions, including
Twister, *SlimeTime Live* and
the Green Slime Geyser

29°N

Orlando
Tee off at Dubsdread Golf Course,
favored by golf legends
Ben Hogan and Sam Snead

ATLANTIC

OCEAN

Kennedy Space Center
Gape at the massive Saturn V moon
rocket, then drop your kids off
at Space Camp to learn rocket science

28°N

Space Coast
Surf the breaks between
Cocoa Beach and Sebastian Inlet

Walt Disney World
Mickey, Minnie and the gang –
and all the wonder and enchantment
here, the theme park by which
other theme parks are measured

Crescent City
Crescent Lake
Bunnell
Lake George
Astor • Barberville
St John's River
Cassadaga
Lake Monroe
Sanford
Lake Jessup
Lake Harney
Orlando
East Lake Tohopekaliga
Kissimmee
Lake Tohopekaliga
Florida's Turnpike (toll)
Lake Kissimmee
Lake Weohyakapka
Lake Istokpoga
Daytona Beach
Edgewater
Titusville
Cape Canaveral
Cocoa Beach
Cocoa Village
Melbourne
Sebastian Inlet
Blue Cypress Lake
Yeehaw Junction
Kissimmee River
St John's River
Mount Dora

81°W

Elevation
3000ft
2000ft
1000ft
500ft
Sea Level

Contents – Text WITHDRAWN

WALT DISNEY WORLD RESORT 88

UNIVERSAL ORLANDO RESORT 116

SPACE COAST 126

NORTH OF ORLANDO 142

SOUTH OF ORLANDO 157

INDEX 188

MAP LEGEND back page

METRIC CONVERSION inside back cover

Contents – Maps

MAP INDEX

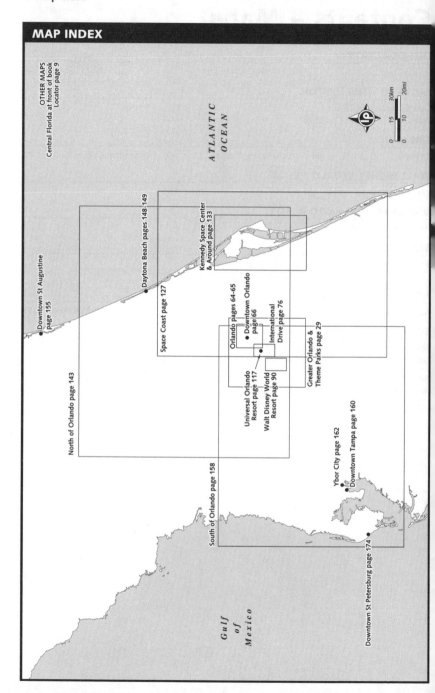

OTHER MAPS
Central Florida at front of book
Locator page 9

ATLANTIC OCEAN

Downtown St Augustine page 155

Daytona Beach pages 148-149

Kennedy Space Center & Around page 133

Space Coast page 127

North of Orlando page 143

Orlando pages 64-65

Downtown Orlando page 66

International Drive page 76

Greater Orlando & Theme Parks page 29

Universal Orlando Resort page 117

Walt Disney World Resort page 90

South of Orlando page 158

Ybor City page 162

Downtown Tampa page 160

Gulf of Mexico

Downtown St Petersburg page 174

30km
20mi
0   15
0   10

The Author

Wendy Taylor was born in October 1971, the same month Walt Disney World was born, and was so christened because of the Peter Pan story. At heart, she's most like Belle, a dreamer and a bookworm who's drawn to underdogs and other strange people.

She's lived in Alaska, Russia and even Delaware, but she now resides in Berkeley, California and works as a freelance travel writer, editor and actor. Until 2002, she worked on staff for Lonely Planet as an editor in the so-hip and exciting Oakland, California office. As an LP author, she contributed to *Russia & Belarus*. More recently, she traveled to Thailand to research *Thailand's Islands & Beaches,* where she enjoyed the fact that she didn't have to stand in any lines for a good two months.

FROM THE AUTHOR

A huge thank you to *Florida* writers Kim Grant, Elaine Merrill and especially Paige Penland, whose text and advice were instrumental in putting together this book. And an extra thank you to Paige for her wonderful boxed text on the *Columbia*.

More LP thanks go to Michele Posner, Susan Rimerman and Erin Corrigan, who were instrumental in getting me this assignment and in guiding me along. Also, editor Danielle North's patience and great editorial instincts had a tremendous positive impact on this book's production.

Barry Sollenberger deserves a big *spasibo* for his boxed text on the Buccaneers, as well as for his support and priceless friendship.

Last but not least, Rebecca Terry and Matthew Wood were my excellent travel companions for parts of this trip and spared me the embarrassment of having to ask 12-year-old boys if I could sit with them on the rides. Thanks to both of you for the laughter and for your patience.

This Book

This 1st edition of *Orlando & Central Florida* was written by Wendy Taylor. Wendy drew on material from the 3rd edition of Lonely Planet's *Florida* by Kim Grant, Paige R Penland and Elaine Merrill.

FROM THE PUBLISHER

This title was commissioned and developed in Lonely Planet's US office by Erin Corrigan and Jay Cooke; Graham Neale commissioned and developed the maps. In the Melbourne office, Danielle North coordinated the editing and proofing, with invaluable assistance from Melanie Dankel, Stefanie Di Trocchio, Kate James, Stephanie Pearson, Cecilia Thom, Katrina Webb and Simon Williamson. Anneka Imkamp coordinated the mapping. Sally Darmody coordinated the colour and layout. Simon Bracken designed the cover. Glenn Beanland assisted with the images. Alison Lyall assisted with last minute map corrections. Adriana Mammarella and Kate McDonald did the layout checks. Project managers Huw Fowles and Eoin Dunlevy streamlined the whole process.

Foreword

ABOUT LONELY PLANET GUIDEBOOKS

The story begins with a classic travel adventure: Tony and Maureen Wheeler's 1972 journey across Europe and Asia to Australia. There was no useful information about the overland trail then, so Tony and Maureen published the first Lonely Planet guidebook to meet a growing need.

From a kitchen table, Lonely Planet has grown to become the largest independent travel publisher in the world, with offices in Melbourne (Australia), Oakland (USA), London (UK) and Paris (France).

Today Lonely Planet guidebooks cover the globe. There is an ever-growing list of books and information in a variety of media. Some things haven't changed. The main aim is still to make it possible for adventurous travellers to get out there – to explore and better understand the world.

At Lonely Planet we believe travellers can make a positive contribution to the countries they visit – if they respect their host communities and spend their money wisely. Since 1986 a percentage of the income from each book has been donated to aid projects and human rights campaigns, and, more recently, to wildlife conservation.

UPDATES & READER FEEDBACK

Things change – prices go up, schedules change, good places go bad and bad places go bankrupt. Nothing stays the same. So, if you find things better or worse, recently opened or long-since closed, please tell us and help make the next edition even more accurate and useful.

Lonely Planet thoroughly updates each guidebook as often as possible – usually every two years, although for some destinations the gap can be longer. Between editions, up-to-date information is available in our free, monthly email bulletin *Comet* (W www.lonelyplanet.com/newsletters). You can also check out the *Thorn Tree* bulletin board and *Postcards* section of our website, which carry unverified, but fascinating, reports from travellers.

Tell us about it! We genuinely value your feedback. A well-travelled team at Lonely Planet reads and acknowledges every email and letter we receive and ensures that every morsel of information finds its way to the relevant authors, editors and cartographers.

Everyone who writes to us will find their name listed in the next edition of the appropriate guidebook. The very best contributions will be rewarded with a free guidebook.

We may edit, reproduce and incorporate your comments in Lonely Planet products such as guidebooks, websites and digital products, so let us know if you don't want your comments reproduced or your name acknowledged.

How to contact Lonely Planet:
Online: e talk2us@lonelyplanet.com.au, W www.lonelyplanet.com
Australia: Locked Bag 1, Footscray, Victoria 3011
UK: 72-82 Rosebery Ave, London, EC1R 4RW
USA: 150 Linden St, Oakland, CA 94607

Introduction

Take a deep breath, and prepare yourself for one of the most attraction-packed places on Earth. With the possible exception of snow-capped mountain peaks, Central Florida has everything anyone could ever want.

The most common reason people from all over the world come to this region is, of course, because it's home to the magical, mindblowingly expansive Walt Disney World. With four different major parks, two water parks, a huge arcade and shopping mall area, and several other minor attractions, Walt Disney World is the king of theme parks. But that's only the beginning. Universal Studios has moved in on the action, and its Islands of Adventure packs more cutting-edge, unforgettable thrills than any other park in North America. Wet 'n' Wild and SeaWorld are splashy attractions too, and great for a midsummer Orlando afternoon. To top it off, the resorts for the main parks are world class, and if you dig deep and carefully, you can come up with some great values.

Meanwhile, downtown Orlando has its own thing going on. It's quiet in the daytime, with a cute historic area paved with bricks

and shaded with trees covered in Spanish moss. At night, the clubs and bars open their doors with music and dancing, and all those people who work so hard for you vacationers during the day bust out and have a little fun of their own.

Not much more than an hour's drive away is the Kennedy Space Center, where even if you can't witness a launch, you can see for yourself the gargantuan Saturn V rocket; amble through the innards of a space shuttle's orbit; have lunch with an astronaut; and see some of the best 3D IMAX movies yet made. And even if you don't see a spacecraft take flight, you may very well see the rare American bald eagle do so, as nearby Merritt Island is home to several endangered species of birdlife.

In fact, you may be surprised at just how much land is still left pristine with so much going on in Central Florida. But you need only drive out less than an hour north to see the Ocala National Forest, a 400,000 acre wilderness with plenty of opportunity for camping, hiking, biking, swimming and fishing. At Blue Spring State Park the endangered, gentle

manatee, also known as the sea cow, can be easily seen floating in the springs' warmth and grazing on underwater vegetation. Alligators can be seen in the wild without much effort – just don't get too close! – and keep an eye out for adorable little prehistoric-looking armadillos crossing the roads.

Water and warmth is what has made Florida a popular destination since before recorded history. Apart from the thousands of natural springs and lakes that dot the land, there's coastline galore – it's a fact that you'll never be more than 60 miles away from either the Atlantic Ocean or the Gulf of Mexico. Daytona Beach is famous for more than fun in the sun – yes, it's a spring-break mecca, but it's also home to America's race-car history,

and thousands make a pilgrimage to the city every year to witness the Daytona 500 and satiate their need for speed. And in March bikers young and old, rich and degenerate, flood the streets with their hogs and Hondas and plenty of rowdiness during Bike Week. In the west, the Gulf coast is quieter, and the beaches reflect it. Tranquil, turquoise waters and the whitest, finest sand you've ever seen will make you want to never turn back home.

Who knows? Maybe you won't return home. Maybe you'll join the ranks of countless others who didn't, making the state one of the fastest-growing spots in the world – even beating out India and Mexico. And how could millions of relocated new Floridians be wrong?

Facts about Central Florida

HISTORY
Prehistoric Inhabitants
Even during the Ice Age, Florida drew in the crowds. Because of the warm ocean waters, the area's climate remained relatively moderate, luring mastodons, mammoths and eventually Paleo-Indians, who migrated across a strip of land that at the time connected northeastern Asia with Alaska but is now covered by the Bering Strait.

Over time, the Paleo-Indians moved southward and eventually showed up in Central Florida about 12,000 years ago. The region's mild climate and abundant water supply enabled human society here to remain more settled than societies in other parts of North America. Year-round, plants and seafood were available, which came in handy for survival once the aforementioned large mammals became extinct.

From 7500 BC to 5000 BC, fishing became more and more important as the ice melted to create rivers, and gourds, nuts, berries and deer were added to the local diet. A burial ground discovered near Windover Pond, in Titusville, shows evidence that people living at that time had religious beliefs and cared for crippled tribe members.

From 5000 BC to 3000 BC, people settled inland, and along the coast and St John's River. At this time, larger, more permanent camps, as well as small hunting camps, were developed. Hunters made points from chert (a type of rock), heating it to make a glassy substance that was easier to shape.

From 3000 BC to 500 BC, the climate in Central Florida was similar to today's. There are scores of middens remaining from this era, but many have been destroyed by mining. The small shells found in these middens show that the food source was being depleted, as people must have been eating mollusks that were not fully grown. The first samples of pottery showed up around this time.

The St John's People lived along the river of the same name, as well as around lakes and the Atlantic coast. There, they farmed corn, squash and pumpkins – successfully enough to create a food surplus, which enabled them to focus on pottery and other cultural activities.

First European Contact
Little written history exists on the various groups of Florida natives, but it seems clear that by the time the first Europeans arrived, in the 16th century, distinct groups of Indians had settled in the region. Much of what we know about these cultures is from the records and diaries of European (primarily Spanish) shipwreck survivors, who joined with the natives and had families.

Europeans brought with them citrus, cattle, new tools and weapons – all of which had beneficial influences on the natives – but they also brought smallpox and other diseases, to which the natives' immune systems were previously unexposed and countless numbers perished.

The largest group in Central Florida at the time of European contact was the Timucua (tim-**oo**-kwa), who descended from the St John's People. They were described as being very tall (it is said that height was selected for, by mating the tallest males and females) and very beautiful. Drawings of Timucuans show long nails, piercings and ornate full-body tattoos. Although they were united by one language, Timucuans identified with their village as opposed to their tribe, and villages often warred with one another, using arrows tipped with flaming Spanish moss to set fire to palm-leaf rooftops. They seemed to get along with the Europeans, and were able to improve their craft of canoe-making with the tools they obtained from their new neighbors. Northern Timucuan chiefs had several wives and were thought by Timucuans to have supernatural abilities. Timucuan religion involved gods of sun, rain and thunder, and during spiritual ceremonies, they drank a black tea that made them vomit and hallucinate. After smallpox and other diseases began to wipe them out – while the number of white faces around them continued to increase – they began to doubt their religious beliefs. Go figure.

The 20,000 or so Calusa were the largest group on the southwest part of the peninsula, around Tampa. Tantalizing speculation concerning the origin of the Calusa's hatred of the Spaniards suggests that there was contact earlier than what is recorded, but one thing is clear: the Calusa readily demonstrated their dislike of the Spanish.

European Colonization
When the first Europeans arrived in Florida, they could not have imagined a less welcoming place. Aside from hostile natives and the unforgiving heat, the land itself was swampy,

overgrown and fraught with dangers. Early settlers had to contend with alligators, poisonous snakes, thick undergrowth and vegetation, and – perhaps worst of all – biting insects in such prodigious quantities that the explorers wondered if they had arrived in hell.

As settlers pushed southward in Florida, workers related stories about black clouds of mosquitoes swarming from sunrise to sunset. And the swamplike conditions throughout the state, especially in the south, made reclaiming land a nightmare.

Nevertheless, before it was finally ceded to the USA by Spain in 1821, Florida would become to North America what Poland was once to Europe: the flattest piece of land between battling superpowers. The Florida area was occupied by several armies – a total of eight flags have flown over Amelia Island, in the northeast corner of the state.

In Come the Spaniards For the most part, historians agree that the first European explorer to reach Florida was Juan Ponce de León, who was a member of the crew on Christopher Columbus' second voyage (1493) and a fighter in the Spanish siege of Puerto Rico (1506–7). When sailing northwest from Spanish settlements in the Caribbean, Ponce de León wound up running smack into Central Florida's Atlantic coastline in 1513, probably near present-day Cape Canaveral. In honor of Pascua Florida, the Easter Feast of Flowers, he named this new land Florida.

Ponce de León didn't see anyone on the shores of what he thought was an island, but he claimed the land for Spain just in case and then tried to sail around it. After making his way around the Florida Keys, he ended up at San Carlos, near present-day Tampa, where he was welcomed by the Calusa with arms – not open ones, just arms.

The Calusa attacked until he sailed away, but Ponce de León had discovered a good source of freshwater and, he presumed, a line on all the riches the area undoubtedly held. He returned to Spain, and on the way he discovered the arid keys west of Key West and named them Las Tortugas for the huge numbers of turtles there.

King Ferdinand V named Ponce de León governor of Florida in 1514. Ponce de León was unable to return to the land until 1521, when he brought settlers, animals and missionaries back to San Carlos. You can guess what the Calusa did. Ponce de León died shortly thereafter in Cuba from a poison-arrow wound. But this did not discourage the Spanish, who were convinced – based on their experiences in South America and Mexico – that Florida was a land of untold mineral wealth.

After Ponce de León's death, several other attempts were made by the Spanish to suss out just what Florida (which then encompassed much of present-day southeastern USA) had to offer. Attempts were made by the feckless Pánfilo de Narváez, who blew it in 1528 and lost everything – four ships, 400 men (including himself) and 80 horses. Despite the disaster, a greater understanding of the land was gained from the diaries of Narváez's treasurer, Álvar Núñez Cabeza de Vaca, who survived among the Indians for eight years before rejoining his own people in Mexico City. Considerably more successful was the approximately 4000-mile expedition by Hernando de Soto in 1539. De Soto explored a huge area of southeastern USA, and when he died in 1542, he was buried in the Mississippi River.

Over the next 20 years, the Spanish were still unable to make a permanent settlement in Florida. Meanwhile, the British and French were sniffing around the region, looking for minerals and possible colonial lands.

The French Home In Despite the Spanish claim on the region, the French arrived in 1562 under the command of Jean Ribault and established a colony on Parris Island, at the southern end of present-day South Carolina. It failed, and Ribault's deputy, René de Laudonnière, pushed on to establish Fort Caroline in 1564 on the St John's River near present-day Jacksonville.

Never one to let the French pull a fast one, Spain's King Philip II sent Pedro Menéndez de Avilés to stomp the French and establish a fort of his own. In 1565 Menéndez arrived at Cape Canaveral with about 1500 soldiers and settlers. They made their way north and established St Augustine, named for the day on which they arrived on the Florida coast: August 28, the Feast Day of Saint Augustine. St Augustine was established on September 4; it was the USA's first permanent European settlement (although the problem-plagued and short-lived British settlement of Jamestown, Virginia, in 1607, is often given this honor in America's Anglocentric textbooks).

Menéndez and his troops headed north, where they were whupped by the French; they then retreated south to St Augustine. Soon after, the French, in an effort to fight *fuego* with *feu*, launched a fleet to take on the pesky

Spaniards. But the French fell victim to a coastal storm, and their fleet was destroyed. Menéndez, always optimistic, immediately forged north to the relatively unpopulated French fort and destroyed it. He executed all prisoners, as well as survivors from the French fleet washed ashore south of St Augustine. In all, almost 600 people were killed, giving the inlet its name: Matanzas (massacres).

And so a full 50 years before the Pilgrims lurched upon Plymouth Rock, and 40 before the establishment at Jamestown, Florida was finally settled for the Spanish by Menéndez.

In addition to chasing away Frenchmen and seeking to get rich, Menéndez also sought to convert the Indians to Christianity and to generally show them what swell folks the Spanish were. His goal was to establish a territory-wide series of missions, forts and trade posts.

All did not go as planned. Missionaries were murdered, and Indian uprisings became as common as one would expect when a new force comes in and tells you everything you believe in is wrong, and in any case your land belongs to them.

The Brits Make Their Move In the late 16th century, Spanish St Augustine was under constant pressure from the Brits: the city was attacked and burned by troops led by Sir Francis Drake in 1586. Later, in 1702, the British returned and attacked the city for 52 days, burning it down – but the Castillo de San Marcos fort in St Augustine held, and remains to this day (see the boxed text 'Excursion to St Augustine' in the North of Orlando chapter).

Unlike the French and Spanish, the British tended to interact less with the natives – instead, they started the long-lived tradition of restricting the Indians' land and creating plantations. New Smyrna, south of Daytona Beach, was the most famous plantation and was colonized by people from Menorca (the Spanish island that at the time belonged to Britain).

Spain Falters During the 17th century, the shape of the world superpowers was altered, with Spain losing control of many colonies and possessions, and Britain and France gaining more power. While the British and French sent troops and explorers scurrying all over the new territories, the Spanish seemed perfectly content to maintain their itsy-bitsy settlements at St Augustine and Pensacola, at the western end of the state.

By the end of the 17th century, the Brits, who were in possession of well-established colonies in the northeast, were continually pressing the Spanish on the southern boundaries of the British territory. In 1670 a demarcation line was established on what are roughly the present-day borders of Georgia and South Carolina, but the line was taken more as a suggestion than a rule, and the Brits repeatedly ran raids into the Spanish territory – both overtly and covertly.

To the west, the French were quickly establishing colonies along the Mississippi River, trying to link up the South with their new Canadian territories. Alliances between the powers were formed as quickly as they were scrapped – and they were scrapped as soon as they were formed.

Throughout the 18th century, the very proximity of the British in Georgia, the French in Louisiana and the Spanish in Florida heightened tensions. By 1700 there were 12 British colonies, and the British were definitely setting their sights on Florida. In 1732 James Oglethorpe settled Savannah, Georgia, and after a trip to England for supplies and armaments, he attacked St Augustine in 1740. That attack, which resulted in a 27-day siege before Oglethorpe's troops ran out of supplies and were forced to retreat, led the Spanish to build tiny Fort Matanzas, at the southern end of St Augustine. Even so, the Spanish position continued to be under constant pressure from the British.

The French & Indian War As England and France began feeling the urge to stretch their legs to the west and east, respectively, hostilities broke out between them in 1754. Known as the French & Indian War because of the French alliance with Indian groups against the British, it was the first war between European powers fought outside Europe.

Choosing the marginally lesser of two evils, Spain chose to side with France in 1761, to which England replied, 'Fine, and by the way, we hope you liked Havana, 'cause we just took it.' Under the First Treaty of Paris (1763), which ended the seven-year war, Spain jumped at the chance to swap Cuba for Florida.

American Revolution Officially declared in 1776, the American Revolution barely affected Florida, which remained avidly loyal to the British Crown. Florida's governor at the time even invited other loyalists to move down to the region.

But after just 20 years of British rule – during which Florida developed a social structure the Spanish had never succeeded in creating – the Second Treaty of Paris (1783) ended the revolution and returned Florida to the hands of Spain.

The War of 1812 As the superpowers – and the US was fast on its way to becoming one – squared off for what was to become the War of 1812 (1812–15), the Spanish ended up allied with the British against the US and France. The War of 1812, aside from being a power struggle between the Americans and the British, was an aggressive campaign of US expansion – north into Canada, westward across the plains and south into Florida.

In Alabama, the 1814 Battle of Horseshoe Bend proved pivotal for Florida. There, notorious (and heroic to his compatriots) Indian-hunter Andrew Jackson (1767–1845) defeated the Creek Indians in an overwhelming massacre, and then took half of their huge territory for the US. The battle also gave him an excuse to chase fleeing Creeks into Spanish Florida under the guise of defense. In late 1817 Jackson, who had earned the Indian nickname Sharp Knife, instigated the First Seminole War (see The Seminole Wars later in this section).

Spain Throws in the Towel As the US sent more and more troops into the region on Indian-hunting and Spanish-harassing missions, the pressure became too much for Spain. It gradually lost its grip on East Florida settlements (Amelia Island, north of Jacksonville, was a Sodomlike den of smuggling, piracy, prostitution and debauchery), and the Spanish government's inability to adequately supply and police the area led to its decision to cede the territory to the US in 1819.

But an itchy Spanish King Ferdinand VII began to waver. After the US told the Spanish to give up and get out or face US troops, a renegotiated treaty was signed, specifying, among other things, that the US would assume Spanish debt in the region. The Spanish finally gave up control of Florida in 1821. The debts, by the way, were never repaid. And who do you think was made governor of the new American territory? Yep, Andrew Jackson himself.

The Seminole Wars The treaty signed in 1814, at the end of the Battle of Horseshoe Bend, opened to white settlers some 20 million acres of land in the region owned by the Creeks. Tensions ran very high, and skirmishes periodically broke out. There would be a total of three Seminole Wars (see the boxed text 'Who Are the Seminole?').

Instigated by Andrew Jackson, the First Seminole War began in 1817, when Indians in the Miccosukee settlement of Fowltown had the audacity to respond to an attack by whites, killing about 50, including women

Who Are the Seminole?

The native group with the most recognized name in Florida, the Seminole, is neither a single tribe nor one that existed when the first Europeans landed in Florida. Instead, the Seminole began as a group of breakaways from other Indian tribes, as well as all kinds of runaways, including black slaves. The origin of the name Seminole is a tricky one: the Florida Department of State says it derives from the Spanish *cimarrone*, while most historical texts claim it was a Creek Indian word, sim-in-ole or sem-in-ole. In any case, in both languages it means 'wild one' or 'runaway' or even 'one who camps at a distance' and reflects the origins of the Seminole nation.

The Muskhogean Indians once existed all around the Gulf Coast of present-day USA. A subgroup, the Creek Confederacy, settled in Georgia and Alabama and gained in number and strength by the turn of the 19th century, when skirmishes with the ever-encroaching Americans escalated into mass killings on both sides. Andrew Jackson enlisted the help of the American-friendly Lower Creeks against the Upper Creeks in the Battle of Horseshoe Bend, on March 27, 1814. It all but wiped the Upper Creeks out. The surviving Red Sticks, a faction of the Upper Creeks, escaped south into still-Spanish Florida, where they were joined by other groups of Indians escaping similar treatment. The Seminole welcomed them, as well as runaway slaves, with open arms.

Some of these groups eventually became the Seminole Nation, and though technically in Spanish territory, they were not safe from Andrew Jackson's purges. Partly in the interest of reclaiming escaped black slaves living among the Seminole, the Americans continued to pursue the Indians across the border.

and children. Enter Jackson, who late that year stormed through Florida with a force of 5000, destroying Seminole villages and, while he was at it, engaging in an unsanctioned attack on Pensacola. (He actually took it, but the US gave it back.)

Jackson was elected president of the USA in 1828, and the extermination of American Indians was accelerated by his Indian Removal Act of 1830. The Treaty of Moultrie Creek of 1823 and the Treaty of Payne's Landing of 1832 were both signed by *some* Seminole, who agreed to give up their Florida lands and move west to reservations, but the provisions of the treaties were flouted by both sides. When the US began moving troops in 1835 to enforce the Treaty of Payne's Landing, Osceola, a Seminole leader, planned an attack on an army detachment. Major Francis Dade and 108 of his men were ambushed by the Seminole as they marched between Tampa and Fort King – only three survived. The attack triggered the beginning of the Second Seminole War, which lasted seven years. The battlefield is preserved at Dade Battlefield Historic Park (see the Orlando chapter).

The war dragged on so long because it was fought guerrilla-style by the Seminole in swamps and hammocks. (This was highly atypical of the traditional European tactics employed by US soldiers.) Creek Indian warriors from Alabama were engaged to fight for the US in exchange for promises of federal protection of their families while they were away fighting. Boy, were they surprised when they returned to pillaged homes!

Osceola was captured on October 27, 1837, as he approached US Major General Thomas Jesup, commander of the Florida troops, both traveling under white flags. Jesup snatched Osceola, who later died at Fort Moultrie in South Carolina.

By 1842 thousands of Seminole had been displaced and marched to reservations in the west by army troops. As the war wound down, the surviving Florida Seminole took refuge in the Everglades. Despite their relegation to the swamps, the Seminole weren't really left alone, and in 1853 they were actually outlawed – a law proclaiming Indians illegal in Florida called for their removal to any place west of the Mississippi River.

In 1855 a party of surveyors were killed after they encroached on Seminole territory. The resulting backlash turned into the Third Seminole War, which ended after Chief Billy Bowlegs agreed to go west (he was paid) in 1858. He and about 100 Seminole did migrate, but about 200 or 300 refused to acknowledge the agreement and retreated into the Everglades. There was never a full treaty ending the war, and some Seminole today say they are technically still at war with the USA.

Statehood & the Civil War

With the Indians out of the way, Florida became the 27th state admitted to the Union on March 3, 1845, only to secede 16 years later with the onset of the Civil War. Admitted to the Union as a slave-owning, agricultural state, Florida seceded from the USA along with the Confederacy on January 10, 1861.

The US Civil War (1861–65) stemmed from a number of issues, but one comes to the fore: the profound debate over the moral and economic issues surrounding slavery.

Aside from providing troops, Florida's role in the Civil War was mainly one of supplying the ever-growing food needs of the Confederate war machine. As Yossarian explained to Milo in *Catch-22,* troops just can't eat cotton (even when chocolate covered), and since cotton was the South's main crop, the Confederate army pressed Florida's citrus and cattle farmers into heavy overtime.

All did not go well. Cattle ranchers and packing plants were heavily overburdened. Florida's cattle were so valuable to the Confederates that the Union's attentions focused on Florida in an effort to cripple the South – the largest battle of the war held on Florida soil, at Olustee, began as a Union effort to cut off beef supplies. Still, at the end of the war, Tallahassee was the only Confederate state capital that hadn't fallen to federal troops.

Reconstruction

The Civil War was one of the bloodiest conflicts in the history of modern warfare, and wounds ran very deep. From the early stages of the conflict until his assassination, President Abraham Lincoln (1809–65) had been putting together a framework for reconstruction of the Union – the 10% Plan. Under it, the Union would federally recognize states in which as few as 10% of the populace had taken oaths of loyalty to the USA – a plan designed to grant political viability to dependable groups (in the Union's opinion) as quickly as possible.

But with Lincoln's assassination, all bets were off, and a political void opened; Florida was ruled by martial law under Union troops. Any semblance of a state government disappeared after the war. Florida's governor, John

Milton, killed himself, preferring death to re-construction. The state was then run by troops carrying out orders from Washington. In the confusion that followed, dozens of factions struggled for power – from labor organizers to the Ku Klux Klan, an organized gang of white supremacists that exists to this day.

But as the federal government established and maintained order, the return to normalcy progressed. Farmers scrambled to reestablish farms, and Florida blacks, though technically free, found themselves working as hired hands for the same plantations as before. As businesspeople and former politicians struggled to re-create a state government, heated arguments arose on what role, freedoms and recognition blacks in Florida would receive.

President Andrew Johnson, a Southerner and former slave owner who succeeded Lincoln, devised a compromise between Lincoln's scheme and the more radical Southern proposals. While his reconstruction granted many concessions, it required state constitutions to ratify the 13th Amendment, abolishing slavery, before being readmitted to the Union.

The contentious issue was black suffrage, something the Southern states were loath to grant, but under the congressional reconstruction plan, martial law was eventually imposed to install it. When Florida was readmitted in 1868, it had technically granted the vote to blacks, but the state's new constitution was carefully worded to ensure Florida did not get a 'Negro government.' After federal troops left, discriminatory laws were enacted – including one forbidding a black man to testify at a white man's trial – and a poll tax was imposed, which kept droves of black and poor white voters away from the voting booth.

The new Florida government began what in many ways continues to this day: an agenda of probusiness, prodevelopment activities to open

up Florida's natural resources to exploitation at the expense of social programs. While schools were underfunded and overcrowded, developers and tourists were enticed to the area – the former by criminally cheap land prices (25¢ an acre was not unheard of) and the latter by hotels and resorts built by the former.

The Railroad Boom
At the end of the 18th century, real-estate developers were busily creating holiday resorts throughout Florida. As the state's agricultural trade – especially citrus and cattle – expanded, the need for railroads increased.

The greatest development was due to three railroad barons: William Chipley in the Panhandle; Henry Plant on the Gulf of Mexico (see the South of Orlando chapter); and Henry Flagler on the Atlantic Coast. In addition to laying down tracks, they built hotels and roads, giving birth to new towns and more tourism. Flagler, who was partner with John D Rockefeller in Standard Oil, was arguably the most important developer, turning Florida into a holiday-destination juggernaut.

World War I & the Roaring '20s
By the time the USA entered WWI in 1917, there was a large naval presence at Key West, Pensacola, Tampa and Jacksonville. By the time the war was over, Florida's new permanent residents led the state into the '20s with great momentum.

During Prohibition (the ban on the sale or manufacturing of alcohol in the USA), Florida became a smuggler's haven. The entire state was booming on a huge scale, one never before seen in the USA. Hundreds of thousands of people were migrating to Florida; land prices soared. Railroads and roads were popping up everywhere, and cities were expanding at staggering rates.

Tin Can Tourists

With the advent of the automobile, intrepid American travelers packed their cars or their Model T Kampkars and headed south toward this so-called paradise in the southeastern corner of their country. They were budget travelers who could have taught today's backpackers a thing or two. Eating from tin cans and sleeping in fold-out cots, the Tin Can Tourists braved looming potholes, road-clogging cattle clusters and puzzling road guides (unfortunately for them Lonely Planet wouldn't be around until about 50 years later). They traveled south on the Dixie Hwy, a paved, two-lane road that stretched 5706 miles from Ontario, Canada, to the southern tip of Florida. Because of the Tin Can Tourists, the route became so popular that the government made the Dixie a National Highway in 1925, granting it a speed limit of 45mph – at the time, the highest in the nation.

And indeed, some tourists still drive at that speed.

The Land Bust
In a manner similar to the stock markets of the '20s, buying Florida land on margin was the ticket; shysters bought land with incredibly small down payments and shucked it onto settlers at huge profits. With such buying and construction, transportation became ever more important. But several disasters were straining the limits of existing communications – among them, a debilitating rail strike and a sunken supply ship in Miami harbor that blocked the entrance to the Miami River and kept other boats from dropping off their loads.

But the end came in a flash: a major hurricane hit South Florida in late 1926, wiping out construction, killing 400 and injuring thousands. In the aftermath, hordes of people who thought they were getting the deal of a lifetime found the catch – deadly storms. They pulled out quickly, taking their money with them. Land prices plummeted, and banks folded like books. And as if to hammer the nails into the coffin, the area was hit by another devastating hurricane and several smaller storms a little more than a year later.

The Great Depression
Florida businesses pretty much followed the national trend during the Great Depression, after the stock market crash of 1929. As banks failed, businesses failed, and many of Florida's rich developers ran home with their tails between their legs. Since Florida's economy was already suffering because of the land bust, the Depression hit it harder than other states, and as such, it needed more federal bailouts.

Florida was a major supporter of Franklin Delano Roosevelt. In the president's first '100 days,' he called an emergency session of Congress to create dozens of new government agencies that would have a profound effect on Florida and the rest of the nation. As part of Roosevelt's New Deal, the Works Progress Administration (WPA) and the Civilian Conservation Corps (CCC) were created. The WPA sent armies of workers to construct buildings, roads, dams, trails and housing, while the CCC worked to restore state and national parks. It was the largest campaign of government-created jobs in the USA, and while critics at the time called it busywork, projects by the WPA and CCC stand today, many as national landmarks.

World War II
Though it sounds cruel, WWII was just what Florida needed. In early 1942, U-boats off the coast of Florida were sinking US freighters at an alarming rate. Almost overnight, Florida turned into one of the biggest war factories and training grounds in the Union: almost every US pilot who flew in WWII trained in Florida; the army's anti–U-boat school was in Miami; and Key West's naval base overflowed with sailors.

As the war ended, soldiers and sailors returned to settle in the region. Once again, Florida experienced a boom initiated by war.

The area was also the beneficiary of increased demand for agricultural products, and Florida farmers raked in big bucks. During the war, Florida's citrus production was the highest in the nation.

The Aerospace Industry
Florida was a natural choice for America's aerospace industry, and in 1947 the US Army chose to set up in Cape Canaveral – the flat landscape, the open water and the offshore islands, which could be used for tracking purposes, made the location ideal. Soon, an entire 'Space Coast' was created to support the highfalutin goals of the National Aeronautics & Space Administration (NASA) in its race to beat the Russkies into space – see the Space Coast chapter for a full history of the US space program.

The Disney Invasion
Something happened to Florida in the 1970s that would change the face of its tourism market forever: Walt Disney World. Hundreds of thousands of tourist-related, service-sector jobs spurted up around this massive entertainment and resort center. Hangers-on and imitators also moved in.

Walt Disney World opened in October 1971, and within only two years, over 20 million visitors (more than the entire population of Florida at the time) came to see it. Orlando's 'mouse boom' made Silicon Valley's Internet boom look like a blip. In some places, the price of land went from $6 an acre to $16,000 an acre. For more on the history of the World, see the Walt Disney World Resort chapter.

The 1980s & '90s
While technology began booming throughout the country, the Space Coast and its support industries between the Kennedy Space Center and Orlando began gaining importance as simulation-technology businesses set up shop. This, and the continued rise of Walt Disney World, its offshoots and all that comes with

theme-park mania, allowed Central Florida to continue to prosper significantly. The population of Orlando tripled in the 20 years following Walt Disney World's grand opening, and tax revenues increased 23-fold in the same period of time.

In the 1990s tourism was affected by a couple of 'bumps.' On August 24, 1992, Hurricane Andrew, with sustained 145mph winds and gusts of up to 170mph, slammed Homestead, near Miami Beach. By the time it passed, the costliest disaster to ever hit the USA had damages pegged at $30 billion. It could have been worse, but people had had time to prepare and evacuate, and the Category 4 storm was obliging enough to keep moving and not sit on the area.

There was also a heavily publicized spree of foreign-tourist-related crimes in 1993. With several shootings and many robberies, Florida was in an understandable panic over the potential loss of its tourism market, which was fast becoming the state's most important industry. Heightened security and the creation of the Tourist Police Force helped to substantially reduce attacks against tourists.

21st Century

At the outset of the new century, Florida is poised to be a state with both clout and complex problems. From oil drilling in the Gulf of Mexico to reclaiming the Everglades; from gay adoptions to terrorists training at flight schools; from failed educational policies and the nation's first anthrax attack to the high cost of prescription drugs for the bursting elderly population; from recognising the interests of agriculture and developers to acknowledging the interests of Cubans and Hispanics and African Americans – Florida has its hands full. But the money pumping into the state is sure to keep its arms strong enough to hold and handle all those heavy problems indefinitely.

Orlando is still the powerhouse tourism draw (Miami takes a second seat), but Tampa and St Petersburg have been seeing an uptick recently, thanks to downtown renewal and renovation. Theme parks account for a huge percentage of visitors. While Disney is still decidedly king of the hill, there's tough competition from Universal Studios, SeaWorld, Islands of Adventure, Busch Gardens and smaller entries, such as Wet 'n' Wild and Splendid China. Furthermore, folks are discovering just how accessible and incredible the state and national parks can be.

GEOGRAPHY

Florida's terrain is mainly flat, with coastal lowlands. Although it's slightly hilly in the center, you won't find anything over 350ft above sea level in Florida. The south-central portion is all wetlands and reclaimed wetlands. The coasts are buttressed by natural barrier islands. And it's a watersport-lover's delight: thousands of springs and lakes freckle the state, and no spot is more than 60 miles from the Gulf of Mexico or the Atlantic Ocean. The St John's River, which cuts through Central Florida, is the state's largest, and its shores were home to the first citrus growers.

GEOLOGY

On the face of it, geologically speaking, Florida's not much to jump up and down about. It's essentially an enormous arched slab of porous limestone. However, when the seas receded and exposed the Florida peninsula – recently enough that dinosaurs never made it here – the limestone caused some interesting things to happen.

First, the salt water that saturated the limestone was forced out by freshwater from rainfall. Decaying plant matter that was washed into the ground by rainfall created a carbonic acid, which ate away at the limestone, forming tunnels and caverns and eventually entire underground freshwater systems of rivers and streams. This created a system of aquifers, which hold and store freshwater like a sponge. There are three aquifer systems in Florida, the most significant of which is the Floridan Aquifer. The Floridan covers about

The Sinkhole That Ate Winter Park

On May 10, 1981, a funny thing happened in ritzy Winter Park, just north of Orlando. The earth opened up a hungry mouth and, over the course of the next couple of days, it ate its fill: several cars (it seemed to like Porsches best – it gobbled up four), whole businesses, a home and a swimming pool. By the time it stabilized, the sinkhole had swallowed almost an entire city block and had dropped 10 stories into the ground.

82,000 square miles (including parts of Alabama and Georgia), averages 1000ft thick and is never much further than 200ft under the surface in Central Florida.

Weaknesses and cracks in the limestone, combined with the pressure of the circulating water, result in springs, of which Florida has hundreds, if not thousands. And those same weaknesses are responsible for sinkholes – amusing when they're not on your property – which occur when the carbonic acid eats away at a section of limestone that's not thin enough to become a spring. When enough stone is dissolved (or when the water table drops, lessening ground support), entire sections of ground simply sink into, well, a hole. See the boxed text 'The Sinkhole That Ate Winter Park.'

CLIMATE

It's warm year-round in Central Florida, but there are two distinct seasons – wet and dry. June to September is wet and November to April is drier, with October and May being transitional months. The temperature is warmer in the wet season and cooler in the dry season.

Florida summers are summed like this: very hot and humid, with thunderstorms at 3pm. There's a cats-and-dogs quality to Florida rain, and it comes on quickly. Summer rainstorms are preceded by inhuman rises in humidity, closely followed by fantastically ominous clouds, which sweep in and reduce daylight to twilight in a matter of minutes. The rain – copious doses of fist-sized raindrops – has a ferocity that floods streets in minutes and causes drivers to pull over and cower. But the rains rarely last very long, and the raindrops are so warm that they can actually be refreshing. Also, more lightning strikes Central Florida than anywhere else in the world.

June is the rainiest month, with an average of over nine inches, and temperatures average between 75° and 88°F (24° to 31°C). August is probably the hottest month, with average temperatures between 77° and 89°F (25° to

31°C), but with all these temperatures you have to take into account the heat index, a product of heat and humidity. It feels a *lot* hotter than 89°F when there's 90% humidity!

See the climate chart for more detailed information.

ECOLOGY & ENVIRONMENT

While what follows will sound grim, keep in mind that things are improving and that the government is now taking an active role in limiting and repairing damage and managing land use.

The *Encyclopedia of Florida* says that Florida's state motto, 'In God We Trust,' was 'evidently taken from the inscription on American currency.' In that spirit lies the fundamental philosophy behind Florida's environmental and ecological policies. The destruction of vast tracts of Florida's natural balance was a direct result of the government's encouragement.

While the Floridan Aquifer has the capability to supply huge quantities of water, ground contamination from sources such as pesticides, heavy metals, sewage and gasoline (leaking from underground storage tanks) has drastically affected the quality of Florida's drinking water in many areas of the state. Similarly, Florida's rivers, streams and lakes have been polluted to the extent that largemouth bass from several lakes are inedible.

Beaches are relatively clean, but the coast has seen high levels of bacteria at times. Health authorities monitor conditions and are good about letting people know when limits are exceeded.

FLORA
Cypress Trees

Although the bark is similar to pine, these deciduous trees grow out of water. The knobs that poke out of water around the trunk are called 'knees' and help the trees breathe. The Timucuans used cypress trees for dugout canoes because the wood is moisture- and insect-resistant. Homes made of it last for decades with little maintenance. As it ages, it takes on a silver hue.

Mangroves

Mangrove trees are halophytes, plants that tolerate salty conditions. Located where the land meets the sea, they stabilize the shoreline and reduce inland flooding during storms, simply because they prevent sand and dirt from washing away. Silt builds up, forming more and more land; eventually the mangroves are

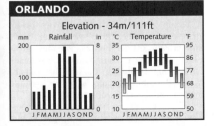

ORLANDO

Elevation - 34m/111ft

strangled by the very land they've created, and they die. Another special quality of mangroves is that their seeds sprout while still on the tree.

Sea Oats

Sea oats *(Uniola paniculata)* get their name from the large plumes they produce. They're protected vegetation in Florida because they trap wind-blown sand and thereby stabilize sand dunes. It's illegal to pick or disturb them in any way.

Sea Grapes

Sea grapes *(Coccoloba uvifera)* are coastal landscape plants native to Florida that stand up to wind and salt water. They have large, round leaves and produce a small, purple, edible fruit that braver people eat or make into jelly.

Pine Flatwoods

Pine flatwoods usually don't have very rich soil and are home to mainly slash pine and saw palmetto, though sometimes cabbage palms grow in these as well.

Spanish Moss

The most surprising thing about Spanish moss *(Tillandsia usneoides),* the ubiquitous, spooky stuff attached to trees in the northern areas of Florida, is that it's not a moss at all. It's an air plant and a member of the pineapple family. That's right, pineapple. Its seeds have tiny parachutes that carry them from tree to tree. In some areas, Spanish moss can get so thick and tangled that it jumps from treetop to treetop across roads, creating a canopy.

Saw Grass

Named for its fine teethlike edges, saw grass is the principal Everglades vegetation, but it grows wherever it's wet. It's rough, firm, stiff and green.

Strangler Figs

The ropelike roots you'll see growing on cypress trees or cabbage palms are the strangler fig *(Ficus aurea),* whose seeds start growing as an air plant. As the strangler fig grows, it sends off roots, which wrap around the trunk of its host, eventually strangling and killing it.

Palms

Florida has many species of palm, which are tropical evergreen trees and shrubs with branchless trunks and fanned leaves in clumps at their tops. You see them in many varieties virtually everywhere.

Fruit Trees

Throughout Florida, you'll run into orange, grapefruit, lemon, lime and tangerine groves (see Economy later in this chapter). You may even find a banana, mango or papaya tree. Most people are a little touchy about strangers walking up to their trees and snatching fruit, so ask first.

FAUNA
Crocodilians

Crocodilians are the world's largest living reptiles, and two species are native to the USA: the American alligator *(Alligator mississippiensis)* and the American crocodile *(Crocodylus acutus).* Crocodiles are very rare in Florida, so if you see a crocodilian here, it's probably an alligator. This can be considered a good thing by visitors: crocs are the more aggressive of the two.

Alligators The name derives from the Spanish *el lagarto,* the lizard.

Diet Alligators are carnivorous; hatchlings eat insects, frogs, small fish, snails and the like. As they grow, they move on to bigger game, but they're never above small snacks like crickets or grasshoppers. Alligators' jaws close on reflex: when open (the muscles that open their mouths are far weaker than those that close them), their closing mechanisms are triggered by anything touching the inside of their mouths.

When that something is edible, the alligator clamps down upon it, raises its head and gulps – swallowing prey small enough in one gulp, and crushing and tearing larger prey repeatedly until swallowable. Stories of alligators dragging prey underwater to drown are hooey.

Appearance Alligators indeed look like long and scary lizards. Most males grow to between 9ft and 12ft, females 6ft and 8ft; the largest found in Florida was a terrifying 17½ft. Alligators generally live to an age of 30 to 35 years in the wild, longer when raised in captivity.

Young alligators are black, with bright stripes and blotches of yellow on their backs and cream-colored bellies. As they grow older, they lose the stripes, but the stomach remains light-colored. It's said that Indians believed rubbing a gator's stomach would make it fall asleep – volunteers?

Alligators have a broad snout (the most obvious difference between alligators and crocodiles, which have narrow ones) and a socket in the upper jaw hides their fourth tooth (which is visible on crocs). There's nothing external to distinguish male and female alligators to the casual observer.

Alligators have large corneas that enhance their night vision. They can see underwater, too: transparent, protective membranes cover their eyes when submerged.

Habitat Alligators are usually (but not exclusively) found in freshwater such as shallow lakes, marshes, swamps, rivers, creeks, ponds and man-made canals. American alligators are found primarily in Louisiana, Florida and southern Georgia. They're a common sight along Florida riverbanks, where they like to sun themselves, and occasionally you can catch a glimpse of the lazy reptiles swimming across rivers and streams.

Gators are warm-weather fans and will rarely feed when the temperature dips below 68°F; their metabolism slows considerably in cold weather. But gators are cold-blooded and can die when the temperature is more than 100°F. To cool themselves, alligators sit on riverbanks or in the shade with their mouths wide open, which dissipates heat.

Nesting occurs in June and July; hatching in August.

In the dry season, alligators become a crucial factor in the survival of many species by digging 'gator holes' – artificial ponds. They dig with their mouths and legs, sweeping out mud and vegetation with lashes of their tails. As the hole fills with water, the gators keep it free of vegetation with further tail-lashing housekeeping. When the dry season comes, gator holes are often the only source of freshwater for many other animals, and many come to hang out. Rent, however, can be expensive: some of the visitors become gator dinner.

Threats to Alligators While alligator eggs and infants are eaten by raccoons, otters and sometimes even other alligators, generally speaking, humans are the alligator's only natural enemies. Formerly abundant in the wild in Florida, an estimated 10 million alligators were killed from hunting and the draining of wetlands in the late 19th century until the Mason-Smith Act, which banned the sale of endangered species in 1969. Alligators had been considered endangered since the mid-1940s. Thanks to protection, the alligator population has recovered to such an extent that it was reclassified as 'threatened' in 1985. Al-

though alligator farms are present in Florida, it is still illegal to hunt or molest alligators in the wild, and strict penalties apply to violators.

Current threats to alligators include cars and loss of habitat.

Crocodiles The crocodile is classified as an endangered species. While there have never been as many crocs as alligators in Florida, there are only an estimated 400 to 500 left in the wild, and their numbers are not substantially increasing.

Crocodiles are more aggressive than alligators (though the American crocodile is not particularly aggressive) and will attack humans with less provocation. They can be smaller than alligators but range in size from 3ft to 15ft; males are larger than females. Crocodiles nest on marl banks, porous sand or shell beaches.

American crocodiles prefer coastal, brackish and saltwater habitats (but they can live in freshwater). Their snouts are more tapered and triangular than those of alligators, and their fourth tooth is exposed. Their bodies are grayish-green, with a light-colored underside; young crocs have dark bands on their backs and tails.

Adult crocodiles feed at night in the water. They eat fish, crabs, birds, turtles, snakes and small mammals. In the daytime they rest in creeks or in dens, which they build within vegetation.

Females build their nests – which you really don't want to approach, okay? – near deep water. They lay eggs April and May, and after they hatch in July and August, mothers carry their newborns to the water in their mouths.

As with alligators, humans are the full-grown croc's only natural enemies.

Turtles

Florida turtles, both sea and land, are either threatened or endangered species, protected by state and federal law. The sea turtle most commonly found in Florida is the threatened loggerhead turtle *(Caretta caretta)*. Also seen, but far more rarely, is the green sea turtle *(Chelonia midas)* and, rarer still, the leatherback *(Dermochelys coriacea)*, the largest of the sea turtles. Both of the latter are endangered. Disturbing turtle nests or possession of live or dead turtles can result in fines or imprisonment.

Nesting Florida's beaches are a perfect nesting ground for sea turtles. Nesting occurs from May to September. Turtles swim ashore at night, preferably onto a wide beach, and pull themselves forward using their fore flippers to find a suitable (the drier the better) area for laying eggs. They hollow a pit with their front flippers, which helps them settle into the sand, and then dig a cylindrical cavity of about 20 inches with their rear flippers.

The turtle raises its hind flippers and releases two to three eggs at a time; she'll lay about 100 in all, each about the size of a ping-pong ball. The eggs have a leathery shell, which prevents them from breaking when they hit the sand. Using her front flippers, the turtle covers the eggs with sand and returns to the water. Sea turtles don't guard their nests. Loggerheads build four to five nests per season at intervals of 10 to 12 days.

Some eggs fall victim to raccoons and other small animals that dig them up for food. Surviving to the hatching stage is really a matter of luck, and only one in 1000 turtles will reach maturity.

Hatching After about 60 days, hatching occurs. Baby turtles orient themselves by moonlight to find the water, and here is yet another instance of human development leading to tragedy for nature: turtle hatchlings are frequently disoriented by the lights from the condominiums and hotels that line the beaches, and often crawl off in the wrong direction.

Volunteers in Turtle Watch programs throughout Florida stand by at hatching time and try to point the turtles in the right direction, employing any method they can – including flashlights and search lights – to get them into the sea.

Manatees

The endangered Florida manatee *(Trichechus manatus)*, also called the sea cow, is a subspecies of the West Indian manatee. Once abundant throughout the Caribbean waters, only an estimated 4000 to 5000 manatees are left in the wild today. Manatees have large, plump, grayish-brown bodies with two small forelimbs and a tail shaped like a beaver's. Their large, upper lip is covered with small whiskers. Manatees range in size from about 9ft to 12ft and weigh between 1000lb and 2500lb. These herbivores consume 10% to 15% of their body weight daily. After 13 months of pregnancy, females give birth to only one calf – every two to five years. They have no natural enemies except humans.

You can find manatees in the wild at Blue Spring State Park (see the North of Orlando chapter), where they winter (November to March) in the 72°F springs. In warmer periods they also swim in the St John's River. Also, SeaWorld (see the Orlando chapter) has a good exhibit and some rescued manatees.

Dolphins & Porpoises

Florida's most common dolphin species is the bottle-nosed dolphin *(Tursiops truncatus)*, which isn't as shy as a common dolphin. They're commonly seen throughout Florida: if you notice playful critters leaping out of the water alongside your boat, you may be looking at bottle-nosed dolphins or porpoises – look for the long snout (bottle-nosed) or no snout (porpoise).

Birds

Pelicans are large birds that live to an average age of 30 years, weigh 5lb to 8lb and eat

---

Mad about Manatees

A cute little nose barely breaks the surface of the water, with a 'pfft' and a spray of water and air. Below that nose stretches a big gray mass with a walruslike body that tapers to a beaverlike tail. For all their size and weight, West Indian manatees, which are related to the elephant, are shy and elusive. So shy, in fact, that early explorers who glimpsed them thought they were mermaids. Later, after they'd been seen grazing on underwater vegetation, they were called 'sea cows.'

These slow, nearly blind mammals are protected by federal and state laws, but their numbers are threatened by loss of habitat, careless anglers and increasing boat traffic. When they come to the water's surface to breathe, manatees are vulnerable to being hit by boats. It's not uncommon to see propeller scars across their backs. Frequently they are also injured or killed by fishing lines, which strangle them or tangle their fins.

There are several organizations throughout Florida that rescue and rehabilitate injured manatees; they are kept busy. The two largest are SeaWorld in Orlando (see the Orlando chapter) and Seaquarium in Miami.

about half their body weight in fish daily. They're also prehistoric-looking, resembling pterodactyls, and are hilarious – especially when one of them has grabbed a fish and is carrying it around in the sac beneath its chin.

Florida has several types of heron, long-necked wading birds who fold their necks over their backs in flight. Throughout the state you'll see snowy egrets and great white herons, along with ibis and the pink-and-orange roseate spoonbill. You'll only find pink flamingos in zoos, on lawns and in John Waters movies, and in the latter two instances, they're made out of plastic.

There are only about 600 pairs of endangered bald eagles, the US national symbol, left in Florida. Adults have a white head and tail, a dark body, and yellow eyes, legs and bill. They grow to about 3ft high and have a wingspan of up to 8ft. Although they're visible in several Atlantic coast state parks, you'll have to be patient.

Wood storks, large wading birds with dark featherless heads, stout bills and 5ft wingspans, have been classified as endangered since 1985, when they were recognized as victims of wetland draining.

GOVERNMENT & POLITICS

With the exception of its long and proud history of open and seemingly encouraged graft, corruption and conflict of interest (which dates back to Spanish explorers and pirates of all nationalities), the Florida state government is a miniature replica of the US federal government. The US legislature is made up of the bicameral Congress – the Senate and the House of Representatives. The Senate has two senators from each of the 50 states, while the 435-member House has at least one member from each state, depending on the state's population. Florida, the USA's fourth most populous state, has 23 representatives.

The Florida legislature mimics the national one. Bills are introduced by representatives and go through several subcommittees before being argued and amended on the floor of the House, which then passes them on to the Senate, which sends them through several subcommittees and argues and amends them further. They're then sent back to the House for *further* amendment, and, finally, to the governor, who can sign the bills into law or veto them. About half of all bills die in the process.

The capital city of Florida is Tallahassee, in the northwest central section of the state, a geographical compromise reached when Florida had two capitals, St Augustine and Pensacola.

Governor Jeb Bush, brother of the current President Bush (No 43, or the 43rd president of the USA, also know as 'W') and son of the former President George Bush (No 41), holds the highest office in Florida and certainly has the ear of the nation's commander in chief, and President George Bush seems to have had Jeb's ear when it came to those crucial presidential electoral votes in 2000. Ah, brotherly love.

ECONOMY

Florida's economy relies heavily on tourism, its most lucrative and important business. Almost 1.2 billion tourists have visited Central Florida in the last 30 years, spending enough money to make a Florida state income tax unnecessary. Tourism is not the only major industry in the region, but it definitely has the most staying power; even the attacks of September 11 didn't keep travelers away from Orlando for long.

Other important economic activities in Florida include the $8-billion-a-year citrus industry, which produces much of the country's frozen concentrated orange juice, bottled juice, grapefruit sections and citrus salad. There are more than 12,000 orange growers and 107 million citrus trees in the state (more than anywhere in the world except Brazil), and Florida is the world's leading producer of grapefruit. Florida is also among the top 10 cattle-producing states in the nation. Other important industries are electronics, programming, simulation technology, space exploration and space-related industry.

Minerals are important to Florida's economy as well. In fact, Florida mines about a quarter of the world's phosphate. Other products extracted from the earth include limestone, peat, zircon, dolomite and sulfur. Until quite recently, oil and gas exploration were also big in three wildlife areas and the Gulf of Mexico, about 25 miles south of Pensacola. Under the terms of a federal agreement reached during Governor Jeb Bush's reelection year (2002), and perhaps as payback for Jeb's help in the 2000 presidential elections, George W Bush and Jeb are buying back those oil leases. Furthermore, they're paying the leaseholders more than what they paid in the first place. Great deal: Jeb looks good to environmentalists (and, more importantly, the majority of Florida voters, who oppose drilling) *and* to oil companies. That's what politicians call a 'win-win situation.'

POPULATION & PEOPLE

The official census 2000 pegs Florida's population at about 16 million, a 26% increase from 1990. That's a lot of extra people in one decade. Most of Florida's populace is concentrated on the coasts, and of those, more than a quarter live south of Alligator Alley (Hwy 84/I-75). Despite its reputation for having a large senior-citizen population, the median age in Florida is 31.3.

In the metro Orlando area, whites account for about 57% of the population, about 25% are black, 15% are Latino and 3% are of Asian descent.

Native Americans number 49,200, constituting 0.3% of Florida's population. Only one federally recognized Indian tribe in Central Florida has reservations: the **Seminole Tribe** (*☎ 800-617-7516;* Ⓦ *www.seminoletribe.com).* These reservations are located in Hollywood, Tampa, Dania, Big Cypress National Preserve and Brighton, near Lake Okeechobee. The Seminole Tribe has expanded its efforts to preserve and interpret the culture, language and customs of the Florida Seminole (see their website for more information).

EDUCATION

Florida's public grade schools and Florida's students fall short of the national average in many areas, notably in Scholastic Aptitude Tests (SATs), the criterion for college and university admissions in the USA. And the number of students who drop out before graduation is higher than the national average. It's not surprising: Florida spends less than almost any other state on its education system, though it spends more than any other state on prison construction. As one local said, 'You can't blame the state for that; they're executing prisoners as quickly as they can!'

Central Florida has several state and private universities: Embry-Riddle University, in Daytona Beach; Stetson University, in DeLand; University of Central Florida, in Orlando; University of South Florida, in St Petersburg; University of South Florida, in Tampa; and the University of Tampa.

ARTS

Orlando's Cultural Corridor is home to many artistic pleasures; see the Orlando chapter for details.

Literature

The following are works by Florida authors – for additional books about the Central Florida region, see the Books section of the Facts for the Visitor chapter.

Fiction No list of Florida writers would be complete without mention of Florida's best known: Marjorie Kinnan Rawlings, Ernest Hemingway and Zora Neale Hurston. Most contemporary Florida writers hail from Miami and do the mystery/suspense/thriller thing – there are many of them, some of them prize-winning, but we've stuck mainly to the Central Florida region here.

Marjorie Kinnan Rawlings' books contain beautiful descriptions of rural Florida life. She's best known for *The Yearling,* the story of how Jodie Baxter's love for a fawn alienates the boy from his family. It's been made into a movie that will break your heart. But Rawlings is also author of books including *Cross Creek,* which describes her home in a town near Gainesville, and *Jacob's Ladder.*

Ernest Hemingway, known as much (in Florida, anyway) for his drinking in Key West bars as for his distinctive style and riveting tales of moral dilemmas, lived in Key West during one of his most fertile periods. It was there that he completed many of his best-loved works, including *A Farewell to Arms.*

Author of seven books, Zora Neale Hurston is best known for *Their Eyes Were Watching God,* her 1937 feminist novel about an independent black woman in rural Florida. Hurston, born in Eatonville, also compiled Southern black folklore. See the boxed text 'Fiction & Folklore: Zora Neale Hurston' for more information.

Known for his snarling satires on Florida tourism and development, Carl Hiaasen's *Team Rodent: How Disney Devours the World* is an eminently readable rant against the Magic Kingdom.

Tampa-based Randy Wayne White writes richly detailed thrillers set on Sanibel Island, an enclave of weirdness on the Florida gulf coast; his hero, Doc Ford, stars in books including *North of Havana, Captiva* and *Sanibel Flats.*

Nonfiction Those short on time, or who can't read on the beach, might pick up *The Florida Reader,* edited by Maurice O'Sullivan & Jack Lane, an anthology of writings, both historical and literary, that lead through the major events in the state from 1530 to the present. David Leon Chandler's *Henry Flagler* chronicles the story of Miami's 'Robber Baron,' who laid out the city. John Rothchild's

Fiction & Folklore: Zora Neale Hurston

Zora Neale Hurston (1901–60) was born in Eatonville, the first black incorporated town in the US, about 5 miles from Orlando. Her family broke apart when she was young, and she supported herself from the age of 14, working odd jobs and finding her way in 1919 to the all-black Howard University in Washington, DC. In 1925 she moved to Harlem, the cultural capital of black America, and distinguished herself quickly as a bright young literary voice. Along with poet Langston Hughes and others, she rose to the forefront of what came to be known as the Harlem Renaissance, a flowering of black creative and intellectual achievement and a celebration of the African-American experience.

Hurston came from a background of storytelling. As a child she'd listened to the men gathered on the porch of Joe Clark's store tell their 'big ol lies' to entertain one another. In later years, she became a good storyteller herself, which made her the life of every party in Harlem. Her interest in storytelling also led her to Barnard College, where she met Franz Boas – the father of modern American anthropology – and discovered the study of folklore. Under Boas' guidance, Zora won a research fellowship from Columbia University and headed back to the South to record the songs, tales, superstitions, games and traditions she'd grown up with.

In pursuit of folklore, she traveled from Florida to New Orleans and eventually into the rich culture of the Caribbean; she posed as a runaway bootlegger's moll, lived in the shantytowns of migrant turpentine workers and was poisoned nearly to death by a voodoo witch doctor in Haiti. But despite her travels and wild, far-flung adventures, Eatonville and the porch of Joe Clark's store would remain at the center of her work, appearing again and again in both her folklore and her fiction.

Mules and Men was published in 1935 and is considered by many the greatest work on black American folklore ever written. In Southern vernacular, it recounts tales of conjure men and hoodoo cures; Ol Massa and his favorite slave, John; Brer Rabbit and Brer Gator (like Disney has never seen them); and more. Before Hurston, white folklorists had portrayed black culture as the product of childish, silly and unsophisticated minds. Hurston instead revealed its wit, humor, imagination and complexity.

Her most famous novel, *Their Eyes Were Watching God,* was published in 1937. It is one of the earliest black feminist novels, telling the story of Janie Crawford, an independent black woman who loved who and how she wanted. The book was savaged by contemporaries such as Richard Wright, author of *Black Boy* and *Native Son,* because it did not address race relations and black oppression but rather black community and black folk.

Hurston died in a welfare home in 1960 and was buried in an unmarked grave in the Garden of Heavenly Rest, in Fort Pierce. In the 1970s, a few dedicated black writers and scholars began the 'Hurston renaissance' – her seven books were reissued, and Alice Walker made a pilgrimage to Fort Pierce to place a memorial stone on her grave. It reads:

> Zora Neale Hurston
> 'A Genius of the South'
> Novelist/Folklorist/Anthropologist
> 1901–1960

Up for Grabs exposes the state's wacky commercial transactions. *Dreamers, Schemers & Scallawags: The Florida Chronicles,* by Stuart McIver, gives the lowdown on the state's colorful underground characters. Michael Gannon's *The New History of Florida* tells the state's story by way of historical themes.

Performing Arts

Throughout the state, regional orchestras, such as the Florida Symphony and the Jacksonville Symphony, perform classical concerts regularly; performances and venues are listed in this book.

The biggest dance companies in Florida are in Miami. Still, the **Orlando Ballet** (W) *www .orlandoballet.org)* can put on some lovely performances, which are held at Bob Carr Performing Arts Centre. See the Orlando chapter for details.

Theater and stand-up is popular in Central Florida (thousands of actors are employed by Disney too!); see the regional chapters for specific venues.

Painting & Sculpture

St Petersburg boasts a trip of powerhouse collections including the Salvador Dalí Museum, the St Petersburg Museum of Fine Arts and the Florida International Museum, with rotating international blockbuster exhibitions. Orlando's Cultural Corridor and the towns surrounding the city have more than one wonderful art museum. For example, stained-glass lovers should make sure to visit the Charles Hosmer Morse Museum of American Art, in Winter Park.

Film

At the turn of the 20th century, before Hollywood, California, became Filmmaking Central, places such as Jacksonville and even Hollywood, Florida, were cranking out films. These days, filmmakers are flocking back to the area with a vengeance. Today, many of Florida's films come out of Miami, but believe it or not, Disney-MGM Studios and Universal Studios Florida are both operational.

Architecture

Central Florida's architecture can be referred to as 'prosaic,' but we'd rather call it 'spectacularly unspectacular.' With few exceptions – Ybor City in Tampa and St Augustine – the architecture you'll run into in Central Florida is run-of-the-mill, post-1950s urban sprawl.

The Spanish colonial and revival styles, predominant in St Augustine, resemble more the grand buildings of Mediterranean Spain (with archways, adobe and terra-cotta tile) than the relatively stark version of Spanish mission architecture found in the USA's Southwest.

Pockets of Victorian and Queen Anne architecture pop up here and there, recognizable by their riotous colors and baubles, gingerbread towers and doodads. If you feel as if you've just walked into an expensive soap shop – or a B&B – it's probably a Victorian building.

Cracker architecture, also called Florida vernacular, is classic pioneer homesteading architecture with a twist: enormous sun porches. Early 'single pen' houses – simple boxes with porches – were later expanded by adding a wall that either straddled the existing chimney (saddlebag) or was adjacent to the wall opposite the fireplace (double pen). Cracker homes run from quaint to enormous and are wood inside and out.

SOCIETY & CONDUCT

Between good ol' Southern hospitality and tourism-trained cheer ('Have a Magical Day®!'), you'll find people in Central Florida to be really very warm and friendly, with waitresses calling you Sugar and Darlin' and men holding doors open for women.

Smoking

The USA, which gave the world tobacco, is now mostly a huge no-smoking zone. Government regulations have banished smokers from virtually all public spaces except bars and the outdoors, and have also banished most tobacco advertising from the media. Several state governments banded together and sued tobacco companies in order to reclaim the millions of public-health dollars they have had to spend dealing with tobacco-related illnesses. The trial revealed that the tobacco companies had indeed designed their products to be particularly addictive and had suppressed evidence that tobacco use causes various diseases. In short, tobacco products, their manufacturers and their uses are now in high disrepute.

Many Americans find smoking unpleasant and know that heavy or habitual smoking is unhealthy and harmful not only to the smoker, but also to those nearby (particularly children and people with asthma or other pulmonary impairments). If you are a smoker from a country that permits smoking in public places, you should be aware of American regulations and social customs.

Smoking is prohibited in most public buildings, such as airports, train and bus stations, offices, hospitals and stores, and on public conveyances, such as subways, trains, buses, planes. Except for the designated smoking areas in some restaurants, bars and a few other enclosed places, you must step outside to smoke.

Most cities and towns require restaurants to have nonsmoking sections, but there is no requirement that there be smoking sections. Hotels offer 'nonsmoking' rooms – that is, rooms used only by nonsmoking guest so that the rooms have no stale tobacco smell.

If you are in an enclosed space (a room or car, for example) with other people, it's polite to ask permission of all others before you smoke and to refrain from smoking if anyone protests.

Yes, indeed, Southern hospitality is as good as its reputation, but remember, the further *north* you go, the further *South* you get.

Outside the major cities, especially in rural areas, Floridians tend to be more conservative: their politics and attitudes are old-fashioned and right wing. In rural areas, travelers should avoid behavior or dress that may be considered offensive. It's also not a good idea for women to wear revealing clothing or go braless. Gay and lesbian travelers in these areas should do their best to behave as 'straight' as possible.

Rednecks, who refer to themselves as just that, can be found in many areas of Central Florida and are easily identified by their foul and racially derogatory language. Leave them in peace to wallow in ignorance, and don't go striking up any debates. In fact, if someone tries to engage you in one, you may want to nod, smile and say 'uh-huh' – it's just not worth the effort. Even a well-traveled American (they do exist!) can suffer from intense culture shock in more rural areas. The number of children showing indisputable signs of fetal-alcohol syndrome is truly depressing.

RELIGION

Floridians are mostly Christians and are somewhat more devout than many other Americans. For example, Lent is taken much more seriously here – you may see many people with a dark smudge on their foreheads on Ash Wednesday.

There are significant numbers of Jews too, most of whom are transplants from northeastern USA. Many Jews are Reform (they don't adhere as strictly to religious and social teachings of the Torah) as opposed to Conservative (more religious and ceremonial) or extremely religious Orthodox. Unlike in Miami, you won't see much evidence of Afro-Caribbean or Afro-Brazilian religions in Central Florida.

Facts for the Visitor

SUGGESTED ITINERARIES

Even a weekend is a worthwhile amount of time to visit attraction-packed Central Florida, whether you spend it all at a theme park or two, on the educational and exciting Space Coast, or in lovely and romantic Winter Park, north of Orlando. Any destination in Central Florida isn't much more than a two-hour drive from Orlando, so you can see many different aspects of the region in a short period of time. Oh, and don't forget: no matter where you are, the beach is never more than 60 miles away.

Three Days

All Disney, All the Time With just three days, it's best to stay at a Disney resort to maximize your time and minimize your travel.

Day 1 Magic Kingdom, break for dinner/nap, see Epcot Future World at night
Day 2 Animal Kingdom, break for dinner/nap, see Epcot World Fair at night, stay for IllumiNations fireworks
Day 3 MGM Studios, stay for Fantasmic! at night

Everybody Wins If you have both kids and teens, you'll be pulled in different directions if you don't let people go their separate ways. For this (packed) itinerary, consider staying at one of the excellent Universal Orlando resort hotels and getting a shuttle to Walt Disney World. If you want to forego the Space Coast and concentrate on theme parks, do a second day of Disney, especially if you'll be staying at a Universal resort.

Day 1 Islands of Adventure and Universal Studios
Day 2 Everyone does a Disney park of choice, meet at MGM Studios for Fantasmic! at night
Day 3 Kennedy Space Center (get there early!)

Four Days

All Disney, All the Time Spend each day at one of the Disney parks, saving the one you consider to be the best until last. Unless you already know you love Epcot, plan that for the first day, especially if you have kids, to avoid anticlimax syndrome. Consider doing Magic Kingdom on the last day if you have very small kids, or figure out what will be the best for you and your cohorts, and save it for last. Even if you don't think it will be the highlight of your trip, see MGM Studio's Fantasmic! on the night of your last day – it

really is the best way to cap off your Disney experience.

Everybody Wins Unless this is a trip for your small children, consider doing two days of Universal Studios and Islands of Adventure and two days of Disney – the Universal Orlando parks are better for young adults.

If you or your kids are really into space exploration, set aside one day for the Kennedy Space Center, and get there early – there's lots to see and do.

One Week

All Disney, All the Time Yes, you can actually spend an entire seven days at Walt Disney World and not feel as if you're stagnating. Spend a full day at each of the major parks, with possibly a second day at your favorite parks, and make sure to take a dip at one of the two wonderful Disney water parks.

Two Weeks

If you have two weeks, you could spend it all at Disney, but your time would be better spent venturing out a bit more. Spend no more than six or seven days at Disney, and get a FlexTicket for Universal Studios/Islands of Adventure and other major Orlando attractions (SeaWorld and Wet 'n' Wild) plus Tampa's Busch Gardens.

If you're not *that* into theme parks, do a few Disney days, check out what Universal has of interest, and skip over to the Kennedy Space Center for a day or two. Take a nice drive out west to see the crystal blue waters and perfect white sands of Clearwater Beach, where you

GREATER ORLANDO & THEME PARKS

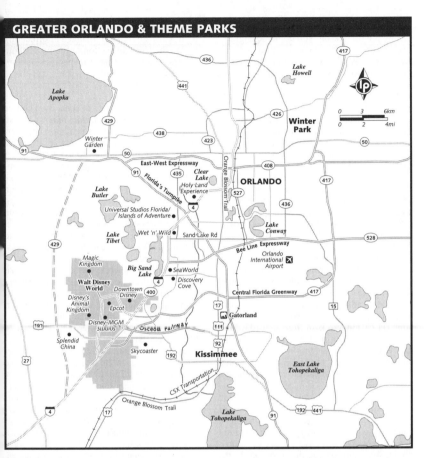

can relax and let all that stocked-up adrenaline from the thrills seep out of your body before heading home satiated and well rested.

One Month

Ah, lucky you. If you have a month to kill in Central Florida, you'll have plenty of time to see all the theme parks you can handle, and then manage to squeeze in enough time to work on your tan lines (or on getting rid of them) before venturing back home. Spend a couple of weeks taking your time with Walt Disney World, Universal Orlando, SeaWorld and any of the minor parks that strike your fancy, then move on to Kennedy Space Center. Get a place in Cocoa Beach and enjoy the wonders of NASA at your leisure. Make arrangements for an outdoor activity you enjoy, such as fishing or golfing. Do make a point to take an excur-

sion to historic, quaint St Augustine for a couple of days – there's no other place like it in the USA, and the Castillo de San Marcos there is something you'll always remember.

If there's still time, head west through Tampa and on to Clearwater Beach, maybe hitting Busch Gardens on the way, just to compare the rides with what Orlando had to offer. At Clearwater Beach lounge on the fine bright-white sand and enjoy a delicious grouper sandwich and a crisp cold beer. It'll only take you a couple of hours to get back to Orlando to fly home, knowing you had it all in Central Florida.

PLANNING
When to Go

The Orlando area is a year-round destination, but the rules that define peak and off-season aren't particularly hard or fast. For example, during the off-season, you could be engulfed by a huge flock of intensely spirited cheerleaders in town for a national competition. A day of beautiful weather during the lowest season could have everyone within driving distance crawling out of the woodwork, and you'll find yourself negotiating crowds that were nonexistent the day before. That said, even on heavily peopled days, it is possible to enjoy yourself – the parks just run at full hilt, with rides running more frequently and with more staff on hand.

Apart from the obviously busy (not to mention hot and rainy) mid-June to mid-August period, the most crowded times for the theme parks are during American holidays. Thanksgiving (in late November); Christmas through New Year's Day; and President's Day weekend (in February) are very busy, as both school vacations and the warmth-in-winter factors combine. College spring break time (mid- to late March) is also pretty crowded and changes the dynamic of the parks, for the better or worse, depending on whether you enjoy a college crowd. Also, popular park events such as Gay Day (first week of June; see the Walt Disney World Resort chapter), the Walt Disney World Marathon (first week of January) and special events for Halloween (October 31) are enough to affect the crowd situation for the worse.

Generally, the best times to go are from January to early March, during the month of May, and from September to mid-November. But if you can't visit during those times, don't despair, you can still have a great vacation – obviously, many people do! Just take in the rest of the advice this book has to offer, plan carefully but remain flexible, and remember to *breathe*. A relaxed attitude on a hot crowded day at a theme park can make the difference between a fun and memorable time and a not-fun, but memorable, meltdown.

Theme parks aside, the rest of Central Florida is a safe bet pretty much any time of year. However, unless you're a college-age party animal or a biker, avoid coastal areas – especially Daytona Beach – in March, when spring break can coincide with Bike Week (see the Daytona Beach section of the North of Orlando chapter). You'll notice that accommodations on the coast will shoot up in price during this time. Although no space shuttle launches were scheduled at the time of writing due to the loss of *Columbia,* launches of unmanned spacecraft cause lodging prices on the Space

Coast to rise in the days surrounding the event (call ☎ 321-867-4636 for launch information).

See the Climate section in the Facts about Central Florida chapter for specifics on temperature and rainfall.

Maps

Free state maps are easy to come by. The free *Official State Transportation Map* is a road map that's probably better than most commercial maps covering the same area. It's available through Visit Florida (see Tourist Offices later in this chapter) and through some larger convention and visitors bureaus. Members of the American Automobile Association (AAA) can request free Florida maps from their local AAA office; members of foreign affiliates can pick up maps once they arrive in the States.

For city maps, many tourist offices and chambers of commerce have free tourist maps; these are less reliable and less detailed with regards to street linework, but are helpful in that many attractions, lodgings and restaurants are indicated. If you want a real city or regional map, try an official tourist information center, or a drugstore or convenience store.

What to Bring

Keep in mind that this is one of the most heavily visited places in the world, so people have gone to much effort to make sure virtually anything and everything is available for purchase. So don't fret if you've forgotten your favorite shampoo, and definitely do not overpack (chances are, you'll need some extra room for things you'll buy during your visit).

The most important things to have are a great, and broken-in, pair of walking shoes, and sunglasses with 100% UV protection (anything else will just make your eyes think they're being protected and relax them, exposing them all the more to UV light). Sunscreen, of course, is also a necessity, but is also easily found if you don't want to pack it.

Clothing should be light and casual, especially if you're going to theme parks, where you're likely to get wet. Bring both shorts and light pants, as well as a light sweater or jacket for cooler days; if you're coming in winter, a pair of jeans or warmer pants, as well as a warm sweater or jacket (water-resistant is even better) may come in handy on a particularly cold day, especially if you plan to go on rides that will up your wind-chill factor. No matter what the weather, bring a bathing suit, even if you only have one and you hate it – there is a good chance you'll want to use it before you muster up the wherewithal to shop for a new one on the trip.

If you'd like to include some fine dining in your plans, bring a nice outfit, preferably one that doesn't wrinkle too easily, and some dress shoes. (Of course, if you have time for shopping, you can always go to one of the myriad malls and purchase some styling duds to make you feel brand-new.) Rain is always a possibility, so you can bring your favorite umbrella or poncho, or purchase that sort of thing onsite, on an as-needed basis.

TOURIST OFFICES

Beware: In the Orlando area, and in fact throughout Central Florida, there are many time-share operations disguised as 'tourist offices' or 'information centers.' These vary from a podium inside a restaurant to official-seeming offices. These places are fine for obtaining pamphlets and some information, but they will try to get you to listen to a 90-minute seminar in exchange for (often illegal) discounted or free theme-park tickets and/or cash. Even if you're on a low budget, and even if you think you have a strong stomach for smarmy salespeople – it's just not worth it. Let's put it this way – we've never received a reader's letter on the subject from someone who didn't say that the whole thing was a nightmare. In this book, the address and telephone number of each chamber of commerce and/or *official* tourist office is given in the information section under the relevant town.

Visit Florida (☎ 850-488-5607, 888-735-2872; W *www.flausa.com*) is the state's privatized tourism agency. Upon request, they will send you a shiny, colorful folder of information about the state.

VISAS & DOCUMENTS
Passport & Identification

Canadians can use either a passport or another piece of photo identification that proves their citizenship. Visitors from all other countries must bring a passport. Everyone, including Americans, should bring their driver's license and any health- or travel-insurance cards.

Anyone who appears to be under 30 will be asked for photo identification at bars and nightclubs, as well as when buying alcohol, or even cigarettes, at a store. This is taken seriously.

Visas

Apart from Canadians, and those entering under the Visa Waiver Program, all foreign visitors need to obtain a visa from a US consulate or embassy. In most countries, the process can be done by mail or through a travel agent, or online at W www.usais.org/visas.htm.

The most common visa is a Nonimmigrant Visitors Visa, and the ones you'll probably require are B1, for business purposes, or B2, for tourism or visiting friends and relatives.

Visa Waiver Program Citizens of certain countries may enter the USA without a visa for tourism- or business-related stays of 90 days or less under the Visa Waiver Program *(VWP;* W *www.travel.state.gov/vwp.html).* Currently these countries are Andorra, Austria, Australia, Belgium, Brunei, Denmark, Finland, France, Germany, Iceland, Ireland, Italy, Japan, Liechtenstein, Luxembourg, Monaco, the Netherlands, New Zealand, Norway, Portugal, San Marino, Singapore, Slovenia, Spain, Sweden, Switzerland, the United Kingdom and Uruguay. Under this program, you must have a round-trip ticket from a participating airline and a machine-readable passport. Also, you will not be allowed to extend your stay beyond 90 days. Check with the US embassy in your home country for any other requirements.

Visa Extensions If you're not visiting on the Visa Waiver Program and would like to stay longer than the time you've been allotted, you should apply for an extension before your visa expires to avoid additional hassle. Your best bet is probably to do this online at W www.usais.org/extendstay.htm.

As a result of the September 11, 2001 terrorist attack on the USA, what was formerly known as Immigration & Naturalization Services (INS), and part of the US Government Justice Department, is now called the **Bureau of Citizenship and Immigration Services** *(BCIS;* ☎ 800-375-5283, W *www.immigration .gov)* and is part of the US Homeland Security Department. If you need to visit one of these offices in person (you poor soul), the Orlando location is at 9403 Tradeport Dr (no phone); tickets are handed out from 8am to 1pm, which means you will be seen in the afternoon. Get there early, bring a good book and pack a lunch. Keep in mind that the first assumption will be that you are working illegally, so come prepared with concrete evidence that you've been traveling extensively and will continue to be a model tourist.

Travel Insurance

It's important to consider travel insurance, especially if you don't have health-insurance coverage in the United States. It may seem expensive – but if you think you can't afford it, you certainly won't be able to afford a medical emergency in the USA. Ticket and luggage loss is also covered by travel insurance. Coverage depends on your insurance and type of ticket, so ask both your insurer and your ticket-issuing agency to explain the finer points.

STA Travel (w *www.statravel.com*) offers a variety of insurance options at reasonable prices.

Hint: buy travel insurance as early as possible. If you buy it the week before you fly, you may find, for instance, that you're not covered for delays to your flight caused by strikes or other industrial actions that may have been in force before you took out the insurance.

Driver's License & Permits
International Driving Permit Bring your driver's license if you intend to rent a car; overseas visitors may find it wise to back up their national license with an International Driving Permit (IDP), available from their local auto club for a nominal fee. Note that your foreign driver's license *is* valid in the USA. An IDP is not a license but rather an official translation of yours (valid for one year, and you still need to carry your license), and while the major rental companies are used to seeing foreign licenses, local traffic police are more likely to accept an IDP as valid identification than an unfamiliar document from another country.

American Automobile Association Cards If you plan on driving a lot in Florida, consider joining your national automobile association or the American Automobile Association (*AAA;* ☎ *800-922-8228;* w *www.aaa .com*), which costs $49 a year plus a one-time $17 start-up fee. When signing up, make sure to ask if there are any promotions going on that could lead to savings in membership fees.

Having a AAA (pronounced 'triple A') membership gives you access to roadside service – oftentimes free of charge and covering everything from locking your keys in the car to having major engine problems.

Excellent free maps and free hotel guides are available for members, as well as discounts on attraction tickets, car rental and accommodations. Although AAA discounts are not available at Disney shops and restaurants, they are available at Universal Studios and Islands of Adventure. When it comes down to it, members wanting to save money should always inquire whether a AAA discount is available

when paying for anything – you may be surprised how often the answer is 'yes.'

Hostel Cards
You don't need to be a Hostelling International/ American Youth Hostel (HI/AYH) member to stay at a hostel, but you will save $2 to $3 a night if you are. Membership is $28 a year or $250 for a lifetime membership. In addition to hostels, you'll receive discounts on Greyhound transportation and car rentals through Alamo and Hertz, as well as other benefits.

You can purchase membership on the spot when checking in, although it's advisable to purchase it before you leave home. Some non-HI hostels will also extend a discount to HI cardholders.

See Hostels, under Accommodations, later in this chapter, for more information on staying in a hostel.

Student & Youth Cards
Students should get an International Student Identification Card (ISIC), or bring along a school or university ID card (not as good). You can get an ISIC from STA Travel offices (w *www.statravel.com*) around the world with proof of enrollment. The ISIC secures substantial discounts at museums and tourist attractions and on some airfares.

Seniors Cards
The American Association of Retired People (*AARP;* ☎ *800-424-3410,* w *www.aarp.org*) issues identification cards for seniors, usually people over 55. These are absolutely key in Florida, where almost all major attractions, most hotel chains and some restaurants offer seniors discounts. Discounts can be substantial – up to 20% off on a room. You'll also save on some transport, including airfares.

Copies
All important documents (passport data and visa page, credit cards, insurance policy, air, bus and train tickets, driver's license etc) should be photocopied before you leave home. Leave a copy with someone at home and keep another with you, separate from the originals.

EMBASSIES & CONSULATES
As a tourist, it's important to realize what your own embassy – the embassy of the country of which you are a citizen – can and can't do to help you if you get into trouble. Generally speaking, it won't be much help in emergencies if the trouble you're in is remotely

your own fault. Remember that you are bound by the laws of the country you are in. Your embassy will not be sympathetic if you end up in jail after committing a crime locally, even if such actions are legal in your own country.

In genuine emergencies you might get some assistance, but only if other channels have been exhausted. For example, if you need to get home urgently, a free ticket home is exceedingly unlikely – the embassy would expect you to have insurance. If your money and documents are stolen, it might assist you with getting a new passport, but a loan for onward travel is out of the question.

To find US embassies and consulates in your country, visit W usembassy.state.gov. All foreign consulates in Florida are in Miami (embassies are generally in Washington, DC). Citizens of Australia and New Zealand may contact the British or Canadian consulates for emergency consular assistance, as neither country maintains consular offices in Miami. For $1.25, you can ask directory assistance at ☎ 305-555-1212 in Miami to find the number of your consulate.

CUSTOMS

US customs (now part of the Homeland Security Department) allows each person over the age of 21 to bring 1L of liquor, 200 cigarettes and $100 worth of gifts duty-free into the country. You can bring in, or take out, as much as $10,000 in US or foreign currency, traveler's checks or letters of credit, without declaring it.

It's forbidden to bring in to the USA chocolate liqueurs, pornography, lottery tickets, items with fake brand names and goods made in Cuba or Iraq. Most food items are prohibited to prevent the introduction of pests and diseases. You may not import or export products made from endangered species, including ivory, tortoiseshell, coral, and many fur, skin and feather products. Alligator-skin boots might be a great souvenir, but be ready to convince customs authorities that they're not made from endangered gators.

MONEY
Currency

The US dollar is divided into 100 cents with coins of one cent (penny), five cents (nickel), 10 cents (dime), 25 cents (quarter) and relatively rare 50 cents (half dollar). There are even a few $1 coins in circulation; they're either gold-colored and feature an image of Sacagawea (a Native American woman who served as a guide, among other things, for explorers Lewis and Clark) or are silver-colored and feature an image of women's-suffrage champion Susan B Anthony (the latter can be easily mistaken for a quarter, hence its small circulation).

Banknotes are called bills. Be sure to check the corners for amounts, as they're all the same size and color. Circulated bills come in denominations of $1, $2 (rare), $5, $10, $20, $50 and $100. The US has two designs of bills in circulation, but you'd have to study them closely to notice. On the newer bills central portrait is bigger and off-center.

There are three straightforward ways to handle payments: cash, US-dollar traveler's checks, and credit and debit cards, the latter being the most convenient.

Exchange Rates

These are particularly volatile, but at press time, exchange rates were as follows:

country	unit		US$
Australia	A$1	=	0.55
Canada	C$1	=	0.63
euro zone	€1	=	0.98
Hong Kong	HK$10	=	1.28
Japan	¥100	=	0.83
New Zealand	N7$1	=	0.47
UK	UK£1	=	1.56

Exchanging Money

The best advice for people who want to exchange a foreign currency for US dollars is to do so at home, before you arrive. Exchange rates are generally worse in the US than in other countries. If you must change money in the States, know that stand-alone exchange offices usually have worse rates than banks, but at banks it may take a couple of days for the transaction to be completed.

Traveler's Checks Denominated in US dollars, traveler's checks are often as good as cash in the USA; many establishments (not just banks) take them. The major advantage of traveler's checks over cash is that they can be replaced if lost or stolen. But changing traveler's checks denominated in a foreign currency is rarely practical. Get larger denomination US$100 checks, as you may be charged service fees per check when cashing them at banks.

The following are toll-free numbers for reporting lost or stolen traveler's checks:

American Express	☎ 800-221-7282
MasterCard	☎ 800-223-9920
Thomas Cook	☎ 800-223-7373
Visa	☎ 800-227-6811

ATMs You can usually withdraw money straight from your bank account at these ubiquitous machines. Most ATMs (automated teller machines) accept bank cards from the Plus and Cirrus systems, the two largest ATM networks in the USA, as well as Visa and MasterCard credit cards.

Keep in mind that unless you're using an ATM belonging to your bank, you will be charged a fee. This can add up if you are withdrawing money often. As for credit card cash advances at ATMs, remember that you are charged interest on the withdrawal, often at a significantly higher rate than for a standard purchase, beginning immediately and until you pay it back. Still, if you think you may need to use your credit card for cash, make sure you obtain a Personal Identification Number (PIN) from the card company before leaving.

Credit & Debit Cards Major credit cards are accepted at many, if not most, places in Central Florida. In fact, you'll find it hard to perform certain transactions, such as renting a car or purchasing tickets to performances, without one. Visa and MasterCard are the most widely accepted.

Places that accept Visa and MasterCard are likely to accept debit cards (also called ATM cards), especially if they bear a Visa or MasterCard logo. Unlike a credit card, a debit card deducts payment directly from your checking account. Instead of an interest rate, users are sometimes charged a minimal fee for the transaction. Be sure to check with your bank to confirm that your debit card will be accepted in other states or countries. Debit cards from large banks can often be used worldwide.

If your debit or credit card is lost or stolen, contact the company or bank immediately. Following are toll-free numbers for the main credit card companies:

American Express	☎ 800-528-4800
Diners Club	☎ 800-234-6377
Discover	☎ 800-347-2683
MasterCard	☎ 800-826-2181
Visa	☎ 800-336-8472

Costs

Depending on your lodging choice and what kind of trip you expect to have, you could get by on anywhere from $30 per person per day to well over $300 per person per day. In the following, very *rough,* per person per day prices, it's assumed you'll be sharing accommodations with at least one other adult.

what you get	cost US$
Camp, self-cater, some activities, no rental car	30
Budget motels, some theme parks, frugal dining, rental car	80
Nice motel or cheap hotel, some theme parks, some frugal dining, rental car	130
Nice hotel, theme parks, fine dining, rental car	180
Resort hotel, theme parks, fine dining, nice rental car	250

Following are some average prices for basic necessities:

item	cost US$
Camping	15 per night
Hostel	30 per night
Motel	50 per night
Hotel	100 per night
Resort	150 per night
All-day attraction ticket	35-60 per person
Breakfast	4-8 per person
Lunch	6-12 per person
Dinner	9-20 per person
Snacks	5-9 per person
Beer	3-5 per pint
Cocktail	5-8
Rental car	35/175 per day/week
Gas	2 per gallon

You're on your own when it comes to souvenirs – the sky's the limit. For the cost of travel to and from Central Florida, see the Getting There & Away chapter.

Tipping

Tipping is a US institution that can, initially, be a little confusing for foreign visitors. Waitstaff at restaurants, bartenders, taxi drivers, bellhops, hotel cleaning staff and others are paid a mere stipend. Customers are expected to compensate these people directly: tips are actually part of their salary, and people in the service industry are taxed on tips the government expects them to make, so if they're not making them, they will pay tax on money they never earned.

The service has to be absolutely *appalling* (ie, you've asked for a manager) before you should consider not tipping. In a bar or restaurant, a tip is customarily 15% (for a standard tip, double the tax and add a smidge) of the bill; a tip for outstanding service in a restaurant is 20% or more. You needn't tip at fast-food restaurants or self-serve cafeterias. Hotel cleaning staff should be tipped about

$2 a day (leave it on the bed). Tip daily, as they rotate shifts. Add about 10% to taxi fares even if you think your driver should be institutionalized. Hotel porters who carry bags a long way expect $3 to $5, or add it up at $1 per bag. Valet parking is worth about $2, to be given when your car is returned to you.

Special Deals

The USA is probably the most promotion-oriented society on earth. Though the bargaining common in many other countries is not generally accepted in the US, you can work angles to cut costs. For example, at hotels in the off-season, casually and respectfully mentioning a competitor's rate may prompt a manager to lower the quoted rate. Artisans may consider a negotiated price for large purchases. Apart from Disney and Universal, virtually all attractions, as well as many restaurants, have coupons out there somewhere, so keep an eye out for them at pamphlet stands and in tourist booklets. (See the Walt Disney World Resort and Universal Orlando Resort chapters for tips on lowering the ticket prices for those places.)

Taxes

There is no national sales tax (such as VAT) in the USA. Most states levy sales taxes (Florida's is 6%), but some communities also tack on a bit more for their fair share. States, cities and towns also usually levy taxes on hotel rooms and restaurant meals. Rooms and meal taxes are not normally included in prices quoted to you, even though (or perhaps because) they may increase your final bill by as much as 9.5% to 11.5%. You must add tax to rates listed in this book. If you eat and drink in a hotel, the same percentage tax is also added. Rental cårs are subject to the 6% sales tax and myriad other surcharges, which add up quickly.

POST & COMMUNICATIONS
Postal Rates

Private shippers such as **United Parcel Service** (UPS; ☎ 800-742-5877) and **Federal Express** (FedEx; ☎ 800-463-3339) ship much of the nation's load of parcels and important time-sensitive documents to both domestic and foreign destinations, although the **US Postal Service** (☎ 800-275-8777; Ⓦ www.usps.gov) can do this just as well and more cheaply.

Currently, rates for 1st-class mail within the USA are 37¢ for letters up to 1oz (28g; 23¢ for each additional ounce) and 23¢ for postcards. Parcels airmailed anywhere within the USA are $3.85 for 1lb or less. For heavier items, rates differ according to the distance mailed. Books, periodicals and computer disks can be sent by a cheaper 4th-class rate.

With the exception of mail to Canada and Mexico, international airmail rates start at 80¢ for a 1oz letter; postcards cost 70¢. Aerograms to anywhere are 70¢. Letters to Canada and Mexico are 60¢ for a 1oz letter and 85¢ for a letter up to 2oz; postcards cost 40¢.

Sending Mail

Mail within the USA generally takes two to three days, and mail to destinations within Florida takes from one to two days – except in St Augustine, where the delivery time ranges from three days to never. It helps to speed delivery if you put the correct nine-digit zip (postal) code on the envelope (though the first five digits will usually suffice). If you know the address but not the zip code, you can find a list at the post office or on the Internet (Ⓦ www.usps.gov/ncsc).

Allow mail at least a week to reach Europe or Australia and up to two weeks at peak times of the year such as Christmas. If you have the correct postage, you can drop your mail into any official blue mailbox, found in such places as shopping centers and on street corners. Mail pickup times are written on the inside of the mailbox lid.

Receiving Mail

You can have mail sent to you care of General Delivery at any post office that has its own zip (postal) code. It's best to have your intended date of arrival (if the sender knows it) clearly marked on the envelope. Mail is usually held for 30 days before it's returned to sender; you might request that your correspondents write 'hold for arrival' on letters. Have them address mail to you like so:

```
Your Name
c/o USPS Orlando General Delivery
46 E Robinson St
Orlando, FL 32802
```

Alternatively, have mail sent to the local representative of American Express or Thomas Cook, both of which provide mail services for their members. Call ☎ 800-275-8777 for postal zip codes and post offices nearest you.

Telephone

If you are calling locally, you may have to dial the area code + the seven-digit number. (leave off the preceding 1 before local calls)

In some places, dialing the area code isn't necessary. So how do you know when to dial it? Make the call using the area code, and if it goes through, great. If it doesn't, a recorded voice will tell you to hang up and dial again without using the area code.

If you are calling long distance, dial ☎ 1 + the three-digit area code + the seven-digit number. If you're calling from abroad, the international country code for the USA is 1.

The ☎ 800, 888, 877 and 866 area codes are toll-free numbers within the USA and sometimes from Canada as well.

The ☎ 900 and 976 area codes have a reputation for catering to sleazy operations – a smorgasbord of phone sex at $2.99 a minute, perhaps. Regardless of the nature of the business, you will be charged a fee when calling ☎ 900 or 976 numbers.

Directory assistance is reached locally by dialing ☎ 411. This costs as much as $1.25 from a private phone. For directory assistance for people and places outside your area code, dial ☎ 1 + the three-digit area code + 555-1212.

Pay Phones & Hotel Calls Local calls cost 50¢ at pay phones, which don't give change. Most hotels add a service charge of 50¢ to $1 for each local – and sometimes toll-free – call made from a room phone. Many also add hefty surcharges for long-distance calls – 50% or even 100% on top of their carrier's rates. Public pay phones, which can be found in many lobbies, are always cheaper. Many pay phones accept incoming calls; the number will be posted on the phone. If incoming calls are not accepted, this will be posted on the phone.

Long-distance rates vary depending on the destination and which telephone company you use. There are literally hundreds of long-distance companies in the US, and rates vary by several hundred percent – call the operator (☎ 0, 3050 or 00) for rate information. Don't ask the operator to put your call through, however, because operator-assisted calls are much more expensive than calls dialed directly. Generally, nights (11pm to 8am) and all day Saturday and Sunday are the cheapest times to call. Smaller discounts apply in the evening from 5pm to 11pm daily.

International Calls To place an international call direct, dial ☎ 011 + country code + area code (dropping the leading 0) + number. From a pay phone, dial all those numbers before inserting coins; a voice will come on telling you how much to put in the phone after you dial the number. For international operator assistance and rates, dial ☎ 00. Calls to Canada are treated as domestic calls.

In general, it's cheaper to make international calls at night, but this varies with the country you're calling and the long-distance company. Calls from a private phone to Australia or Europe, from a nondiscounted long-distance carrier, should be about $1 for the first minute and 50¢ for each subsequent minute. Calls to other continents usually cost about twice that. From private phones with a discount plan for long-distance service, the cost could be as low as 20¢ a minute to Europe or 50¢ a minute to Australia – check before you dial!

ekno Communication Service Lonely Planet's ekno global communication service provides low-cost international calls – for local calls, you're usually better off with a local phonecard. Ekno also offers free messaging services, email, travel information and an online travel vault, where you can securely store all your important documents. You can join online at ⓦ www.ekno.lonelyplanet.com, where you will find the local access numbers for the 24-hour customer service center. Once you have joined, check the ekno website for the latest access numbers for each country and for updates on new features.

Collect & Country Direct You can call collect (reverse charges) from any phone. There are increasing numbers of providers, but be aware that there really is a difference in price, so check before you dial. The main players at the time of writing were **AT&T** (☎ 800-225-5288) and **MCI** (☎ 800-265-5328). You can also just dial ☎ 0 + the area code and number, eg, 0+212+555-4567, but this is generally the most expensive option of all.

Country-direct service connects you, toll-free, with an operator from another country and allows you to make collect calls via that country's phone system, which may be cheaper than doing it from the USA. With country direct, you may also use your phone-company charge card from home.

The following are some country-direct numbers:

Australia	☎ 800-682-2878
Austria	☎ 800-624-0043
Belgium	☎ 800-472-0032
Denmark	☎ 800-762-0045
France	☎ 800-537-2623
Germany	☎ 800-292-0049

reland	☎ 800-562-6262
taly	☎ 800-543-7662
apan	☎ 800-543-0051
Netherlands	☎ 800-432-0031
Norway	☎ 800-292-0047
New Zealand	☎ 800-248-0064
Portugal	☎ 800-822-2776
Spain	☎ 800-247-7246
Sweden	☎ 800-345-0046
JK	☎ 800-225-5288

Cell Phone & Two-Way Rentals Many families like to use cell phones or two-way radios to communicate with each other while n the parks. Your rental car agency may be ible to rent you a phone for about $1 a day plus a $10 one-time rental fee, plus expensive air time ($1 per minute).

Cell U Rent (*☎ 407-522-6565; phones & radios $10/50 per day/week; pagers $8/day; open 24hr*) offers free delivery within the hour to the Orlando area. For phones, there is a $1.95 per minute charge, so consider going with the radios. A major credit card is needed for rentals.

Fax & Telegram
Fax machines are easy to find in the USA; they're at shipping outlets such as Mail Boxes Etc, as well as most hotel business service centers, and photocopy shops such as Kinko's. Be prepared to pay high prices (more than $1 a page to US numbers, $4 or more to Europe and elsewhere). Prices for incoming faxes are usually half the outgoing domestic rate. You can send telegrams from Western Union (*☎ 800-325-6000*).

Email & Internet Access
Public libraries often grant access to email and the Internet, and often for free. If you have your own gear, you can plug into the telephone socket in your room. Remember that if you use a hotel's phone line to access the Internet, you may be (over)charged for a long phone call.

DIGITAL RESOURCES
The Internet is a rich resource for travelers. You can research your trip, hunt down bargain airfares, book hotels, check on weather conditions and chat with locals and other travelers about the best places to visit (or avoid!).

There's no better place to start your Web exploration than the Lonely Planet website (W *www.lonelyplanet.com*). Here you'll find

succinct summaries on traveling to most places on earth, postcards from other travelers and the Thorn Tree bulletin board, where you can ask questions before you go or dispense advice when you get back. You can also find travel news, and the subWWWay section links you to the most useful travel resources elsewhere on the Web.

BOOKS
Most of the books listed here are available locally, some nationally and internationally. One of the best publishers of books on Florida and its regions is **Pineapple Press** (*☎ 800-746-3275;* W *www.pineapplepress.com; PO Box 3889, Sarasota, FL 34230*). See the Facts about Central Florida chapter for works by local writers.

Lonely Planet
Lonely Planet publishes *Florida; Miami & the Keys; USA; Louisiana & the Deep South;* and *Diving & Snorkeling Florida Keys* – as well as guides to nearby destinations, including *Eastern Caribbean, Cuba* and *Mexico.* Lonely Planet's excellent *Travel with Children* is a parent must-read for preparation and strategy.

Guidebooks
One of our favorites is Frank Zoretich's *Cheap Thrills Florida* (Pineapple Press), written by an admittedly very stingy man and containing lots of cheap things to do around here. Chelle Koster Walton's excellent *Fun with the Family in Florida* is just what it sounds like.

History
The best book on Florida history is *The New History of Florida* (University Press of Florida), edited by Michael Gannon and written by Gannon and many experts on Florida history. The book is a concise and complete, beautifully written, flawlessly edited masterpiece of a good read – many chapters actually reading more like a novel than a history.

Disney
Sci-fi fans will especially appreciate Cory Doctorow's *Down & Out in the Magic Kingdom* – a futuristic look at the park's politics long after the world has gone through a major revolution, and death and money have been eliminated from human society. You can buy the book, or download it for free (don't you love rebels?) from W www.craphound.com.

NEWSPAPERS & MAGAZINES

National papers like the *New York Times* and *Wall Street Journal* are widely available. For excellent, unbiased and thoughtful coverage of international news, pick up a copy of the *Christian Science Monitor*. Most major Western European newspapers are available at good newsstands, which are not easy to find – ask at your hotel.

The *Miami Herald,* the flagship of the Knight Ridder newspaper group, has the largest circulation of any paper in the state, and is available in many cities around the state. The *Orlando Sentinel* is Orlando's daily.

RADIO

National Public Radio (NPR) is an excellent source of relatively balanced news coverage, with a more international approach than most US stations; it broadcasts on the lower end of the FM dial.

TELEVISION

American television is a hodgepodge of talk shows, cop shows, dramas, melodramas, sit-coms, soap operas, game shows and commercials. The five major broadcast television networks are ABC, CBS, Fox, NBC and PBS. Of them, Fox shows the most sensationalistic – but also the most groundbreaking – TV shows. CBS, ABC and NBC all show a mix of quasi-current films, news and news-magazine shows, sit-coms and dramas. They broadcast national news at 6:30pm eastern standard time (EST). PBS, the Public Broadcasting System, shows mainly educational programs, foreign programs and films, and excellent current-affairs shows such as *Newshour with Jim Lehrer.* And the best part of it all is, it's mostly viewer supported – there are no standard commercial interruptions but rather a list of corporate sponsors is read at the end of each program.

Cable TV is available at almost every hotel, which gives you access to, at the very least, ESPN (sports), CNN and CNN Headline News, the Weather Channel and Comedy Central. Some offer premium channels such as HBO and Showtime (feature films).

PHOTOGRAPHY & VIDEO

Color print film is widely available at supermarkets and discount drugstores, while B&W and slide film is most likely to be found at camera shops. Both B&W film and slide film are rarely sold outside of major cities and, when available, are more expensive.

Drugstores process film cheaply. If you drop it off by noon, you can usually pick it up the next day. Processing a roll of 100 ASA 35mm color film with 24 exposures costs about $6 to $8. One-hour processing services are listed in the Yellow Pages under 'Photo Processing.' Expect to pay double the drug-store price.

Film can be damaged by excessive heat, so don't leave your camera and film in the sun (next to you on the beach towel) or car on hot days (read: most of the year).

Remember that the USA uses the National Television System Committee (NTSC) color TV and video standard, which, unless converted, is not compatible with the PAL and SECAM standards used in Africa, Europe, Asia and Australia.

Since the terrorist attacks of September 11 security is *very* serious business at US airports. Video and camera equipment, as well as cell phones and laptops, will probably be examined separately – this may also take place at the Kennedy Space Center. Film under 1600 ASA is safe in the X-ray scanners.

TIME

Central Florida is in the US eastern time zone, which is three hours ahead of San Francisco and Los Angeles and five hours behind GMT/UTC. Daylight saving time takes place from the first Sunday in April through the last Sunday in October. The clocks 'spring forward' one hour in April and 'fall back' one hour in October. Clocks are reset at 1am.

ELECTRICITY

Electric current in the USA is 110V–115V 60Hz. Outlets may be suited for flat two- or three-prong plugs. If your appliance is made for another electrical system, you will need a transformer or adapter; if you didn't bring one along, check a local Radio Shack or another consumer electronics store.

WEIGHTS & MEASURES

The US continues to resist the imposition of the metric system. Distances are in feet, yards and miles; weights are in ounces, pounds and tons. Gasoline is measured in US gallons, about 20% smaller than the imperial gallon and equivalent to 3.79L. Temperatures are given in degrees Fahrenheit. See the conversion chart on the inside back cover for more information. Clothing sizes differ from UK and European sizes, but European sizes are often printed along with the US size.

LAUNDRY

There are coin laundries at most motels. Generally, the cost is $1.50 to wash, and there is either a flat rate (like $1.25) to dry, or it costs 25¢ for each five or 10 minutes in dryers. Some motels will wash, dry and fold your clothes for a hefty charge. To find a laundry in town, look under 'Laundries' or 'Laundries – Self-Service' in the Yellow Pages. Dry cleaners are also listed under 'Laundries' or 'Cleaners.'

RECYCLING

It is illegal to litter highways, streets, sidewalks or other public spaces. Fines can be stiff, though enforcement is usually lax. Virtually all commercial beverage containers sold in the USA are recyclable. Some campgrounds and a few roadside rest areas have recycling bins next to the trash bins. Materials accepted are usually plastic and glass bottles, aluminum and tin cans, and newspapers.

Perhaps better than recycling is reducing your use of these products. Many gas stations and convenience stores sell large plastic insulated cups with lids, which are inexpensive and ideal for hot and cold drinks. You can usually save a few cents by using your cup to buy drinks.

WOMEN TRAVELERS

For the most part, solo female travelers in Central Florida will feel perfectly safe and totally comfortable, but in more rural areas, such as around Ocala, this is not necessarily the case. In such areas – and you'll know them if you come upon them – trust your instincts, don't try to be a bad ass, and spend the night watching television in your room. There are much better ways to exercise your independence.

If you get stuck on a road and need help, it's a good idea to have a premade sign to signal for help. At night, avoid getting out of your car to flag down help; turn on your hazard lights and wait for the police to arrive.

If despite all precautions you are assaulted, call the police. In any emergency, phoning ☎ 911 will connect you with the emergency operator for police, fire and ambulance services.

Never accept drinks offered by strangers in bars unless you've seen the bartender make it. In the mid-1990s (especially), Rohypnol, a tasteless sedative 10 times more powerful than Valium, was being added to women's drinks in Florida bars by the men who bought them – the women were sedated and raped.

To deal with some potential dangers, many women protect themselves with a whistle, Mace, cayenne-pepper spray or some self-defense training. If you do decide to purchase a spray, contact a police station to find out about regulations and training classes. Laws regarding sprays vary from state to state, so be informed based on your destination. It's a federal felony to carry sprays on airplanes (because of their combustibility).

Check the Yellow Pages under 'Women's Organizations & Services' for local resources.

GAY & LESBIAN TRAVELERS

Florida has a history of discrimination against homosexuals, despite the income that gay tourists bring in to the state. There is a small but enthusiastic gay scene in Orlando, and a huge and very enthusiastic celebration at Walt Disney World every June (see the Walt Disney World chapter). Still, even in Orlando, it might be wise to keep the closet door slightly closed. In rural areas especially, gay travelers may occasionally find hostility or open rudeness. Gay-bashing is not common in Florida, but it's not unheard of anywhere in the USA. You should always use caution in strange situations.

In this book, we list gay and lesbian resources wherever possible. On the Internet, head to **QueerAmerica** (W *www.queeramerica .com*), which lists gay and lesbian resources and community groups within specified areas – enter a zip code or area code, and the website will spit out as much as it knows (which is usually a lot!). Other good sources are college and university campuses.

Try Damron's *Women's Traveller,* with listings for lesbians; *Men's Travel Guide,* for men; and *Damron Accommodations,* listing gay-owned and gay-friendly hotels, B&Bs and guest houses nationwide. All three are published by **Damron Company** (☎ 415-255-0404, 800-462-6654; W *www.damron.com*). *Ferrari's Places for Women* is also useful. **Out & About** (☎ 212-645-6922, 800-929-2268; W *www.outandabout.com*) publishes books and a newsletter.

The **Gay & Lesbian Yellow Pages** (☎ 212-674-0120; W *www.glyp.com*), another good resource, has national and regional editions. You can also contact the **National AIDS/HIV Hotline** (☎ 800-342-2437), the **National Gay and Lesbian Task Force** (☎ 202-332-6483; W *www.ngltf.org*) or the **Lambda Legal Defense Fund** (☎ 212-995-8585 in New York City, ☎ 213-937-2728 in Los Angeles).

DISABLED TRAVELERS

The Orlando area in particular is very accessible, as are the theme parks. Of course, the more populous the area, the greater the likelihood of facilities for the disabled, so it's important to call ahead to see what is available.

There are a few local agencies that rent wheelchairs and electric scooters (see Senior Travelers later in this chapter).

A number of organizations and tour providers specialize in the needs of disabled travelers:

Access-Able Travel Source (☎ 303-232-2979; W www.access-able.com) PO Box 1796, Wheat Ridge, CO 80034. An excellent website with many links

MossRehab ResourceNet (☎ 215-456-9900; W www.mossresourcenet.org/travel.htm) 1200 W Tabor Rd, Philadelphia, PA 19141. A concise list of useful contacts for disabled travelers

Society for Accessible Travel & Hospitality (SATH; ☎ 212-447-7284; W www.sath.org) 347 Fifth Ave, No 610, New York, NY 10016. Lobbies for better facilities and publishes *Open World* magazine

For wheelchair, walker, and cane users alike, *Wheelchairs on the Go: Accessible Fun in Florida,* by Michelle Stigleman & Deborah Van Brunt, is a wonderful 424-page guide that includes information on theme parks, beaches, accommodations and lots more. To order, call ☎ 888-245-7300 or ☎ 727-573-0434 or go to W www.wheelchairsonthego.com.

See Camping under Accommodations later in this chapter for information on Golden Age Passports.

SENIOR TRAVELERS

Though the age at which seniors benefits kick in varies, travelers aged 50 and up can expect significantly cut rates at such places as hotels, museums and restaurants. Be sure to inquire about these rates at hotels and restaurants *before* you make your reservation (for purposes of space, senior prices are not included in this book). See Seniors Card earlier in this chapter for information on AARP. See Camping under Accommodations later in this chapter for information on Golden Age Passports.

If mobility is an issue, electric scooters, oxygen and wheelchairs can be rented from **Walker Medical & Mobility Products** (☎ 888-726-6837; open 9am-5pm Mon-Fri), which offers free delivery to Orlando and Disney hotels seven days a week. Wheelchair rentals are for seven days only and cost $50 to $70. Electric scooters for people weighing 275lb or less are $30/200 per day/week, and scooters for heavier people are $39/250. There is a two-day minimum.

FLORIDA FOR FAMILIES WITH CHILDREN

Will somebody, *please,* think of the children?!? Well, we have. You'll note throughout the book that rides and other attractions are approached from a kid- and parent-oriented point of view. Consider picking up Lonely Planet's excellent *Travel with Children* for general information and encouragement.

Kid's Nite Out (KNO; ☎ 407-827-5444) provides professional nannies and sitters to take children to attractions. It's insured and bonded, and sitters are trained in CPR and first-aid. The price for one child is $13.50 an hour (four-hour minimum); add $2 per child after that or if the session starts at 9pm or later.

Also, ask at your hotel about babysitters. Many high-end hotels and most resorts offer some sort of service. If you really need a day (or week) of peace, there are a variety of cool programs that'll take the kids off your hands. The US Space Camp is a fantastic weeklong educational program for kids interested in science and space exploration; see the Titusville section of the Space Coast chapter.

DANGERS & ANNOYANCES
Crime

The cities of Florida generally have lower levels of violent crime than larger, better-known cities such as Washington, DC, New York and Los Angeles. Nevertheless, violent crime is present, and you should take the usual precautions.

Always lock cars and put valuables out of sight, whether leaving the car for a few minutes or longer, and whether you are in town or in the remote backcountry. Split up your money and credit cards to avoid losing everything, and try to use ATMs in well-trafficked areas.

In hotels, don't leave valuables lying around your room. Use safety deposit boxes, or at least place valuables in a locked bag. Don't open your door to strangers – check the peephole or call the front desk if unexpected people are trying to enter.

Credit Card Scams

Try to limit the situations in which you give your credit card number out over the phone. People can charge anything they want if they

Parental Guilt Be Gone!

So if you're one of many families who couldn't bear to visit Central Florida during crowded school vacation periods, you may be instead bearing the burden of a guilty conscience.

But there's really no reason to suspect that your child's education will be deficient because of this trip – actually, the region is packed with wonderful children's museums and exhibits that may well teach them lots more than their schools will (especially if they attend an American public school).

Following are some suggested places to take your kids:

- WonderWorks
- Epcot
- Orlando Science Center
- Titanic – Ship of Dreams

Also, in addition to checking with teachers to see if your students can do any vacation-related projects to turn in upon returning to class, you can create some things for them to do that will keep their brains ticking like a roller coaster up that first hill. Give them a disposable camera and let them be the photojournalist for the trip. When you return home, have the film developed and have your child fill an album, telling the story of the vacation and writing captions.

Involving your child in planning the trip can be very educational as well. If you're driving, let your child help plan your routes, calculate the number of miles, the budget for gas, and where to stop along the way. These are only a few ideas to get you going – use what you know will interest your children most and involve them accordingly. Kids love to feel useful, and endowing them with responsibilities during the trip of their dreams may help them stay well-behaved.

have your name, card number and expiration date. Destroy any carbons generated by a credit card sale.

Hotels customarily ask for a credit card imprint when you check in to cover incidental expenses. Make certain that this imprint is destroyed if not used.

Enter a '$' sign before, and make certain there's a decimal point in, numbers written in the 'total' box on a credit card slip. You don't want to be charged $1500 for a T-shirt instead of $15.

Hurricanes

Hurricanes are generally sighted well in advance, and there's time to prepare. When a hurricane threatens, listen to radio and TV news reports. Give credence only to forecasts attributed to the National Weather Center (shortwave radio listeners can tune to 162.55MHz), and dismiss anything else as rumor. There's a **hurricane hot line** (☎ 305-229-4483), which will give you information about approaching storms, storm tracks, warnings, estimated time till touchdown…all the things you need to make a decision about if and when to leave.

There are two distinct stages of alert: a hurricane watch is given when a hurricane *may* strike the area within the next 36 to 48 hours; a hurricane warning is given when a

hurricane *is likely* to strike the area. If a hurricane warning is issued during your stay, you may be placed under an evacuation order. Hotels generally follow these orders and ask guests to leave. The Red Cross operates hurricane shelters, but they're just that – shelter. They do not provide food. You must bring your own food, first-aid kit, blanket or sleeping bag – and hey, bring a book.

Tornadoes

For a brief period after a hurricane, as if to add insult to injury, conditions become just ducky for a tornado. A tornado watch is generally issued as standard operating procedure after a hurricane, but actual twisters do pop up in Florida even without hurricanes. There's not much you can do about a tornado except to be aware of the situation and follow the instructions of local radio and television stations and police.

Ocean Dangers

Florida's Atlantic coastline isn't, for the most part, very rough. But there are a few areas of rough surf, rip tides and undertows. The entire coast is dangerous before and after storms, when it is inconceivably stupid to go in the water. The most important thing to keep in the water is your calm. And use your head: human versus ocean is no contest.

Take a peek into the water before you plunge in to make certain it's not jellyfish territory. These gelatinous creatures with saclike bodies and stinging tentacles are fairly common on Florida's Atlantic coast. They're most often found drifting near the shore or washed up on the beach. The sting of a jellyfish varies from mild to severe, depending on the type of jellyfish. But unless you have an allergic reaction to jellyfish venom, the stings are not generally dangerous. The Portuguese man-of-war is the worst type to encounter. Not technically a jellyfish, the man-of-war is a colonial hydrozoan, or a colony of coelenterates, rather than a solitary coelenterate like a true jellyfish. Its body consists of a translucent, bluish bladderlike float, which generally grows to about 4 to 5 inches long. A man-of-war sting is very painful, similar to a bad bee sting, except you're likely to get stung more than once from clusters of their incredibly long tentacles, containing hundreds of stinging cells. Even touching a man-of-war a few hours after it's washed up on shore can result in burning stings. If you do get stung, quickly remove the tentacles and apply vinegar or a meat tenderizer containing papain (derived from papaya), which neutralizes the toxins. For serious reactions, including chest pains or difficulty in breathing, seek medical attention.

Snakes

Before you freak out, you should know that encountering poisonous snakes in Florida is rare. In the unlikely event of a bite by a snake, the main thing is to stay calm – easy for us to say! If you can get to a telephone, call ☎ 800-222-1222 to be connected to the nearest Poison Control Center. If you can, find a ranger. If you're alone, stave off panic with knowledge: snake bites don't, no matter what you've seen in the movies, cause instantaneous death. But they are dangerous, and you need to keep a good, clear head on your shoulders.

Wrap the bitten limb as you would a sprained ankle (not too tightly), and then attach a splint to immobilize it. Get medical help as soon as possible, and if you can, bring along the dead snake for identification – but *do not* attempt to catch the snake if there's *any* chance of being bitten again. Sucking out the poison and attaching tourniquets have been widely discredited as treatment for snakebites, so do not apply ice or a tourniquet and do not elevate the limb or attempt to suck

out the poison yourself. Instead, keep the affected area below the level of the heart and move it as little as possible. Do not ingest alcohol or any drugs. Antivenins are available in hospitals.

Alligators

Alligators generally only eat when they're hungry – unless they think they're being attacked. They've been known to munch on small animals or things that look like them, such as small children or people crouching down real small to snap a photo. Fairly common in suburban and rural lakes, alligators move around but generally mind their own business. 'Nuisance alligators' – those that eat pets or livestock – become the bailiwick of the police (call ☎ 911 if you see an alligator in a city) and often end up at SeaWorld. Generally speaking, the best thing to do with an alligator is stay away from it completely.

Biting Insects

Florida has about 70 types of mosquitoes and other biting insects such as deerflies and fleas. They're bloody annoying, but there are some steps you can take to minimize your chances of getting bitten.

Prime biting hours are around sunrise and sunset. Cover up – wear long pants, socks and long-sleeved shirts. The better brands of insect repellent in the USA are Off! and Cutter for city use, and industrial-strength products like REI Jungle Juice or any repellent that contains a high percentage of DEET for more severe situations, such as the Everglades or the backwoods. If you've been bitten, drugstores sell various products to alleviate the itch.

EMERGENCIES

Dial ☎ 911 for police, fire and ambulance emergencies – it's a free call from any phone. Check the inside front cover of the White Pages for a slew of emergency numbers.

If you're robbed, report the theft to police on a nonemergency number. You'll need a police report in order to make an insurance claim back home.

If your credit cards, debit cards or traveler's checks have been stolen, notify your bank or the relevant company as soon as possible. See Money earlier in this chapter for telephone numbers.

Foreign visitors who have lost their passports should contact their consulate. Having a photocopy of the important pages of your passport will make replacement much easier.

LEGAL MATTERS

Possession of small quantities of marijuana or speed (amphetamines) is a misdemeanor and technically punishable by up to one year in prison *and* a $1000 fine.

It's illegal to walk with an open alcoholic drink – including beer – on the street. If you're driving, all liquor has to be unopened (not just sealed, but new and untouched) and, technically, stored in the trunk of the car.

If you are stopped by the police for any reason, there is no system of paying fines on the spot. Attempting to pay the fine to the officer is frowned upon (at best) and may lead to a charge of attempted bribery to compound your troubles. Should the officer decide you need to pay up front, he or she can take you directly to the magistrate instead of allowing you the usual 30-day period to pay the fine.

Everyone arrested legally has (and should be given) the right to remain silent, to make one phone call and to representation by an attorney. If you don't have a lawyer or family member to help you, call your embassy. The police will give you the number upon request. You are presumed innocent until proven guilty.

Note that police officers in Florida are allowed to search you if they have 'probable cause' – an intentionally vague condition that can almost be defined as 'if they want to.' The police will likely be able to search your car, under many different circumstances. There is no legal reason for you to speak to a police officer if you don't want to (although the officer may try to offer compelling reasons – like handcuffs – if they wish to speak with you and you ignore them).

Florida law upholds the death penalty for capital crimes.

Driving Laws

The maximum permissible speed is 70mph on interstate highways and between 55mph and 65mph on state highways unless otherwise posted. You can usually drive about 5mph over the limit without much likelihood of being pulled over by the police, but if you're doing 10mph over the limit, you'll be caught sooner or later.

Speed limits on smaller highways are 55mph or less, and in cities they can vary from 25mph to 45mph. Watch for school zones, where speed limits can be as low as 15mph during school hours – these limits are strictly enforced. Passengers should wear a seat belt (mandatory) and motorcyclists a helmet (not mandatory).

Drinking & Driving

The USA is one of the least tolerant countries in the world when it comes to drunk driving. During festive holidays and special events, police roadblocks are sometimes set up to check for drunk drivers.

While alcohol levels vary from person to person, generally speaking, if you have *one* beer, you're pushing Florida's legal limit (0.08%). If you're pulled over and an officer suspects you're drunk, you'll be given a 'field sobriety test.' If you fail, you'll be placed under arrest immediately. In the police station, you'll be offered a breath test. If you fail or refuse to take the test, your license will be immediately suspended pending a hearing, and you'll be fined hundreds of dollars. Depending on alcohol level and whether you've had an accident, this fine could easily reach $5000. Don't bother drinking and driving; it's not worth it.

BUSINESS HOURS

Office hours are generally 9am to 5pm, though there can be a variance of half an hour or so. In large cities, a few supermarkets and 'convenience stores' (selling food, beverages, newspapers and some household items) are open 24 hours a day. Shops are usually open from 9am or 10am to 5pm or 6pm but are often open until 9pm in shopping malls, except on Sundays, when hours are generally noon to 5pm.

Post offices are generally open Monday to Friday from 8am to 5pm, and some are also open Saturday from 8am to 3pm. Banks are usually open Monday to Friday from 9am or 10am to 4pm or 5pm. A few banks are open Saturday from 9am to 2pm (hours are decided by the individual bank branches).

Gas stations on major highways are open 24 hours a day, seven days a week. City gas stations usually open at 6am or 7am and stay open until 8pm or 9pm. In small towns and villages, hours will probably be slightly shorter.

PUBLIC HOLIDAYS

The following national holidays are observed:

New Year's Day January 1
Martin Luther King Jr Day January – third Monday
Presidents' Day February – third Monday
Easter late March/April – Easter Sunday
Memorial Day May – last Monday
Independence Day July 4
Labor Day September – first Monday
Columbus Day October – second Monday
Veterans Day November 11
Thanksgiving November – fourth Thursday
Christmas Day December 25

On these days, schools and government offices (including post offices) are closed, and transportation, museums and other services are on a Sunday schedule.

SPECIAL EVENTS

There are special events all the time in Florida; the Florida Division of Tourism has a complete list, updated annually, and each city's convention and visitors bureau (CVB/VCB) or chamber of commerce publishes a list of its own celebrations. Following are some of the more major events in Central Florida:

January

Outback Bowl (Tampa; ☎ 813-874-2695, 813-223-1111) This football match takes place at the Raymond James Stadium on January 1.

Florida Citrus Bowl (Orlando; ☎ 407-849-2020) This college football game is played at the Florida Citrus Bowl Stadium on or close to New Year's Day.

February

Speed Weeks (Daytona; ☎ 386-253-7223; W www.daytonabeach.com) This three-week auto-race celebration begins in early February and leads up to the Daytona 500 at Daytona International Speedway.

Florida State Fair (Tampa; ☎ 800-345-3247) During the second week of February, fruits, vegetables, and arts and crafts are displayed and sold at the Florida State Fairgrounds.

March

Bike Week (Daytona; ☎ 386-255-0981; W www.bikeweek.com) During the first week in March, lawyers, Hell's Angels, speed heads, accountants and others saddle up for a wild party, based around motorcycle races at the Daytona International Speedway.

April

Festival of the States (St Petersburg; ☎ 727-898-3654; W www.festivalofstates.com) Taking place in early April, this 50-year tradition offers competitions, music performances, an antique car show and the like.

Fun 'n' Sun Festival (Clearwater; ☎ 727-562-4804) Sport contests, musical events and lots of action on the beach and in town mark this mid-April to early May attraction.

Kissimmee Jazz Festival (☎ 407-908-3263) This free two-stage festival takes place on the last Sunday in April at Kissimmee Lakefront.

October

Biketoberfest (Daytona Beach; ☎ 800-854-1234; W www.daytonabeach.com) Mid-October sees another week of motorcycle celebration.

November

Lincolnville Festival (St Augustine; ☎ 904-829-8379, 904-825-1000) This early-November festival features ethnic foods, live entertainment, and arts and crafts shows.

December

Grand Illuminations/Night of Lights (St Augustine; ☎ 904-824-9550) The entire historic district is lit with tens of thousands of little lights from late November until early February – you'll feel as if you're in a fairy tale. There are also re-enactments and other shows and events.

ACCOMMODATIONS

For the most part, you get what you pay for with Central Florida lodging, so first determine how important luxury is as opposed to cost.

Accommodation prices fluctuate, especially during shoulder season. Call hotels directly for up-to-date prices. The 'rack rate' is the standard price a person walking in off the street will pay for hotel accommodations. It is not necessarily the final price, though. This is especially true in the larger, more expensive places. Sometimes a simple 'Do you have anything cheaper?' will result in an immediate price reduction. Sometimes, in chain hotels, it may help to walk to the telephone booth in the lobby and call that chain's toll-free reservation number and ask for specials. At other times, the toll-free line may quote you a price much higher than that particular hotel offers. Always try both tactics whenever possible. It's never bad form to negotiate in an American hotel, and the savings can be substantial if you do.

Now, if you're doing Disney or Universal, you'll need to decide whether or not to stay 'on campus.' The only reason you shouldn't would be if you really can't afford it, but don't be too quick about deciding it's too expensive. Rates at a Disney value resort can be as low as $75, and there are lots of ways to score great bargains if you plan well enough. Remember that if you stay at the resort and don't plan to venture out of the park, you won't need to pay for a rental car or parking or gas, but dining may be more expensive than if you were to stay 'off campus.' Now, superbudget visitors can find accommodations for as low as $30 a night in the Kissimmee/Hwy 192 area, so if that's all you can afford, that's where you'll end up. In the $75 to $100 range, you could probably find nicer accommodations off campus than on, and food will be cheaper outside the parks, so if having the full park experience isn't that important to you, and you plan on renting a car anyway, staying offsite may be the best solution for you. See the Orlando, Walt Disney World Resort and Universal Orlando Resort chapters for more information on those accommodations.

Reservations

Make these well in advance, even if you're not traveling during a peak season – you never know what sort of special event will pop up in town. Normally, you have to give a credit card number to hold the room. If you don't show and don't call to cancel, you will be charged the first night's rental. Cancellation policies vary; ask for details when you book. Some places let you cancel at no charge 24 hours or 72 hours in advance; others are less forgiving. Also, tell the hotel if you plan to arrive late – many places will rent your room if you haven't arrived or called by 6pm.

Camping & RV Parks

While it's less convenient than in Europe, opportunities for camping abound in Florida. There are three types of camp grounds available in the state: undeveloped, public and privately owned.

Undeveloped camp grounds obviously have no running water, toilets or any other facilities, and generally accommodate only tents.

Both privately owned and public camp grounds – usually located within or close to state parks – are clean and, generally speaking, very safe. Both usually have hot showers and sewage hookups for recreational vehicles (RVs). Your fellow campers will include an interesting mix of foreigners and rural Americans – American city dwellers tend to camp less than rural dwellers.

Public camp grounds usually cost between $7 and $20 a night. Areas costing several dollars more have showers or RV hookups. Make reservations for Florida state parks by calling ☎ 800-326-3521 or visiting Ⓦ www.florida parks.com. National forest camp ground and reservation information can be obtained by calling ☎ 877-444-6777 or by visiting Ⓦ www .reserveusa.com. For a one-time $10 processing fee, Golden Age Passports allow permanent US residents aged 62 years and older unlimited entry to all sites in the national park system, with discounts on camping (50%) and other fees. Golden Access Passports offer the same benefits to US residents who are legally blind or permanently disabled.

Privately owned camp grounds are the most expensive camping option and are usually located several miles from town, but they also have the most amenities. Most are designed for RVs but will also have a small section for tenters. **Kampgrounds of America** (KOA; ☎ 406-248-7444; Ⓦ www.koa.com), a national network of private camp grounds, sets the standard for quality and price, with sites in or near most Florida cities. In addition to tent and RV sites, Kamping Kabins come in one- and two-bedroom flavors and average about $35 a night. KOA sites average $25 to $35, with electricity, cable TV and sewage hookups costing more.

Hostels

There are two good **Hostelling International/ American Youth Hostels** (HI/AYH; ☎ 800-909-4776; Ⓦ www.hiusa.org) in Central Florida, one in Orlando and one in Clearwater Beach – although a very popular one is not too far away in St Augustine (see the boxed text 'Excursion to St Augustine' in the North of Orlando chapter). See the Orlando and Clearwater Beach Places to Stay sections for details.

Youth hostels are not just for backpackers, you know. Private rooms are usually available and can accommodate small families. If you're a noncamping family who wants to bring lodging and food costs to a bare minimum, hostels are your cheapest bet, and always feature a full community kitchen. Plus, they're fun! You really will meet friendly people from all over the world, and sometimes group activities and meals are planned. Dormitory beds at hostels cost about $12 to $17 nightly. Private rooms cost in the low to mid-$30s for one or two people. Dorms generally have between four and eight single beds, mostly bunk beds, and are often segregated by sex.

B&Bs

Bed & breakfast inns in Florida really try hard to provide personal attention, excellent rooms in pretty houses, great service and local advice. Amenities may include a lovely breakfast, cocktail hour or Jacuzzi. Prices generally range from $90 to $230 a night, and credit cards may not be accepted. The website Ⓦ www.florida-inns.com is a great way to pinpoint the B&B of your choice.

Motels

Motels, a creation of the 1950s, are relatively inexpensive hotels designed for short stays by motorists (the name is a contraction of 'motor hotel') and other travelers, and for trysts (often involving television evangelists). A typical mid-range Florida motel is a one- or two-story building with a large parking lot and is often located just off a highway exit, near an airport or along a major road. The entryway will smell like old coffee and have discount-coupon and pamphlet racks against a wall.

Many motels offer a 'Continental breakfast' – that is, questionable coffee and day-old donuts. It gets old real fast and messes with your blood sugar. There are almost always soda- and snack-vending machines and free ice (wash that ice bucket before you fill it up). Daily maid service is standard, and you should leave a tip if the service is good (see Tipping earlier in this chapter).

Motels in the $30 range are the cheesiest offering, and only to be explored by hardcore budget travelers; **Motel 6** (☎ 800-466-8356; W *www.motel6.com*) usually has rooms in this range.

Rooms from $40 to about $60 are less rundown and more spacious; there may be a clock radio, a fridge and a microwave. If these sorts of things are worth an extra $10 to $20 a night to you, try **Super 8 Motel** (☎ 800-800-8000; W *www.super8.com*), **Days Inn** (☎ 800-329-7466; W *www.daysinn.com*), **Best Western** (☎ 800-528-1234; W *www.bestwestern.com*), **Red Roof Inns** (☎ 800-733-7663; W *www.red roof.com*) or **Econo Lodge** (☎ 800-553-2666; W *www.choicehotels.com*).

The larger and more expensive chains, charging in the $70 to $100 range, make a motel almost as nice as a hotel. Establishments such as these include the **Quality Suites** (☎ 800-228-5151; W *www.choicehotels.com*), **Comfort Inns** (☎ 800-228-5150; W *www.comfortinn.com*), **Sleep Inns** (☎ 800-627-5337; W *www.sleepinns.com*) and **Rodeway Inns** (☎ 800-228-2000; W *www.hotelchoice.com*).

Hotels

Hotels are traditionally located within cities and offer more and better service than motels. This means there will be doormen, valet parking, room service, a copy of *USA Today* in the morning, laundry and dry cleaning, a pool and perhaps a health club, a business center and other niceties. The perks come at a price, to be sure: want a shirt washed? It's gonna cost you six bucks.

The basic hotel room differs little from the basic motel room, except that the furnishings should be newer and cleaner. Surprisingly, rooms at expensive hotels – like Hyatt and Sheraton – usually aren't much nicer than high-quality motel rooms, and they usually cost at least twice as much.

Chain-owned hotels in Florida include the following:

Hilton (☎ 800-445-8667, W *www.hilton.com*)
Holiday Inn (☎ 800-465-4329, W *www.holiday-inn.com*)
Marriott (☎ 800-228-9290, W *www.marriott.com*)
Radisson (☎ 800-333-3333, W *www.radisson.com*)
Ritz-Carlton (☎ 800-241-3333, W *www.ritzcarlton.com*)
Sheraton (☎ 800-325-3535, W *www.starwood.com/sheraton*)

The bottom end for hotels is about $90 a night (peak season) throughout the state, usually at Holiday Inns and Marriotts. These offer basic amenities, room service, restaurants and nightclubs.

Full-service hotels, complete with bellhops and doormen, restaurants and bars, exercise rooms and saunas, room service and concierges, are found in the main cities. Aimed at those with expense accounts, peak season prices range from about $150 to $200 per room per night.

Resorts

Theme-park resorts aim to keep you entertained on the premises for your entire holiday. You could easily stay at the resort and never need to venture out of it for good food, entertainment, shops or services. Prices are usually higher (around $150 to $250) than hotel prices, but good deals, sometimes even under $100 can be found. See the Walt Disney World Resort and Universal Orlando Resort chapters for details on each resort.

FOOD

The number of eateries in the Orlando area will make your head spin. The most abundant type of restaurant in Central Florida is the family-style restaurant, which varies in price and healthy options from low to acceptable. And of course, you can find every single fast-food chain, some of which even an American may have never heard of before. (In this book, we've tended to not include these two kinds of places – but because of their ubiquity and flashy signs, you shouldn't have trouble finding them on your own.) Apart from those options, there are also all kinds of ethnic cuisines and plenty of romantic, upscale and gourmet options.

The first thing that first-time foreign visitors will find surprising is the unbelievable quantity of food you get at American restaurants. Two light eaters may do perfectly well by sharing one main dish, and you may find that two meals a day is enough.

Note that you'll see dolphin on restaurant menus throughout Florida. Don't go reporting to SeaWorld just yet: this is dolphin fish (also called mahimahi), not the friendly and protected sea mammal. The alligator meat that's also served is not from protected alligators but from those raised on federally licensed alligator farms. Although it's mainly served as deep-fried nuggets, marinated and grilled alligator is quite tasty – tastes like chicken.

Main Meals

Breakfast This meal in America is heavier than in many other countries, though Brits and the Irish will feel right at home tucking into eggs, toast, bacon, ham or sausage and fried potatoes. (Home fries are fried chunks of potato; hash browns are shredded fried potatoes.) Grits, a corn-derived white glop, are often served in lieu of potatoes at breakfast, and they're best when totally smooth and very hot. Treat them as a hot cereal and add cream and sugar, or treat them as a side dish and add salt and pepper.

'Continental breakfast' is usually a euphemism for anything from a donut and a cup of coffee at your motel to a European-like spread of cheese, bread, muffins and croissants at your hotel.

Lunch Traditionally, lunch is the least important meal in the USA. Many office workers have lunch at their desks, and most people simply grab something on the run – which is precisely why America has the best sandwiches in the world: Americans know how to eat on the go. Sandwiches are usually packed with stuff, including meats (such as roast beef, ham or turkey), fresh vegetables and cheeses. Subway outlets are everywhere, of course, and actually offer a pretty good garden patty sandwich for vegetarians, although the veggie special isn't much more than lettuce and a roll.

Lunch is almost always a better value than dinner. The same $7 lunch dish will often cost $15 at dinner. Early-bird dinners, offered from around 4pm to 6pm, try to lure customers in by offering similar discounts.

Dinner The main, largest and most social meal of the day in the USA is dinner. Americans tend to eat at about 6pm or 7pm. It's the

time when restaurants are the most expensive and the most crowded.

Remember, if you have an early rise for a long theme-park day planned, it's best to avoid having a large meal right before you go to bed the night before. The food just sits in your stomach if your body isn't using it, and then converts to sugar, creating the same effect as an alcohol hangover. Not the best way to start a long, action-packed and even patience-testing day.

Regional & Interesting Cuisines

Southern cuisine is heavy on fat and meats; typical specialties include biscuits (faintly similar to scones), collard greens (served with hot-pepper-infused vinegar) and black-eyed peas, all of which are prepared with chunks of pork or ham. Main courses include fried chicken, roasted ham, pork in any variety of ways and gravies with cornbread (a dry cake-like bread made from yellow cornmeal). If you're here on New Year's Day, have a plate of black-eyed peas for good luck in the coming year (every restaurant will be serving them; it's a Southern tradition).

Another tradition is barbecue (purists say the proper pronunciation is '**buh**-buh-kyu'), which consists mainly of seasoned pork, chicken and baby back ribs cooked over an open flame and served with sweet-and-tangy sauce that has smoky overtones.

Jamaican, Creole, Haitian and especially Cuban dishes are worth trying if you haven't

---

Boiled Peanuts

As you crisscross the county roads of Central Florida, you're bound to come across steaming kettles of the region's favorite treat, boiled peanuts. They're cheap, packed with protein and often a vegetarian's best option in the outback, but...boiled peanuts?

The key to enjoying your first taste of this unusual item is to think of them not as nuts, but as something more akin to boiled potatoes: they're soft and flavorful (green peanuts are a tad firmer), and even tastier with Cajun seasoning.

You'll be presented with a crock-pot (or giant metal barrel, or anything else that can be kept warm over an open flame) of the nuts: grab the requisite Styrofoam cup, stacked to the side, and ladle them in. Then enjoy!

Barracuda Danger

Do not eat barracuda in Florida no matter what size – they may carry ciguatera toxin (CTX), produced by microscopic algae. This is eaten by smaller fish, then travels up the food chain and accumulates in larger fish, who pass it on to humans. It can cause severe illness, with symptoms including diarrhea, nausea, cramps, numbness of the mouth, chills, headaches, dizziness and convulsions. Don't believe local legends about the weight of the fish or cooking tests using a dime in the boiling water – this toxin can be deadly.

before. Note that Cuban and Haitan food often uses goat meat, which can be stringy.

Seafood

Florida has more than 8000 miles of coastline, so it's no surprise that seafood is omnipresent. Most common are grouper, dolphin fish (mahimahi), tuna, salmon and swordfish, all served grilled or deep-fried. Blackened seafood is thrown into a hot frying pan filled with black pepper so the outside is burned to a crisp while the inside is cooked to medium. Incidentally, one indicator of a town's sophistication is the availability of non-deep-fried foods – in some towns, everything is fried.

Another Florida favorite is stone crab, indigenous to South Florida and available in the winter only. Florida lobster doesn't hold a candle to Maine lobster, so if you like the latter, avoid the former.

Vegetarian Food

Apart from Indian and Asian restaurants, which can easily be found in the Orlando area, vegetarian options aren't so hot, and vegans will have even more trouble. Theme parks in particular have this problem, so if you don't eat meat, you may want to bring snacks in with you, especially if you're burnt out on Caesar salad and the occasional low-quality veggie burger. In places that don't obviously cater to vegetarians, you may need to ask twice about whether something contains meat – some southerners don't consider things like sausage seasoning, bacon bits, turkey or chicken to be meat! Asking whether a soup contains chicken or beef stock will probably lead to a perplexed or even exasperated look from the server. Salad bars are a good way to stave off hunger, and many restaurants serve large salads as main courses (usually with chicken or bacon, but just request a dollop of your favorite salad topping instead of the meat – after all, the price of the salad is mostly for the meat). If you have kitchen facilities at your disposal, you'll find lots of vegetarian favorites, such as tofu, garden patties, rice milk etc at Publix grocery stores. Be assured that in this book, we've included vegetarian and other healthy options when possible.

Theme-Park Food

It's safe to say that, for the most part, theme-park food is lousy, overpriced and fatty. Hey, what do you expect? They've got you virtually imprisoned within their fences until the last firework has fizzled – who's going to steal your business from them? Burgers, pizza, fries, sad pasta dishes and Henry VIII–style turkey legs dripping with grease await you and your children 'round every bend. If your theme-park visit is only a short one, well, who cares if you are forced to eat like this? On the other hand, if you're staying longer, consider having a large healthy and energy-packed breakfast, bringing snacks with you for the park, and eating dinner back in town.

Buffets

Many family-style restaurants feature all-you-can-eat buffets, which have unfortunately become a popular American pastime. Prices range from about $6 for low-grade breakfasts to over $20 for dinner. If you're really hungry and plan to graze a while, these can be a good deal, but they can also work out to be more expensive than a large meal if you don't stuff yourself to the gills. Especially consider whether the value is what it seems if you have children in tow – even the hungriest of 10-year-olds usually won't eat $15 worth of buffet food. The upside of these smorgasbords is that, yes, you can feast like a king and not need another bite until the next day, but if you're planning a theme-park visit later that day, you will probably feel weighed down – and what if your six-year-old insists you go on the spinning teacup ride with her?

Supermarkets

To the first-time visitor, American supermarkets are daunting and over-the-top. Often large enough to house a regulation football field, American supermarkets are one-stop shopping extravaganzas that stock everything from auto parts to garbage cans, electronics to pharmaceuticals, school supplies to contraceptives, wine to beer, and, oh yes, food (including fresh produce, seafood and meats).

The two biggest supermarket chains are Publix and Winn-Dixie. Most supermarkets have bakeries, but they also sell dozens of types of packaged breads. Some supermarkets also have full-service delicatessen counters; newer ones have full-service cafés.

DRINKS
Nonalcoholic Drinks
Familiar soft drinks are readily available, although they sometimes are called 'tonic' or 'pop' rather than soda or soft drinks. You can also select from a host of bottled fruit juices, iced tea and spring water. Most drinks come in cups or glasses filled with ice, so you're paying mostly for frozen water. You might want to order your drinks without ice or with 'just a little' ice (it's more healthy to drink liquid that's not ice-cold anyway). Tap water is safe to drink virtually everywhere and usually is palatable.

Smoothies are made from yogurt and fresh fruits blended into a type of shake. A shake, or milkshake, is fast-blended ice cream, milk and flavoring (usually chocolate, vanilla or strawberry). The biggest surprise for many non-Latino foreign visitors is *guarapo,* or sugarcane juice.

Traditionally, American coffee comes from a light-brown roasted bean and is weaker than that preferred in Europe. In some parts of Florida, 'regular' coffee means coffee with sugar and milk or cream, so specify 'black coffee' if that's what you want.

Tea comes in bewildering varieties It is often served with lemon, unless milk is specified. Herbal teas of many kinds are readily available, as is decaffeinated tea. Iced tea with lemon is a popular summer drink. Sweet tea is *heavily* sugared iced tea.

Alcoholic Drinks
The strictly enforced minimum drinking age in Florida is 21. Carry a driver's license or passport as proof of age to enter a bar, to buy alcohol or to order it at a restaurant. Servers have the right to ask to see your ID and may refuse service without it – they're instructed to proof anyone who appears to be under 30. Minors are not allowed in bars and pubs, even to order nonalcoholic beverages. Unfortunately, this means most dance clubs are also off-limits to minors, although a few clubs have solved the under-age problem with a segregated drinking area. Minors are, however, welcome in the dining areas of restaurants where alcohol is served. Beer and wine are sold in supermarkets in Florida, while harder stuff is sold in liquor stores.

Beer Most commercially available American 'beer,' for lack of a better term, is weaker and sweeter than its equivalent around the world, perhaps to encourage drinking more of it. Indeed, the marketing of 'light' beer – with fewer calories than regular beer – stalled until savvy marketers were able to convince the public that 'less filling' meant one could suck down many more beers on the same stomach.

Six-packs of major brands (eg, Budweiser and Miller) cost $4 to $5 in supermarkets. You can visit the Anheuser-Busch Hospitality Center at SeaWorld in Orlando or at Busch Gardens in Tampa for free samples. Brits, Germans and other people who like *real* beer will find Anheuser-Busch products pathetic and should look for microbrews when outside of British or Irish pubs.

Wine Wine is also available in supermarkets and liquor stores, and foreign visitors will often find that wine from their home country is cheaper here — many Australian wines are about 20% less in Florida than in Australia.

ENTERTAINMENT
Bars
Bars range from down-and-dirty to chic, and the prices range accordingly. Most American bartenders (except in tonier places that spend money on automatic pourers) free-hand pour in a manner that would make British publicans blanch. A 'shot,' ostensibly 1oz, is often larger than that. American custom says that you tip the bartender for each drink – generally $1 – and that (except in very crowded nightclubs, when you should hand the tip to the barkeep) you place your cash on the bar and leave it there while you drink.

'Happy hours,' usually a lot longer than an hour and sometimes all day, are periods in which drink prices are reduced, sometimes substantially. Two drinks for the price of one is a common deal. 'Ladies' night' – a clever ploy that allows women to drink for free, thus luring horny, thirsty males – is held once a week at many places.

Clubs
In Orlando, admission to hootchaterias (with loud music and cheap alcohol) around Church St and on Pleasure Island is about $15 to $20; smaller clubs charge less to compete.

SPECTATOR SPORTS

Sports in the USA developed separately from the rest of the world, and baseball (with its clone, softball), football and basketball dominate the scene. Football and basketball, in particular, are huge. Orlando's professional basketball team is the Orlando Magic.

Florida has three National Football League (NFL) teams: the winning Miami Dolphins, the Tampa Bay Buccaneers and the Jacksonville Jaguars. If you've ever wondered whether it was true that the word fan derives from 'fanatic,' attend a Florida pro football game. And if you think that's bad, wait till you see the fanaticism associated with *college* football. The state has several good college teams, chief among them are the University of Miami Hurricanes and the FSU Seminoles.

Baseball is so embedded in the country's psyche that – despite its complex rules, the difficulty and expense of maintaining playing fields with an irregular configuration, and labor-management problems at the highest professional levels – the sport continues to flourish. Many of the most meaningful metaphors in American English and even political discourse – such as 'getting to first base' or the debased 'three strikes and you're out' – come from baseball. Many professional baseball teams come to the warmth of Florida for spring training in March, and minor-league teams play here throughout the baseball season, from April to October. There are major-league baseball teams in Miami (Marlins) and St Petersburg/Tampa Bay (Devil Rays).

Soccer (aka 'football') has made limited inroads and will probably remain a relatively minor diversion until the Americans can consistently make a name for themselves at the World Cup.

Jai alai, a fascinating and dangerous Basque game in which teams hurl a pelota – a *very* hard ball – at more than 150 mph, can be seen (and wagered on) in Florida stadiums.

SHOPPING

If you like to shop, you'll feel right at home in Central Florida, especially in the Orlando area. In Kissimmee, along Hwy 192, flea markets occur daily, but they are there for the tourists, so they're not as cheap as one might expect. Shops with rock-bottom electronics prices also dot Hwy 192. Off the freeways are regular shopping malls, with stores such as Macy's, Neiman-Marcus etc, and outlet malls, which sell old or overstocked goods that manufacturers are trying to unload. It could be last season's gear, ugly as sin, damaged or 'irregular,' but sometimes you can find great deals on perfectly unshabby items – for as much as 70% lower than retail.

Tourist-crap stands abound in major cities and in gas stations along highways. Disney stores (mostly unofficial) are everywhere in Orlando and are frequently spotted throughout Central Florida.

Local specialty items are oranges and other citrus fruits and small alligator heads, culled from alligator farms (yuk). Lots of manatee-related paraphernalia is on offer, too.

Cheaper in the States

While you'll have trouble finding a jar of Vegemite, the USA has the world's best prices (with the possible exception of Hong Kong) on some other items. They include:

Jeans New blue jeans (like unwashed Levi's and faded Gap jeans) start at $35.

Sunglasses Ray-Bans and other premium brands can be found for as low as $35.

Zippo lighters These flashy babies start at about $12.

Running shoes Name-brand sneakers start at $40.

Camping equipment From tents and sleeping bags to heavy-duty backpacks, everything costs less here.

Computers Though you'll probably have to pay an import tariff when you get home, it will certainly be offset by great American bargains. Between falling prices and equipment upgrades, it doesn't do any good to quote prices here.

Cameras Ditto on cameras, especially digital.

CDs If you're lucky, the new CDs you want will cost $12 to $14; harder-to-come-by titles reach up to $20, though.

If you're buying electric or electronic appliances here (such as kitchen gadgets, telephones, CD players, etc), you'll need a step-down transformer – not an adapter – to allow the item to work at home.

Getting There & Away

AIR
Airports

Central Florida's major international airport is Orlando International Airport (MCO). And it's a happening place too: *Newsweek* voted it 'Top US Airport for Just Hanging Around.' Also, the smaller Orlando Sanford Airport is growing steadily, in large part due to the increasing number of British chartered flights to Orlando. See Ⓦ www.orlandoairports.net for details.

Other regional airports with increased international traffic include Tampa/St Petersburg (TPA) and Daytona Beach (DAB) Airports, which are becoming important domestic hubs as well.

With the exception of Orlando, there is usually no public transportation between airports and downtown; you're at the mercy of car rental agencies, taxis or shuttle services.

Airlines

US-based airlines and international airlines fly into MCO.

US-Based Airlines Following are airlines based in the US that fly into MCO:

Air Tran (☎ 800-247-8726, Ⓦ www.airtran.com)
Alaska Airlines (☎ 800-252-7522, Ⓦ www.alaskaair.com)
America West (☎ 800-235-9292, Ⓦ www.americawest.com)
American Airlines (☎ 800-433-7300, Ⓦ www.aa.com)
ATA (☎ 800-225-2995, Ⓦ www.ata.com)
Champion Air (☎ 800-225-5658, Ⓦ www.championair.com)
Continental Airlines (☎ 800-525-0280, Ⓦ www.flycontinental.com)
Delta Air Lines (☎ 800-221-1212, Ⓦ www.delta.com)
Frontier (☎ 800-432-1359, Ⓦ www.frontierairlines.com)
Jet Blue Airways (☎ 800-538-2583, Ⓦ www.jetblue.com)
Martinair (☎ 800-627-8462, Ⓦ www.martinairusa.com)
Miami Air (☎ 305-871-3300, Ⓦ www.miamiair.com)
Midwest Airlines (☎ 800-452-2022, Ⓦ www2.midwestexpress.com)
Northwest Airlines (☎ 800-225-2525, Ⓦ www.nwa.com)
Omni Air International (☎ 877-718-8901, Ⓦ www.omniairintl.com)

Ryan International Airlines (☎ 800-727-0457, Ⓦ www.flyryan.com)
Southwest Airlines (☎ 800-435-9792, Ⓦ www.southwest.com)
Spirit Airlines (☎ 800-772-7117, Ⓦ www.spiritair.com)
Sun Country Airlines (☎ 800-359-6786, Ⓦ www.suncountry.com)
TransMeridian (☎ 770-732-6900, Ⓦ www.transmeridian-airlines.com)
US Airways (☎ 800-428-4322, Ⓦ www.usairways.com)

International Airlines Following are international airlines that fly into MCO:

Aeromexico (☎ 800-237-6639, Ⓦ www.aeromexico.com)
Air Canada (☎ 800-247-2262, Ⓦ www.aircanada.ca)
Air Jamaica (☎ 800-523-5585, Ⓦ www.airjamaica.com)
Air Transat (☎ 877-872-6728, Ⓦ www.airtransat.com)
ANA (☎ 800-235-9262, Ⓦ www.ana.co.jp)
Bahamasair (☎ 800-222-4262, Ⓦ www.bahamasair.com)
British Airways (☎ 800-247-9297, Ⓦ www.britishairways.com)
CanJet (☎ 800-809-7777, Ⓦ www.canjet.com)
Copa Airlines (☎ 800-359-2672, Ⓦ www.copaair.com)

Preboarding with Children

Unlike many airports, MCO generally does not allow people with small children – even babies – to preboard. When so many passengers leaving Orlando have small children, what would be the point anyway?

Iberia (☎ 800-772-4642, Ⓦ www.iberia.com)
Iceland Air (☎ 800-223-5500, Ⓦ www.icelandair.com)
Japan Airlines (☎ 800-525-3663, Ⓦ www.jal.com)
LTU (☎ 800-888-0200, Ⓦ www.ltu.com)
Mexicana (☎ 800-531-7921, Ⓦ www.mexicana.com)
Skyservice (☎ 866-232-4722, Ⓦ www.skyserviceairlines.com)
Virgin Atlantic (☎ 800-862-8621, Ⓦ www.virgin-atlantic.com)
United Airlines (☎ 800-538-2929, Ⓦ www.ual.com)

Buying Tickets

The plane ticket will probably be the single most expensive item in your budget, and buying it can be intimidating. Research the current state of the market and start shopping for a ticket early – some of the cheapest tickets must be bought months in advance, and some popular flights sell out quickly. Bargain 'last-minute' airfares are for the most part nonexistent, although if you have to book at the last minute, you may find some prices that are comparable to, if not lower than, advance-purchase tickets. If you're planning to use frequent-flyer miles for the trip, book well in advance, as there are few seats available per flight for those tickets.

Use the fares quoted in this book as a guide only – you will probably find something much cheaper with a little research. Quoted airfares are approximate and based on the rates advertised by travel agents and airlines at press time. They do not necessarily constitute a recommendation for the carrier.

Note that peak season in the USA is mid-June to mid-September (summer) and the two weeks around Christmas. The best rates for travel to and within the USA are offered November through March, except for major holidays – especially Thanksgiving (the third Thursday in November) – which account for the heaviest travel days of the year.

If you think you're saving money by booking through the airline directly instead of through an independent travel agent, think again – even if you have to pay the travel agent for services, the amount they can save you will probably cover the expense. Call travel agents for bargains; airlines can supply information on routes and timetables, but they don't supply the cheapest tickets, except during fare wars.

The cheapest tickets are often nonrefundable and require an extra fee for changing your flight. (Many insurance policies will cover this loss if you have to change your flight in an emergency.) Round-trip (return) tickets usually work out cheaper than two one-way fares – often *much* cheaper.

Once you're ready to buy your ticket, if you're booking by phone, make sure to ask for the *total* amount being charged to your credit card (after all taxes and fees have been added on). You don't want any surprises.

Once you have your ticket, make copies of it and your itinerary, and keep them separate from the originals (it doesn't hurt to leave extra copies with someone at home). If the ticket is lost or stolen, the copies will help you get a replacement.

Remember to buy travel insurance as early as possible (see 'Visas & Documents' in the 'Facts for the Visitor' chapter).

Travel Websites

Commercial reservation Web networks offer airline ticketing as well as information and bookings for hotels, car rental and other services. To buy a ticket via the Web, you'll need a credit card; this should be straightforward and secure, as card details are encrypted.

Popular websites such as Expedia and Travelocity, and browser websites such as Yahoo and Excite, are usually not the best places to go for the lowest airfares. The following are lesser-known sites that might help your research. Once you've found the lowest fare on the Web, see if a travel agent can beat it.

Atevo Travel (Ⓦ www.atevo.com)
Cheap Tickets (Ⓦ www.cheaptickets.com)
Lowest Fare (Ⓦ www.lowestfare.com)
Onetravel (Ⓦ www.onetravel.com)
Orbitz (Ⓦ www.orbitz.com)
Travel Library (Ⓦ www.travel-library.com)

Getting Bumped

Airlines try to guarantee themselves consistently full planes by overbooking, assuming some passengers will not show up. When everyone who's booked actually does show up, some passengers can be 'bumped' off the full plane, but they are usually compensated for the inconvenience. Getting bumped can be a nuisance because you have to wait around for the next flight, but if your schedule is flexible, you might be able to make the system work for you.

When you check in at the airline counter, ask if they will need volunteers for bumping, and ask what the compensation will be. Depending on the desirability of the flight, this can range from a $200 voucher toward your next flight to a fully paid round-trip ticket. Try to confirm a later flight so you don't get stuck in the airport on standby. If you have to spend the night, airlines frequently foot the hotel bill for their bumpees. All in all, it can be a great deal, and many people plan their trips with a day to spare, hoping to get a free ticket that will cover their next trip.

Be aware that, due to this same system, being just a little late for boarding can get you bumped with none of these benefits.

Visit USA Passes

Many domestic carriers offer Visit USA and Visit North America passes to non-US citizens. The passes are actually coupons that you buy – each coupon equals a flight. You have to book each of these, including your return flight, outside of the US. This is usually cheaper than buying flights in the US.

Contact the bigger carriers like Continental, American and Delta Airlines in your home country (see 'Airlines,' earlier in this chapter, for contact details). Some will let you fly standby, while others require you to reserve flights in advance (and penalize you if you need to change the fare). When flying standby, call the airline a day or two before the flight and make a 'standby reservation.' This way you get priority over others who just appear at the airport and hope to get on the flight the same day.

Travelers with Special Needs

If you have special needs of any sort – dietary restrictions, wheelchair dependence, responsibility for a baby, fear of flying – you should let the airline know as soon as possible so they can make arrangements accordingly. You should remind them when you reconfirm your booking (at least 72 hours before departure) and again when you check in at the airport.

Guide dogs will often have to travel in a specially pressurized baggage compartment with other animals, away from their owners, though smaller guide dogs may be admitted to the cabin. Guide dogs are not subject to quarantine as long as they have proof of vaccination against rabies. Deaf travelers can request airport and in-flight announcements in written form.

Children under the age of two can travel for 10% of the standard fare (or free on some airlines), as long as they don't occupy a seat. (They don't get a baggage allowance.) 'Skycots' should be provided by the airline if requested in advance; these will take a child weighing up to about 22lb. Children between two and 12 years old can usually occupy a seat for half to two-thirds of the standard fare, and they do get a baggage allowance. Strollers usually must be checked in at the aircraft door; they are returned at the door upon disembarking.

Departure Tax

A departure tax is charged to all passengers bound for a foreign destination from the USA. A North American Free Trade Agreement (NAFTA) tax is charged to passengers entering the USA from a foreign country. Depending upon the airport, there may be other small airport usage and security fees (you can almost count on these, as the ramifications of September 11 continue to impact the airlines' bottom line). Departure taxes are normally included in the cost of tickets bought in the USA. If you bought your ticket outside the USA, you may have to pay the tax when you check in for your departure flight.

Baggage & Other Restrictions

Baggage regulations are set by each airline, but usually they allow you to check in two bags of average size and weight and to carry one smaller bag (in addition to a purse or computer) onto the plane. If you are carrying many pieces of luggage, or pieces that are particularly big, bulky, fragile or heavy (such as a bicycle or other sports equipment), check with the airline about special procedures and extra charges.

If your luggage is delayed upon arrival (which is rare), some airlines will give you a cash advance to purchase necessities. If sporting equipment is misplaced, the airline may pay for rentals. Should the luggage be lost, it's important to submit a claim. The airline does not have to pay the full amount of the claim; rather, it can estimate the value of your lost items. It may take anywhere from six weeks to three months to process the claim and pay you.

A number of items are illegal to carry on airplanes in checked-in baggage or on your person. These include weapons, knives of *any* kind, scissors, aerosols, tear gas and pepper spray, camp-stove fuel canisters and full oxygen tanks. Regulations have tightened since September 11, and anything bizarre (like a stapler) or pointy (like a nail file) may be confiscated. All bags are subject to random searches.

Smoking is prohibited on all domestic flights within the USA and on most international flights to and from the USA. Most airports in the USA prohibit smoking except in designated areas.

Only ticketed passengers are allowed beyond the X-ray machines.

Within the USA

Check the weekly travel sections of major newspapers like the *New York Times*, *Los Angeles Times*, *Chicago Tribune*, *San Francisco Examiner* and *Boston Globe* for discount fares. From Miami, scan *New Times* and the *Miami Herald* advertisements for discounted flights that leave from Miami. Also check the websites listed earlier. Finally, see if a travel agent can beat all offers.

The following are some very rough figures for flights to Orlando from some major cities:

Departure	January ($)	July ($)
Anchorage	700	600
Atlanta	215	190
Chicago	190	175
Cleveland	300	225
Dallas	245	245
Denver	250	240
Detroit	250	250
Honolulu	620	620
Los Angeles	360	215
New York City	155	155
Salt Lake City	380	230
San Francisco	355	355
Seattle	310	240

Canada

Travel CUTS, the excellent Canadian Federation of Students' organization (☎ 416 966 2887; W www.travelcuts.com) has offices in major Canadian cities. Also check the Toronto *Globe & Mail* and *Vancouver Sun*, which carry travel agents' advertisements. With a little luck, you might find a round-trip fare of C$475 from Toronto and C$625 from Vancouver, regardless of season (usually midweek, with a 14-day advance purchase and seven-day stay). All prices quoted below are in US dollars.

Departure	January ($)	July ($)
Calgary	470	480
Edmonton	540	465
Halifax	510	435
Montreal	440	400
Ottawa	430	400
Toronto	390	340
Vancouver	510	435
Winnipeg	520	445

Central & South America

The following are some rough estimates of what you can expect to pay to fly to Orlando from some major Latin American cities.

Departure	January ($)	July ($)
Asunción	980	940
Bogotá	610	570
Brasilia	900	900
Buenos Aires	740	800
Caracas	560	560
Guayaquil	750	750
La Paz	1080	1060
Lima	685	680
Mexico City	520	500
Montevideo	885	840
Quito	695	695
Rio de Janeiro	910	875
Santiago	1050	1050

The UK

Start by perusing the travel sections of *Time Out*, *Evening Standard* and *TNT*. UK travelers will probably find the cheapest flights are advertised by obscure bucket shops. Many are honest and solvent, but some are rogues who will take your money and disappear. If you feel suspicious about a firm, don't give them all the money at once – leave a deposit of 20% or so and pay the balance on receiving the ticket. If they insist on cash in advance, go elsewhere. Once you have the ticket, ring the airline to confirm that you are booked on the flight.

Good, reliable agents for cheap plane tickets in the UK include **Trailfinders** (☎ 020 7938 3939; W www.trailfinders.co.uk; 194 Kensington High St, London W8 7RG) and **STA Travel** (☎ 020 7581 4132; W www.statravel.co.uk; 86 Old Brompton Rd, London SW7 3LQ).

Don't forget that most British travel agents are registered with the **Association of British Travel Agents** (ABTA; W www.abta.com) and are bonded under agreements such as the Air Transport Operators License (ATOL). If you buy a ticket from a registered agent and the airline then goes out of business, ATOL guarantees a refund or an alternative flight.

In January a round-trip plane ticket from London to Orlando might cost up to £395. In July the same ticket would cost £665.

Continental Europe

Most major European airlines service Orlando, many with nonstop service. In January/June, expect to pay round-trip €550/845 from Amsterdam, €595/875 from Paris, €555/600 from Madrid and €555/810 from Munich or Frankfurt.

NBBS (☎ 0900 10 20 300; ⓦ www.nbbs.nl), the Dutch Student Travel Service, is probably your best bet in the Netherlands, but also check out ⓦ www.budgettravel.com/amsterda .htm for a complete list of Dutch travel agents near you.

STA Travel (☎ 049 69703 035; ⓦ www.sta travel.de) and **Travel Overland** (☎ 089 27276 370; ⓦ www.travel-overland.de) are popular choices and have many offices throughout Germany.

For great student fares from France, contact **USIT** (☎ 01 42 44 14 00; ⓦ www.usit connections.fr) in Paris, which has many outlets in the city and around the country. For USIT locations around the world, check out ⓦ www.usitnow.ie.

Australia & New Zealand

Neither Qantas nor Air New Zealand have direct service to Florida; you'll have to change planes (and perhaps carriers) in Los Angeles or San Francisco on the West Coast. From Auckland to Los Angeles it takes 12 to 13 hours; from Sydney to Los Angeles, 13½ to 14½ hours. From the West Coast to Orlando, it takes four to eight hours, depending on the connections (or lack thereof).

From the Australian east coast to Orlando, typical round-trip fares vary from A$2500 to A$2800. With Air New Zealand, expect to spend about NZ$2200 to NZ$2600 December to April from Auckland to America's West Coast, but don't forget to add another NZ$600 for the last leg from Los Angeles or San Francisco to Orlando with another carrier. The whole trip is about NZ$200 less expensive during the US winter (November to February).

STA Travel (in Australia ☎ 1300 360 960, 03 9347 6911; 224 Faraday St, Carlton South, Melbourne • in New Zealand ☎ 0800 100 677, 09 309 0458; 10 High St, Auckland) has numerous offices that sell tickets to everyone but has special deals for students and travelers under 30.

In Australia, don't forget to peruse the Saturday editions of newspapers like the *Sydney Morning Herald* and the *Age*. In New Zealand, pick up the *New Zealand Herald*.

South Africa

A reasonably easy-to-get discounted flight between Johannesburg and Orlando would be about R5000/5800 in off-season/peak season. **STA Travel** (☎ 021 418 6570; ⓦ www.sta travel.co.za) has offices all over the country, as does **Rennies Travel** (☎ 011 407 3343).

Asia

Hong Kong is Asia's discount plane ticket capital, but its bucket shops can be unreliable. Ask other travelers for advice before buying a ticket.

The dependable **STA Travel** (ⓦ www.sta travel.com) has branches in Hong Kong, Tokyo, Singapore, Bangkok and Kuala Lumpur.

United Airlines, Northwest Airlines and Japan Airlines have daily flights to the West Coast, where you can get a connecting flight to Orlando. Airfares as low as HK$7400 may be available from Hong Kong to Orlando, with a West Coast connection, but more normal fares hover around HK$9400. See 'Airlines' earlier in this chapter for contact details.

Arriving in the USA

As you approach the USA, the cabin crew on your flight will hand out a customs and immigration form for you to fill in.

Arriving from outside North America, you must complete customs and immigration formalities at the airport where you first land, whether or not it's your final destination. Choose the proper immigration line: US citizens or non-US citizens.

After passing through customs, you are officially in the country. If your flight is continuing to another city or you have a connecting flight, it's your responsibility to get your bags to the right place. Normally, there are airline counters just outside the customs area that will help you. See 'Customs' in the 'Facts for the Visitor' chapter for more information.

Leaving the USA

You should check in three hours prior to departure for international flights. All passengers must present photo identification at check-in. During check-in procedures, you may be asked questions about whether you have packed your own bags, whether anyone else has had access to them since you packed them and whether you have received any parcels to carry. These questions are for security reasons.

LAND
Bus

Greyhound (☎ 800-231-2222; Ⓦ www.greyhound.com) is the main bus (coach) operator in the USA and is the only scheduled statewide service. In other words, Greyhound is the car-less traveler's best friend, serving all major cities and many second-tier ones. Having said that, bus travel can often be tiring, inconvenient and expensive, so look at all your options.

Getting to places off Greyhound's main routes is impossible without a car. Furthermore, buses tend to run infrequently, schedules are often inconveniently timed, buses are often late, and stations are sometimes in sleazy areas. Fares can also be relatively high: bargain airfares can undercut buses on long-distance routes; on shorter routes, renting a car can be cheaper. Nonetheless, long-distance bus trips are often available at bargain prices by purchasing or reserving tickets three to seven days in advance. Then, once you've arrived at your far-flung destination, you can rent a car to get around.

In an effort to boost ticket sales, Greyhound offers a series of incentive fares to a variety of locations around the country. These change frequently, so it pays to ask.

Train

Amtrak (☎ 800-872-7245; Ⓦ www.amtrak.com) has been, since 1971, the US national railway system. It connects Florida with cities all over the continental USA and Canada, and two main routes serve Florida. The pricing structure is based on the date you're traveling, not just the time of year. You should always ask Amtrak if you can get a better deal by leaving a couple of days later or earlier. Having said that, in the winter months it's generally cheaper to go north and

pricier to go south, and vice versa in spring. The cheapest period is usually summer.

On Amtrak trains, each adult paying full fare can bring two children aged two to 15 for half-price. Seniors 62 years and over get a 15% discount on tickets. There are two types of seating: reclining airline-style seats, and cabins. Cabins come in four flavors: single, double, family (sleeping two adults and two children under 12) and 1st class. Cabins always command a surcharge, which varies depending on the date you're traveling.

Florida residents are eligible for the Florida Rail Pass, which allows unlimited travel throughout the state for just $199 a year.

Car & Motorcycle

Central Florida is served by three main interstate highways, which connect it with the north and the west. Highway I-95 is the main East Coast interstate highway, extending from Miami to Maine. Highway I-75 runs west from metro Miami through the Tampa area and northward to Michigan. These two are connected horizontally by I-4, which passes through Orlando and is probably the one you'll use most in your travels in the area. Following are a few sample distances and times from other points in the USA:

city	distance (miles)	driving time (hrs)
Atlanta	658	11½
New Orleans	863	14½
Washington, DC	1064	18
New York City	1282	21½
Chicago	1394	23½
Los Angeles	2754	46
San Francisco	3108	52½

ORGANIZED TOURS

Organized tours – from Disney cruises to horse-drawn carriages to airboat rides to behind-the-scenes theme-park tours – are available throughout Central Florida. See the regional chapters for details on organized tours in a given area.

Getting Around

The best way to get around most US states – and Florida is no exception – is by car. But most modes of transportation are possible; it might even be desirable to combine a couple.

AIRPORT TRANSFER

Many vacation packages include an airport transfer, but if yours doesn't, there are many companies waiting to assist you.

Mears Transportation (☎ 407-423-5566; W www.mearstranportation.com; open 24hrs) has a virtual monopoly on airport and theme-park shuttles. The company participates in airport transfers that are part of vacation package deals, but they also handle private requests. For trips to I-Drive and downtown Orlando, the one-way/round-trip prices are adult $14/24, child four to 11 $10/17. For trips to Walt Disney World and Hwy 192, the prices are adult $16/28, child four to 11 $12/20. Children under three ride free. No reservation is required for service from the airport (shuttles leave every 20 minutes or so), but if you've scheduled a round-trip service, call the day before to set a pick-up time. Be prepared to make several stops along the way. Mears also provides a limo service; plan on $50 to $60 for four people and $110 to $120 for five or six.

Fun Time Transportation (☎ 407-262-2785) is a smaller company and is less expensive. One-way transport to Orlando International Airport is $10 per person or $40 for up to six people.

SHUTTLE & BUS

The ubiquitous **Mears Transportation** (☎ 407-423-5566; W www.mearstranportation.com; open 24hrs) will also pick you up and take you to Walt Disney World, Universal Orlando, SeaWorld, Wet 'n' Wild, the dinner shows and downtown Orlando from your accommodations. Resort and pricier hotels offer free or paid service to many theme parks.

It's not a big surprise that there's virtually no public bus service out to the parks – who would ever pay $8 for parking if there were?

Greyhound (☎ 800-231-2222 or 01342-317-317 in the UK; W www.greyhound.com) offers bus service between all major Florida cities. Intercity bus travel in the US is inexpensive, but it's often an unsavory experience – consider renting a car instead.

CAR & MOTORCYCLE

By far the most convenient and popular way to get around Florida is by car. In fact, in many cities it's nearly impossible to get by without one. Even if you're in a small town like St Augustine, getting to a supermarket will require a car or an expensive taxi. Motorcycles are very popular in Florida, and with the exception of the rain in the summer, conditions are perfect: good flat roads and warm weather.

Overseas visitors: Unless you're coming here from Saudi Arabia or Indonesia, American gasoline prices are a gift from heaven. But remember to always use self-service gas pumps, as full-service ones cost about 25¢ more per gallon.

Road Rules

Americans drive on the right (and yes, that also means *correct*) side of the road and are supposed to pass on the left. (In Florida, that means that they pass on both sides!) Right turns on a red light are permitted after a full stop. At four-way stop signs, the car that reaches the intersection first has the right of way. If it's a tie, the car on the right has the right-of-way. Flashing yellow lights mean caution; flashing red lights mean stop. Speed limits in the city are between 15mph and 45mph. Be especially careful in school zones, which are limited to 15mph when the lights are flashing, and on causeways, which – no matter how fast cars actually travel – are limited to no more than 45mph.

Florida police officers are merciless when it comes to speed-limit enforcement; see

> ### Toll Roads
>
> Many Florida highways, such as Florida's Turnpike, are toll roads, which means you'll be stopping periodically (as frequently as every few minutes) to pay a toll of anywhere from 25¢ to $1.75. Make sure you have enough money to pay several tolls when you venture out! The best thing to do is to keep a very large handful of quarters in your car at all times. If you need change, there are special lanes for that. Otherwise, you can stay in the Exact Change lane and toss your quarters in the bucket at the toll gate (your kids will probably be clamoring to do this for you).

Legal Matters in the Facts for the Visitor chapter for more information on speed limits. Speeding tickets are outrageous: for example, if you're clocked at 50mph in a 40mph zone, the fine is about $150. Radar detectors are legal in Florida (hint-nudge-wink).

All passengers in a car must wear seatbelts; the fine for not wearing a seatbelt can be as high as $150. All children under three must be in a child safety seat (the rental car companies will rent you one for about $5 a day).

Parking

Always park in the shade if possible. Furthermore, it may pay to invest in a windshield shade – even a cardboard one – to filter sunlight. Cars heat up to unbelievable temperatures very quickly.

Outside cities, park wherever you want within reason. A red-painted curb means that no parking is allowed. Parking in designated handicapped parking spaces or in front of a fire station, fire hydrant, taxi stand or police station is always illegal and your car may be towed. Believe it or not, in many cases it's also illegal to park in front of a church.

In cities, parking is often a challenge. In those places, look for metered parking or, if none is available, city or private parking lots. In city lots, parking is generally about 75¢ an hour; private lots can charge a lot more, especially during special events.

Valet parking is available at many finer restaurants and in front of nicer hotels. It's usually $8 or so.

There's always free parking in supermarkets and shopping malls, and parking is usually available for a small fee (perhaps $5) at stadiums and theme parks.

Floridians are generally careful about not knocking over motorcycles parked on the street, but there aren't many motorcycle-only parking lots.

Towing

If your car is towed, call the nearest police station and ask them which towing company they use. Or look for a phone number plastered on a nearby sign (that you probably ignored) that says 'if your car has been towed, call XYZ.' The tow will cost at least $80 plus the cost of the ticket to unimpound your car. It's not a pleasant experience, and the location of the towing contractor is seldom convenient. Downtown Orlando is especially notorious for towing people *very* quickly (see Getting Around in the Orlando chapter).

Theft

If you own a car, it may pay to invest in an antitheft device such as the Club – it's cheap and quite effective. There is a method of getting around the Club: by hacksawing through your steering wheel. But this sort of thing is more a problem in Miami than anywhere else, and it's unlikely you'll be a victim of car theft.

Obviously, don't tempt thieves by leaving your keys in the car or your doors unlocked, and remove valuables from plain sight before leaving your vehicle. Put everything in your trunk if you don't want to carry it with you.

If, despite all precautions, you come back and find your car gone, call the police on a nonemergency number (call ☎ 411 for directory assistance) to see if they had it towed. If they didn't, don't hang up; report it stolen immediately.

Breakdown

Most rental cars are covered for breakdown; your rental agreement will have a toll-free breakdown number. Depending on the company, someone will come rescue you soon or next to soon. If they can't get to you until the next day, ask if your motel costs can be covered. Even if they say no, keep your receipts for food and lodging while you wait, and take the matter up with a manager when you return the car. You may get reimbursed, or perhaps get a coupon for a free rental next time.

If you break down in a privately owned vehicle and you're not a AAA member (see the Facts for the Visitor chapter), check the Yellow Pages under 'Towing.' If you're on the road, find a pay phone, call ☎ 411 for directory assistance and ask them for a towing company. If they argue and say they can't (they're instructed not to make suggestions so as not to show favoritism to certain companies), ask for a supervisor and explain your situation. They'll usually look up a company in the Yellow Pages for you. Members of the

Exit Number Changes

The Florida Department of Transportation has begun to change exit numbers on Florida's Interstates. A dual posting period will exist until April 2004 on I-4. You may want to try to make a point of finding out both the old and the new exit numbers for your destination before getting in the car, just to avoid any unnecessary confusion.

AAA and its foreign affiliates can call ☎ 800-222-4357 and a tow truck will be sent out quickly.

It may pay to rent or buy a cellular telephone, especially if you'll be traveling to remote areas (see Telephone in the Facts for the Visitor chapter).

Car Rental

All major US car rental companies have offices throughout Florida. Rates go up and down like the stock market, and it's always worth phoning around to see what's available. Booking ahead usually ensures the best rates – and booking ahead can mean calling the company's 800 number from the pay phone in the rental office. (Sometimes the head office can get you a better price than the branch office.) If you're a member of a frequent-flyer club, be sure to find out which rental agencies can give you miles. When booking your flight, ask if you can book a rental car at the same time – they may be able to offer a good deal. Usually, you can cancel the car booking with no charge if you find a better deal later – just ask.

Most car rental agencies require that you be at least 25 years of age and have a major credit card in your own name.

Orlando International Airport has all the major agencies onsite, making pick-up and drop-off very convenient.

Major rental companies in Florida include the following:

Alamo (☎ 800-327-9633, Ⓦ www.alamo.com)

Avis (☎ 800-831-2847, Ⓦ www.avis.com)

Budget (☎ 800-527-0700, Ⓦ www.budget.com)

Dollar (☎ 800-800-4000, Ⓦ www.dollar.com)

Enterprise (☎ 800-325-8007, Ⓦ www.enterprise.com)

Hertz (☎ 800-654-3131, Ⓦ www.hertz.com)

National (☎ 800-227-7368, Ⓦ www.nationalcar.com)

Thrifty (☎ 800-367-2277, Ⓦ www.thrifty.com)

Rates & Fuel In Florida, a typical small car costs $25 to $45 a day or $129 to $229 a week. On top of that there is a 6.5% state sales tax, $2.05 per day Florida road surcharge, $0.43 per day 'license recoupment charge,' and $7 to $18 a day for each insurance option you take (see Insurance later).

Generally speaking, the best deals are for weekly or weekend rentals. It pays to shop around carefully; the same car can vary from company to company by as much as $20 a day or $75 a week. If you're planning on dropping off at a different location than the one you picked up from, make certain there won't be any penalty. Enough companies offer this option that you shouldn't have to pay additional charges.

Most car rental companies in Florida include unlimited mileage at no extra cost. Be sure to check whether you get unlimited mileage, as you can rack up hundreds of miles *within* a city. At 25¢ per mile, this could be an unhappy surprise.

You may be offered a choice of 'fuel plans': you can pick up and return the car with a full tank of fuel, or you can pay for the gas that's in the car and return it empty. The former is always the better choice. As it's virtually impossible to return a car empty of gas, you will end up turning over several gallons of fuel to the rental company, which will then try to sell it to the next renter.

Gas stations are ubiquitous and many are open 24 hours a day. Small-town stations may be open only from 7am to 8pm or 9pm. At some stations you must pay before you pump; at others, you may pump before you pay. The more modern pumps have credit/debit card terminals built into them, so you can pay with plastic right at the pump. At more expensive, 'full service' stations, an attendant will pump your gas for you; no tip is expected. Plan on spending $1.40 to $1.60 per US gallon, more for higher-octane fuels.

Insurance Note that in Florida, liability insurance is not included in rental costs. Some credit cards cover Loss/Damage-Waiver (LDW, sometimes called CDW, or Collision/Damage Waiver), which means you won't have to pay if you damage the car itself. But liability insurance means you won't have to pay if you hit someone and they sue you. If you own a car and have insurance at home, your liability insurance may extend to coverage of rental cars, but be *absolutely* certain before driving on the roads in the litigious USA.

Note that in the case of damage, a rental company might require that you not only pay for repairs, but also that you pay normal rental fees for the time that the rental car is off the road for repairs. Your policy should cover this loss as well.

If you aren't already covered, you should seriously consider paying the extra money for liability and/or LDW insurance (at $7 to $18 daily).

Motorcycle Rental

Be a biker – or just look like one. To rent a motorcycle, you have to be at least 21 years old and possess both a motorcycle license and a major credit card with enough credit left to make a deposit of $1000 or more.

CruiseAmerica (☎ *800-327-7799;* W *www .cruiseamerica.com)* has several Florida locations and rents Honda motorcycles from $149 to $179 per day, including unlimited mileage, CDW and liability insurance. Helmets are also mandatory with CruiseAmerica.

Harley-Davidson (☎ *407-423-0346, 877-740-3770;* W *www.orlandoharley.com; day/week $70-140/350-750)* has a few Orlando locations. Check pamphlet counters at the airport, tourist center or your hotel for discounts.

RV Rental

A recreational vehicle (RV) can be a great way to get out into Florida. Renting an RV makes sense if you meet one of two conditions: a) you're as rich as Croesus or b) there are several of you chipping in to pay for it. RVs are surprisingly roomy and flexible, and even the smaller ones can sleep four comfortably – as long as you're close friends. If you're not, don't despair: many RV sites are large enough to accommodate the RV and still leave room for a tent outside.

The downside is you'll probably need additional transportation when you get to where you're going. At an average highway gas consumption of between 8 and 10 miles per gallon, RVs are not exactly a good method of city transport. You can, of course, get a bicycle rack or, if you also have a car, a tow-hitch to bring it along, but that makes your already dismal gas mileage even worse.

CruiseAmerica (☎ *800-327-7799;* W *www .cruiseamerica.com)* is the largest of the nationwide RV rental firms. It has a huge variety of RVs available. The standard – 21ft to 25ft with two double beds and a dinette that converts to a single bed, a bathroom with shower, and a kitchen – costs $875 a week during off-season and $1095 in peak season (three weeks around Christmas). A thousand miles are included; after that you're billed 29¢ a mile. You can prepurchase additional miles at 500 miles for $130, but there is no refund for unused miles. One-way drop-off charges within Florida add another $50. Inquire about their long-term rentals and buy-back programs.

El Monte RV (☎ *888-337-2228;* W *www.el monterv.com)*, a smaller company, also has many offices nationwide.

Recreational Vehicle Rental Association *(RVRA;* ☎ *703-591-7130, 800-336-0355;* W *www.rvra.org)* is a great resource for anyone considering renting an RV. Or, consult the Yellow Pages of the phone book under 'Recreational Vehicles-Renting & Leasing,' 'Trailers-Camping & Travel' and 'Motor Homes-Renting & Leasing.'

BICYCLE

If you can stand the heat, Florida's not a bad place for cycling. Absolutely flat roads make it easy going, and biking is a convenient mode of transportation. Helmets are not required under Florida law, but they're a good idea, as are highly reflective everything-you-can-think-of. Since Florida drivers are not used to seeing bicyclists, the more you can do to make them see you, the better chance you have of getting where you're going.

If you do get tired of biking, you can pack your bike. Most international airlines, and flights within Florida, allow you to bring a bike at no extra charge as checked luggage. They charge a fee ($50 to $100) if it's in addition to your checked-luggage limit. Bike boxes cost about $10 if you buy them from an airline, Greyhound or Amtrak (but Amtrak doesn't always require them – it depends on the route). You'll have to remove the handlebars and pedals to box it, but you may also get away with bagging it. Greyhound charges an additional $15 for your boxed bike.

Bike Florida (☎ *407-343-1992;* W *www.bike florida.org)* is the best all-around source for information about bicycling in the state. They'll assist with reservations for accommodations, help you plan itineraries, and counsel you on the realities of a bike trip through Florida.

HITCHHIKING

It is never entirely safe to hitchhike anywhere in the world, and we don't recommend it. Travelers who decide to hitchhike should understand that they are taking a small but potentially serious risk – creeps and criminals might see a hitchhiker as easy prey.

BOAT

All coastal cities, and even some inland ones, have sightseeing boats that cruise rivers, lakes, harbors and coastlines. See individual city sections in this book for details.

Cruises

A number of websites specialize in cruising, a multibillion-dollar business. Check out the following, and look for last-minute specials for multi-night and -day cruises (see the Walt Disney World Resort chapter for Disney Cruise Line information):

w www.cruise.com
w www.vacationstogo.com
w www.bestpricecruises.com
w www.cheapncl.com
w www.cruisesonly.com

Here is a list of some of the lines cruising out of Florida:

Carnival Cruise Lines (☎ 800-327-9501, **w** www.carnival.com)

Celebrity Cruises (☎ 800-437-3111, **w** www.celebritycruises.com)

Cunard Line (☎ 800-528-6273, **w** www.cunard.com)

Disney Cruise Line (☎ 800-951-3532, **w** www.disneycruise.disney.go.com)

Holland America (☎ 800-426-0327, **w** www.hollandamerica.com)

Norwegian Cruise Line (☎ 800-327-7030, **w** www.ncl.com)

Princess Cruises (☎ 800-421-0522, **w** www.princesscruises.com)

Royal Caribbean (☎ 800-327-6700, **w** www.royalcaribbean.com)

Royal Olympic Cruises (☎ 800-368-3888, **w** www.royalolympiccruises.com)

Sea Escape Cruises (☎ 800-327-2005, **w** www.seaescape.com)

Port Canaveral As the closest port to Orlando, Port Canaveral (☎ 321-783-7831, 888-767-8226; **w** www.portcanaveral.org) has been giving Miami a run for its money as the number-one port in the world since Scandinavian World Cruises established a home base here in 1982. Its mainstay is popular three- and four-night cruises with the Carnival, Norwegian, Disney, Holland America and Royal Caribbean lines.

Port of Tampa The Port of Tampa (☎ 813-905-7678, 800-741-2297; **w** www.tampaport.com; 1101 Channelside Dr) is still a small player by Florida standards, but it's rapidly gaining a foothold in the market. Currently it has berths for Carnival Cruise Lines, Celebrity Cruises, Holland America and Royal Caribbean.

PUBLIC TRANSPORTATION

See individual city sections for information about local public transportation.

Wheelchair-bound passengers should contact the local bus company to inquire about special transport services. Most buses in Florida are wheelchair accessible, though some bus companies offer individual transit services in addition to regular service for those with physical or mental disabilities. See the Facts for the Visitor chapter for information on organizations that assist with travel for the disabled.

Orlando

pop 186,000

No city in the world is quite like Orlando. Designed for pleasure and entertainment, the sheer…*Americanness* of it is enough to make some people glow with pride and others shudder in shame. It is, indeed, the world's largest tourist trap, and humans pour in from all four corners of the earth like Disney's poor misrepresented lemmings over a cliff (see the boxed text 'Fact or Disney?' in the Walt Disney World chapter). And they love every second of it and come back for more, as may you.

But that's really just part of it. There's plenty of Orlando that seems like just a regular American city. Believe it or not, even if every last theme park was shut down, there would still be plenty of reason to visit O-Town and its surrounding environs. The downtown area of the city is clean, and Lake Eola is beautiful for a midday stroll. Just north is a lovely historic district, populated with well-maintained older homes, bricklined streets, and plenty of huge shady trees dripping with Spanish moss. Restaurants, bars and clubs abound in all varieties, and the museums and theaters of the Cultural Corridor are excellent civic attractions.

For Winter Park and other areas surrounding the city, see Around Orlando later in this chapter. For Walt Disney World and Celebration, see the Walt Disney World Resort chapter; Universal Orlando has also earned its own chapter (and deservedly so!).

HISTORY

At the end of the Second Seminole War, settlers and traders made their way here, eager to build homes and farms in the fertile region. Originally named Jernigan (after settler Aaron Jernigan), the settlement here grew up around Fort Gatlin and became the Orange County seat in 1856. In 1857 the city was renamed Orlando for Orlando Reeves, a soldier killed by Seminole Indians on the shores of Lake Eola.

The city boomed several times; a railroad boom (which fueled a population boom), a real-estate boom and a citrus boom all brought prosperity to the area. And the late 1950s saw a technology boom, as Orlando manufactured the hardware for Cape Canaveral's launches.

With the establishment of Walt Disney World in 1971, the area became theme park central. Almost overnight, the median income rose by 50% and development exploded. Orlando is now the third-ranking destination of overseas visitors, after Los Angeles and New York City. To get a better idea of the drawing power of the Mouse and others, consider that Honolulu, San Francisco and Miami are all in this city's dust.

See the Facts about Central Florida chapter for more history.

ORIENTATION

I-4 is the main north–south connector, though it's labeled east–west: to go north, take I-4 east (toward Daytona); to go south, hop on I-4 west (toward Tampa).

The main east–west thoroughfares are Hwy 50 and Hwy 528 (Bee Line Expressway; toll road), which connect Orlando to the Space Coast. The Orlando International Airport is accessible from the Bee Line Expressway.

Highlights

- Strolling along a quiet brick-paved street under a shady canopy of Spanish moss in downtown Orlando's historic residential area
- Feeding the dolphins and fighting off the birds at SeaWorld
- Taking in the views on a scenic boat tour in Winter Park
- Plunging over 300ft and then flying like Superman on the Skycoaster in Kissimmee
- Walking around Lake Eola followed by a fine dinner and some cocktails at Church St Station

Where Do You Draw the Line?

The borders of the municipality of Orlando are…interestingly drawn. Often, when the sprawling city reaches a working-class, Hispanic or black neighborhood, the city limits mysteriously end, leaving the folks beyond the borders without city services or voting power. Decades of selective annexations of wealthy areas point to a city government that's been more interested in increasing tax revenues than building a diverse community. Orlando is not unique to this sort of redlining, but it could be argued that few other cities are so blatant about it – you need only drive a few blocks west of the well-manicured downtown area before you're dodging potholes and empty shopping carts in a rundown poor black area.

In the 2003 mayoral elections this was a hot topic, with both candidates promising changes to incorporate more areas. However, candidate Pete Barr, whose losing campaign was tarred with accusations of racial slurs, claimed that previous annexations had been colorblind. Meanwhile, winner Buddy Dyer criticized officials for cherry-picking prime property.

So Orlandoans (at least those who were allowed to vote) made their voices heard. But what actually *happens* in the coming years to the fringes of Orlando remains to be seen.

A good map is essential, as the area is so spread out, and you'll have to spend some money if you want to explore. Especially if you're driving in downtown Orlando, which is a one-way nightmare, you should consider getting a detailed nontourist map. Dolph, Universal and Rand McNally all produce useful maps ($3 to $5 at any area gas station). The maps put out by AAA are also good and are free for members.

The best way to think about Orlando (and this chapter for that matter) is to break it down into a few basic categories.

Downtown Orlando

Quaint in the daytime and a bar-lover's haven at night, downtown Orlando is centered on north–south Orange Ave and east–west Central Blvd, which divide the city's addresses into north, south, east and west. The main drags are Orange Ave and Church St.

Outer Orlando

From the downtown area, Orlando expands to some degree in all directions: **northward** you'll find the Cultural Corridor and, along Colonial Dr, plenty of Vietnamese eateries; **eastward** is ritzy and residential; **westward** is an unincorporated poor African-American area that belies the city's real concerns (see the boxed text 'Where Do You Draw the Line?'); and **southward** is partly working-class residential and partly a trendy area.

International Drive

Also in the area south of downtown is International Dr, or I-Drive, which is home to Sea-World, Universal Studios/Islands of Adventure,

Wet 'n' Wild and dozens of other minor attractions – and therefore, it's also home to more hotels and restaurants than you can count. Several buildings flanking the strip have made their own personal attempts at grabbing your attention – some buildings were built to look upside-down or lopsided, and even the McDonald's has a bright, flashy marquee. The International Dr strip is bookended by Universal Studios and SeaWorld; there are three exits to International Dr from I-4.

Hwy 192

If International Dr is Las Vegas, Hwy 192 is Reno. About 25 miles southwest of downtown Orlando, this is often referred to as Kissimmee (pronounced kih-**sih**-mee), which is a town further east. Hwy 192 is where you'll find the cheapest motels and plenty of

Driving on Hwy 192

Pick up a tourist map of Kissimmee, which will feature popular attractions, restaurants and motels along Hwy 192. Because of the glut of eye-grabbing signs crammed in on the street, it's extremely easy to pass what you're looking for on the highway, and it's a real pain to have to make two U-turns on the busy highway to backtrack. So to help you, big blue highway markers have been posted. Before journeying out to your destination, you may want to call the place and ask for the location's position with regards to the markers and/or any super-visible landmarks, and then keep your eyes peeled.

ORLANDO

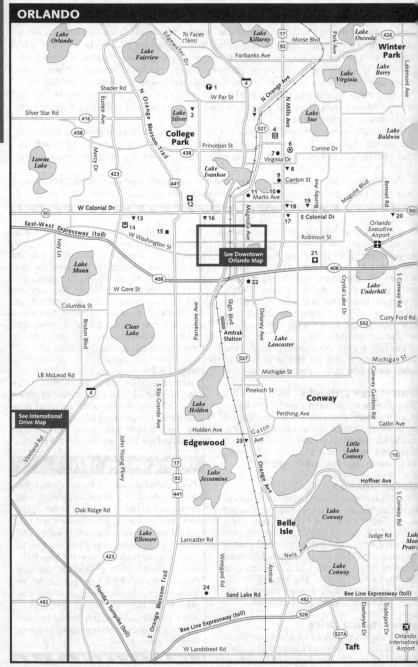

To Faces (1km)

Lake Orlando

Lake Fairview

Lake Killarny

Lake Osceola

426

Winter Park

Morse Blvd

17
92

Park Ave

Lake Berry

Lake Virginia

Lakemont Ave

Fairbanks Ave

Shader Rd

W Par St

4

Silver Star Rd

416
438

Eunice Ave

N Orange Ave

N Orange Blossom Trail

Lake Silver

▼2

1

W Par St

3

527

N Mills Ave

4

6

Lake Sue

Lake Baldwin

College Park

Princeton St

438

Corrine Dr

7

Virginia Dr

▼8

Lawne Lake

Mercy Dr

423

441

Lake Ivanhoe

9

Canton St

11

10

Marks Ave

19

Bumby Ave

Maguire Blvd

Bennet Rd

12

▼18

50

W Colonial Dr

East-West Expressway (toll)

▼13

14

15

W Washington St

▼16

Magnolia Ave

17

E Colonial Dr

50

20

Orlando Executive Airport

Robinson St

See Downtown Orlando Map

21

408

Crystal Lake Dr

Lake Underhill

S Conway Rd

Ivey Ln

Lake Mann

W Gore St

22

408

Columbia St

Bruton Blvd

Clear Lake

Parramore Ave

Sligh Blvd

Delaney Ave

Lake Lancaster

552

Curry Ford Rd

Amtrak Station

527

Michigan St

Michigan St

LB McLeod Rd

4

S Rio Grande Ave

Pineloch St

Conway

Conway Gardens Rd

Lake Holden

Pershing Ave

Gatlin Ave

See International Drive Map

Vineland Rd

John Young Pkwy

Holden Ave

Edgewood

23 ▼

Gatlin Ave

Little Lake Conway

15

Oak Ridge Rd

17
92
441

Lake Jessamine

Hoffner Ave

S Conway Rd

Belle Isle

423

Lake Ellenore

Lancaster Rd

Winegard Rd

Amtrak

Lake Conway

Judge Rd

Lake Mary Jane Prairie

Nela Ave

Lake Conway

482

Florida's Turnpike (toll)

S Orange Blossom Trail

24

Sand Lake Rd

482

Bee Line Expressway (toll)

528

Daetwyler Dr

Tradeport Dr

Orlando International Airport

527A

Taft

W Landstreet Rd

budget restaurants to go with them. It's an awful eyesore, but it's very close to Walt Disney World.

The area around Kissimmee was once a peaceful landscape of swamps and green, but the extraordinary growth of theme parks has had a profound effect on the surroundings. Hwy 192 (also called Irlo Bronson Memorial Hwy and Vine Ave) is a sprawling ribbon of endless concrete, motels, shopping malls, wannabe attractions and discount ticket stands of dubious reliability (see Tourist Offices later in this chapter).

INFORMATION
Tourist Offices

There are lots of unofficial 'tourist information centers' concentrated along International Dr and Hwy 192 in Kissimmee. Most offer a hard sell on free or discounted tickets in exchange for looking at some pricey property; however, tours are tedious and tickets are often restricted or falsified. If you're promised free parking or the right to go to the front of long lines, it's almost certainly a scam. Should you fall for it, please don't complain to harried amusement park staff; it's not their fault you thought you were slick. Call the police instead. Other venues offer deals on partially used multiple-day passes for Walt Disney World and Universal Studios. These are *usually* real and can result in considerable savings, but it's illegal to purchase or use them. Really, it's best to just go to the official tourist centers and not have to deal with the anxiety of wondering whether you're being hoodwinked.

The most official and helpful place to go is the **Official Tourist Information Center** (☎ 407-363-5871, 800-551-0181; W www.go2orlando .com; 8123 International Dr; open 8am-7pm daily), at the corner of Austrian Row. Here, staff sell legitimate discount attraction tickets (you'll save about 5%) and racks and stacks of free coupon books and handouts.

If you're staying in the Kissimmee/Hwy 192 area, the **Kissimmee/St Cloud Convention & Visitors Bureau** (☎ 407-847-5000, 800-327-9159; W www.floridakiss.com; 1925 W Hwy 192; open 8am-5pm Mon-Fri) may be more convenient.

Money

Bank of America (☎ 407-244-7041; 390 N Orange Ave) is right downtown, but there are branches everywhere. Also downtown, **American Express** (☎ 407-843-0004; 2 W Church St) has a full-service office in Sun Trust Bank.

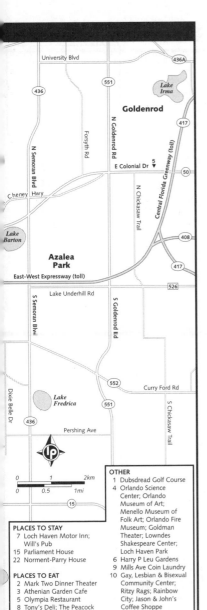

University Blvd

Goldenrod

Azalea Park
East-West Expressway (toll)

Lake Underhill Rd

Curry Ford Rd

Lake Fredrica

Pershing Ave

Cheney Hwy

Lake Barton

N Semoran Blvd

Forsyth Rd

N Goldenrod Rd

N Chickasaw Trail

Central Florida Greenway (toll)

E Colonial Dr

S Semoran Blvd

S Goldenrod Rd

S Chickasaw Trail

Dixie Belle Dr

Lake Irma

436 | 436A | 551 | 417 | 50 | 408 | 417 | 526 | 552 | 551 | 436

| 0 | 1 | 2km |
| 0 | 0.5 | 1mi |

PLACES TO STAY
7 Loch Haven Motor Inn; Will's Pub
15 Parliament House
22 Norment-Parry House

PLACES TO EAT
2 Mark Two Dinner Theater
3 Athenian Garden Cafe
5 Olympia Restaurant
8 Tony's Deli; The Peacock Room
13 Caribbean Sunshine Bakery
16 Garden Cafe
17 Little Saigon; Ahn Hong
18 Moodswing Café
19 Thanh Thanh; Thai House
20 Sweet Tomatoes
23 Le Coq au Vin

OTHER
1 Dubsdread Golf Course
4 Orlando Science Center; Orlando Museum of Art; Menello Museum of Folk Art; Orlando Fire Museum; Goldman Theater; Lowndes Shakespeare Center; Loch Haven Park
6 Harry P Leu Gardens
9 Mills Ave Coin Laundry
10 Gay, Lesbian & Bisexual Community Center; Ritzy Rags; Rainbow City; Jason & John's Coffee Shoppe
11 Orlando Opera & Orlando Ballet Box Offices
12 Full Moon Saloon
14 Greyhound Bus Station
21 Southern Nights
24 Sandlake Rd Maytag Laundry

DOWNTOWN ORLANDO

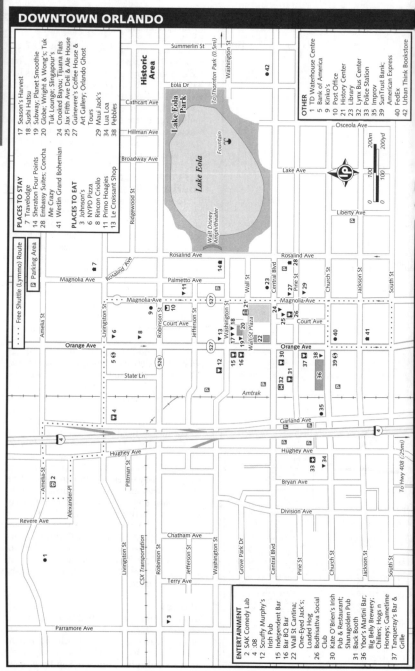

PLACES TO STAY
7 Travelodge
14 Sheraton Four Points
28 Embassy Suites; Concha Me Crazy
41 Westin Grand Bohemian

PLACES TO EAT
3 Johnson's
6 NYPD Pizza
8 Rincon Criollo
11 Primo Hoagies
13 Le Croissant Shop
17 Season's Harvest
18 Sushi Hatsu
19 Subway; Planet Smoothie
20 Globe; Wright & Wong's; Tuk Tuk Lounge; Slingapour's
24 Crooked Bayou; Tijuana Flats
25 Jax Fifth Ave Deli & Ale House
27 Guinevere's Coffee House & Art Gallery; Orlando Ghost Tours
29 Maui Jack's
34 Lua Loa
38 Pebbles

OTHER
1 TD Waterhouse Centre
5 Bank of America
9 Kinko's
10 Post Office
21 History Center
23 Library
32 Lynx Bus Center
33 Police Station
35 Improv
39 SunTrust Bank; American Express
40 FedEx
42 Urban Think Bookstore

ENTERTAINMENT
2 SAK Comedy Lab
4 :08
12 Scruffy Murphy's Irish Pub
15 Independent Bar
16 Bar BQ Bar
22 Wall St Cantina; One-Eyed Jack's; Loaded Hog
26 Bodhisattva Social Club
30 Kate O'Brien's Irish Pub & Restaurant; Shanagolden Pub
31 Back Booth
36 Ybor's Martini Bar; Big Belly Brewery; Chillers; Hogs n Honeys; Gametime
37 Tanqueray's Bar & Grille

Most theme parks have ATMs and foreign exchange desks.

Post

The **main post office** (46 E Robinson St) is downtown. Opposite is **Kinko's** (☎ 407-839-5000; 47 E Robinson St; open 7am-10pm Mon-Sat, 7am-7pm Sun), which has fax, photocopier and desktop publishing services. There is also a downtown office of **FedEx** (W www.fedex.com; 201 S Orange Ave; open 9:30am-7:30pm Mon-Fri).

Bookstores & Libraries

Urban Think Bookstore (☎ 407-650-8004; W www.urbanthinkorlando.com; 625 E Central Blvd; open 10am-9pm Mon-Sat, 10am-6pm Sun) is a wonderful independent bookstore with a great and knowledgeable staff.

The main **library** (☎ 407-835-7323; 100 E Central Blvd; open 9am-9pm Mon-Thur, 9am-6pm Fri & Sat, 1pm-6pm Sun), downtown, offers Internet access for $5 per week; call to ask about other library locations.

Media

The most popular daily is the *Orlando Sentinel* (W www.orlandosentinel.com). Lots of free weeklies and monthlies cover local events, politics and the music scene: *Groove* (W www.yougotgroove.com) hits the dance scene; *Axis* (W www.axismag.com) is about alternative rock; *Orlando Weekly* (W www.orlandoweekly.com) and *Connections* are the major free weeklies; and *Impact Press* publishes left-wing rants.

Commercial radio in Orlando is actually OK (the playlists have more than four songs in rotation). There's alternative FM rock at 101.3, 104.1 and 105.9; dance at 101.9 and 106.7; classic rock at 96.5, 98.9 and 101.5; golden oldies at 100.3; and country at 97.5. National Public Radio (NPR) is at 90.7 FM and 89.9 FM.

Gay & Lesbian Travelers

The **Gay, Lesbian & Bisexual Community Center** (☎ 407-228-8272; W www.glbcc.org; 946 N Mills Ave; open noon-5pm Mon-Thur & Sat) has a library and resource center, plus tips on local hot spots and social events. **Rainbow City** (☎ 407-898-9069; 930 N Mills Ave) has a huge selection of g/l/b/t literature and friendly staff; one salesperson, Matt, was only half kidding when he noted wryly that these few blocks along N Mills Ave were 'Orlando's best stab at West Hollywood.'

Laundry

Most motels have a coin laundry, and for a large fee, you can often have your hotel do your laundry for you.

Mills Ave Coin Laundry (☎ 407-898-9059; 1030 N Mills Ave; open 24hrs) is a good choice for insomniacs. **Sandlake Rd Maytag Laundry** (☎ 407-438-8911; 811 Sand Lake Rd; open 7am-7pm Mon-Sat; 8am-6pm Sun) is convenient to International Dr.

Police & Medical Services

Call ☎ 911 in an emergency. In a nonemergency (eg, to report something stolen), call ☎ 321-235-5300; that is indeed for Orlando, despite the area code. The main police station is downtown at 100 S Hughley Ave, near Central Blvd.

Ask-A-Nurse (☎ 407-303-1700) is a free service that provides 24-hour information on how to treat nonemergency injuries and symptoms.

Main St Physicians (☎ 407-396-1195; 8324 International Dr; open 8am-3:30pm Mon-Fri, 8am-8pm Sat & Sun) is a walk-in clinic; see the International Dr map for location. A visit costs at least $95, and you have to pay up front. They also offer a 24-hour service that sends doctors to most hotels in the area, starting at $185. They accept very few insurance carriers.

Sand Lake Hospital (☎ 407-351-8550; 9400 Turkey Lake Rd) is a full-service medical facility; see the International Dr map for location.

Curfew

A curfew is in effect from midnight to 6am in downtown Orlando for anyone under 18 years old. Offenders will be detained, and perhaps worse, their parents will be summoned to fetch them. This is not a joke.

SEAWORLD ORLANDO

A fun combination of amusement park, aquarium and beer garden, SeaWorld (☎ 407-351-3600; W www.seaworld.com; 7007 SeaWorld Orlando Dr; adult/child 3-9 $52/43; hours vary) is excellent family entertainment. It's a little pricey – more than a Disney park – but some of that money does go to very good causes: the SeaWorld Orlando Animal Rescue Team is one of the best in the country. And if you're the sort of person who likes leaping dolphins, sliding sea lions and crashing whales, you're going to have an incredible time.

Orientation & Information

SeaWorld Orlando is near the intersection of I-4 and the Bee Line Expressway, at the bottom of the International Dr strip.

Guest Services, to your left as you enter the park, has an ATM and exchanges foreign currency 10am to 4pm daily. They also have a lost and found, foreign-language guides, kennel services ($7; bring your own food) and lockers ($4).

SeaWorld participates in the 14-day, five-park **FlexTicket** program (adult/child $203/165), which includes the two Universal Orlando parks, Wet 'n' Wild and Busch Gardens in Tampa. Discount tickets and package deals are available. Parking is $7/8 per car/recreational vehicle (RV).

All attractions are wheelchair accessible. Single/double strollers can be rented for $8/14, manual/electric wheelchairs for $8/25. There are air-conditioned child-care centers throughout the park with diapers, formula and other necessities for sale, and changing tables in all restrooms.

Rides

SeaWorld is primarily a show-based park, but there are a few options for those who are craving a little energy boost.

Kraken It's a darn good roller coaster, but not the best in Orlando. Named after a legendary sea monster, the ride gives you an idea of what it might feel like to ride on top of the writhing beast. There's a little mist and some silly Kraken eggs at the end of the ride, but the theme is played up enough.

Journey to Atlantis This roller coaster cum flume ride has special effects aplenty, but the reason why everyone's screaming is the 60ft vertical drop. Will you get wet? No, you'll get soaked – enough to make Shamu feel a little work-related pressure. Since this ride doesn't go upside down, you might think it's better for children. And in that sense it is, but young ones (especially girls who adore Ariel) could get freaked by the creepy evil mermaids.

Wild Arctic You're traveling to Base Station Wild Arctic in an incredibly high-powered helicopter as a bad storm front moves in. The nature-loving pilot brings you very close to some polar bears before setting down on thin ice. Of course, after hearing an awful rumbling sound, you fall through the ice, and it's touch and go for a while, but...

This ride is interesting in that you can experience it either as a simple IMAX movie or as a Star Tours–like ride. The ride is far from scary, but if you have doubts, get in the Walk line, as opposed to the Fly line. After the show/ride, you walk through a cave and maybe get to glimpse some polar bears and other Arctic life.

It is c-c-c-cold in this area. Even if it's a hot day, you will get chilly within minutes.

Shows

Seating at SeaWorld shows is on ridged metal benches that are low to the ground. You might have to sit on a jacket to keep the blood flowing to your feet.

Shamu Adventure Killer whales are the stars at SeaWorld, and this is where you watch them do their thing. TV animal expert Jack Hanna hosts the show on a large high-resolution video screen. The first 15 rows – sometimes more – of Shamu Stadium are the 'splash zone,' and both whales and trainers enjoy soaking the crowd with icy seawater. If you go to SeaWorld, you can't miss this show.

Cirque de la Mer If you *are* going to miss a show, this one should be it, especially if you've been to (or plan to see) a Cirque du Soleil show. Although there are highlights – some of the acrobatics are stunning – a lot of it is a not-very-funny, headache-inducing clown show (will someone *please* take away that clown's whistle?!?).

Key West Dolphin Adventure Atlantic bottlenose dolphins and their trainers work together so beautifully in this show – you can really get a sense of the deep, fond relationship between the animals and the humans. Bet you didn't think a dolphin could get you soaked, either! Rarely seen false killer whales, which look like skinny dark-grey killer whales, are also featured.

Pets Ahoy! Featuring the talents of cats, birds, rats, pot-bellied pigs and other animals, this show will delight the little ones. Many of the showpets went from a final cage to the grand stage (they were rescued from local animal shelters).

Clyde & Seamore Take Pirate Island Also a must-see, this is a truly delightful show starring sea lion, otter and walrus 'comedians.' It's excellent for kids, who find it screamingly funny – and the humans in it are pretty funny too. In fact, they may be the only ones in Orlando who can perform a schlocky script with panache. Take the tots to **Shamu's Happy Harbor** afterward, to work off some of that excitement.

Shamu Rocks America SeaWorld's daily grand finale combines splashes in the water and splashes in the sky, with both Shamu and fireworks to bring the day to a close. Get there early!

Other Attractions

Dolphin Nursery Is there anything cuter than a bunch of baby dolphins leaping and playing? Red balls bounce around the water as the little grey tikes learn to earn their fins. It's shady too, so if you just want to relax for a while, it's a good place to come.

Key West at SeaWorld You can take an up-close look at endangered sea turtles at **Turtle Point**. Nearby, **Tropical Reef** is home to exotic fish, parrots, macaws and flamingos. Banyan trees and 30ft bamboo trees make you feel like you're in Southeast Asia. For $6, you can feed the dolphins (or just pet them for free) at **Dolphin Cove**, and you can do the same to slimy little de-stingered baby stingrays at **Stingray Lagoon**.

Pacific Point Preserve California sea lions, fur seals and harbor seals make merry (and plenty of noise) in this area, created to look like the rugged Pacific coastline. There's underwater viewing as well.

Shark Encounter Menacing sharks, rays, barracudas, lionfish and skates swim all around the 60ft-long Plexiglas tube that you're carried through on a conveyor belt. Aren't you glad Orlando doesn't have a beach?

Clydesdale Hamlet You can walk through the stables of these enormous and proud horses, which are the symbol of Anheuser-Busch products. There are good photo opportunities (when the horses are decked out in all their finery) from 12:30pm to 1:30pm; or at Wild Arctic at noon and the Games Area, north of the Shamu Stadium, at 4pm.

Manatees: The Last Generation? The heroic SeaWorld Orlando Animal Rescue Team rescues injured and sick manatees, and this is where you'll see the recuperating cuties.

It begins with a heart-wrenching film and finishes with a fine view of manatees bearing the scars of human encroachment. As much as possible, the SeaWorld manatees are eventually released back into the wild.

If you want to see manatees in the wild, see the Blue Springs State Park section of the North of Orlando chapter.

Penguin Encounter People movers take you past penguin tanks with manufactured snow, the sounds of penguin calls barely audible over the hilarious and appropriate *oom-pah-pah* music. Dig the wild rockhopper penguins, who look very much like mid-1980s Rod Stewart.

Anheuser-Busch Hospitality Center A favorite of harried single dads trying to cope with the hyperactive kids they haven't seen in six months, this 'educational' attraction teaches you a little about the brewing of Anheuser-Busch products and a lot about the self-acclaimed greatness of the company itself. Afterward, you'll sample several to make sure they're OK. You'll also get to do a taste test between a stale Bud and a fresh one (hint: the stale one actually has more flavor). All in all, it feels like one big Budweiser commercial. If you get bored of the corporate propaganda, try to count how many times you hear the phrase 'king of beers.' Yes, you get free beer, or some derivative thereof.

Shamu's Happy Harbor Slides, plastic bubbles, nets and tunnels for the kiddos. Splash Attack lets them soak each other for kicks. Whee!

Animal Interaction Programs

Yes, these are pricey, but for many, this is a dream come true. Call SeaWorld to find out if any new or temporary programs will be available during your visit. All these programs are limited to four people per day, so make reservations early. For all of these, participants must be at least 13 years old.

Animal Care Experience ($389) gives you a chance to work with SeaWorld's animal rescue and rehabilitation team; it teaches basic marine animal care and feeding. **SeaWorld Trainer for a Day** ($389) is just what it sounds like, and participants must be at least 52 inches tall. **False Killer Whale Interaction Program** ($200) is the only program of its kind in North America; it lets you swim with Shamu. A guardian must accompany those

Orlando FlexTicket

If you'd like to visit Wet 'n' Wild, Busch Gardens, both Universal Orlando parks and/or SeaWorld, it pays to get a five-park FlexTicket (adult/child 3-9 $203/165), which gets you *unlimited* entry to all of those places within a 14-day time period, plus a free express bus to Busch Gardens. If Busch Gardens is not on your agenda, there's a four-park FlexTicket (adult/child 3-9 $170/135) that excludes that more distant park.

Even if you visit each place only once, you will save significantly. The official tourist centers (see Information earlier in this chapter) sell FlexTickets at a slight discount.

under 18, and participants must be at least 52 inches tall.

Discovery Cove (☎ 407-370-1280; W www .discoverycove.com; admission $219), adjacent to its parent park SeaWorld, is an innovative and elite attraction and is limited to only 1000 guests daily; make reservations well ahead. Private beaches, a complimentary lunch and an exotic bird aviary are just a few of the diversions. As part of your day, you'll get some hands-on basic training and then swim with dolphins! There are also snorkeling opportunities in a lagoon packed with rays and tropical fish. Reviews of Discovery Cove are mixed. One participant was disappointed that, after an hour of training, she only got to spend a few minutes with the dolphins. Other people felt it was the best vacation they'd ever had.

Places to Eat

Cypress Bakery has pastries, coffee, juices and cold sandwiches. For ice cream, get yourself over to **Polar Parlor**. Fried yumminess is at **Captain Pete's Island Eats**, which serves funnel cake, fritters, chicken tenders, hot dogs and smoothies. **Mama Stella's Italian Kitchen** has pasta, pizza, sandwiches and salads. **Smoky Creek Grill** does BBQ – you'll smell it from afar. Burgers and hot sandwiches are the fare at the **Waterfront Sandwich Grill**; similar food is offered at **Dockside Cafe** and **The Deli**, which also has beef stew in a bread bowl and salads. The food at **Mango Joe's Cafe** is slightly more healthful – fajitas, fish sandwiches and entrée salads. For full-service dining, head to **Sharks Underwater Grill**, which has a dining area in an underwater grotto, seafood, steaks, pizza and two age-related kids menus.

Now, for more money, you can have a special SeaWorld dining experience. The **Polynesian Luau** (adult/child under 13/child 3-8 $38/28/17) features dancing, drumming and an 'exotic' banquet.

Dine with Shamu (adult/child under 10/child 3-10 $32/18) is a very popular, one-hour buffet meal that puts you just a splash away from SeaWorld's biggest star.

WET 'N' WILD

Wet 'n' Wild (☎ 407-351-1800, 800-992-9453; W www.wetnwild.com; 6200 International Dr; adult/child 3-9 $32/26; hours vary, open year-round) is one of Florida's first water parks, and it's still a refreshing way to spend part of your vacation.

Wet 'n' Wild participates in the FlexTicket program (see the boxed text in this chapter). Parking is $7/8 per car/RV. It's perfectly located right at the heart of International Dr and is clean, safe and family oriented – not to mention packed with great rides.

Some of the attractions include **The Storm**, which dumps you into a huge whirlpool; **Mach 5**, a superslick mat ride; **Black Hole**, enclosed for maximum disorientation; and **Hydra Fighter**, which involves bungee cords and fire hoses in a two-person car. At the center of the park is a wave pool; **Lazy River** meanders around the perimeter. There's also an artificial beach. The whole place can be quite the pick-up scene.

HOLY LAND EXPERIENCE

Did you ever wonder where Rod and Todd Flanders spent their vacation while the Simpson family, through a series of hilarious mishaps, ends up performing at Gay Day in the Magic Kingdom? They came to Holy Land Experience (☎ 407-367-2065; W www .theholylandexperience.com; 4655 Vineland Rd; adult/child 6-12 $30/20, hours vary), Orlando's only Christian theme park, and the only theme park with a mission (other than to take your money and to keep you coming back for more) – it's focused on showing Jews that Jesus Christ was indeed the son of God, and to explain why Christianity may be better for them. The publication and website for the organization Zion's Hope (W www.zionshope .org) will spell it out for you.

The park is designed to look like Jerusalem c. 33 AD, and staff (who are born-again Christians) wear flowing Bedouin robes and hawk Middle Eastern food treats ($5 to $7) such as mint tea, tabouli and falafel, as well as Goliath burgers and fries, and chicken fajitas (not sure about that one). Even more prevalent are the shops selling Holy Land Experience gear and Christian- and Jerusalem-themed tchotchkes – everything from carved wooden camels to Jesus-fish neckties. There aren't any rides, despite obvious Old Testament candidates like the Parting of the Red Sea.

You have to be really interested in Biblical history or very devout to enjoy this. Otherwise, it's as boring as spending a day in church. If you're going for the novelty and to ogle, that wears off quickly and isn't worth the admission.

Gospel choirs come from all over the Southeast to perform here, and there's a daily musical performed at the six-story, blindingly white **Plaza of the Nations**.

The **Jerusalem Model AD 66** is an impressive scale model of ancient Jerusalem, blending history, archaeology and New Testament tales in a somewhat dry but educational way. The **Theater of Life** has continuous showings of *The Seed of Promise,* a 25-minute film that's about – well, it's not really clear what the through-line is on this one, but Abraham's near-sacrifice of Isaac is particularly moving. Also featured are Adam and a deferential, blonde and bodacious Eve running (discreetly) naked through Eden's foliage, with God yelling after them 'Where are you, Adam?!' For a minute, you might feel like you're watching one of the *Friday the 13th* movies. At the end is the crucifixion of Christ, followed by a scene where people of all races and professions (?) stand agog and teary-eyed, looking at what must be the Second Coming.

The **Wilderness Tabernacle** takes you back 3400 years to see the nine different ways Aaron (Moses' older brother) sacrificed sheep to God, complete with a light-and-sound spectacular reminiscent of *Raiders of the Lost Ark*. Although that part only lasts a few seconds and doesn't show any melting faces or angry spirits, this could scare young ones just a bit.

The **Scriptorium** is a 55-minute tour of biblical antiquities such as Babylonian tablets that are more than 4000 years old, ancient Egyptian scrolls, and an exact replica of the Gutenberg Press. To get you juiced and amped and in the mood, there are monitors so you can try your hand at some *serious* Bible trivia (for example, 'Which Biblical woman lived to be 127 years old – Eve, Sarah or Ruth?').

Rules, as you might imagine, are strict: Dress conservatively and don't smoke. Anyone yelling about evolution, gay rights or abortion will be politely escorted to the parking lot. You can rent strollers for $5 and arrange tours for the deaf and blind in advance. Parking costs $5.

Oh, and make sure to anoint yourself aplenty with sunscreen – some of the shows have uncovered seating, and no amount of faith will save you from a Florida sunburn.

To get to Holy Land Experience, follow the signs from I-4 exit 78; it's at the corner of Conroy and Vineland Rds.

SKULL KINGDOM

You can't miss the giant skull motif on this souped-up haunted house (☎ 407-354-1564; W www.skullkingdom.com; 5933 American Way; adult/child under 8 $15/7.50; open 6pm-11pm Mon-Fri, noon-11pm Sat & Sun), at the corner of International Dr. It's not high-tech or anything, but some love went into this palace of horrors, and you are very likely to scream a few times; it's not recommended for children under 8. It's the by-product of the once-great, now-defunct Terror on Church St, which was one of the most remarkable haunted houses ever. If you decide to go to Skull Kingdom, try to get your hands on a coupon.

VANS SKATEBOARD PARK

Adrenaline junkies will love this enormous skateboard and BMX park (☎ 407-351-3881; W www.vans.com/skateparkorg/orlando.html; 5220 International Dr; 2-hour session $14; open 10am-11pm daily), at the intersection of Touchstone Dr. You can rent a skateboard ($5) and all the necessary safety equipment, right after you (or your legal guardian if you're under 18) sign a comprehensive waiver.

SPLENDID CHINA

This Chinese-owned-and-operated theme park (☎ 407-396-7111, 800-244-6226; W www.flor idasplendidchina.com; 3000 Splendid China Blvd; adult/child 5-12 $29/19; hours vary) is definitely a different sort of dazzling. Exhibits, arranged throughout the manicured grounds, are miniature replicas of famous Chinese sights done in meticulously detailed, hand-painted ceramic. It attracts lots of Chinese-American families hoping to force-feed the kids some history, and they've come to the right place: the Stone Forest, Great Wall, Temple of Confucius and Forbidden City are just a few of the dramatic displays populated by five-inch-tall inhabitants.

A recorded history of each site is provided in English and Spanish, and a free tram circles the park, hitting most sites. There are also performances of folk music, martial arts and traditional theater, including a 90-minute show called *Mysterious Kingdom of the Orient*, featuring Chinese circus acts. Admission includes a meal at one on-site restaurant. If you're just interested in the 90-minute show, it's $15 (including dinner).

To get to the park, take I-4 exit 64B and go west (toward Disney) on Hwy 192. Near Mile Marker 5, you'll see a sign.

GATORLAND

You're in Florida, so you've got to see gators. And this is a fine place (☎ 407-855-5496, 800-393-5297; W *www.gatorland.com; 14501 S Orange Blossom Trail; adult/child 3-12 $20/ 10; open 9am-dusk daily*) to do it. A warning though: this place probably isn't PETA (People for the Ethical Treatment of Animals)-approved, and the **Wrestlin' Gator Show** may have more empathic folks squirming. If you can handle it, however, try to catch Babs Steorts, Gatorland's first female wrestler, take on one of the toothy critters.

Ethical issues aside, Gatorland is fun. The **Jumparoo Show** has 10ft-long alligators leaping almost entirely out of the water to grab chunks of rotting meat from the trainer's hand – like Shamu, only creepy. The **breeding marsh**, with 100 females and 25 lucky guys, is, well, one whole heck of a lot of alligators. The **Gatorland Express Train** will give you a tour of the place for an extra $1. There are also lots of crocodiles and other reptiles imported from all over the world.

Hungry? Gatorland breeds alligators for food, and you can get the freshest gator nuggets and smoked gator ribs around at **Pearl's Smokehouse**.

SKYCOASTER

By far, the most adrenaline-pumping experience in Central Florida is the Skycoaster (☎ 407-397-2509; W *www.skycoaster.com; Hwy 192 btwn I-4 & Seralago Blvd; 1/2/3 people $37/32/27*).

Picture this: you and up to two other people are wrapped in an apron that's hooked on to a long rope, which pulls you more than 300ft straight up into the air. You dangle helplessly for a few moments, and then a voice from below commands a designated faller to yank the release. Then you shoot down, straight at the pond below, head first, at speeds of up to 85mph. At the last second before impact, you're suddenly soaring above

the water, and now you can enjoy a minute of swinging to and fro over the water while you catch your breath, try to relocate your stomach and whisper a few 'Holy Sh*ts!' to your companions in a voice that's now weak and hoarse from your full-throttle screaming. It's over fast, but worth every penny. Students fall for $25 before 8pm, and videos of the experience cost $16. It's open late (often until midnight) but if there's a chance of lightening, falls will be delayed until the storm passes.

CLASSIC AMUSEMENT PARKS

Feeling nostalgic? International Dr has a few attractions reminiscent of small-town touring carnivals, right down to the creaking machinery and carnies.

Fun Spot Action Park (☎ 407-363-3867; W *www.fun-spot.com; 5551 Del Verde Way; all-inclusive armbands $30/10 adult/child 2-6; open 2pm-11pm Mon-Fri, 10am-midnight Sat & Sun, 10am-midnight daily in summer*) has a Ferris wheel, go-karts and the awesome Zipper, as well as the opportunity to win giant stuffed animals. You can also purchase rides separately ($3 to $6).

Magical Midway (☎ 407-370-5353; W *www .magicalmidway.com; 7001 International Dr; all-inclusive armbands $29, ride tickets $3-6, laser tag $4; hours vary*) has a better location but less-ambitious attractions.

CULTURAL ATTRACTIONS

Make sure to check out the Winter Park section under Around Orlando later in this chapter for some very nice museums.

Harry P Leu Gardens

This 50-acre estate (☎ 407-246-2620; W *www .leugardens.org; 1920 N Forest Ave; adult/ youth 18 & under $4/1, Mon 9am-noon admission free; open 9am-5pm daily*) is famous for its camellias (more than 2000 varieties) and roses. Twenty-minute tours of the **Leu House**, an 18th-century mansion listed on the National Register of Historic Places, are available every half-hour from 10am to 3:30pm.

Harry P and Mary Jane Leu had planned to grow tea here on their estate, but it didn't work out. Instead, they planted flowers that they'd collected from all over the world. Their lush creation was donated to the city in 1961 to be used as a public botanical garden. It's a wonderful place for an hour stroll, or for enjoying all day.

From I-4, take exit 43 to Princeton St and follow the signs.

Loch Haven Park

This part-cultural, part-industrial park off Mills Ave is home to two museums, the Orlando Science Center and Orlando Museum of Art, several galleries and two performance halls (see Entertainment later in this chapter). There's also a Fire Museum, with old fire trucks, but you may have to peek through the windows; funding is short so hours are unpredictable.

Orlando Science Center This well-done museum (☎ 407-514-2000, 888-OSC-4FUN; W www.osc.org; 810 E Rollins St; adult/child 3-12 $10/7.50; open 9am-5pm Tues-Thur, 9am-9pm Fri & Sat noon-5pm Sun) combines actual science with special effects (several exhibits are spruced up with props donated by Disney). Highlights include a nuclear reactor you operate – complete with sirens and smoke if you screw up – and a dinosaur room with fossils, plus animatronic beasties that move and growl. You can even design your own roller coaster.

A small IMAX theater and planetarium cost an extra $7/5 a show, and an all-inclusive combo ticket runs $16/13.50. Separate entrance to the observatory costs $3.

You can park in the garage across the street ($3.50 per day).

Orlando Museum of Art Founded in 1924, this sprawling museum (☎ 407-896-4231; W www.omart.org; 2416 N Mills Ave; adult/child 4-11 $6/3; open 10am-5pm Tues-Sat, noon-5pm Sun) has a great collection of modern art, with a pronounced focus on female and minority American artists. Huge rooms lend themselves to drastic installation pieces and highlight impressive collections of African and pre-Columbian pieces. On the first Thursday of each month, the museum holds a dress-up gala (admission $7) dedicated to Florida artists who inspire the theme.

Mennello Museum of American Folk Art Small and bright, this collection (☎ 407-246-4278; W www.mennellomuseum.com; 900 E Princeton St; adult/child under 12 $4/free; open 11am-5pm Tues-Sat, noon-5pm Sun) features paintings by Earl Cuningham, a self-taught artist (and pilot and anthropologist) with an eye for color. Wonderful rotating exhibitions focus on other folk art themes; definitely check this place out.

History Center

This regional historical museum (☎ 407-836-8500; W www.thehistorycenter.org; 65 E Central Blvd; adult/senior/child $7/6.50/3.50; open 10am-5pm Mon-Sat, noon-5pm Sun) has three floors devoted to the history of Central Florida. Permanent exhibits cover prehistoric Florida, European exploration and settlement, and citrus production, among other things. The excellent History of Florida Tourism exhibit pays special homage to Walt Disney (referring to swampy, backwater Orlando as 'BD' and the bustling town it is today as 'AD').

International Train & Trolley Museum

Home to the most extravagant model train set you could imagine, this museum (☎ 407-363-9002; 8990 International Dr; adult/child 3-12 $4/3; open 10am-6pm Mon-Thur, 10am-7pm Fri & Sat) is well worth the price if you're into that sort of thing.

Flying Tigers Warbird Air Museum

A must for WWII buffs, this museum (☎ 407-933-1942; 231 N Hoagland Blvd, Kissimmee; adult/child 8-12 $9/8; open 9am-5pm daily), in Hangar No 5 at Kissimmee Regional Airport, displays WWII fighter planes in various stages of restoration. Workers can take up to several years per plane, and some of the finished products can be seen before they fly away to join air shows and air-tour-company fleets.

From I-4, go east on W Hwy 192 to the second light after the Medieval Times dinner theater and turn right; the entrance to the airport is about three-quarters of a mile down.

Fun Exhibitions

Head along International Dr for a museum-type experience with an edge.

Hard Rock Vault The ubiquitous café has found a new way to receive money from music fans at this museum (☎ 407-599-7625; W www.hardrock/vault; 8437 International Dr; adult/child 5-12 $15/9; open 9am-midnight daily), which has rock-star guitars and costumes, interactive exhibits and a high-tech listening room. You have to really love music memorabilia to feel this was money well spent.

Titanic – Ship of Dreams This temporary exhibition (☎ 407-248-1166; W www.titanicshipofdreams.com; The Mercado on International Dr; adult/child 6-11 $17/12; open 10am-8pm daily) has been held over by popular demand. It's really fun and worth the ticket price if you have the time to visit. All staff are professional actors in period costume. You will receive a ship admission ticket with the name of an actual Titanic passenger, and you are to assume the role of that person for the duration of the wonderful and emotional tour. At the end, you can look at a board listing information on all the passengers to find out whether you survived the shipwreck.

WonderWorks If you're feeling guilty about pulling the kids out of school, take them to this upside-down building (☎ 407-351-8800; Ⓦ www.wonderworksonline.com; 9067 International Dr; adult/child 4-12 $17/13, magic dinner show $18/15). Earthquake and hurricane simulators, hands-on exhibits, laser tag and more offer all ages hours of delight. The **Outta Control Magic Show** includes dinner and is lots of fun. There are combo tickets available that include the magic show and/or laser tag games.

OUTDOOR ACTIVITIES
Golfing
Florida is probably the nation's premier golfing destination, and there are countless places to tee off in the Orlando area. The courses are least crowded from May to October, when you can pick your tee time and be confident that you can play as leisurely as you like. Also during those months, many private courses are available to the public. The number of courses at your disposal goes far beyond the scope of this book, so to get the full spectrum, go to Ⓦ www.golfingorlando.com.

Following are a few golfers' favorites; see the Walt Disney World Resort chapter for more.

Falcon's Fire Golf Club (☎ 407-239-5445; 3200 Seralago Blvd; $40-110) flaunts a country-club atmosphere and a 6900-yard, par-72 Rees Jones course; it's just 3 miles east of Walt Disney World, just off Hwy 192.

Dubsdread Golf Course (☎ 407-246-2551; 549 W Par Ave; $13-21) is a bunker-happy course designed way back in 1923 and has seen the likes of legends Sam Snead, Ben Hogan and Claude Harmon.

The following places are further away but worthy of the drive.

Golden Bear Club-Keene's Point (☎ 407-876-5775; 6300 Jackson Nicklaus Pkwy, Windermere; $60-115) may be going private, so get in there, and bring your A-game. Tiger Woods, Mark O'Meara, Lee Janzen and Ken Griffey Jr have frequented these greens.

Orange Country National Golf Center & Lodge (☎ 407-656-2626; 16301 Phil Ritson Way, Winter Garden; $60-105) offers excellent links-style play. Panther Lake is a rolling-hills 18-hole course, and Crooked Cat features Bermuda greens and some challenging par-3s. A decent short game and accurate iron play are important here.

Fishing
Central Florida is famous for its freshwater fishing (especially largemouth bass), and the Orlando area is no exception. For licenses, rules, tips and other information, contact **Fish Orlando** (☎ 407-317-7329; Ⓦ www.state.fl.us/fwc/fishing). March and April are peak months for bass.

Lake Tohopekaliga
Day trips by pontoon boat to Lake Tohopekaliga (south of Kissimmee) for fishing, picnicking and birdwatching are becoming more popular. Contact **Aquatic Wonders Boat Tours** (☎ 407-846-2814; Ⓦ www.florida-nature.com; 101 Lakeshore Blvd, Kissimmee).

ORGANIZED TOURS
See Winter Park under Around Orlando later in this chapter for information on scenic boat tours there.

Airboat Rides
Blazing through reedy waters and spotting wildlife along the way can be a fun, relaxing way to spend an afternoon. Make sure to bring your sunglasses and sunscreen on these trips, as well as some warmer clothing (you'll be going up to 45mph). There are lots and lots of these companies, but here are a couple.

Boggy Creek (☎ 407-344-9550; Ⓦ www.bcairboats.com; adult/child 3-12 $18/13) offers 30-minute tours or 45-minute private tours ($45 per person) as well as night tours ($25 per person; March to October only). A three-day advance reservation is recommended.

Old Fashioned Airboat Rides (☎ 407-568-4307; Ⓦ www.airboatrides.com; adult/child under 13 $35/15) is further away (about 45 minutes east) but the remoteness adds to the experience. The tours are 90 minutes long.

Orlando Ghost Tours
This 90-minute walking tour (☎ 407-992-1200; Ⓦ www.orlandohauntings.com; tours $10) features 'true' ghost stories, Orlando history, and creepy guides in period costume and bearing lanterns. Tours depart at 8pm Friday

and Saturday from Guinevere's Coffee House (Pine St & Magnolia Ave). For each adult, a child under 11 goes free.

PLACES TO STAY

Hotels in downtown Orlando are geared to business travelers. It's usually a much better deal to stay on International Dr, close to the theme parks, or (even cheaper) in Kissimmee, along Hwy 192. The rack rates quoted here vary widely according to demand, and can usually be lowered by bargaining, or as part of a package deal.

Also see Wekiwa Springs, under Around Orlando later in this chapter, for more campsites – they're further away, but they're prettier, and see Accommodations in the Facts for the Visitor chapter for information on camping and RV parks.

Downtown

Budget and mid-range hotels right downtown are scarce, so if you want to stay here, be prepared to shell out big bucks.

Travelodge (☎ 407-423-1671; W www travelodge.com; 409 N Magnolia Ave; rooms $55-65) is pleasant and has a pool.

Sheraton Four Points (☎ 407-841-3220; W www.sheratonfourpointshotels.com; 151 E Washington St; rooms $99-129) is well located right on Lake Eola, but the rooms are somewhat aged; it's a little too expensive for what you get.

Westin Grand Bohemian (☎ 407-313-9000; W www.grandbohemianhotel.com; 325 S Orange Ave; singles/doubles weekends $109/ 139, weekdays $159/189) is downtown's most luxurious option, with spas, restaurants and lovely rooms. And it's got one of two gold-plated Bösendorfer pianos in the world, played nightly along with a jazz quartet.

Embassy Suites (☎ 407-841-1000; W www embassysuites.com; 191 E Pine St; rooms $169-199) is right downtown and features an indoor atrium, a 24-hour fitness center and the popular Concha Me Crazy restaurant (see Places to Eat).

Outer Orlando

KOA (☎ 407-277-5075, 800-562-3969; 12343 Narcoossee Rd; sites without/with hookups 25/30) has a campground 5 miles south of the Bee Line Expressway at exit 13.

Loch Haven Motor Inn (☎ 407-896-3611; 820 N Mills Ave; rooms $40), north of downtown, is clean enough, friendly and convenient to Winter Park and the Cultural Corridor.

Parliament House (☎ 407-425-7571; W www.parliamenthouse.com; 410 N Orange Blossom Trail; rooms summer $59-99, Gay Day $99-139) is a gay resort and an Orlando institution. It features six clubs and bars, a restaurant, and some of the best female impersonators this side of the Mississippi.

The **Norment-Parry House** (☎ 407-648-5188, 800-444-5289; W www.orlandohistoric inn.com; 211 N Lucerne Circle E; rooms $89-120) is a friendly, Victorian B&B with colorful and comfortable rooms. The house, which is Orlando's oldest, dates from 1883 and is furnished throughout with excellent antiques.

International Drive

Hotels lining International Dr usually include a 'free' (you'll actually pay about $10 more per room for this service) shuttle to area amusement parks. Unless otherwise noted, all of the following are on International Dr.

Comfort Suites Orlando (☎ 407-351-5050; W comfortsuitesorlando.com; 9350 Turkey Lake Rd; rooms summer/winter $49/89) is very comfortable.

Days Inn (☎ 407-351-1200; W www.days inn.com; No 7200; rooms summer/winter $39/99) has basic rooms but no free shuttle.

Holiday Inn International Drive Resort (☎ 407-351-3500; W www.holidayinn.com; No 6515; rooms summer/winter $49/69) is nicer than average, with shuffleboard courts!

Howard Johnson (☎ 407-351-2000; W www .howardjohnsonhotelorlando.com; 7050 S Kirkman Rd; rooms summer/winter $45/79) has a free shuttle and miniature golf course ($1).

La Quinta (☎ 407-345-1365; W www.lq .com; 8504 Universal Blvd; rooms summer/ winter $69/109) has rooms with microwaves and fridges.

Quality Inn Orlando (☎ 407-996-8585; W www.qualityinn.com; No 9000; rooms $89) has standard rooms, a free shuttle and a big pool.

Landmark Sheraton (☎ 407-351-2100, 800-327-1366; W www.sheratonstudiocity .com; No 5905; rooms summer/winter $99/ 119) is flashy.

Doubletree Castle (☎ 407-345-1511; W www.doubletreecastle.com; No 8629; rooms summer/winter $79/199) wins for presentation – a huge castle with lots of kid-oriented amenities.

Peabody Hotel (☎ 407-352-4000; W www .peabodyorlando.com; No 9801; rooms $345-1400) is the big exception. It's got all the

ORLANDO

INTERNATIONAL DRIVE

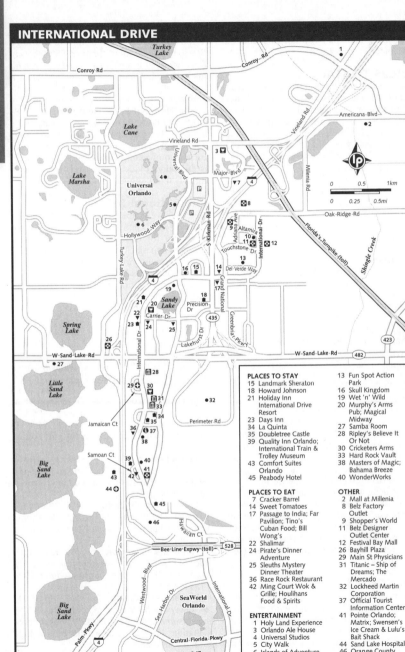

PLACES TO STAY
15 Landmark Sheraton
18 Howard Johnson
21 Holiday Inn
    International Drive
    Resort
23 Days Inn
34 La Quinta
35 Doubletree Castle
39 Quality Inn Orlando;
    International Train &
    Trolley Museum
43 Comfort Suites
    Orlando
45 Peabody Hotel

PLACES TO EAT
7 Cracker Barrel
14 Sweet Tomatoes
17 Passage to India; Far
   Pavilion; Tino's
   Cuban Food; Bill
   Wong's
22 Shalimar
24 Pirate's Dinner
   Adventure
25 Sleuths Mystery
   Dinner Theater
36 Race Rock Restaurant
42 Ming Court Wok &
   Grille; Houlihans
   Food & Spirits

ENTERTAINMENT
1 Holy Land Experience
3 Orlando Ale House
4 Universal Studios
5 City Walk
6 Islands of Adventure
10 Vans Skateboard
   Park

13 Fun Spot Action
   Park
16 Skull Kingdom
19 Wet 'n' Wild
20 Murphy's Arms
   Pub; Magical
   Midway
27 Samba Room
28 Ripley's Believe It
   Or Not
30 Cricketers Arms
33 Hard Rock Vault
38 Masters of Magic;
   Bahama Breeze
40 WonderWorks

OTHER
2 Mall at Millenia
8 Belz Factory
   Outlet
9 Shopper's World
11 Belz Designer
   Outlet Center
12 Festival Bay Mall
26 Bayhill Plaza
29 Main St Physicians
31 Titanic – Ship of
   Dreams; The
   Mercado
32 Lockheed Martin
   Corporation
37 Official Tourist
   Information Center
41 Pointe Orlando;
   Matrix; Swensen's
   Ice Cream & Lulu's
   Bait Shack
44 Sand Lake Hospital
46 Orange County
   Convention Center
47 Discovery Cove

amenities you'd expect at these prices, plus one famous extra: at 11am a line of ducks marches into the lobby fountain, then they head single file back to their ceiling nests at 5pm. And yes, you can just drop by to see the parade.

Hwy 192

For those seeking supercheap, if a tad tattered, accommodations, this is the place. The further west you get from I-4, the less you'll pay. Of more than 100 hotels and motels along the W Hwy 192 strip, the following (just their street numbers are given in the contact information) are as good as any.

HI/AYH Orlando/Kissimmee Resort (☎ 407-396-8282, 800-909-4776; No 4840; dorm beds HI/AYH members/nonmembers $16/19, rooms $28/31) looks more like a motel than a hostel, but it has a laundry, large lockers, a swimming pool, a porch, a lake for fishing, a game room, and a large common area and kitchen. It's clean, safe and fun, but it's inconvenient to get here without a car. From downtown, take Lynx bus No 50 to Disney and transfer to No 56, which stops right by the hostel. Private rooms can hold from one to four people. You may spot some exciting wildlife such as armadillos and sandhill cranes (more than 3ft tall with red heads, they travel in pairs and mate for life). Publix across the street is open till 11pm and the kitchen is open till midnight. A Mears shuttle from the airport costs $16. Hey, best of all – across the street is the **Big Bamboo Lounge**, a fun South Pacific divey bar where former (read: burnt out and ready to spill beans) Disney castmembers are reported to hang out.

Raccoon Lake (☎ 407-239-4148, 800-776-9644; sites without/with hookups $15-18/25, cottages $39-50) has sort of shoddy little cabins, but they're clean and the sites are fine.

Casa Rosa Motel (☎ 407-396-2020; W www .hotel4you; No 4600; rooms $50) has friendly service but no free shuttles.

Gator Motel (☎ 407-396-0127; No 4576; rooms summer/winter $25/60) has room fridges and a giant alligator next door, but no free shuttles.

Howard Johnson (☎ 407-396-4762; W www .hojo.com; No 4836; rooms summer/winter $44/79) has a picnic area by the lake and a free shuttle to Disney.

Knights Inn (☎ 407-396-8186; W www .knightsinn.com; 2880 Poinciana Blvd; rooms summer/winter $35/60) has spacious rooms and a free shuttle to Epcot.

Magic Castle Inn & Suites (☎ 407-396-1212; W www.magicorlando.com; No 4559;

rooms summer/winter $34/39) looks like a castle and has a free shuttle to Disney. There's another, even cheaper one further east on Hwy 192.

Masters Inn (☎ 407-396-4020; W www .mastersinnorlando.com; No 5367; rooms summer/winter $35/50) has a free shuttle to Disney and lots of French tourists.

Ramada Inn (☎ 407-396-1111; W www.ram adainneastgate.com; No 9200; rooms summer/ winter $49/99) has miniature golf, tennis courts and a free shuttle.

Sevilla Inn (☎ 800-367-1363; W www .sevillainn.com; No 4640; rooms summer/ winter $30/60) is attractive, but offers no free shuttles.

Sun Motel (☎ 407-396-6666; W www.sun motel.com; No 5020; rooms summer/winter $37/55) is cleaner than average.

PLACES TO EAT

Fast-food joints and family-style chain restaurants such as Denny's and Chili's abound in Orlando and its environs. If these places suit your fancy, you often need not drive a mile in any direction before you find one, especially along Hwy 192 in Kissimmee and along International Dr. You can save bundles by stocking up on snacks and drinks and keeping them in your hotel room and in your day bags. Publix and Winn-Dixies pop up frequently just outside of downtown Orlando, but not so much in the tourist-trap areas (gee, I wonder why?).

Downtown Orlando

The fabulous Orlando **Farmers Market** takes place downtown in front of the History Center every Saturday from 8am to 2:30pm.

American/Continental From pizza joints to Tex-Mex burritos to a simple deli sandwich, anyone could be pleased with downtown's offerings. **Subway** and **Planet Smoothie**, on Wall St Plaza, are good for a quick bite or a healthful slurp.

NYPD Pizza (☎ 407-481-8680; 373 N Orange Ave; open 11am-9pm Mon-Thur, 11am-10pm Fri, 5pm-10pm Sat) is a local favorite. Slices start at $2.40 and 14-inch pies start at $10.

Jax Fifth Ave Deli & Alehouse (☎ 407-841-5322; 11 Court Ave; dishes $3-7; open 11am-1am Wed-Fri, noon-2am Sat, noon-1am Sun) has a great selection of sandwiches, salads and pita pizzas. Crunchy folk will appreciate the Skid Row sandwich – peanut butter, honey, banana and granola on (you guessed it) whole-wheat bread. And if you haven't plunked down enough cash in these parts, the Park Avenue – steak tartare with caviar and a bottle of Dom Perignon – is on offer if you provide 24 hours notice and $375.

Primo Hoagies (☎ 407-423-0123; 223 Magnolia Ave; dishes $3-$14.50) has lots and lots of sandwiches, including the infamous hard-salami sandwich: 'the Viagra.'

Tijuana Flats (☎ 407-839-0007; 50 E Central Blvd; dishes $4-9; open 11am-6pm Sun & Mon, 11am-9pm Tues-Thur, 11am-midnight Fri & Sat) is a solid bet for a Tex-Mex lunch. Huge burritos and gooey quesadillas come with your choice of 12 different hot sauces, from 'Georgia Peach & Vidalia Onion' to 'Smack My Ass and Call Me Sally.'

Maui Jack's (☎ 407-447-5225; 100 E Pine St; mains $5-13; open 11am-2am daily) features a raw bar, beer on tap, American sandwiches and burgers, and some Hawaiian cuisine as well. Sports are shown on its TVs (there are more than two dozen).

Pebbles (☎ 407-839-0892; W www.pebbles worldwide.com; 17 W Church St; dishes $7-19; open 11:30am-10pm Mon-Thur, 11:30am-11:30pm Fri, 5pm-11:30pm Sat) has upscale Continental cuisine such as duck morel linguine ($14.50) in a sleek dining room that still somehow exudes a chainy ambience.

Asian It's mostly sushi that you'll find.

Sushi Hatsu (☎ 407-422-1551; 24 W Washington St; mains $8-13; open 11am-2:30pm Mon-Fri, 5pm-10pm Mon-Sat) gets several thumbs up. It's a Korean-Japanese place that serves excellent kimchi and sushi.

Wright & Wong's (☎ 407-849-9904; 25 Wall St Plaza; dishes $3.25-6), in the back of Slingapour's (see Entertainment later in this chapter), seems like an afterthought – the sushi bar is about four stools wide, and that's all there is of the place. Both traditional and Westernized rolls are available.

Cafés & Bakeries Café nesting is especially popular in yuppie Thorton Park, east of the downtown area.

Guinevere's Coffee House & Art Gallery (☎ 407-992-1200; 37/39 S Magnolia St; open 8pm-midnight daily) has caffeine in all its guises, sugary treats and live acoustic music.

Le Croissant Shop (☎ 407-648-8316; 111 N Orange Ave; pastries $1-3, dishes $3-6) has fresh-baked savory and dessert croissants, croissant sandwiches, pastries, wraps and salads.

Season's Harvest (☎ 407-426-7607; 20 E Washington St; breakfast $3, salads $4-6, lunch $5-6; open 7am-3pm Mon-Fri) offers supercheap but yummy breakfast sandwiches and gourmet sandwiches, such as smoked turkey and smoked gouda with cranberry mayo on a croissant.

Regional Ethnic Cuisine Downtown Orlando has soul food, Creole cuisine and Cuban sandwiches for you to test your tastebuds on.

Crooked Bayou (☎ 407-839-5852; 50 E Central Blvd; dishes $4-7; open 11am-2pm Mon-Sat) has good pressed sandwiches with a Creole zing. Jambalaya, red beans and rice, and several salads are also available.

Rincon Criollo (☎ 407-872-1128; 331 N Orange Ave; sandwiches $5-7; open 8am-3pm daily) does vegetarian Cuban cuisine such as meatless meatball sandwiches and pressed veggie Cubans, as well as plenty of meat-laden ones.

Concha Me Crazy (☎ 407-246-0011; 191 E Pine St; dishes $12-28; open 11am-10pm Mon-Fri, 11am-11pm Sat & Sun), in the Embassy Suites hotel, features the Caribbean cuisine of renowned Disney chef Johnny Rivers but gets mixed reviews. At least there's free valet parking.

Lua Loa (☎ 407-426-0566; 301 W Church St; dishes $6-13; open noon-3pm & 6pm-11pm Wed-Fri, 6pm-2am Sat, noon-5pm Sun, is a popular downtown place for soul food.

Outer Orlando

If you have a car, these places are worth a drive.

American/Continental Reliable food is easy to find in O-Town.

Moodswing Café (☎ 407-895-9777; 815 N Mills Ave; mains $7-13; open 11:30am-9pm Mon-Thur, 11am-10:30pm Fri & Sat) has great burgers, sandwiches and Lonnie's famous meat loaf. On the first and third Monday of the month, it becomes a 'drag diner,' with extra-dazzling servers, entertainers and even customers ($5 cover).

Sweet Tomatoes (☎ 407-896-8770; W www .souplantation.com; 4678 E Colonial Dr; buffet $7-8.50; open 11am-9pm Sun-Thur, 11am-10pm Fri & Sat) has a big all-you-care to-eat salad bar, pasta bar and dessert bar, with soups and fresh breads to boot. The fare is generally better and more healthful than at other buffet places (this is great for vegetarians). There's another location on International

Dr (☎ 407-363-1616; 6877 S Kirkman Rd; open 10:30am-9pm Sun-Thur, 10:30am-10pm Fri & Sat).

Le Coq au Vin (☎ 407-851-6980; 4800 S Orange Ave; dishes $13.50-22; open 11:30am-2pm & 5:30pm-10pm Tues-Fri, 5:30pm-10pm Sat, 5pm-9pm Sun) is a local favorite for French food, and area chefs are known to frequent it. The place's eponymous signature dish is available year-round. The food is elegant, but the atmosphere is relaxed.

Asian Japanese steakhouse chain Kobe can be found all over greater Orlando. Of course, Splendid China (see that section earlier in this chapter) has Chinese food and a dinner show, but the food is made for the masses, and it shows.

Thai House (☎ 407-898-0820; 2117 E Colonial Dr; dishes $1-10; open 11am-2am Mon-Fri, 5pm-10pm Sat) is very good – and very spicy.

The area around E Colonial Dr, east of N Mills Ave, is freckled with all sorts of Vietnamese shops and great, affordable restaurants.

Little Saigon (☎ 407-423-8539; 1106 E Colonial Dr; dishes $5-9), just off N Mills Ave, is an Orlando institution (the menu is on display at the History Center). It's got excellent service and quality charbroiled beef and *pho* (delicious meat and noodle soup flavoured with lemongrass and basil).

Ahn Hong (☎ 407-999-2656; 1124 E Colonial Dr; mains $5-9; open 9am-9:30pm daily), nearby, serves more traditional Vietnamese food – have a durian smoothie with your meal. The spring rolls are excellent.

Thanh Thanh (☎ 407-894-5225; 2101 E Colonial Dr; dishes $5-13; open 10am-10pm daily) is dinky in size but huge in flavors. There is a hefty list of veggie dishes, too.

Garden Cafe (☎ 407-999-9799; 810 W Colonial Dr; dishes $5-10; open 11am-10pm Tues-Fri, noon-10pm Sat & Sun) is an all-veggie delight with a Chinese twist.

Mediterranean Don't forget that Holy Land Experience (earlier in this chapter) offers a theme-park version of Mediterranean cuisine.

Olympia Restaurant (☎ 407-273-7836; 8505 E Colonial Dr; dishes $7-15; open 5pm-10pm Tues-Thur, 5pm-2am Fri & Sat) doles out calamari, roast lamb and spanakopita to Orlando's Greek community – a great sign. Belly dancers round out your meal on Friday and Saturday nights.

Athenian Garden Cafe (☎ 407-898-2151; 2918 N Orange Ave; dishes $8-12; open 10:30am-10:30pm Mon-Sat) is cheery, casual and authentic, with moussaka, souvlaki and kebabs.

Tony's Deli (☎ 407-898-6689; 1323 N Mills Ave; dishes around $6) has yummy Lebanese food. Falafel, hummus, tabouli, baklava – you got it.

Regional Ethnic Cuisine Both of these are Orlandoan faves.

Johnson's (☎ 407-841-0717; 692 W Robinson St; dishes around $7) gets the honor of being the city's favorite place for soul food.

Caribbean Sunshine Bakery (☎ 407-839-5060; 2528 W Colonial Dr; dishes $4-10; open 8am-9:30pm Mon-Thur, 8am-10pm Fri & Sat, 8am-7pm Sun) gets rave reviews.

International Drive

Most of the restaurants on International Dr are chains.

American/Continental Soothe your sweet tooth for the night at **Swensen's Ice Cream** (☎ 407-370-9770; No 9101, cones $3-7; open 10am-9pm Mon-Thur, 10am-10pm Fri & Sat).

Cracker Barrel (☎ 407-248-6260; 5859 Caravan Ct; dishes $3-13; open 6am-10pm Mon-Thur, 6am-11pm Fri & Sat) is a rampant chain in the Orlando area. Part kitschy gift shop, part restaurant, it's a good place to go to try some traditional Southern cuisine for breakfast. Make sure to get a taste of the hash-brown casserole. Also try the catfish, chicken 'n' dumplings and perfect fried okra. If you don't stop by here, well, they're everywhere.

Race Rock Restaurant (☎ 407-248-9876; No 8186; mains $7-15; open 11:30am-11:30pm daily) is a Nascar-themed eatery with cars hanging from the ceiling, a museum-quality collection of racing memorabilia, burgers, fried chicken and steaks.

Asian Authentic it ain't, but it'll do the trick. For the real thing, see the Outer Orlando section earlier.

Bill Wong's (☎ 407-352-5373; No 5668; lunch $7.50-8.50, dinner $7.50-14; opens at 11am Mon-Fri, noon Sat & Sun, last seating 10:30pm) is a Chinese buffet-style restaurant.

Ming Court Wok & Grille (☎ 407-351-9988; No 9188; dishes $4.50-40; open 11am-2:30pm & 4:30pm-midnight daily) has great dim sum, but like many great dim sum places, it gets noisy. The interior is impressive.

Indian There are quite a few Indian places along International Dr, if not elsewhere.

Passage to India Restaurant (☎ 407-351-3456; No 5532; lunch $8-13, dinner $13-22; open 11:30am-10pm daily) is heaven sent for vegetarians needing a break from the salad bars. It's a little pricey but worth it – try the *bhaigan bharta* (baked eggplant) or tandoori chicken.

Far Pavilion (☎ 407-351-5522; No 5748; dishes $9-19; open 11:30am-2pm & 5:30pm-11pm daily) is so popular that even Orlandoans venture into this tourist trap to enjoy it.

Shalimar (☎ 407-226-9797; No 7342; dishes $12.50-15; open 3pm-midnight Tues-Thur, noon-midnight Fri-Mon) has all the standard vegetarian and meat curries. If you stop by the Tourist Information Center on International Dr, they may have coupons.

Regional Ethnic Cuisine Try one of these for something different.

Tino's Cuban Food (☎ 407-345-5660; 6917 Municipal Dr; dishes $6-9; open 7am-8:30pm Mon-Sat) has sandwiches, pork and steak.

Lulu's Bait Shack (☎ 407-351-9595; No 9101; dishes $8-16; open 11am-10pm Mon-Thur, 11am-midnight Fri & Sat) has it all: Cajun, Creole, alligator, burgers, steaks and more.

Bahama Breeze (☎ 407-248-2499; No 8849; dishes $10-27; open 4pm-1am Sun-Thur, 4pm-2am Fri & Sat) has Floribbean food and all the color that goes with it. The 'fish in a bag' is the house special: mahimahi baked in parchment. The paella is also a crowd-pleaser. And make sure to try the Key lime pie, a Florida specialty.

Samba Room (☎ 407-226-0550; 7468 W Sand Lake Rd; dishes $14-25; open 11:30am-11pm Sun-Wed, 11:30am-midnight Thur-Sat) is pre-Castro Havana come to life, with white-jacketed waiters, lively music and a cigar lounge. The menu is unique: sugar-cane beef tenderloin with chipotle mashed potatoes, for example.

Hwy 192

Hwy 192 has lots of fast-food chains and gut-busting buffets that will unite body and soul.

Dinner & a Show

Kissimmee and International Dr are both dinner-theater central. *Always* check the tourist rags for coupons, which will save you a bundle.

WonderWorks Outta Control Magic Show (☎ 407-351-8800; W www.wonderworksonline.com; 9067 International Dr; adult/child $18/15) is a 90-minute comedy and magic show that includes all the pizza, popcorn, beer and soda you can make disappear. It's great for kids.

Mark Two Dinner Theater (☎ 407-843-6275; W www.themarktwo.com; 3376 Edgewater Dr; tickets $35-50) does daily performances such as *Titanic* and *Annie Get Your Gun* while you eat.

Capone's Dinner & Show (☎ 407-397-2378; 4740 W Hwy 192; adult/child $40/24), a mile east of Hwy 535, is a gangland revue set in a 'cabaret and speakeasy' in Prohibition-era Chicago. There's an unlimited Italian buffet.

Sleuths Mystery Dinner Theater (☎ 407-363-1985, 800-393-1985; W www.sleuths.com; 7508 Universal Blvd; adult/child 3-11 $42/24) has 11 different shows, each about 2½ hours long. You are an invited guest to a dinner party, at the end of which someone dies. You interrogate while you eat. They also have special shows for kids.

Pirate's Dinner Adventure (☎ 407-248-0590; 6400 Carrier Dr; adult/child $44/27) has a full-sized Spanish galleon where actors swing from ropes, have sword fights and rescue damsels in distress while you eat mediocre food. It's actually pretty enthralling, especially for kids, who get to partici-pate in all the action. Check the tourist rags for coupons offering 50% discounts.

Medieval Times (☎ 407-396-1518; W www.medievaltimes.com; 4510 W Hwy 192; adult/child $44/28) takes you back to the Middle Ages, when everyone ate with their hands (kids dig this) while watching jousting tournaments. There's also a **museum** (adult/child $8/6; open 4:30pm-8:30pm daily) with torture devices used during the Spanish Inquisition.

Arabian Nights (☎ 407-239-9223, 800-553-6116; 6225 W Hwy 192; adult/child $46/27) is the best choice for children. It has acrobats, gypsies, unicorns and, according to a horse trainer I spoke to, some impressive equestrian stunts. Dinner is your choice of prime rib or vegetable lasagna. Small children love the pretty horses.

Orlando signage

Splendid China theme park

Dolphin, SeaWorld Orlando

Heron, Lake Eola, Orlando

NEIL SETCHFIELD

Journey to Atlantis, SeaWorld Orlando

The number of places to eat are overwhelming, so here are just a few.

Havana's Cafe (☎ 407-846-6771; No 3628; lunch $6-8, dinner $7-13) includes pepper steak and chicken filet skillet on the menu.

Giordano's Pizza (☎ 407-397-0044; No 7866; dishes $10-13; open 11am-midnight Mon-Sat, noon-midnight Sun), close to Splendid China, has great stuffed and thin-crust pizzas plus hearty pasta dishes.

Kosher Korner (☎ 407-787-3344; No 4944; dishes $10-23; open noon-10pm Sun–Thur, 10am-3pm Fri) is very pricey and is run by the Chabad Lubavitchers, a faction of Orthodox Judaism that proselytizes within the Jewish faith. But where else are you going to find falafel on Hwy 192?

ENTERTAINMENT

Orlando has a taste for fun, not to mention a healthy local music scene – Creed came up through these bars. From the manufactured merrymaking at Universal's CityWalk and Disney's Pleasure Island (see those chapters) to downtown's excellent and organic collection of clubs, there's just no reason to stay home at night. Local theater and dance troupes entertain at some spectacular venues, too.

The collection of bars, shops and nightclubs on Church St near Garland Ave is housed in beautifully renovated, century-old buildings called Church St Station, done up in an Old South/Grand Ole Opry theme. It was closed during research for much-needed renovations but all should be back in order by late 2003.

Bars & Clubs

Happy hours abound downtown. Church St has loads of places: **Chillers** (a daiquiri bar), **Hogs n Honeys** (a wannabe biker bar) and **Gametime** (three guesses) are just a few.

On Wall St Plaza, there's a slough of yuppie bars and brewpubs all owned by the same folks: **Globe** (a brewpub), **Slingapour's** (cocktails), **Tuk Tuk Lounge** (cocktails), **Wall St Cantina** (Tex-Mex), **One-Eyed Jack's** (pub) and **Loaded Hog** (pub). Once a month, these places hold a joint block party and feature live music.

Bodhisattva Social Club (☎ 407-872-3136; 23 S Court Ave) attracts the alternative folks.

:08 (☎ 407-839-4800; W www.8-seconds .com; 100 W Livingston St) is an insanely popular country bar – you have to stay on the mechanical bull for eight seconds, get it? There's no electric bull inside, but call to find out about upcoming rodeo events, which are staged outside.

Independent Bar (☎ 407-839-0457; 68 N Orange Ave; cover $10; open 9pm-3am Wed-Sat) is hip, crowded and loud, with DJs spinning underground dance and alternative rock until the wee hours; ladies drink free until midnight on Wednesday.

Tanqueray's Bar & Grille (☎ 407-649-8540; 100 S Orange Ave; open 11am-2am Mon-Fri, 6pm-2am Sat & Sun), a few steps down from street level, is friendly, packed with regulars and has live music, usually reggae or blues, on weekends ($2 cover).

Scruffy Murphy's Irish Pub (☎ 407-648-5460; 9 W Washington St) is the best Irish place, and has a great selection of Irish beers and a fun crowd.

Bar BQ Bar (☎ 407-648-5441; 64 N Orange Ave; open 6pm-2am daily) has cheap beer and a menu worth reviewing. Local bands get busy Tuesday and some other nights; there's never a cover.

Back Booth (☎ 407-999-2570; W www .backbooth.com; 37 W Pine St; open 9pm-2am Sat-Wed; 5pm-2am Thur & Fri) is a great place to see local and national bands. There's usually a cover.

Big Belly Brewery (☎ 407-649-1270; 33 W Church St; open 4pm-2am daily) has scantily clad servers and a mostly male clientele who only come here for the happy-hour buffet, really.

Ybor's Martini Bar (☎ 407-316-8006; 41 W Church St; open 5pm-2am Mon-Fri, 7pm-2am Sat) is upscale, with cigars in the humidor and premium drinks such as Louis 13th cognac, Macallan 18-year-old scotch and 45 types of martini.

Jax Fifth Ave Deli & Ale House (☎ 407-841-5322; 11 Court Ave; open 11am-1am Wed-Fri, noon-2am Sat, noon-1am Sun) is a comfy place with 200 different beers.

Kate O'Brien's Irish Pub & Restaurant (☎ 407-649-7646; 42 W Central Blvd; open 11:30am-2am Mon-Sat, 7pm-2am Sun) has live music Thursday to Saturday (no cover), lots of good beer on tap and standards like fish & chips on the menu. **Shanagolden Pub** is next to Kate O'Brien's and owned by the same people. It's newer but doesn't have as much character.

There are some decent choices outside of downtown as well.

Will's Pub (☎ 407-898-5070; W www.wills pub.com; 1850 N Mills Ave) is off the beaten path but worth it for the great live music and atmosphere refined to the tastes of Orlando's tattooed masses.

Cricketers Arms (☎ 407-354-0686; 8445 International Dr; open until 2am) is an English-style pub with English-style grub and 17 draught beers. Entertainment performs nightly and the theme is cricket, cricket and cricket.

Matrix (☎ 407-370-3700; 9101 International Dr; $5 after 10pm), at Pointe Orlando, is loud, flashy and popular with 20-somethings. Techno to Top 40 is played.

Gay & Lesbian Venues

Orlando's gay and lesbian scene is growing, and explodes during the weeks around Gay Day (see the boxed text 'Gay Day at Disney' in the Walt Disney World Resort chapter). Before you transgendered cuties head out on the town, stop by **Ritzy Rags** (☎ 407-897-2117; W www.ritzyrags.com; 928 N Mills Ave), where owner and performer Leigh Shannon offers makeup and wardrobe tips for making the most of what you were born with. Wigs, dresses and size-14 pumps are also available.

John & Jason's Coffee Shoppe (☎ 407-447-1578; 932 N Mills Ave; open 7am-10pm Mon-Thur, 7am-2am Fri & Sat, 10am-11pm Sun) serves coffee and sandwiches alongside acoustic entertainment most weekend nights.

Southern Nights (☎ 407-898-0424; 375 Bennet Rd), just north of the Orlando Executive Airport, attracts more of a mixed crowd.

Faces (☎ 407-291-7571; 4910 Edgewater Dr), north of downtown on the west side of I-4, is a well-established lesbian bar.

Parliament House (☎ 407-425-7571; 410 N Orange Blossom Trail) is a gay resort (see Places to Stay earlier in this chapter) with cruisey country, piano and poolside bars, along with drag shows and other live entertainment.

Full Moon Saloon (☎ 407-648-8725; 500 N Orange Blossom Trail) is a fun leather and Levi's place in close proximity to Parliament House.

The Peacock Room (☎ 407-228-0048; 1321 N Mills Ave) is great for a drink or two and makes the best martinis in town.

Performing Arts

The **Orlando Fringe Festival** (☎ 407-648-0077; W www.orlandofringe.com) features performance art, community theater and other (stranger) offerings at venues throughout the city in May.

The **TD Waterhouse Centre** (☎ 407-849-2001 events listings, 407-849-2020 box office; 1 Magic Place, 600 W Amelia Ave) hosts sporting events and concerts. It also holds two more major performing arts venues, the

Bob Carr Performing Arts Centre and the **Civic Theater of Central Florida**, both of which stage performances of opera, classical music and theater.

Orlando Opera (☎ 407-426-1700; W www.orlandoopera.org; 1111 N Orange Ave) is a major regional company, representing 19 communities.

Orlando Ballet (☎ 407-426-1739; W www.orlandoballet.org; 1111 N Orange Ave) offers dance performances year-round at various locations in the area.

SAK Comedy Lab (☎ 407-648-0001; 398 W Amelia St) is a comedy/improv troupe that packs 'em in on weekends; make reservations.

Improv (☎ 321-281-8000; 129 W Church St) sometimes has popular names in stand-up comedy, and the best of local talent.

Masters of Magic (☎ 407-352-3456; 8815 International Dr; adult/child $20/15) stages a 90-minute magic show starring Typhoon Low, who served in the Navy for 22 years and also attended clown school. He disappears in midair on a Harley!

Loch Haven Park The Cultural Corridor here has lots to enrich your senses.

Goldman Theater (☎ 407-447-1700; 812 E Rollins St) is a 120-seat venue that stages locally produced plays and musicals as well as hosting touring troupes. Also here is **Studio B**, a black box theater specializing in performance art.

Lowndes Shakespeare Center (☎ 407-836-5540; 812 E Rollins St), in the same complex, is home to the UCF Shakespeare Festival (W www.shakespearefest.org), which has performances here and at the **Walt Disney Amphitheater** on lovely Lake Eola in downtown Orlando.

The **University of Central Florida Theatre Guild** (☎ 407-823-1500; 4000 Central Florida Blvd; adult/student $10/6) stages performances at the University of Central Florida and other area venues.

Orlando Philharmonic Orchestra (☎ 407-896-6700; W www.orlandophil.org) is the best in Central Florida.

SPECTATOR SPORTS

Orlando Magic (☎ 407-896-2442; W www.nba.com/magic) is Orlando's powerhouse professional men's basketball team and plays home games at the TD Waterhouse Centre (see Performing Arts earlier in this chapter).

The **Orlando Miracle** (☎ 407-916-9622; W www.wnba.com/miracle), a Women's National Basketball Association team, plays here as well.

The TD Waterhouse Centre is also home to the Arena Football League's **Orlando Predators** (☎ 407-447-7337; W www.orlandopredators.net).

SHOPPING

All the museums have gift shops, as do all the theme parks – probably more shops than rides by a factor of ten – packed with tempting, overpriced merchandise. Be careful out there.

International Dr is lined with grungy storefronts hawking everything from discount Disney gear and cheap electronics to specialty stores for science fiction, movie and beanie baby buffs. It's bookended by two malls.

The Mercado (☎ 407-345-9337; 8445 International Dr; W www.themercado.com) has shops, restaurants and the Titanic – Ship of Dreams exhibit.

Pointe Orlando (☎ 407-248-2838; W www.pointeorlandofl.com; 9101 International Dr), to the south, is a popular mall that was clearly designed by someone who'd done way too much acid at Walt Disney World.

Belz Factory Outlet (☎ 407-354-0126; 4949 International Dr) is an enormous place with discount designer duds; you too could score a pair of DKNY leather pants for $55, marked down from $230. There are also great Disney buys there.

Eli's Orange World (☎ 800-531-3182; W www.orangeworld192.com; 5395 Hwy 192) allows you to give the gift of citrus. In addition to orange, tangelo and grapefruit packages, you can have citrus preserves sent anywhere you want. You might be surprised how pricey it is though.

GETTING THERE & AWAY

See the Getting There & Away chapter for information on air, bus and train travel to Orlando. For getting to Orlando from the airport, see the Getting Around chapter.

I-4 runs north–south through Orlando, though it's labeled east–west; head north to Daytona on I-4 East and south to Tampa via I-4 West.

From Miami, the fastest and most direct route to Orlando is via Florida's Turnpike (toll), about a 4½-hour drive. Both the Bee Line Expressway and Hwy 50 will take you to the Space Coast; the expressway has frequent tolls, but is about an hour faster than Hwy 50.

GETTING AROUND
Car & Motorcycle

Downtown Orlando has an infuriating one-way street system that would seem to have been taken right out of either Kafka or Boston. Bring a map and expect to do a loop or two while looking for the freeway on-ramps.

The major car rental companies all have offices at the airport and many hotels (see the Getting Around chapter). If you're in the midst of a midlife crisis, **Orlando Harley Davidson** (☎ 407-944-3938; W www.orlandoharley.com) will drop off and pick up rental bikes at your hotel.

Note that many major throughways are toll roads, including Hwy 528, which connects International Dr with the airport and Space Coast. Bring quarters: if you have correct change (50¢ to $1.75), you can breeze through the booths a lot faster.

Parking There are lots of public parking garages in the downtown area, as well as meters. There are also lots of tow trucks: take no risks (see the boxed text). Remember that the downtown area is full of one-way streets, so be patient. Meters are enforced Monday to Friday 8am to 6pm and Saturday 2pm to 6pm. Unless otherwise posted, there is no charge for on-street metered parking after 6pm.

Taxi

Fares are $3 for the first mile plus $1.50 for each additional mile. You need to call for a cab (as opposed to hailing one on the street). Major

Illegal Parking – A Risky Business

Tow trucks in downtown Orlando literally hide in wait for people parking in private or company spots that are labeled tow-away zone. If the parking spot is labeled for 'Jane's Salon' and you're going to 'Ricky's Sandwiches,' you'll likely be towed within minutes of entering Ricky's. Consider this: parking garages abound in downtown Orlando. Even if you have to walk a bit, that's much better than spending a full day and a lot of money retrieving your rental car from some far-off tow lot and dealing with the seedy and unscrupulous behavior that often comes with these places.

ORLANDO

companies include **City Cab** (☎ 407-422-5151) and **Checker & Yellow Cab Co** (☎ 407-699-9999).

Shuttle & Limo Services
The biggest shuttle service in the area is **Mears Transportation** (☎ 407-423-5566), which runs vans between most major hotels, the youth hostel, campsites and the major theme parks. Expect to pay between $10 and $15 round-trip for shuttle service, unless your hotel has a special deal – many do.

Trolley
I-Ride Trolley (☎ 407-248-9590; W www.iride trolley.com; rides adult/senior/child under 12 75¢/25¢/free, 1-/3-/5-/7-/14-day pass $2/3/5/7/15; 24hrs) operates trolleys (buses in drag) that run along International Dr and Universal Blvd every 15 minutes. It serves Universal Studios, Wet 'n' Wild, SeaWorld, and the gazillion hotels, restaurants and tourist traps in between. Day passes can be bought at the Official Tourist Information Center on International Dr (see Information earlier in this chapter).

Bus
Lynx (☎ 800-344-5969 general information, 407-841-8240 route information; W www.go lynx.com; rides $1, transfers 10¢; buses run 4am-3am Mon-Fri, 4am-1am Sat, 4am-10pm Sun) covers all of Orlando. Bus stops are marked with a sign bearing a Lynx paw print of sorts along with the number of the route(s) that stop there. **Lymmo** is their free bus service, which circles downtown Orlando.

The **Lynx Bus Center** is in the alley between W Pine St and W Central Blvd, one block west of Orange Ave. You can buy tickets and get maps and specific route information from the **information booth** (open 6:30am-8pm Mon-Fri, 7:30am-6pm Sat, 8am-6pm Sun).

Lynx serves Orlando International Airport (Nos 11 and 42), Winter Park (Nos 1 and 9, hourly), Kissimmee (Nos 4 and 18), Walt Disney World (Nos 50 and 56), International Dr (No 38) and Colonial Dr (No 30), among many other places.

Around Orlando

WINTER PARK & AROUND
The self-proclaimed Venice of America, so named for its many canals, is one of Florida's best-kept secrets, a favorite weekend destination for the state's Epicurean leisure seekers.

Shaded cobblestone streets are lined with posh shops and restaurants, historic buildings and a handful of remarkable museums. Exclusive Rollins College – worth a stroll for its impressive architecture – adds an intellectual flavor. It's Flagler-era Florida still thriving right down to the picturesque Amtrak station in the pedestrian-friendly city center. It makes for the perfect vacation from the frantic glitter of the theme parks.

Information & Orientation
Winter Park is about 4 miles north of downtown Orlando. The city's main drag is Park Ave, bisected by Morse Blvd downtown. Rollins College is at the intersection of Park Ave and Osceola Ave (Hwy 426).

Winter Park Chamber of Commerce (☎ 407-644-8281; W www.winterparkcc.org; 150 N New York Ave; open 9am-5pm Mon-Fri) has free maps and a pamphlet outlining self-guided tours to the town's historic landmarks.

There's a **Bank of America** (☎ 407-646-3524; 250 Park Ave) downtown. Next door to the chamber of commerce is the **post office** (300 New York Ave).

The **library** (☎ 407-326-6600; 460 E New England) does not offer free Internet access. **Brandywine Books** (☎ 407-644-1711; 114 E Park Ave; open 10am-5:30pm Mon-Sat) has a huge collection of new and used tomes.

Charles Hosmer Morse Museum of American Art
You will be astounded by this beautiful museum (☎ 407-645-5311; 445 Park Ave N; adult/child under 12 $3/free; open 9:30am-4pm Tues-Sat, 1pm-4pm Sun, also open 4pm-8pm Fri Sept-May) and its unparalleled collection of Tiffany glass. Lamps are the least of the treasures you'll see: the *Four Seasons* may be the pinnacle of the art form, but the elaborate (some say garish) Tiffany Chapel is certainly the most impressive. Oh yeah, there's lots of other art here, too, mostly from the 1920s.

Cornell Fine Arts Museum
The collection at this small museum (☎ 407-646-1595; 1000 Holt Ave; admission free; open 10am-5pm Tues-Fri, 1pm-5pm Sat & Sun), on the impressive Rollins College campus, easily outclasses many larger, more famous galleries: Oldenburg, De Kooning and Rauschenberg works are just part of the permanent file. Rotating exhibitions are usually spectacular.

ORLANDO

Albin Polasek Galleries

Scattered through the grounds of this stately home and serene garden (☎ 407-674-6294; W www.polasek.org; 633 Osceola Ave; adult/child $4/2; open 10am-4pm Tues-Sat, 1pm-4pm Sun) are the works of Czech sculptor Albin Polasek, an artist obsessed with our ability to carve our own destiny. The sculptures are heavy, thoughtful and, in some cases, quite moving. Impromptu tours through the statues and small chapel are available from informative docents at the door, as long as they're not too busy.

Audubon Center for Birds of Prey

Fierce feathered friends are taken care of when wounded and are available for observation at this center (☎ 407-644-0190; 1101 Audubon Way; adult/child $5/4; open 10am-4pm Tues-Sun) in Eatonville, just down the road from Winter Park. The center also offers classes on the basics of bird watching ($10).

Maitland Art Center

Since 1937, this art center (☎ 407-539-2181; W www.maitartctr.org; 231 W Packwood Ave; admission free; open 9am-4:30pm Mon-Fri, noon-4:30pm Sat & Sun) has provided classes and studio space to area artists, as well as galleries where they can display their work for the public. The facilities also have some lovely gardens where live music, usually classical, is performed on an irregular basis.

Scenic Boat Tours

This company (☎ 407-644-4056; W www.scenicboattours.com; 1 E Morse Ave; adult/child $8/4; open 10am-4pm daily) takes you down through 12 miles of tropical canals, lined with mansions and the stunning campus of Rollins College. Be warned, however: Sandra, who now works at the Park Plaza Hotel, had to uproot her family and move here after taking this trip. They also rent canoes, $5 for the first hour, $1 for each additional hour.

Places to Stay

Winter Park's hotels don't exactly cater to the budget traveler.

Best Western Mt Vernon Inn (☎ 407-647-1166; W www.bestwestern.com; 110 S Orlando Ave; rooms $97) takes full advantage of its location by charging premium prices for clean, standard rooms.

Park Plaza Hotel (☎ 407-647-1072, 800-228-7220; W www.parkplazahotel.com; 307 Park Ave S; rooms without/with a view $100/194) is definitely the most elegant property in the Orlando area. Its 1920s ambience is palpable, and some lushly appointed rooms have balconies overlooking the cobblestoned downtown.

Thurston House (☎ 407-539-1911; W www.thurstonhouse.com; 851 Lake Ave; rooms $140-150), in nearby Eatonville, is a rambling Victorian B&B on the shores of Lake Eulalia.

Places to Eat

Winter Park is home to some of the best restaurants in the Greater Orlando area.

Power House Cafe (☎ 407-645-3616; 111 E Lyman Ave; dishes $4-6; open 9am-7pm Mon-Fri, 10am-5pm Sat) serves truly outstanding sandwiches with a vegetarian focus and Middle Eastern flavor. The fruit smoothies are excellent.

Briarpatch Restaurant (☎ 407-628-8651; 252 Park Ave N; dishes $7-12; open 7am-9pm Mon-Sat, 8am-5pm Sun) does great specialty omelettes and homemade breads, plus lots of vegetarian dishes for lunch and dinner.

Restaurant du Parc (☎ 407-647-4469; 348 Park Ave N; prix fixe $45; open 11.30am-2pm & 6pm-9pm Mon-Sat) is a fine French restaurant tucked into a hidden garden off Park Ave. The same proprietors offer more affordable crepe-based cuisine at **Maison des Crepes** (mains $15 to $20) next door.

Brandywine's Delicatessen (☎ 407-647-0055; 505 N Park Ave; dishes $4-7) has deli sandwiches.

Siam Garden (☎ 407-599-7443; 1111 W Webster Ave) is a local's favorite for Thai food.

Black Bean Deli (325 S Orlando Ave) has excellent Cuban food.

PF Chang's (407-622-0188; 436 N Orlando Ave) is the place to go for Chinese food.

Coldstone Creamery (601 N Orlando Ave) spells trouble. The made-to-order ice cream sundaes at this chain are to die for.

Speaking of trouble, **Fuji Sushi** (☎ 407-645-1299; 1499 Lee Rd) has added tempura cheesecake to its nice sushi menu.

Getting There & Away

Lynx buses (see Getting Around in the Orlando section earlier) run between downtown Orlando and Winter Park; bus Nos 1 and 9 make the trip hourly.

Amtrak (☎ 407-645-5055; 150 Morse Blvd) stops right downtown and offers regular service to Orlando, Miami and all points on the Eastern Seaboard.

By car, head north on I-4 to exit 46, go east on Lee Rd and take a right on Orlando Ave (Hwy 92). Make a left onto Morse St, which takes you right downtown.

DADE BATTLEFIELD HISTORIC PARK

Just west of Orlando, this small state park (☎ 352-793-4781; 603 S Battlefield Dr; adult/ child $2/1; open 8am–sunset daily) has a few small nature trails, a great little **museum** (open 9am–5pm daily) and probably the most interesting historical reenactment in Florida.

In 1835 the US government tried to move the Seminole Nation to concentration camps …er, reservations in Oklahoma. Seminole chief Osceola was not about to go quietly, and organized 180 warriors and escaped slaves to fight back. On December 28, they ambushed a column of soldiers led by Major Francis L Dade, killing all but two of them; Osceola lost three men. Every year, on the anniversary of the battle, reenactors (including several enthusiastic Seminole Indians) gather here to re-create the carnage, which incited the beginning of the Second Seminole War (see the History section of the Facts about Central Florida chapter).

There's great camping nearby at **Withlacoochee Trail State Park** (☎ 352-726-2251; 3100 Old Floral City Rd; sites without/with hookups $10/13) on the shores of Silver Lake next to an awesome rail trail.

To get here, take US Hwy 50 (Colonial Dr) west of downtown about 40 miles; Withlacoochie Trail State Park is at the intersection with I-75, Dade Battlefield Historic Park is about 10 miles north on the interstate.

YEEHAW JUNCTION
pop approximately 100

There's not much going on at Yeehaw Junction, about 60 miles south of Orlando on Florida's Turnpike, but the town has two diehard tourist attractions that pack 'em in. First is the **Yeehaw Travel Center** (☎ 407-436-1616, 800-493-3492; 3100 State Route 60; open 7am–8pm Sun–Thur, 7am–9pm Fri & Sat), which sells discount tickets to Orlando attractions and specializes in getting good deals on rooms. They also have free coffee.

The second attraction has charm, character and the dignity of having been placed on the National Register of Historic Places. The **Desert Inn** (☎ 407-436-1054; W www.desert innandrestaurant.com; 5570 S Kenansville Rd; rooms $39) was once Central Florida's favorite bordello. Room service isn't what it used to be, but you can still stay the night, or just stop at the **restaurant** (dishes $3-5; open 9am–10pm Mon–Thur, 8am–11pm Sat, 9am–11pm Sun) for a burger or a beer.

Ask owner Beverly Zichek to show you the **museum** (admission $1). In several of the rooms, it shows the bedrooms as they looked during the place's heyday from 1889 to 1953, complete with red satin bedspreads, swings and saddles.

WEKIWA SPRINGS STATE PARK

If Orlando is your only stop in the region, do yourself a favor and see this sliver of the real Central Florida (☎ 407-884-2006; 1800 Wekiwa Circle; pedestrian/car $1/4). It's got miles of hiking, bicycle and canoe trails through palmetto wilderness, not to mention a natural spring welling up at 72°F year-round. You can rent bikes ($9 for two hours, $18 all day) and canoes ($14 for two hours, $25 all day) to better take it all in. Best of all, the only mice you'll see will be trying to raid your picnic basket.

Before European settlers arrived, the area including this park was inhabited by Timucuans, and middens found around here date back as far as 3000 BC. As a tourist destination, Wekiwa Springs has been a popular since the late 19th century, when vacationers started to swim in the springs and imbibe their healing waters. They called it Clay Springs back then, and an early proprietor built a hotel here, but it fell into a state of disrepair by the very beginning of the 20th century. Later, other owners added a bathhouse, a slide, picnic areas, a dance pavilion and a new hotel, and in 1906 they changed the name to Wekiwa Springs.

Wekiwa Springs (☎ 407-884-2006; W www .abfla.com/parks/WekiwaSprings/wekiwa.html; 1800 Wekiwa Circle; sites without/with hookups $17/19) is a beautiful place to pitch a tent. There are also free walk-in sites 4 miles from the parking lot.

Head north from downtown Orlando on I-4 East about 6 miles, and take exit 49 west on Sanlando Rd. Make a right at Wekiwa Springs Rd and follow the signs three more miles to the park.

MT DORA

Quaint little Mt Dora attracts tourists eager to escape urban Orlando. It's a sugary concoction of gingerbread Victorian B&Bs, shady parks, a beautiful lake plied by photogenic pontoon boats and a cutthroat knickknack market that has elegant matrons providing free coffee and fresh-baked cookies to lure you inside their adorable shops and galleries.

It really is a taste of what awaits visitors who have the time to explore Central Florida's hinterlands, complete with that sense of luxurious indolence endemic to this beautiful region. But it's all right here, an hour from Orlando, perfect for visitors budgeting their time.

Orientation & Information

Mt Dora's main drag is Donnelly St, which runs from US Hwy 441 south to the shores of Lake Dora. East–west avenues are numbered, beginning at the lake's shore; shops and restaurants are concentrated between 3rd and 6th Aves. The train station, which is now defunct, is a block south of Donnelly on 3rd St.

The **chamber of commerce** (☎ 352-383-2165; W www.mountdora.com; 341 Alexander St), in the 1915 Atlantic Coastline train depot, has racks of pamphlets and colorful free maps of town.

Bank of America (163 W 5th St) is at the corner of Alexander St.

Dickens-Reed (☎ 352-735-5950; 140 5th Ave; open 9am-6pm Mon-Sat, 11am-5pm Sun) is an excellent bookstore with an attached coffee shop that serves outstanding apple pie. They show free foreign flicks at 8pm Saturday.

Organized Tours

The **Mt Dora Road Trolley** (☎ 352-357-9123; 100 N Alexander St; adult/child under 13 $8/5.50) offers a one-hour tour that takes you to the 'lighthouse,' along a small nature trail and past lots of historic buildings. It leaves several times daily from the Lakeside Inn; you can also get package deals that include a meal or room at the hotel.

Places to Stay

For a complete list of lodging options (with a heavy emphasis on B&Bs) contact the chamber of commerce.

Mt Dora Inn (☎ 352-735-1212; W www.mountdorahistoricinn.com; 221 E 4th St; rooms $75-135) is a typically lovely 1880s Victorian mansion within walking distance from downtown.

Lakeside Inn (☎ 352-383-4101; W www.lakeside-inn.com; 100 N Alexander St; rooms $92-210) is a rustic hotel that packs in the tourists; it's a little rough around the edges but has ambience to spare.

Coconut Cottage Inn (☎ 352-383-2627; W www.coconutcottageinn.com; 1027 McDonald St; rooms $129-149), in a 1920s Arts and Crafts home, is a bit different: rooms are decorated with African, Asian and Middle Eastern motifs.

Places to Eat

If you're looking for local gems undiscovered by tourists, you've come to the wrong place.

Sunshine Mountain Bakery (☎ 352-735-5227; 115 W 3rd Ave; dishes $3-8; open 7am-4pm daily) has pastries, sandwiches and salads.

The **Frosty Mug** (☎ 352-383-1969; 411 N Donnelly St; dishes $6-20; open noon-midnight Tues-Thur & Sun, noon-1am Fri & Sat), in the Renaissance Mall, is a cozy Icelandic pub serving gravlax (cured salmon), pickled herring and more. There's live jazz and blues on Wednesday and Thursday night.

O'Neil's Irish Pub (☎ 352-735-7755; 421 Baker St; lunch $6-10, dinner $10-20; open 11am-midnight Sun-Wed, 11am-2am Thur-Sat) has all the Irish standards (cottage pie, bangers and mash etc), plus burgers, steaks and tasty buffalo wings. There's live acoustic music Thursday through Saturday.

The **Mt Dora Kringle Co** (☎ 800-733-2214; W www.kringleco.com; 3985 N Hwy 19-A) is just one mile north of Mt Dora. It specializes in a traditional Danish pastry called the kringle, something like a flaky PopTart.

Getting There & Away

Take Hwy 441 (Orange Blossom Trail) north from downtown Orlando and make a left on County Road 44B (Donnelly St) shortly after the turnoff to Eustis. There's lots of free parking downtown.

Walt Disney World Resort

When Disneyland opened in Southern California, it took off in a huge way, fundamentally transforming the concept of theme parks. Walt Disney, however, was unsatisfied, and irritated at the hotels and concessions that were springing up around his property in a manner that he felt was entirely parasitic. So in the mid-1960s, under the nom de guerre Reedy Creek Development Company, Walt bought up 27,000 acres of land in Central Florida. One of the main reasons he selected the spot (besides the dirt-cheap land) is that it is crossed by both Florida's Turnpike and I-4. The latter was built in the '60s under much controversy – people thought it was unnecessary and would not be used enough to justify the cost. Well, Disney certainly changed that, as you'll notice on I-4 at rush hours.

His goal was no less than the creation of a family vacation 'city,' every aspect of which – hotels, resorts, restaurants, parking and transportation – he controlled. Walt hired retired General William Potter, who helped design the 1964 World's Fair, to build the park. Then he somehow convinced the state of Florida to grant Disney the right to self-govern the municipality. The park opened in October 1971 and in its first year saw more than 10 million visitors. Today, the park's almost 40,000 employees welcome an average of 70,000 people daily.

It is indeed its own city, complete with an elaborate transportation system (featuring buses, trams, ferries, shuttles and a monorail), a fire department, several medical centers, an efficient and incorruptible police force, an energy plant – even a florist. All this is designed to make the theme park as isolated, self-sufficient and perfectly happy as it can be.

What follows is just a description of the main features of the park, and in no way covers all the seemingly infinite options for entertainment, dining, shopping and more. You could easily vacation here for two weeks without ever seeing the same thing twice. And you'd never even know that Orlando was there.

PLANNING

Before you start planning, you can order a free copy of the *Walt Disney World Vacations Brochure* online (W *www.disneyworld.com*) or by calling ☎ 800-327-2996. You can also request a free vacation-planning video.

Highlights

- Witnessing first-hand the pure joy of children (and some adults!) meeting Mickey
- Getting a glimpse of the almost eerie utopia in the Disney town of Celebration
- Seeing it all from above at the front of the monorail
- Receiving a flirtatious hug from your favorite Disney character
- Taking your child on your very favorite ride and reliving the wonder vicariously
- Debating with friends and family, at the end of the day, over which is the best attraction

Orlando ●

Walt Disney ■
World Resort

When to Go

As far as accommodations go, the cheapest time of year is from the beginning of August to mid-December. July and August are hot, but cooling (and line-shortening) downpours occur frequently. Visiting between late June and early August, or around the Christmas and New Year's holidays, guarantees spending an extra three hours per day in line. During the summer, weekends are the least crowded days; the rest of the year the opposite is true.

No matter what season you arrive, get to the parks early. They open about an hour before the schedule (available at W www.disney world.com or by calling ☎ 407-939-62442) says they do, and staff get the most popular rides running early. Note that certain night events such as fireworks and laser shows are seasonal, so if you have your heart set on seeing something, check with Disney early to make sure it will be on when you visit.

Prices for everything are raised regularly, so pay for accommodations and tickets as soon as possible to beat the hikes. If you know you're going next year, buy and book everything before December 31st, after which new rates are usually established. See the Facts for the Visitor chapter for more tips on the best times to go.

Buying Tickets

There are several different ticket options, and the selection can get confusing. The prices below, with the exception of the single-day pass, were Disney's advance-purchase, online, pre-tax rates at the time of research. All child prices listed below are for children aged three to nine, and children under three are free. For single admission to the minor parks (such as the water parks and Disney's Wide World of Sports), see those sections, later in this chapter.

Single-Day Adult/child $50/40. Good for admission to only one of the four major parks for one day. These are available only at the front gate of the park, not online or through other companies.

Park Hopper Adult/child four-day pass $192/152, five-day pass $217/172. These come with a four- or five-day option and admit you to all four major parks as often as you like during that time period. Unused days never expire, and can be saved for future use.

Park Hopper Plus Adult/child five-day pass $247/197, six-day pass $277/222, seven-day pass $307/247. These give you unlimited access to all four major parks, plus limited visits to Pleasure Island, the water parks and Disney's Wide World of Sports for the duration of the ticket purchased. Unused days never expire.

Ultimate Park Hopper Adult/child prices range from $114/91 to $435/348 for one to 11 days. These are purchasable only by visitors who are staying at Disney World accommodations. Unlimited access to all parks, major and minor, is granted, and you will receive a card that functions as an admission pass and as a credit card (purchases are billed to the hotel room). The downside is that it expires upon checking out of the accommodations, and that it's more expensive than Park Hopper passes. Consider going with a Park Hopper or Park Hopper Plus instead if you're not planning on spending much time at the minor parks.

Annual Pass Adult/child $369/314. Good for admission to any park, any time for 365 days from the date of purchase.

Discounts The only thing crazier than getting your tickets by surviving a timeshare lecture is to purchase them in line at the parks. Get your tickets before going to the park, even if you get them from Disney directly. You'll be waiting in enough lines once you get in the park – why wait in line to buy your ticket? Plus, there are ways to save money if you buy tickets in advance.

- Check out W www.mousesavers.com for truly excellent information on discounted tickets and other deals.
- We do not recommend buying leftover days on Park Hopper passes on eBay, but some people do this and have no trouble. Just keep in mind that if your tickets are duds or if they're ripped up in front of you at the gates, you'll basically have no recourse.
- Lucky Florida residents get a special deal called the Orlando Magical Getaway Travel Club. Visit W www.orlandoinfo.com/floridaresidents for details.
- The Official Tourist Information Center on International Dr (see the Orlando chapter) offers

E-Ride Nights

Although early entry for resort guests was halted after September 11 for security reasons, there is now a program called E-Ride Nights, where for an additional charge, Disney resort guests who've purchased multiday tickets may stay three hours past closing at Magic Kingdom to ride nine of the best attractions there: Astro Orbiter, Big Thunder Mountain Railroad, Buzz Lightyear's Space Ranger Spin, Country Bear Jamboree, The ExtraTERRORestrial Alien Encounter, The Haunted Mansion, Space Mountain, Splash Mountain and the Tomorrowland Transit Authority.

E-Ride Nights cost $12/10 per adult/child 3 to 9 and are available on a first-come, first-served basis. You must show resort ID and your multiday ticket at purchase, which can be done at a resort hotel's guest services desk.

Keep in mind that this program is offered sporadically, and usually during periods when the park closes early anyway.

WALT DISNEY WORLD RESORT

WALT DISNEY WORLD RESORT

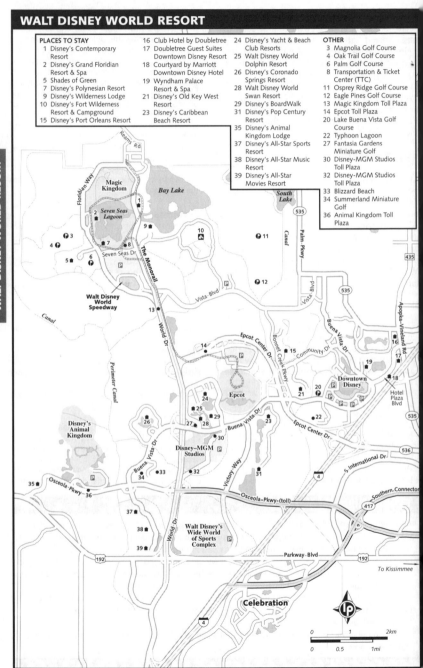

PLACES TO STAY
1 Disney's Contemporary Resort
2 Disney's Grand Floridian Resort & Spa
5 Shades of Green
7 Disney's Polynesian Resort
9 Disney's Wilderness Lodge
10 Disney's Fort Wilderness Resort & Campground
15 Disney's Port Orleans Resort

16 Club Hotel by Doubletree
17 Doubletree Guest Suites Downtown Disney Resort
18 Courtyard by Marriott Downtown Disney Hotel
19 Wyndham Palace Resort & Spa
21 Disney's Old Key West Resort
23 Disney's Caribbean Beach Resort

24 Disney's Yacht & Beach Club Resorts
25 Walt Disney World Dolphin Resort
26 Disney's Coronado Springs Resort
28 Walt Disney World Swan Resort
29 Disney's BoardWalk
31 Disney's Pop Century Resort
35 Disney's Animal Kingdom Lodge
37 Disney's All-Star Sports Resort
38 Disney's All-Star Music Resort
39 Disney's All-Star Movies Resort

OTHER
3 Magnolia Golf Course
4 Oak Trail Golf Course
6 Palm Golf Course
8 Transportation & Ticket Center (TTC)
11 Osprey Ridge Golf Course
12 Eagle Pines Golf Course
13 Magic Kingdom Toll Plaza
14 Epcot Toll Plaza
20 Lake Buena Vista Golf Course
22 Typhoon Lagoon
27 Fantasia Gardens Miniature Golf
30 Disney-MGM Studios Toll Plaza
32 Disney-MGM Studios Toll Plaza
33 Blizzard Beach
34 Summerland Miniature Golf
36 Animal Kingdom Toll Plaza

official Disney and other park tickets at a slight (about 5%) discount. They also sometimes have promotions with even better deals, so it's worth calling to ask (☎ 407-363-5872). You can also purchase the tickets online at Ⓦ www.orlando ticketsales.com.

• Special folks, such as members of the Disney Club, Disney Vacation Club and AAA (contact the club); military and government employees (contact personnel); employees of Disney and corporate sponsors (contact personnel); and Canadians (contact a local Disney store) receive discounts.

• Ticketmania (☎ 877-822-7299, Ⓦ www.ticket mania.com) offers legal discount tickets to all Central Florida attractions, even Cirque du Soleil.

• The Wal-Mart (☎ 800-669-0913) on Hwy 192 near mile marker 15 gives a decent – and legal – discount on Disney tickets and other attractions.

Now, as for those fake tourist center operations that offer super-discounted or free tickets in exchange for your attending a lecture about timeshares, don't do it. We have never heard of anyone coming out of that experience saying it was worth it, but we have plenty of readers' letters including the phrases 'tricky bastards' and 'sheer torture.' There are better ways to save money than subjecting yourself to this.

Leftover Days Unused days on Park Hopper and Park Hopper Plus tickets never expire, so you are welcome to hold on to the tickets until you come back (or give them to family or friends, which isn't *technically* allowed by Disney).

But also, know that those same fake tourist centers that sell illegal tickets will buy those leftover days for cash. We're not saying this is OK or anything– in fact, it's a misdemeanor.

What to Bring
Even when it's raining, temperatures are (usually) warm, so bring a lightweight rain poncho, comfortable clothing that you don't mind getting wet, a bathing suit, sunscreen and sunglasses. Carry it all in a backpack compact enough to keep on your lap during rides. Bring a solidly resealing bottle of drinking water (refills are free). Food from outside is technically not permitted in the parks, but this is generally not enforced. See the Facts for the Visitor chapter for more information on what to bring.

Maps
The free *Walt Disney World Resort Map,* available throughout the park and at any Orlando visitors center, has an overview of the whole resort, breakdown maps of the main parks, and a useful transportation network chart. You'll get free handout maps of each particular park at the entrance.

ORIENTATION
Walt Disney World Resort is north of Hwy 192, roughly west of I-4 and skirted on its east and some of the north by Hwy 535. It's about 23 miles southwest of Orlando and 4 miles northwest of Kissimmee.

There are four main parks (Magic Kingdom, Epcot, Disney-MGM Studios and Disney's Animal Kingdom), two water parks (Blizzard Beach, Typhoon Lagoon), a shopping and entertainment district (Downtown Disney), several specialized attractions (such as Disney's Wide World of Sports) and numerous other destinations. There are dozens of Disney-owned resorts on the property.

The main Ticket & Transportation Center (TTC) is off Seven Seas Dr, as are the main bus station and parking lots for Magic Kingdom. Many Orlando and Kissimmee hotels provide shuttle buses to this complex, which is simple to find by car from either I-4 or Hwy 192.

INFORMATION
Walt Disney World (☎ 407-934-7639; TDD 407-939-7670; Ⓦ www.disneyworld.com) does not have a toll-free information or reservations telephone number. The information and reservations line is also usually backed up at least fifteen minutes, especially for English-speaking operators. The website, however, is easy to use and often has better prices on accommodations. By mail, send requests for brochures or other information to **Walt Disney Guest Communications** (PO Box 10000, Lake Buena Vista, FL 32830-1000).

Note that there is no paging or loudspeaker system that is available for guests – no matter what.

Autograph Books & Passports
These things are very popular with kids; you can buy them here or bring your own. They are used to collect character autographs and stamps from the different 'lands' in Epcot. Do the characters a favor and bring a large, thick pen – it's hard to grab a skinny little ballpoint in a 50lb rubber suit.

Baby Care Centers & Sitters
Excellent baby centers are located in every park. They're air-conditioned, packed with toys and run Disney cartoons constantly (for

WALT DISNEY WORLD RESORT

the older kids). They also sell diapers, formula, baby powder, over-the-counter medicine – the works. Nursing rooms are also available. Note that nursing children in public may attract uncomfortable stares in this part of the USA.

For private baby-sitting for kids under 12, call **KinderCare** (☎ 407-827-5437); if you're staying at a Disney resort, they can watch children under 12 in your hotel room (☎ 407-827-5444). Disney also offers supervised activities for potty-trained tots ages four to 12, which run $5 to $8 hourly between 5pm and midnight. Call ☎ 407-939-3463 for more information.

You can rent strollers ($8/15 single/double). This is a good idea – you'll be walking a lot more than you think, and even active kids over five will get tired.

Disabled Travelers
The excellent *Guidebook for Guests with Disabilities,* available at Guest Services, has maps and ride-by-ride guides with information on closed captioning and accommodating wheelchairs and seeing-eye dogs. On many rides, wheelchair-bound folks (plus all ten of their friends) will be waved to the front of the line. You can borrow braille guides and audiotape guides from Guest Relations with a $25 deposit. All over the resort, manual wheelchairs are available for $7 plus a $1 deposit; electric ones are $30 plus a $10 deposit (all chairs are first-come, first-served; reservations are not possible). All public transportation is wheelchair accessible.

Kennels
There are kennels at the four major parks. They are available to pets with proof of vaccinations for $6 daily, $9 overnight (checkout is at 1pm). You must pay extra for food, and dog owners are expected to return twice daily to walk their pets. Pets can also stay with you at Fort Wilderness full-hookup campsites.

Meeting Characters

You can meet any of more than 250 Disney characters for free at the parks, or you can pay to have a meal with them at one of the character dining options.

Free Meetings
These can be arranged by consulting your *Times Guide* (given to you at the park's entrance). If there's a particular character you must see, ask a cast member (any Disney staff member) to call the character hotline to find out if he or she is out and about at the moment, and if so, where.

The best park for seeing characters is at Magic Kingdom, especially at Fantasyland and Mickey's Toontown Fair (see those sections). You can also see characters at Epcot, but not as frequently; the upside is that the characters there are not mobbed like they are elsewhere, so it's easier to get in for an autograph etc. MGM Studios has lots of shows featuring characters, but you can also do the meet-and-greet thing; try the end of New York St on the backlot or in front of the Animation Building. At Animal Kingdom, Camp Minnie-Mickey is specially designed and well organized for character meetings. The characters at Animal Kingdom are usually from *The Jungle Book*, *The Lion King*, or *Pocahontas*. You can also see characters at the resorts, but there's no set schedule; it's very random.

Character Dining
This is incredibly popular, so call way in advance for priority seating (☎ 407-939-3463). Meals (breakfast, brunch, lunch and dinner are all possible) take place at restaurants both in the parks and at the resort's hotels, and are generally all you can eat, even if they're not buffet-style. You can expect around four or five characters to make an appearance; you can find out who'll be there when you book priority seating (this is good to know in case your child is afraid of certain people or animals from the movies – villains do sometimes show up for character dining!).

Now if you want to partake in the character breakfast at **Cinderella's Royal Table**, good luck. The restaurant is small, many of the tables are booked by package deals, and it's probably the most popular character meal. Nevertheless, if you want to make a go of it, you must call ☎ 407-WDW-DINE at 7am EST *exactly* 60 days before the date you'd like to dine with Cinderella. Do anything differently and you won't get in. Yes, that's how popular it is.

Lines

Crowds can get amazing, especially in peak seasons. Approximate wait times (usually slightly overestimated) are posted at the beginning of each line. FastPass (see that section later) lets you swipe your ticket at the entrance to popular attractions, then return at a predetermined time (usually an hour or two later), when you'll be waved to the front of the line – take advantage of this! Disney also has a child-swap program, which allows parents with small children to hand the kid off to one another while the other rides. Single riders often have separate, and much shorter, lines.

The best strategy is to get to the park early and get in line for the most popular rides first. Downpours and parades also tend to shorten lines considerably.

Medical Services

There are excellent, nurse-staffed clinics in all the parks.

Money

Guest Relations in all four parks exchanges foreign currency up to $50, at slightly worse rates than you'd get at the bank. They can point you toward numerous ATM machines.

Disney dollars can be purchased at a 1:1 exchange with US dollars at parks and Disney stores all over the world, then used to buy souvenirs. In fact, Disney hopes you'll keep several of them as souvenirs themselves.

Organized Tours

There are at least a dozen guided tours (☎ 407-939-8687) available throughout the park, ranging from the tempting *Keys to the Kingdom,* which takes you through the Magic Kingdom's network of underground tunnels, to *Epcot Dive Quest,* which lets certified divers frolic with dolphins. Attendance is limited and prices vary widely; call for more information.

Parking

It costs an extra $7/8 per car/recreational vehicle (RV) for parking. If you decide to visit more than one park in a day, flash your previous park's parking ticket – it's good all day for all Disney parks.

FASTPASS

You're crazy if you don't use FastPasses. Don't just use them, plan your day around them. For example, when you enter a new land, go and get a FastPass for the attraction that you're most interested in, then go to non-FastPass attractions while you wait for your appointment time. FastPasses for the most popular attractions can run out by midday, so if you really really want to see something, get your FastPass as soon as possible.

Magic Kingdom

When most people think of Disney World, they're thinking of Magic Kingdom. This is Mickey and Minnie's home base, and where you'll find such classic attractions as Pirates of the Caribbean and Space Mountain. The centerpiece is Cinderella Castle, instantly recognizable to most of the world's population. Magic Kingdom is also the most anticipated destination on the Disney property for the under-12 set. Save it for last or risk eye-rolling aplenty when you drag the kids to Epcot. Teens and thrill-seekers will be disappointed with Magic Kingdom (and other Disney parks for that matter) in comparison to Universal's Islands of Adventure. For adults who've been here (or Disneyland, which is similar to Magic Kingdom), nostalgia is the reason for coming back. But for kidless adults who have never been and aren't Disney fanatics, the Magic Kingdom might be a disappointment.

Many attractions here are of the 'it's a small world' variety, but that doesn't mean they're as annoying as that attraction. For example, the Peter Pan and Winnie the Pooh rides are very adorable.

ORIENTATION & INFORMATION

The Magic Kingdom is divided into seven 'lands' arranged around the central hub with a statue of Walt and Mickey holding hands, right in front of Cinderella Castle, the most useful landmark when orienting yourself in the park.

Don't Miss!

- Pirates of the Caribbean
- Splash Mountain
- The Haunted Mansion
- Hall of Presidents
- Peter Pan's Flight
- The Many Adventures of Winnie the Pooh
- ExtraTERRORestrial Alien Encounter
- Space Mountain
- The Timekeeper

WALT DISNEY WORLD RESORT

Hidden Mickeys

What is a Hidden Mickey? No, it's not something a sneaky criminal slips into your margarita at a busy bar. A Hidden Mickey is an image of the Disney mouse that's been somehow integrated into the environment so as to be noticeable only if you're looking for it – or if you're lucky and happen to see it out of the corner of your eye.

The images are often just one big circle with two tangential smaller circles to form that three-circle triangle associated with Mickey, but just what constitutes a Hidden Mickey is a matter of constant debate – and yes, you can bet your bottom dollar there are plenty of people out there who have much to say on the subject. Websites and newsgroups on Hidden Mickeys abound. There are 'Deliberate Mickeys,' which Hidden-Mickey hunters have determined to be purposely hidden by Imagineers, and 'Serendipitous Mickeys,' which they've determined to be accidental images of Mickey; these are usually disproportioned or otherwise off-kilter, and fall into the 'wishful thinking' category.

Unfortunately, Disney has never kept track of these images. They have been placed pretty much at the whim of park designers, so it's up to fanatics to keep a record of reported sightings. If you'd like to report or confirm a Hidden Mickey sighting, you can go to W www.hiddenmickeys.org.

You enter onto Main Street, USA, with lots of restaurants and souvenir shops. Tomorrowland and Frontierland have most of the big rides (and most of the long lines). Fantasyland and Mickey's Toontown Fair (where characters congregate) have rides for smaller children. Liberty Square and Adventureland seem somewhat neglected, but still have their charms. Walt Disney World Railroad, a steam-driven locomotive, circumnavigates the entire park in a long, boring loop, stopping at Main St, Frontierland and Mickey's Toontown Fair (see Getting Around later in this section for information). Magic Kingdom is on the Monorail line.

Main Street, USA is where most guest services are (see that section).

MAIN STREET, USA

Guest Services and the **lost and found** are in City Hall, immediately after you enter the park.

Wheelchair and stroller rental is immediately on your right before passing under the train station. There are **ATMs** and **storage lockers** at the Main St Railroad Station. **First aid** and the park's **baby care center** are located, as you enter the park, on the left side of Main St by the Crystal Palace restaurant. At the end of Main St, on the left, there's an **information board** with the day's show and parade times, estimated ride waits and other helpful tips.

ADVENTURELAND

This land has some of the least popular attractions, with the exception of Pirates of the Caribbean.

Swiss Family Treehouse

This is worth a quick tour, and there shouldn't be a wait to do so. You'll be walking up plenty of stairs, so it's not something you'll want to do when you're tired, and folks in wheelchairs will have to get a view from the ground.

The attraction is the replica treehouse-home of the shipwrecked family from the book and Disney movie *The Swiss Family Robinson*. In it, you'll see how the Robinsons' MacGyver-type brilliance turned their disaster-stricken lives into a paradisiacal wonderland that makes the folks on *Survivor* look like nincompoops. It'll sort of make you jealous that you're not a castaway yourself.

The Magic Carpets of Aladdin

This ride is the Disney version of One Fish, Two Fish at Universal's Islands of Adventure. That is, riders, going in a circle, are given up and down controls to avoid the waterstream of the spitting camel. Kids will want to ride it, but be prepared to wait; loading on this one is inefficient.

The Enchanted Tiki Room

Now under new management, the Enchanted Tiki Room once rode on adult nostalgia and toddler power alone. Well, the magic of nostalgia is gone – that wonderful song 'In the tiki tiki tiki room...' has been cut down to a couple of verses. Why is Gilbert Gottfried's voice so ubiquitous at these parks? Isn't anyone else annoyed? The toddler power may also be gone – it's now scarier under 'the new management,' with a storm and booming god and goddess voices. Disney blew it on this one. Hey, see if you can guess which actors do the voices of the preshow entertainment birds.

Jungle Cruise (FastPass)

We're going to be honest with you, here and throughout the book. So it must be said that the genius of Disney's Imagineers needs to be redirected, for a day at least, toward rewriting host speeches, which are often some of the most schlocky, wince-inducing spiels known to man. Jungle Cruise is right up there with the worst of them.

Kids might like it and be spared the bad sense of humor, but it's a slow line. Make sure to get a FastPass if you plan on seeing this one. Oh, and you won't really get wet.

Pirates of the Caribbean

Here it is, one of the most popular, nostalgia-invoking rides of Disney. Like the Haunted Mansion, and plenty of other Disney attractions for that matter, fans of this one are rabid on the subject.

Pirates is an indoor boat tour, but you won't get wet. Small children may get scared in the dark, but the whole thing is generally more silly than scary.

Pirates of the Caribbean is proof that Disney can update its attractions to cut out possibly politically incorrect or otherwise tacky aspects without diminishing the magic.

FRONTIERLAND

America's Wild West and Deep South are the themes here.

Splash Mountain (FastPass)

This ride, based on the movie *Song of the South,* depicts the misadventures of Brer Rabbit, Brer Bear and Brer Fox, complete with chatty frogs, singing ducks and other colorful critters along its lengthy, half-mile trail. Then it drops you a screaming 50ft at nearly 40mph into the river, making for one of the biggest thrills in the park. You will get very very wet!

This is one of the most popular rides in the park – there will be a long line, even as soon as the park opens, so get a FastPass.

Riders must be at least 40 inches tall and children under 7 must be accompanied by an adult.

Big Thunder Mountain Railroad

This is a mild roller coaster, in the sense that it doesn't go particularly fast and there aren't any big drops – just very sharp turns.

Riders must be at least 40 inches tall and children under 7 must be accompanied by an adult.

Tom Sawyer Island

This attraction is a kind of escape from the rest of the park: you board a raft that takes you out to an island, where kids can get their ya-yas out climbing hills and exploring windmills and firing airguns. Take their leashes off and let them run free. Meanwhile, park yourself on a bench and relax. You can also enjoy a snack or libation from Aunt Polly's Dockside Inn.

Arrrrr...Get a Life, Matey!

You may have noticed that today's Pirates of the Caribbean is more politically correct than it used to be – for example, toward the end of the ride, there's a woman chasing a pirate who has stolen some food. You may remember that the pirate used to chase the woman, presumably for some...booty.

Or maybe you don't remember. Maybe, just maybe, you have other things to think about.

But others, apparently, don't. The Internet is rife with discussions about updates of and odd facts about Pirates of the Caribbean (and other Disney attractions, for that matter). For example, someone has bothered to notice that the pieces in the chess game being played by skeletons at the beginning of the ride are set to form a stalemate. Of course, there is debate about this too; others think it's a checkmate, and still others are trying to crack some word code they think exists in the pieces' placement.

Where do people get the time?

Rumor has it that Pirates is haunted by George, the ghost of the attraction's designer, who allegedly died on the ride. Cast members claim that if they do not greet George in the morning and say goodnight when they close, the ride will break down (Pirates is notorious for breaking down frequently). Ask about George when you're there; see what they say. And whatever you do, don't repeat 'George isn't real' while on the boat ride – they say it's sure to stop the ride.

Country Bear Jamboree

This is another animatronic attraction; many consider this one to be outdated too. Mounted bear heads singing a hoe-down – you make the call.

Frontierland Shootin' Arcade

No sweat if you miss this one. But if, after standing in one line too many, you're hankerin' for some shootin', pick up a shotgun and take a crack at one of many targets, which come to life if your aim is true. It's 25¢ per play, and don't expect a prize. For a simple pleasure, sit down with a partner at one of the checkers tables in front and play a game or two.

LIBERTY SQUARE

This area of the Magic Kingdom is home to two creepy attractions – a haunted house and robotic politicians.

The Haunted Mansion (FastPass)

This attraction is less a chilling haunted house (even little kids will be fine) than a showpiece for what Disney's special-effects geniuses can come up with when their hearts are in it. Like at MGM-Studio's new Tower of Terror ride, you begin grouped together in a lobbylike area. Eventually, you get into cars that take you through the mansion to witness all of the ghostly guests for yourself. It's not scary, or particularly exciting, but it's the favorite of many Disney fan(atic)s. In fact, Cory Doctorow's book *Down & Out in the Magic Kingdom* focuses on this attraction.

Hall of Presidents

In the waiting area for this attraction, you can view all sorts of presidential memorabilia, including a handwritten 8th grade autobiography of Nixon, an Impressionist portrait of

Gay Day at Disney

Gay Day was conceived in 1991, when Orlando gay activist Doug Swallow and a handful of friends posted an invitation online saying, 'Hey, if you're into Disney, show up and wear red.' Some 2500 gays and lesbians made it. Ever since, the first Saturday in June has seen the 'happiest place on Earth' transformed into the gayest place on Earth. The entire week is one of the busiest times for the area, and one veteran taxi driver in Orlando says he consistently gets better tips from the Gay Day event than he gets any other time of year.

Disney (whose recent record of fair treatment to gay and lesbian employees has been exemplary, going so far as to extend health-care benefits to same-sex partners) stresses very publicly that this is *not* an official Disney event. Still, they tolerate – even help organize – Gay Day, and in 2002 an estimated 125,000 gay and lesbian visitors descended on Cinderella Castle for what is now an entrenched Florida tradition. Inevitably, some families show up unawares of the event and try to demand a refund from Disney for the spoiling of their vacations. While a refund will not be in order, Disney may be so kind as to supply any obliviously red-shirted dads with a free Mickey T-shirt (sorry, 'Gosh, folks, I'm not a homosexual!' is not written on the back). If you have any qualms about homosexuality, do yourself and everybody else a favor and plan your trip around this event.

Despite what some fearful parents might think, while same-sex affection will definitely be visible during this period of time, nudity and 'overtly sexual' behavior is for the most part not something that Gay Day visitors participate in.

At Magic Kingdom at 1pm, bears (um, hirsute gentlemen) head to the Country Bear Jamboree to sing along with their animatronic friends. And at 3pm everyone gathers for the Main St parade, where characters put on an especially enthusiastic show as they navigate a truly awesome sea of red.

The festivities have now grown to encompass almost every attraction in Orlando. On the Thursday before the event, party people pack Pleasure Island, and Friday at SeaWorld is de rigueur. Friday night is the Beach Ball at Disney's Typhoon Lagoon, with DJs and dancing. So much for getting to Magic Kingdom early and beating the lines! Saturday night sees a bash at Arabian Nights Dinner Theater, and Universal Orlando is actively trying to get in on the action, offering discounts on Sunday at Islands of Adventure. And all weekend long, downtown Orlando clubs and bars cater to the crowds.

Log on to W www.gayday.com for more information, and to register for regular email updates. **Good Time Gay Productions** (☎ *888-429-3527, 305-864-9431 fax 305-866-6955)* books Gay Day packages – make reservations early, as this is the most popular event in Disney World history.

Paige R Penland

Tiger, Disney's Animal Kingdom

Spoonbill, Animal Kingdom

Cinderella Castle, Magic Kingdom

Liberty Belle Riverboat, Magic Kingdom

Big Thunder Mountain Railroad, Magic Kingdom

Kali River Rapids, Disney's Animal Kingdom

Epcot

Sunset Blvd, Disney-MGM Studios

Clinton and a bust of Dubya that's close enough to sneeze on. But the excitement doesn't stop there.

Next, you're herded into a theater to watch a virtually incomprehensible and, not surprisingly, superpatriotic flick on US history that mysteriously jumps from the Civil War to recent history, with no real transition. Someone should work on that.

But the final part of this attraction is flawless. The red curtains rise, and every single US president stands or sits before you on stage, all of them shifting and nodding at seemingly random intervals, some of them fiddling nervously with a pen or adjusting their seated rumps, while select presidents say a few words. The level of detail and reality is truly mindboggling (people on the left may think to themselves, 'Was Zachary Taylor just *flirting* with me?'). Each president – even nonames such as Chester Arthur and Millard Fillmore – is duly introduced. We'll leave it up to you whether to boo or cheer them, although the theater's ambience is generally pretty somber. President George W Bush, like President Clinton before him, actually made time to record a message for his animatronic double to lip-sync along with. And that, dear friends, is the power of Disney.

Liberty Belle Riverboat
Like the Walt Disney World Railroad, this attraction is good for just sitting and resting and taking in the Kingdom, although it can't be used for transportation because you end up where you got on. It's a big paddle-wheel riverboat that will take you around Tom Sawyer Island and Fort Sam Clemens.

FANTASYLAND
This land is the epitome of Disney, with its crown jewel, Cinderella Castle, right at the forefront.

it's a small world
Loved by some, hated by many, you only have to see it once to know where you stand. It's a slow boat ride through a land of animatronic creatures designed to look like children from all over the world in very stereotypical aspects. It's another instance of Disney really needing to update an attraction, but at least there are some children 'of color' – kind of, and toward the end. The song will stick in your head for weeks if you don't listen to some AM radio soon afterwards.

Peter Pan's Flight (FastPass)
This is for the wee ones, but it is beautiful, and adults will appreciate it. Board a pirate ship and fly over London, enchanted in stars and fog, to Never Neverland. Delightful, and nothing about it is scary.

Cinderella's Golden Carrousel
This enchanting merry-go-round is a sight to see, especially when it lights up at night.

Dumbo the Flying Elephant
For some reason, kids love this. It's another midway ride. Be prepared for a wait!

Mad Tea Party
Wait until your last meal is well digested before venturing out on this barf-o-rama of a ride – especially if you think your kids have it out for you. It's a simple, carnival-like spinning ride, and you and the people in the teacup with you get to decide just how much you'll be twirling.

The Many Adventures of Winnie the Pooh (FastPass)
Who doesn't love Poohbear? This is a sweet, untacky storybook journey through Hundred Acre Wood, with all the beloved characters, including Tigger (yay!), Piglet, Roo, Eeyore and of course, that darling boy Christopher Robin and his favorite bear Winnie. Only those with the hardest of hearts won't smile.

If you're looking for Mr Toad's Wild Ride, it's no more – this one replaced it in 1999.

Snow White's Scary Adventures
Disney had the sense (or maybe just enough complaints) to add the word 'Scary' to the title of this ride – it's more about the witch than the sweet, animal-loving girl. Some little ones, especially under seven, really can get scared. Shoot, that witch in the movie is mean – do you blame them?

MICKEY'S TOONTOWN FAIR
This land opened as Mickey's Toontown in 1988 and the country-fair aspect was added in 1996. Adults and teens will be bored, but it is one of the most reliable places to see Mickey or Minnie, as well as lots of other characters. Little ones like it a lot.

Mickey's & Minnie's Country Houses
That's right – houses, plural. They don't live together. Hey, why didn't they ever get married? Anyway, you'll get to walk through their

homes, and see how they live and the botched job Goofy did on remodeling Mickey's kitchen. At the end of the tour, you can move on or decide to wait in line to meet Mickey or one of his cohorts at the **Judge's Tent.** If you know that your tike won't let you get out of Orlando alive without meeting Mickey, trying getting here first thing in the morning.

The Barnstormer at Goofy's Wiseacre Farm

Short and sweet and designed for small bodies, this is a roller coaster meant for kids – a perfect initiation for those who've never ridden one before. Riders must be at least 35 inches tall.

Donald's Boat

This is a splashy little playland. Donald the Duck's boat is springing leaks and it's up to your kids to plug up the holes. Some kids don't tire of it for hours. If the weather looks iffy, it may be closed down – kids standing in puddles during a lightning storm doesn't make for a good Disney experience.

TOMORROWLAND

This is the land that spawned Epcot, and it shows – visually at least. But Tomorrowland has all of the Jetsons-style kitsch and none of the corporate propaganda. It's also home to Space Mountain, a Magic Kingdom must-see.

ExtraTERRORestrial Alien Encounter

Whoa. This is Disney?!

After watching a sick and twisted preshow spectacle (an adorable little bug-eyed alien gets fried to a crisp in a transporter experiment gone wrong), you are ushered in to watch the same experiment on a person, but everything goes haywire when a hostile, maneating alien intercepts the transmission and is beamed on board, while you're trapped in utter darkness in the theater seats (you are tightly restrained in your seats, not because the theater moves, but so you don't get out of your seat and make for the door).

Walt is rolling over in his grave right now (not least of all because this replaced Mission to Mars). But that's not to say this is not an…interesting…attraction. It's just out of place. The pros are that there's nothing else quite like it (although a case could be made for Universal's Terminator 2). And Kathy Najimy and Jeffery Jones make surprise appearances in the video part of the attraction.

Alien Encounter seems to be one of Disney's attempts to live down its 'pixie dust and fairytales' reputation so that thrill-heavy Universal won't steal away so many customers. Well, back to the drawing board.

Tomorrowland Indy Speedway

Race gas-powered (pee-yoo) Grand Prix–style cars around a figure-eight track – without your parents!

Riders must be 52 inches tall. Unfortunately, kids shorter than that are the ones who want to ride the most. And no, you don't get to bump into other cars.

Buzz Lightyear's Space Ranger Spin (FastPass)

You're inside the film – well, the spin-off video game for the film – letting loose with your laser cannon at almost anything that moves. Steer your own Star Cruiser (in a 360° circle) as it races through space, with the Evil Emperor Zirg close behind. Tip: If you hold the trigger down, rather than firing in rapid bursts, you'll score much higher.

Space Mountain (FastPass)

It's *the* classic coaster – it even has its own fan club – and it hurtles you through the darkness of outer space. Yes, it's tame by today's standards, but *boy* is it ever bumpy. Isn't space travel supposed to be smooth?

This is probably the most popular ride in the Magic Kingdom, so get a FastPass. Riders must be at least 44 inches tall. A **video-game arcade** is at the end of the ride, but the games aren't particularly great.

The Timekeeper

Witness prehistoric Europe and visions of the future through the nine eyes of a robot in a 360°-vision theater. This is only open seasonally, but shouldn't be missed if it's not closed – it's great, and Robin Williams is featured.

Astro Orbiter

It used to be called StarJets, and it's not much to speak of – just a revolving rocket ride; you can get a nice view of Tomorrowland though.

Tomorrowland Transit Authority

They've updated the name (it used to be WEDway PeopleMover) but not the ride, which is a tram that takes you slowly through Tomorrowland and even into Space Mountain. It's good for a rest, but not much more.

Carousel of Progress

Watch an animatronic American family change and evolve through 100 years of technological progress, from hand-cranked gramophones to high-tech kitchens.

SHOWS & PARADES

Check your *Times Guide* pamphlet for exact show times and parade schedules (you'll receive this list at the entrance). The best show, of course, is the fireworks display during 'Fantasy of the Sky', which takes place toward the end of the evening when the park is open late. It's possible to rent a charter cruise to watch the fireworks from the Seven Seas Lagoon; call ☎ 407-WDW-PLAY for information and pricing.

PLACES TO EAT

As in all the parks, expect lots of perfectly edible fast food, cafeteria cuisine and snacks at premium prices. Don't miss the delicious turkey legs ($5). All the coffee at Disney World is just horrible.

This list only includes sit-down restaurants where priority seating (☎ 407-969-3463) is recommended.

Tony's Town Square Restaurant *(Main St; mains $10-24)* serves Italian cuisine, including good vegetarian options.

Liberty Tree Tavern *(Liberty Square; dishes 8-15; character dinners adult/child $16/9)* serves American cuisine (clam chowder, prime rib etc) and at dinner, a buffet with Minnie Mouse, Goofy, Chip and Dale!

Crystal Palace *(adult/child $16/9)* has a good-looking buffet with the coolest characters in town, Winnie the Pooh and Tigger, too!

Cinderella's Royal Table *(mains $16-30)* is the most popular restaurant in Disney World – make reservations 60 days ahead of time. A host of characters keep the kids entertained while you eat gourmet(ish) American cuisine.

Priority Seating

In Disneyspeak, priority seating means restaurant reservation – kind of. You will not be guaranteed a table at a certain time, but you will be given preference over people off the street at your appointed time. All in all, the system works pretty well, and you shouldn't have to wait too long after your scheduled time to be seated. To obtain priority seating call ☎ 407-969-3463.

GETTING AROUND

If your feet are achin', or if you just want to relax in a shady area and see another side of the Magic Kingdom, take a seat on the **Walt Disney World Railroad**. Hey, it can also be convenient for getting to the other side of the park quickly without dodging strollers and strings of handholding families. The railroad follows the perimeter of the park and stops at Main Street, USA (the park's entrance and exit), Frontierland and Mickey's Toontown Fair (Adventureland is the only land that you won't be able to see by train). There's a recorded and cheezy announcement on the train, and some really outdated and not very politically correct fake Indians and animals are in sight along the way, but Disney kitsch has its own set of rules, doesn't it. Strollers are not allowed on the train (just pick up a new rental at your destination, and don't forget your name card and rental receipt), and wheelchair access is only possible at the Frontierland and Mickey's Toontown Fair stops.

Disney-MGM Studios

Smaller kids – who can't take advantage of the absolutely awesome rides on offer here – could find MGM dull. Adults, unless they're movie buffs, may agree by the end of the day. But there are definitely some diamonds worth digging for.

MGM Studios came about when Disney caught wind that Universal was planning on creating an Orlando version of the extremely popular Universal Studios park in California. Disney got it together and opened this park almost two years before the Universal park opened. Keep in mind that the park is also a working production facility, so some of the land is closed off or accessible only on special guided tours.

ORIENTATION & INFORMATION

Guest Relations, to your left as you enter, also houses the park's **first aid** and **baby care center**. **Banking** facilities are on the right. Also, at the end of Hollywood Blvd, on the right, is a **guest information board**, where you can find the facts on show times and priority seating for meals.

You enter this smallish park on **Hollywood Blvd**, which is basically a cluster of movie-themed gift shops. Then make a right onto

Don't Miss!

- The Great Movie Ride
- Indiana Jones Epic Stunt Spectacular
- Star Tours
- Jim Henson's Muppet Vision 3D
- Who Wants to Be a Millionaire? Play It!
- Voyage of the Little Mermaid
- Rock 'n' Roller Coaster
- The Twilight Zone Tower of Terror
- Fantasmic!

Sunset Blvd to hit the big thrill rides, left toward **New York** for the movie-based attractions. **Mickey Ave**, straight ahead, is designed for kids.

ATTRACTIONS
The Great Movie Ride

This is a headliner at MGM, and lines can be fierce. You'll get into a vehicle that will whisk you past soundstage sets for some of the world's most beloved movies and their animatronic stars. *The Wizard of Oz, Casablanca* and *Raiders of the Lost Ark* are just some of what you'll see. Be prepared for a surprise or two!

Sounds Dangerous

Drew Carey stars in one of the most disappointing attractions in all of Central Florida. Sounds Dangerous is supposed to help you understand how important the element of sound is in a movie production, but this show is so boring that it surely only adds to the underappreciation of the sound industry.

Indiana Jones Epic Stunt Spectacular (FastPass)

Professional stuntpeople show you the tricks of the trade...well, sort of, anyway. At any rate, they blow things up and crash motorcycles while kids scream and gasp. Tip: If you want to be part of the action, sit up front and start jumping around and yelling immediately when they ask for volunteers.

Star Tours (FastPass)

How can you not have a blast on a flight simulator that takes you on a fast and frantic ride through the *Star Wars* saga? It's identical to the one in Disneyland. The gift shop is a budget buster.

Jim Henson's Muppet Vision 3D (FastPass)

Miss Piggy plays a gorgeous diva; Beaker plays with dangerous chemicals; Kermit plays the straight man; and the rat keeps trying to play the audience by putting on fake ears and masquerading as Mickey Mouse. Aging 3-D technology is helped along with animatronic hecklers and live-action trolls, but this movie's so hilarious that it doesn't even need 'em.

Honey, I Shrunk the Kids Movie Set Adventure

To make the little shrimps feel even smaller, everything is oversized in this children's play area. That is, except for the area itself, which isn't expansive enough to accommodate all the screaming miniature humans that want to inhabit it. So you may have to wait a while before your kids can access it. Featured are mountainous weeds, gigantic insects, huge Lego pieces and an oversized water-sprinkling garden hose (oh boy, do kids like this one – there are triggers in the floor).

Disney-MGM Studios Backlot Tour (FastPass)

Earthquakes, artillery fire, tidal waves, flaming oil rigs, the original house from the *Golden Girls* – all this and more awaits you on this entertaining tour. Check out the old spaceship props left to rust in the Florida rain. Volunteers are also sought for this attraction – try getting a FastPass and asking staff if you can be one.

Who Wants to Be a Millionaire? Play It! (FastPass)

Admit it – you've always wanted to face down Regis, the host of the US version of this show. Now you can: everyone gets a 'fastest finger' ticker at their seat, and top scorers compete for pins, hats and even Disney cruise tickets.

Now, we'll admit it. This is *exciting*. No one's really on TV, and your chances of getting into the Hot Spot are slim, but don't be surprised if you find your heart racing in anticipation when the show begins.

There are about 10 seats on the show's floor with fancy monitors, but sitting there doesn't mean you have a better chance for the Hot Spot. If you want to sit there anyway, they select those people from the FastPass line.

Walt Disney: One Man's Dream

This is a biographical exhibit on the great dreamer himself, Walt Disney, with some echnical animation exhibits thrown in for good measure. It's interesting for adults and boring for kids, but they've supplied enough eye candy (TV monitors with cartoon clips and miniature set replicas) to keep them at an even keel until parents have had their fill.

Voyage of the Little Mermaid (FastPass)
This 15-minute musical about Ariel and her finned friends gets rave reviews for the singing, set and underwater effects. Black lighting is used in utter darkness so that the fluorescent sea critters (handled by puppeteers swathed in black so you can just *barely* see them) pop out in a brilliant flash of color. It's a definite 'can't miss' attraction. It's also a perfect retreat from the hot Florida sun – you'll leave refreshed and smiling. Oh, but that sea witch does make a booming appearance – if your kids are scared of her, beware.

The Magic of Disney Animation
You can see animation artists at work during this 35-minute tour, which is bookended by two short films about the history of animation.

Playhouse Disney – Live on Stage
Puppets, song and dance thrill the socks off toddlers and other teeny ones (the stars are from the Disney Channel shows). The effect the characters have on the children is amazing. Seating is on the floor, and the diminutive audience does *not* remain seated, but rather run around singing and yelling. The chaos is good for a chuckle, even for nonparents.

Beauty & the Beast – Live on Stage
Belle, the Beast and all his accoutrement sing and dance and tell you to 'Be Their Guest' at this 30-minute show.

Rock 'n' Roller Coaster (FastPass)
This is the best coaster at Disney World, hitting you with 5Gs around the loop – more than the space shuttle. Even better, the ride is synchronized to Aerosmith's music! Rock on, Steven Tyler. Riders must be 48 inches tall.

The Twilight Zone Tower of Terror (FastPass)
Follow the screams to creepy Hollywood Tower Hotel, where Rod Serling takes you to a strange, new, special-effects-laden dimen-sion – one where you drop 13 stories in two seconds! Or do you? The ride is randomized, so each experience is different – keeps you on your toes, in addition to keeping your buns off the seat. For many, this is their favorite attraction at Disney World.

SHOWS & PARADES
Check the *Times Guide* for the **Disney Stars and Motor Cars Parade**, which is totally missable and a great time to hit up the more popular rides, which will be less crowded because of the parade.

But do not miss **Fantasmic!** Arrive an hour early to get good (or any, on crowded days) seats for what's generally agreed to be the best show at Disney World. It's epic: Mickey Mouse faces Disney's assembled dark side, including a 50ft (15m), fire-breathing dragon. It has a soaring score and light show to match. Characters from virtually all Disney animated movies wave to the audience from their boats during a water parade interval, and clips from *Fantasia* are projected onto huge walls of water – it's breathtaking.

PLACES TO EAT
There are lots of places to eat, and these restaurants recommend making reservations for priority seating (☎ 407-969-3463).

Mama Melrose's Ristorante Italiano *(mains $8-15)*, behind New York St, bakes its pizzas in a brick oven and serves all kinds of other Italian food, including spaghetti just like Lady and the Tramp shared on their big date.

Sci-Fi Dine-In Theater *(mains $9-15)*, across from Star Tours, is a 'drive-in' where you eat in abbreviated Cadillacs and watch classic sci-fi flicks.

Hollywood Brown Derby *(Sunset Blvd; mains $13-25)* serves gourmet cuisine and a great-looking Cobb salad in semiupscale surroundings modeled after the LA original.

Epcot

Epcot, which stands for 'Experimental Prototype Community of Tomorrow,' attempts to infuse high-concept entertainment with educational merit, with a decidedly commercial slant. There are two parts to Epcot, Future World and World Showcase. Epcot was intended by Walt Disney to be a city, but he died and it was instead developed into a theme park. See Celebration, at the end of this chapter, to read about what a Disney community is like.

Don't Miss!

- Mission: Space
- Honey, I Shrunk the Audience
- Body Wars
- Cranium Command
- The Making of Me
- IllumiNations

Half of Epcot is devoted to **Future World**, where rides and attractions have scientific themes and often corporate underwriters. Exxon Mobil, for example, sponsors Ellen's Energy Adventure (see later), which describes fossil fuels in, shall we say, more glowing terms than some experts would use, especially regarding their effects on global warming. The 'education' that you'll be getting is often more corporate propaganda than information on advancements in engineering. If you're expecting cutting-edge technology at Future World, you'll find more at the local RadioShack. It's a strange kind of rip-off to go into an attraction expecting to be inspired and awestruck but to come out feeling as if you just watched an expensive commercial. You'd think that if so many huge companies are sponsoring Epcot, it would show in the surroundings, but the money must be going elsewhere (maybe to the much awaited Mission: Space attraction.)

The **World Showcase**, on the other hand, is better. Disney has done a Disneyrrific job in re-creating 11 countries. Staff members from the nations represented come here on one-year contracts, and operate authentic-feeling villages that serve some of the most interesting food in Disney World.

ORIENTATION & INFORMATION

You enter the park in Future World, centered on the landmark geodesic dome of Spaceship Earth. The World Showcase is further back, arranged country by country around the lagoon where fireworks are held.

Guest Services is to your left as you enter the park, **lockers** and an **ATM** to your right. **First aid** and the **baby care center** are located in the Odyssey Center, on the left before you cross the bridge from Future World to the World Showcase. This park is served by monorail.

FUTURE WORLD

When you first enter Future World, you'll see triangular monoliths jutting out of the ground and, upon closer examination, you'll see the faces of thousands of Epcot visitors etched into the stone and dating back years, un blemished by time. This is called **Leave a Legacy**, and for $25, you too can have your face planted on a rock in Central Florida. Gosh, just think what archaeologists thousands of years from now will say when they find the ruins of Epcot.

Spaceship Earth

This AT&T-sponsored ride is what that big geodesical ball is about. It's sort of fun in a kitschy way – you'll see how communications developed from prehistoric times to the Renaissance to the 19th century to today, and developments into the future. Apart from the darkness, it's a slow-moving ride that's no frightening for kids, but for others, the visions of the future are sort of creepy in that they seem to imply that AT&T will soon control the world. Afterward you'll be dumped into an interactive area that will underwhelm any kid who's ever used a home computer.

Innoventions

The coolest thing about this exhibition is the Segway demonstration. Segways are two-wheeled motorized personal vehicles that you stand on and steer – they're absolutely amazing, but currently go for about $5000 and are only available through Amazon.com or at the Segway store in Celebration (see that section later in this chapter). The rest of Innoventions is for the most part company-sponsored interactive technology demos, although there are some Sega games that will certainly interest the children – maybe for longer than you'd like. There's also the one-sided display celebrating genetically modified organisms (sponsored by agribusiness giant Monsanto). This is a great place to have the 'advertising versus information' talk with your kids.

Mission: Space (FastPass)

Scheduled to open sometime in 2003, this long-awaited interactive attraction is sure to be exciting. You get to become an astronaut, and yes – experience the feeling of zero gravity.

Test Track (FastPass)

This is considered by many to be the most thrilling ride at Epcot, but it leaves much to be desired. The idea is that you become a living crash-test dummy, but afterward, the thinking adult may feel more like a marketing-test dummy. You'll be placed in a General

Motors car to go through heat, cold, speed, braking and crash tests. It's a short ride, and not scary (those who eschew roller coasters could enjoy this), but the lines can be fierce. You can use a FastPass for this, but even better is to split up into singles, as there's a special line for solitary riders, and it moves very quickly.

Riders must be 40 inches tall.

Ellen's Energy Adventure
Join Bill Nye (the Science Guy) and Ellen DeGeneres as they explain various energy sources, from solar to nuclear to fossil fuels – which, of course, necessitates a trip into the Cretaceous period (yes!), because oil and coal and stuff are all made out of really cool dinosaurs. Little kids could be intimidated by the dinosaurs, and they won't follow the 'educational' segments, but that's probably for the best.

Honey, I Shrunk the Audience (FastPass)
It's not just a 3-D film starring the cast of *Honey, I Shrunk the Kids*, it's a full-on sensory experience, much like Jim Henson's MuppetVision at MGM Studios or It's Tough to Be a Bug! at Animal Kingdom. And like those, small children may be frightened by the experience (by the way, someone needs to turn down the volume on this attraction). Most will enjoy this popular show (remember that 3-D works better if you don't sit very close to the screen).

Body Wars
If you like Star Tours, you'll probably like this – it's a fascinating, *Inner Space*–like journey through the human body. You'll mingle with blood cells red and white, spark with neurons, breathe with bronchi and more. If you're easily nauseated by motion-simulators, you may want to steer clear, but otherwise, this is fun and noncommerical.

Cranium Command
Buddhists beware: One of the main sources of Western neurosis – that there's a little person in your head who controls everything – is the foundation of this show, which is sure to make you laugh and leave you smiling.

You'll see a day in the life of a 12-year-old boy who's just met the new girl at school – now who wouldn't want to experience this? Major comedy stars do an excellent job with a delightful script – and they're so well cast! For example, Charles Grodin plays the left brain, Jon Lovitz plays the right brain, Bobcat Goldthwait plays the adrenal (as in 'adrenaline') gland, George Wendt ('Norm!') plays the stomach and Kevin Nealon and Dana Carvey work together as the left and right ventricles.

The Making of Me
Starring Martin Short, this is a Disneyfied version of the sex ed film you watched in grade school. It's very – very – tame: no nudity, no genitalia-related vocabulary and definitely no sex is shown (a kiss is as hot as it gets). There is a delightful cartoon segment that shows the sperms' sprint race to the egg. Actually, it's hard to imagine that uninitiated children would be able to make any sense of it, so if you're not even close to being ready to answer questions on the subject, avoid the show. The message is, 'When two people really *really* love each other, they can get so *close* that they make a baby.'

This is one of those Disney attractions that is great simply because it's so old-fashioned. It'll make you feel all warm and fuzzy inside.

The Living Seas
This aquarium attraction is a major, major Disnappointment. The tank is not huge-seeming, not filled with much of interest, and the 'ride' portion is nothing but a fake elevator, which opens up into – you guessed it, a gift shop.

Living with the Land (FastPass)
This (splash-free) water ride educates you all about – farming! It's much more interesting than it sounds, though, and lots of the herbs and veggies you see growing onshore will soon be served at the Garden Grille restaurant upstairs.

The Circle of Life
Characters from *The Lion King* are featured in this sobering ecological film that shows the delicate balance of interdependency among species.

Food Rocks
Animatronic food and utensils join to put on a musical show about the wonderful world of nutrition. Hit up a Disney hot dog stand afterward, just for irony's sake.

Journey into Imagination with Figment
The five senses and the world of imagination are the theme for this ride, which stars Figment the purple dragon. Little kids will like it, especially the skunk spray toward the end.

Places to Eat

Garden Grille *(adult/child $21/10)*, in the Land section of Future World, serves catfish, barbecue and fresh veggies – with Mickey, Pluto, Chip and Dale! The food didn't look nearly as good as what's on offer in the World Showcase, but your kids won't care. Make reservations 60 days in advance.

WORLD SHOWCASE

This is a hemisphere of nations, all getting along side by side in perfect harmony. If only the real world were like this – but hey, Disney's all about escaping the real world, right? Although there are some rides and the architecture is really fun, the variety of foods is one of the biggest pluses for this side of the park. And hopefully, it will inspire you to visit the countries themselves, if you haven't already. What's shown about these countries is sanitized and stereotypical, and not particularly informative. But if someplace there tickles your fancy, go see the real thing. Oh, and if you do go, buy one of the wonderful Lonely Planet guidebooks for that destination! (When in Epcot...)

The featured countries are Mexico, Norway, China, Germany, Italy, Japan, Morocco, France, the UK, Canada and of course the USA. Each section has architecture unique to that country, at least one restaurant so you can try the national cuisine and gift shops aplenty.

Attractions

Keep in mind that the attractions at World Showcase are hardly worth a long wait.

In Mexico, **El Río del Tiempo** (that's River of Time to you gringos), is an indoor boat ride through the various ancient cultures of Mexico, leading to present day.

Tucked away in the Norway pavilion, **Maelstrom** is a cute little boat ride (you won't get wet) with Vikings, trolls and a couple of good waterfalls. It's probably fine for little kids. Afterward, you'll watch a film put out by a Norway tourism company about the wonders of that Arctic land. It's sweet.

Wonders of China is a 20-minute film on the country that is beautiful to look at, and you'll see no depressing glimpses of any political unrest or human-rights abuses.

Animatronic wisenheimers Mark Twain and Ben Franklin star in **American Adventure**, a patriotic and unblemished rendition of US history. The key word here is 'patriotic.'

Francophiles will enjoy the 12-minute **Impressions de France**, celebrating the nation's beautiful countryside.

Give the Canadians the attention they deserve at **O Canada!**, a 10-minute film show-

---

Mission: Cheese Sauce

Just because this book doesn't kiss Mouse butt, it doesn't mean we don't give credit where credit is due. Yes, we've told you when attractions could do with a renovation or even a complete overhaul, but now we'll say this: nobody, *nobody* does service like Disney. Take this example.

While wandering through the World Showcase at Epcot, we overheard a preteen boy tell his buddy about the huge pretzels he had over in Germany. 'And they have cheese sauce for dipping, too!' he added.

We were sold. We hightailed it over to Deutschland, and spotted the pretzel cart, which was manned by a skinny young German guy and his American manager, Bruce, who had just stopped by to change out the cash register and check up on the pretzel situation in general.

Pretzels there were, fresh and hot and huge, but we saw no bright-orange tublets of cheese sauce. We asked young Johann if he carried the substance, and he said he did not. But Bruce's ears perked up. 'You want cheese sauce? I believe they have it at the cart in front of USA.'

'Hey, thanks!' we replied, and started to turn away, but Bruce said, 'Hold on, let me call over there for you to make sure.' In all seriousness, he proceeded to dislodge his two-way radio from his holster and call some sort of operator to ask for the frequency or number for the cheese-bearing cart. The operator said she would call him back, which she did after a minute. Bruce then connected with the other cart and asked whether cheese was available there.

'Uh huh. Yes. Thanks.' Bruce turned to us and said, 'Yes, I've had confirmation that cheese sauce is indeed available at a small extra charge at the cart in front of USA.'

'Wow. Gee. Thanks,' we replied, sort of in shock.

'No problem,' smiled Bruce. 'Have a Magical Day.'

asing the beauty of the country in a seatless 60° theater.

Places to Eat

If you've got a Park Hopper pass, spend your day anywhere else, but come to World Showcase for dinner at least once.

Make priority seating reservations (☎ 407-939-3462) to eat in any of the lavish dining rooms (Mexico's is outstanding) as soon as you get to the park. Though sit-down meals generally run $14 to $30, all the pavilions have a counter-service option outside that costs about half that. The most popular (read: make reservations *well* in advance) restaurants are as follows:

Le Cellier, in the Canada pavilion, is hands down the most visited eatery. Servers, who bemoan the lack of *poutine* (a French-Canadian creation of french fries, gravy and cheese curds) on the menu, recommend the steak burger ($10) and barbecued beef tips ($16), as well as the *Oh Canada* film next door. Vegetarians shouldn't even bother – head to Morocco's **Tangierine Café** instead.

Mitsukoshi, one of four restaurants at this lavish pavilion, has been serving fine cuisine in Japan (the country, not the theme park attraction) since 1673, and they cook it right at your table ($12 to $30). Other on-site eaters serve sushi ($7 to $10 per roll) and tempura plates ($13 to $28). Try to get there for the drumming demonstrations.

Chefs de France is the obvious choice, with an appropriately snooty staff that likes the *salade niçoise* ($11), foie gras ($19) and *marmite du pêcheur* (Mediterranean seafood casserole; $27). All options come with wine recommendations, *bien sur*.

Don't forget to save room for dessert at Norway's **Kringla Bakeri**.

SHOWS

IlumiNations, which takes place in the center of the park's lagoon, is one of the best things about Epcot. You can see this fireworks show from virtually anywhere in the park, but you may want to stake out a choice spot a good hour before it starts if you want an unencumbered viewpoint. Add this to **Tapestry of Dreams**, an artsy parade featuring gauzy two-story-tall puppets, and that's a great ending to your day.

In addition, each nation in the World Showcase has live-music, comedy, drumming or dancing shows; check your *Times Guide* pamphlet for show times.

Disney's Animal Kingdom

Despite a public relations blitz that claims the contrary, the majority of Animal Kingdom *is* a zoo. Sure, it's the most amazing zoo you could ever imagine, souped up with all sorts of bells and whistles. There are rides and shows, of course, but this place is all about the animals: the safari tours sometimes have to stop in their tracks to let elephants and zebras get by. The Asia and Africa sections display an obsession with detail endemic to Disney, right down to the staff – as in the World Showcase (see Epcot earlier in this chapter), many people working here are on one-year contracts from Cambodia, Côte d'Ivoire and other appropriate countries.

If you are concerned your children might get bored here, think again. It may turn out that they think their heroic parents have somehow provided them with tickets to paradise. Even better, there are staff everywhere – talk to them! They're there to answer your questions, and they're great with kids. There are plenty of games for little ones too, and ask about the *Kids' Discovery Club Guide*, which is a puzzles and stamp booklet that is filled as they explore the park. Stamping stations are marked on the park maps with a 'K'.

You'll enjoy yourself very much here if you don't expect a thrilling amusement park (in comparison with Busch Gardens, Animal Kingdom is loads better zoologically but not as adrenaline-packed). Instead, take it as a grand tour of the world's biodiversity, refracted through that rose-colored Disney lens. The park is also a great tribute to the power of Disney sanitization: despite the lush, tropical surroundings and humid weather, you'll be hard pressed to find any insects or other stray, unwanted life forms in the park.

Disney Trivia

Ponder these puzzlers while waiting in line.

a) What is Donald Duck's middle name?
b) There are only two Disney cartoons that feature two-parent families in which neither parent dies by the end – which are they?
c) What is the name of the lion that roars for MGM?

The answers are: a) Fauntleroy; b) 101 Dalmations and Peter Pan; c) Volney.

Don't Miss!

- It's Tough to Be a Bug!
- Kilimanjaro Safaris
- Kali River Rapids
- Dinosaur
- Festival of the Lion King
- Flights of Wonder

ORIENTATION & INFORMATION

You enter the park at the Oasis, which features lovely gardens and giant anteaters. To your left is Camp Minnie-Mickey, with characters and rides for little kids, and to your right is Dino-Land USA, which caters to the preteen crowd. The park is centered on Discovery Island and its landmark, Tree of Life, which is definitely worth a closer look. You'll have to cross the island to get to Asia and Africa, where the very popular safari begins. Rafiki's Planet Watch is accessible only by a train that leaves from Africa. A new land to feature mythological animals is currently in the works.

Guest Services is to your left as you enter the park, as is an **ATM** and lockers. Both **first aid** and the **baby care center** are on Discovery Island, on your left on the way to Africa.

OASIS

This is the first area you'll see when entering the park. There's a gorgeous waterfall on your left, and tell your kids to find the giant anteater, the boar and the colorful macaw in the lush surroundings.

DISCOVERY ISLAND

This is the park's hub, and like Cinderella Castle at Magic Kingdom, the huge, ornate **Tree of Life** serves as the best landmark for orienting yourself in Animal Kingdom. Even if you think the age of your child will preclude you from seeing the It's Tough to Be a Bug show (see the following entry), spend some time at the tree, which you're sure to remember from the modern Disney classic *The Lion King*. It's 14 stories tall and has over 325 animal images carved into its trunk. It's fun to explore the **trails** around the tree, and you and your kids may spot an exotic animal or two.

It's Tough to Be a Bug! (FastPass)

This is awesome, but if your kids are terrified of darkness or creepy crawlies, keep them out

of this 3-D show, or you'll be wondering why they didn't call it 'It's Tough to Be a Parent!' Even though it's very cute much of the time, you will definitely hear children crying by the end. You can find this attraction right where all the bugs would be if there were any at Animal Kingdom – buried in the root system of the Tree of Life. No matter how old you are, you will scream (and then laugh). There are surprises. And we're giving you no hints.

CAMP MINNIE-MICKEY

Dozens of characters await scores of children in this land, which is also home to two shows (see Shows later in this section).

AFRICA

In area, this is the hugest land in Disney.

Kilimanjaro Safaris (FastPass)

This attraction could compete with almost any zoo in the country for the animals and their 'natural' habitats. And it's got that Disney touch: you're barreling down rutted roads in your rickety bus, past zebras, lions and more when suddenly there's word that poachers are on the loose! Local law enforcement can't do it alone, so you've got to help.

Pagani Forest Exploration Trail

On the first of two walking trails that put a Disney spin (outrageous architecture, nifty exhibits) on the typical zoo experience, this lush and landscaped path passes gorillas, hippos, a great aviary and a hive of naked mole rats, the only mammals who organize themselves like insects. Spend some time watching the gorillas – although one (angry) visitor said that the monstrous silverback who slammed himself against the viewing area's Plexiglas was more terrifying than the Tower of Terror.

RAFIKI'S PLANET WATCH

The adorable, fist-sized tamarins are entirely watchable at **Habitat Habit**, but there's not much more of interest there. The **Affection Section** is a petting zoo with sheep and goats. There's a place for you all to wash your hands afterward. To get there, you'll need to take the **Wildlife Express Train**. The best aspect of this out-of-the-way section of the park is the **Conservation Station**, which, as the park's veterinary and conservation headquarters, could be fascinating if you happen to be there during an interesting project (such as a lion tamarin receiving an exploratory laparoscopy). If you're going to travel out to these boonies, be in

Fact or Disney?

The world of Disney is without a doubt the stuff of legends – including urban legends. For anybody out there who really believes that lemmings commit mass suicide, here's a reality check.

In the late 1950s and before the rise of PETA (People for the Ethical Treatment of Animals), Disney made a number of animal documentaries, and some of them have come under scrutiny.

The most well-known example of this is *White Wilderness*, in which lemmings are shown stampeding off a cliff and to their deaths in the water below – purportedly giving proof of the widespread idea that these rodents commit mass suicides when their population exceeds nature's desires. Actually, this idea has always been false; although lemmings do engage in mass migration when their area becomes overpopulated, and many fall into water along the way and drown, they do not end their lives en masse and on purpose. However, that didn't stop the director of *White Wilderness*, who was determined to show this phenomenon.

The crew bought some lemmings from Inuit children, placed them on a snow-covered turntable in Alberta, Canada and filmed them from different angles to make it seem like there were lots more present than just a few dozen. In the end, the dizzy little bewildered critters were chased off a cliff to their deaths.

Or so the story goes…

quisitive, ask the staff questions, or else you may feel as if you've wasted your time.

ASIA
Maharajah Jungle Trek
See Bengal tigers, huge fruit bats, Komodo dragons and other Asian critters lounging around in habitats designed to look like Angkor Wat. Neat.

Kali River Rapids (FastPass)
Feeling overheated? This ride will get you soaking wet (souvenir shops nearby sell extra socks) while you scream. Bonus: It has some of the best queue entertainment around. Also, there's a weird tribute to the burning of the Earth's rainforests – without any verbal back up, it's just strange and sticks out like…a smoldering tree trunk. But at least they tried.

DINOLAND USA
This carnival-like area is mostly for little kids, but it also features one of the scariest rides of all.

Dinosaur (FastPass)
The most thrilling ride in the park takes you back in time, where you've got to rescue a (huge, scary) dinosaur specimen before a meteor hits….

This is *definitely* not for little kids, unless yours is tough as nails. If you need proof, just look at the riders' photos displayed at the end of the ride, and count how many children you see with tear-stained faces nestled in parental armpits.

Primeval Whirl (FastPass)
Yeah, so it's a kid's coaster. It's still a whirly twirly good time, but it's not super barfy like a tea-cup ride (and you don't control the spins). The coaster on the left is identical to the one on the right, so don't ride it twice, unless you really loved it.

The Boneyard
This may be the most inspired sandbox on Earth. Just try to drag the kids away from their frantic digging for mastodon skeletons, or their seat atop massive rib cages and other fossils.

TriceraTop Spin
Yet another Dumbo-style midway ride but with a dinosaur theme this time. It comes with the requisite slow loading and kid magnetism.

SHOWS
Pocahontas & Her Forest Friends
Any ecological message from Disney is much appreciated, but geez Louise, this Camp Mickey-Minnie show is so corny. A few live critters are featured – just focus on that and try to tune out the rest.

Festival of the Lion King
This excellent show in Camp Mickey-Minnie more than makes up for the Pocahontas debacle. It's got it all – animatronic stars from the movie, great songs, audience participation, beautiful and amazing acrobatics, and glorious costumes. Don't miss it.

Flights of Wonder

This bird show in Asia has some cheezy dialogue, but it's very bearable, and the animals are spectacular. Sit in the middle if you'd like them to fly over you. Owls, peregrine falcons and others will dazzle you, and afterward, you can approach the trainers and their birds with questions and to take photos.

Tarzan Rocks!

Gymnasts and in-line skaters perform to songs based on the movie soundtrack. It's another dud. Tarzan doesn't rock.

PLACES TO EAT

The only restaurant here that takes priority seating reservations is **Restaurantosaurus** (☎ 407-939-3463), which does a character breakfast featuring Donald, Mickey, Goofy and Pluto. Yes, your kids would rather eat with Timon and Simba, but at press time this wasn't an option.

Other Attractions

It would only take, oh, two weeks to experience (almost) everything in the four major parks, but Disney would like you to stick around a little longer. So they've provided you with several other entertainment options, many of which are listed here. There are also six golf courses, parasailing and surfing lessons, waterskiing options and more. See Outdoor Activities later in this chapter for more information.

WATER PARKS

Before September 11 there were three Disney water parks, but River Country has since been closed indefinitely due to security issues and a drop in tourism. These parks are generally open year-round, independent of the weather, but they do close periodically for refurbishment.

Blizzard Beach

This is the home of **Summit Plummet**, Disney's tallest (120ft) and fastest free-fall slide. Themed to look like a ski resort, Blizzard Beach features things such as a ski lift and snowcapped mountains, but mainly it's a slide and raft park that is a great way to spend at least half a day. Don't miss **Run-Off Rapids**, with three crazily curving slides, or **Teamboat Springs**, which increases speed with every person you pile onto your mat.

Typhoon Lagoon

The slides here are a tad less radical than those at Blizzard Beach, but this rain forest–themed water park has a couple of big bonuses: the **Surf Pool** features 6ft-high breakers, and the **Shark Reef** offers instruction and equipment for snorkeling among tropical fish.

WALT DISNEY'S WIDE WORLD OF SPORTS

This huge complex (☎ 407-828-3267; W www .disneyworldsports.com) is home to the **NFL Experience**, where you can take on the same obstacle courses and other challenges as your favorite American football players. The complex also hosts a mind-boggling array of professional and amateur sports events, including games with the Atlanta Braves, Orlando Rays and the Harlem Globetrotters. Events tickets are not included in the price of admission.

WALT DISNEY WORLD SPEEDWAY

This is where you'll find the **Richard Petty Driving Experience** (☎ 800-BE-PETTY), where you can race Winston Cup–style cars (see Daytona Beach in the North of Orlando chapter for more on racing) around a real track. If you've got the money and the juice, you can participate in one of four programs.

The Ride Along Program (starts at $89) will let you ride shotgun in a two-seater stock car driven by a pro; riders must be at least 16 years old. One step up is the Rookie Experience (starts at $349), which is a three-hour program that ends with you driving eight laps on your own; drivers must be 18 or older. If eight laps just aren't enough, double the price and take on the Kings Experience (starts at $699), in which you'll get another 10 laps; drivers must be 18 or older. And finally, the aptly named Experience of a Lifetime (starts at $1199) gives you three sessions and a total of 30 laps, with instruction between sessions on how to increase your speed; riders must be 18 or older.

Yeeeeeehaw!

DOWNTOWN DISNEY

Basically a shopping mall with upscale chain restaurants and venues staging great live music, Downtown Disney eliminates any temptation to leave the resort property should you, say, need to buy a bathing suit, Dominican cigars or museum-quality original art. There are several entertainment options. Downtown Disney is divided into West Side, which has dining, Cirque du Soleil, DisneyQuest, movie theaters and the House of Blues; Pleasure Island, which has lots of dance clubs and an improvisational comedy venue; and Marketplace, which has shops galore.

West Side

This section of Downtown Disney has the most popular nonclub attractions. It's open for dining and entertainment from 11am to midnight; shops are open 10:30am to 11pm.

DisneyQuest This attraction *(adult/child 3-9 $31/25; open 11:30am-11pm Sun-Thur, 11:30am-midnight Fri & Sat)* features five floors of exhibits designed to indulge Ritalin-addled video-game addicts. Virtual reality rides, arcades, alien invasions, flight simulators and other technological delights will satisfy folks with even the most limited attention spans. Note that some rides cost a little extra on top of the admission fee, and you must be over 51 inches tall to hop onto the really good ones.

On slow nights, management may offer discounted tickets ($15) at the gate for the last two hours of operation. Children under 10 must be accompanied by an adult.

Cirque du Soleil: La Nouba One of the biggest draws of Downtown Disney is this unforgettable and breathtaking circus show *(☎ 407-939-7719; ⓦ www.cirquedusoleil.com; adult $72-82, child 3-9 $44-49)*. Many people say this is the best thing at Disney World. Shows start at 6pm and 9pm, Tuesday through Saturday only.

Other Attractions Live shows feature at **House of Blues** *(☎ 407-934-2583; ⓦ www .hob.com)*: Tenacious D, George Thorogood and No Doubt have played here. It's also a Southern-cuisine restaurant.

AMC Pleasure Island has 24 state-of-the-art movie theaters.

Places to Eat Latin music and dancing is featured at **Bongos Cuban Café** Thursday to Saturday. Other eateries include **Wolfgang Puck** and **Planet Hollywood**.

Shopping There is such a thing as exhaustive detail, so we'll just say that there are plenty of places to purchase Disney merchandise, snacks, coffee and all kinds of other stuff.

Pleasure Island

It's New Year's Eve every night at this complex of eight bars and clubs. It's adjacent to Downtown Disney and free for all Disney employees, which means you'll get all the real dirt about the parks over a beer or three. Oh, and you can carry your drinks from bar to bar.

Clubs include **BET SoundStage**, which plays hip-hop; **8Trax**, for disco; **Mannequins**, which has a revolving dance floor; and **Motion**, for Top 40. Restaurants and shops are also scattered around the area.

You must be 21 or older to enter Mannequins on any night, or to enter BET Sound-Stage from Thursday to Saturday. To gain admission to other clubs, you must be 18 or older. An admission fee of $19.95 is charged after 7pm (unless you have a Park Hopper Plus or Ultimate Park Hopper pass).

Shops are open from 10:30am to 1am; everything else is open 7pm to 2am.

Marketplace

Lego, Disney paraphernalia (including a specialty pin store), sports gear and more are here for your purchasing convenience. Restaurants include **Fulton's Crab House**, on a replica paddleboat; **Ghirardelli** (yummy sundaes); and the everpopular **Rainforest Café** (make reservations).

OUTDOOR ACTIVITIES
Golfing

Walt Disney World has six courses, one of which (Oak Trail) is for juniors and beginners. Call 407-WDW-GOLF for tee times or information on instruction, or visit ⓦ www .golf.disneyworld.com.

The remaining five courses, all of which are 72 par and ranked at 4 to 4½ stars by *Golf Digest* are as follows:

Name	No 1 Villain
Palm	Water
Magnolia	Sand
Eagle Pines	Tall grass & pine straw
Osprey Ridge	Large rolling greens
Lake Buena Vista	Narrow fairways

Also, there are two miniature golf courses in the World. **Winter Summerland** (☎ 407-560-3000) is just outside Blizzard Beach and **Fantasia Gardens** (☎ 4007-560-4870) is across from the Swan Hotel.

Water Sports

Cocoa Beach Surfing School (☎ 407-939-7529) gives instruction at Typhoon Lagoon before the park opens. Boards are provided, but there are age and height requirements; call for details.

Finding a Pin in a Haystack

There are various species of Disney fanatics. One is the *informatius junkia,* who spends hours upon hours swapping random trivia via newsgroups and the Internet (see the boxed text 'Arrrr...Get a Life, Matey!' earlier in this chapter). Another, the *mickispotus vigilante,* spends all their free time during park hours seeking out that unmistakable three-circle image (see the boxed text 'Hidden Mickeys' earlier in this chapter). And then there's the collector (a common species in all fanatic families), *gottafindit gottagetit.*

Now, Disney collectors appear in many different breeds, but while in the parks, keep your eyes peeled for the Disney pin collectors. Beanie-baby lovers are put to shame by the devotion of these collectors (although there is an exotic breed of Disney beanie-baby collectors as well). In the parks, you're sure to see people whose shirtfronts are bedecked with glistening metal emblems, or who are holding up lanyards of their little prizes to other fanatics, making trades on the spot. And you'll certainly see the crowds around the special carts that sell the items.

Like any collection series, some items are rare and coveted, while others are ubiquitous and paltry (but still go for around $8 each). The 'Born to Shop' Minnie pin is very hard to find, and the ultimate meta-pin set, 'Pin Trading Mickey & Minnie,' recently went for $2200 on eBay. Disney World has quickly and skillfully picked up on the phenomenon, opening up 40 Official Pin Trading Stations (although there are more than 80 locations where pins are sold throughout the parks). To keep interest bubbling, more than 350 new pins per year are released, including several limited-edition and special-event pins. One of the newest nods at pin-collecting are the larger Magical Moments pins, which 'react' to various events and surroundings with a light display.

At Disney's MGM-Studios, take note of the 'Ooooos' and 'Ahhhhhs' when they announce the second prize for the Who Wants to be a Millionaire game: a 10-pin collector set (just to give you some perspective, first prize, for a million points, is a Disney cruise).

Waterskiing, wakeboarding, parasailing, tubing and riding personal watercrafts are all possible by contacting **Sammy Duvall's Water Sports Centre** (☎ 407-939-0754).

Fishing excursions can also be arranged, as can the rental of various boats for up to 12 people; call ☎ 407-939-7529.

Tennis
The World has eight clay and nine hard courts, as well as clinics and private lessons. Call ☎ 407-939-7529 for details.

SHOPPING
If you live to shop, be prepared to spend several hours doing so at Walt Disney World. At the parks, at the hotels and especially at Downtown Disney, there are scores of stores with all kinds of things Disney, as well as plenty of non-Disney merchandise as well. At Epcot's World Showcase, each country has shops with imported goods that may be hard to find back home.

Keep in mind that 'shopping around for a better deal' isn't necessary at the World – if the Mickey ears are a certain price in one place, they'll be the same price elsewhere in the World; even sale items are discounted to the same price throughout the resort. If you want to find better deals than what you're seeing at Disney, there are countless unofficial stores throughout the Orlando area, and even some scattered about in other parts of Central Florida. But keep in mind that the quality will probably not be as good if it doesn't come direct from Disney.

See the Orlando chapter for more on shopping for non-Disney gear; also, Celebration (see that section later in this chapter) has some interesting high-end stores to browse in.

Places to Stay

If you can afford it, staying on-site at Disney World really adds to the experience. And if you think you can't afford it, don't give up without trying. If you start researching well in advance, you can come up with some really good deals, and remember that by staying in the World, you'll save on parking and possibly even a rental car if you're not planning on going to other Central Florida attractions. Even better, if you're going to be there during the busiest seasons, you can rest assured that you'll never be turned away

t the gates – resort guests are guaranteed
park admission.

You can get resort-by-resort descriptions
and the latest rates online at W www.disney
world.com. Make reservations online or by
calling ☎ 407-934-7639. Always, *always* ask
if there are any special deals; they won't tell
you unless you ask. Don't forget to mention
if you're a member of AAA or any other
clubs that could save you money. See the
boxed text 'Disney Bargain Websites' for information on websites with special deals.

The rack rates quoted are a tad misleading,
as you can get deals on multiple-day packages that include admission to the theme parks
and other attractions. One veteran Disney-
goer said she paid the same price for five
nights at a deluxe resort as was originally
quoted for four nights at a value resort – just
by asking. Still, it's always cheaper to stay in
Orlando or Kissimmee.

Disney accommodations are broken down
into four main categories. Price ranges listed
here are for standard rooms with a double
bed in low and high season; keep in mind
that pricier, fancier rooms are probably
available (and may be all that's available if
you don't book far enough in advance). The
rates are before the 6.5% Florida sales tax
and 5% county resort tax. Extra charges may
apply if there are more than two adults; call
for details.

When booking a room, the representative
is surely going to try to sell you a vacation
package – you'll be paying for convenience
with these, and they're not a better deal than
if you book 'room only' and take care of tickets etc yourself. If the room or discount you
want has been booked up, don't give up! Try,
try again – people cancel reservations all the
time, so call back first thing next morning.

Disney Bargain Websites

The following are websites, apart from the official site (W www.disneyworld.com), where
you can find out about scoring a deal on resort lodging.

- W www.mousesavers.com – great tips, special discount codes and coupons on lodging
and merchandise, as well as Disney news
- W www.wdwig.com – dining covered in exhaustive detail and good tips on accommodations, with fact sheets and photos

VALUE RESORT HOTELS

The least-expensive properties available,
these have thousands of very small motel-
style rooms that may be difficult to maneuver
should you ask for a refrigerator or crib. All
are lavishly (garishly?) decorated according
to the theme. Rates for all four range from
$77 to $124, depending on the season. You
will definitely feel the difference in price.
Service is far from what it is in other, more
expensive resorts, and the staff are younger
and less trained. Instead of proper restaurants, there are only food courts and snack
bars, but there are pools and fun playgrounds.
If you're looking for romance, stay away
from these – they're very family oriented,
with lots of screaming children and sassy
teens.

Disney's All-Star Sports Resort has enormous footballs everywhere.

Disney's All-Star Music Resort has giant
guitars.

Disney's All-Star Movies Resort is perfect
for the cinemaphile in the family.

Disney's Pop Century Resort is the largest,
with more than 5000 rooms.

MODERATE RESORT HOTELS

These hotels have slightly larger rooms, less-
ostentatious themes and access to beaches
and the marina. Rooms run $133 to $184 for
two adults.

Disney's Caribbean Beach Resort has
brightly hued decor.

Disney's Coronado Springs Resort has a
Mexican/Southwestern theme and is convenient to Animal Kingdom.

Disney's Port Orleans Resort includes a
Disneyfied version of New Orleans' French
Quarter.

DELUXE RESORT HOTELS

These upscale resorts have everything: extra
large rooms designed to sleep at least five,
excellent kids' programs, fabulous swimming
pools, room service and health clubs, not to
mention characters in all their plush glory
roaming the lobby and food courts every
morning.

Disney's Old Key West Resort *($254-
1460)* has studios and one- to three-bedroom
villas available.

Disney's Wilderness Lodge *(rooms $199-
324)* has a beach, marina, 'hiking' trails and
easy access to Magic Kingdom. Studios and
one- and two-bedroom villas are available for
$279 to $955.

The Military & the Mouse

Disney will cut you deals galore if you're in the US military or Department of Defense. In fact, **Shades of Green** (☎ 407-824-3400, 888-593-2242; W www.shadesofgreen.org) is a special resort just for military families. During research, Shades of Green was closed for refurbishment and expansion, but they've been taking reservations all the while, and the resort is sure to be open by the time you're reading this. Rates depend on rank (they get more expensive the higher you are in rank), but range from $70 to $116 a night – a steal no matter whether you're a private or a colonel. You'll also get significant discounts on admission to Walt Disney World (including the Richard Petty Driving Experience), Universal Studios, SeaWorld, the dinner shows, Kennedy Space Center and lots of minor parks, such as the Holy Land Experience. Special deals pop up from time to time for the Disney Cruise Line as well – call ☎ 800-511-1333 to find out if there's any cruise bargains out there for you.

Disney's Animal Kingdom Lodge (rooms $199-324) abuts the African Safari section of Animal Kingdom, so you're able to see zebras, giraffes and other exotic critters from your hotel window. This is probably the most exciting accommodations at Walt Disney World, and it shows in the prices, which can go up as far as $2505 for a presidential suite. Sheesh!

Disney's Contemporary Resort (rooms $234-525) has futuristic architecture, character dining and monorail access.

Disney's Polynesian Resort (rooms $299-469) has tropical landscaping and an evening luau feast (adult/child $47/24) Tuesday to Saturday.

Disney's Yacht Club Resort (rooms $289-449) has a nautical theme. Studios and one- and two-bedroom villas go for $289 to $1050.

Disney's Beach Club Resort (rooms $289-650), right next door to the Yacht Club, is very similar. But it's much better if you have young children and offers the best opportunities to participate in water sports.

Disney's Boardwalk Inn (rooms $289-449) has child-care facilities and is convenient to Epcot. Studios and up to three-bedroom villas range from $289 to $1915.

Disney's Grand Floridian Resort & Spa (rooms $339-514), which looks for all the world like the hotel from *Some Like it Hot*, has full kitchens in the rooms, monorail access and almost any other amenity you could dream up. It's gorgeous.

The **Walt Disney World Swan & Dolphin Resorts** ($325-365) are two hotels facing each other on Disney property, but they're actually owned by Sheraton. Still, character breakfasts and other Disney perks are available there.

HOME-AWAY-FROM-HOME RESORTS

These properties, which feature amenities such as a kitchen and video games for the kids, vary widely in price and facilities but generally sleep at least eight people.

Disney's Fort Wilderness Resort & Campground (campsites with partial hookup to full hookup and cable $35-82, cabins $229-329, rooms $289-990) is in a shady natural preserve where programs include hayrides and sing-alongs. Primitive camping is $10 per person, but there has to be a minimum of 20 people; you can rent tents for $30 per night Firewood and cots are available for an extra charge.

Disney's Boardwalk Villas (rooms $289-990) is the most convenient of these choices to the parks.

NON-DISNEY PROPERTIES

There are several non-Disney properties in the area, and some of them are excellent. Rates change dramatically on an almost daily basis, depending on demand.

Club Hotel by Doubletree (☎ 407-239-4646, 800-521-3297; 12490 Apopka-Vineland Rd; rooms $79-139) is an attempt at a budget place.

Courtyard by Marriott Downtown Disney Hotel (☎ 407-828-8888, 800-223-9930; 1805 Hotel Plaza Blvd; rooms $89-139) is a very good deal with standard hotel rooms.

Doubletree Guest Suites Downtown Disney Resort (☎ 407-934-1000, 800-222-8733; 2305 Hotel Plaza Blvd; suites $138-279) is right nearby.

Wyndham Palace Resort & Spa (☎ 407-827-2727; 1900 Buena Vista Dr; suites $189-199) is walking distance to Downtown Disney and a favorite for Gay Day participants.

Jaws IV props, Universal Studios

Marilyn character, Universal Studios

Jurassic Park River Adventure, Islands of Adventure

The Lost Continent, Islands of Adventure

Getting Around

Pick up a copy of the *Walt Disney World Transportation Guide/Map*, which is available at the resorts and probably from Guest Relations at the parks. The **monorail** is definitely a memorable attraction at Walt Disney World; if you've never ridden a Disney monorail, do try it. Also, if you'd like to sit in the front car, just ask. There are extra seats up there by the conductor, the views are splendid, and the conductors can be wonderful about explaining the trains to kids. The **boats** are quiet, comfortable and quick once they leave, and there are often characters on board. Less exciting interpark transport is also provided by **bus**.

Remember that parking at the parks is $7/8 per car/RV, but is good all day for all parks – just keep your receipt pamphlet. Unless you have rock-star, early-bird parking, you'll probably have to board a tram to the park's entrance (or you can sometimes walk if you so choose). Remember where you parked, whether you write it down, text message yourself, or even call your own cell phone and leave a message. No one wants to wander around a gargantuan parking lot at the end of a busy Disney day. If you can't find your car for some reason but think you may be close, try honking the horn with the lock feature on your remote, if you have such a device (just don't hit the trunk or unlock buttons!). If you hear a honk, follow the sound. You'll notice plenty of others doing this too, but it still can work.

DISNEY TRANSPORT

The monorail is fun and efficient but has very few stops. The boat system is also good but service is limited. Buses go almost everywhere and generally leave every 20 minutes, running until 1am.

To Magic Kingdom
From Resorts You can take the monorail from the Polynesian, Contemporary or Grand Floridian resorts. From the Wilderness Lodge and Fort Wilderness Resort, you can reach Magic Kingdom by boat. For other resorts, you'll be taking a bus – ask at the resort for schedule information.

From Parks To reach the Magic Kingdom from MGM Studios or Animal Kingdom, you'll need to catch a bus to the TTC (Trans-

portation & Ticket Center) and then catch either the monorail or ferryboat to the park's entrance. From Epcot, you can take the monorail all the way, or you can take the monorail to the TTC and then catch the ferryboat the rest of the way.

To Disney-MGM Studios
From Resorts You can hop on to the boats leaving from Boardwalk, Yacht Club, Beach Club, Swan and Dolphin resorts. From other resorts, you'll be boarding a bus.

From Parks From Epcot and Animal Kingdom, you'll need to ride a bus to reach the studios; from the Magic Kingdom, you can get on either the monorail or the ferryboat until you reach the TTC, from which point you'll board a bus.

To Epcot
From Resorts You can take the monorail all the way to Epcot from the Polynesian, Contemporary and Grand Floridian resorts, but you'll need to transfer at the TTC. From the Boardwalk, Yacht Club, Beach Club, Swan and Dolphin, you can ride a boat or even walk to Epcot. A bus ride is required to reach Epcot from other resorts.

From Parks Hop on a bus to Epcot from MGM Studios and Animal Kingdom. From the Magic Kingdom, board the monorail or a boat to the TTC, at which point you'll need to transfer to board an Epcot-bound monorail train.

To Animal Kingdom
From Resorts It's a bus all the way, no matter which Disney resort has you. Gotta keep the safari/wilderness theme intact, you know.

From Parks To get to Animal Kingdom from Epcot and MGM Studios, you'll need to take a bus. From Magic Kingdom, take the monorail or ferry to the TTC, then from there, board a bus.

To Other Parks
To get to other parks from all Disney resorts you'll be riding a bus. To reach Downtown Disney, Typhoon Lagoon, Blizzard Beach and Winter Summerland (miniature golf), direct buses are available from all resorts.

To reach Fantasia Gardens (miniature golf), you can take a bus from any resort to

Downtown Disney, then transfer to a Swan/Dolphin bus. From the Swan/Dolphin stop, you can walk to the golf course.

If you want to get to Wide World of Sports, catch an MGM Studios–bound bus from any resort, then transfer to a Wide World of Sports bus.

Resort-to-Resort

You can reach any resort by riding a bus to Downtown Disney, from where you can transfer to a bus heading toward your destination.

Getting There & Away

If you're flying into Orlando International Airport and staying at a Disney Resort, and have no urge to visit Orlando or the surrounding area, you don't need to rent a car. **Mears Airport Shuttle** (☎ 407-423-5566; W www.mearstransportation.com; one way/round-trip $16/28) provides transportation between the airport and Walt Disney World, where you can use free public transportation throughout the park.

Most hotels in Kissimmee and Orlando offer shuttles to Walt Disney World. If yours doesn't, call around to see if you can catch a ride (usually $10 to $12) on a nearby hotel's shuttle.

From Orlando's Lynx Bus Center, in the alley between W Pine St and W Central Blvd, one block west of Orange Ave, you can catch buses to the Disney parks (No 50, every two hours), but it's a long ride.

The entire complex is designed for clueless out-of-town drivers: signage and civil engineering are spectacular. From Orlando, take I-4 south and follow the signs, which are marked for easy access to each of the four major parks. From Kissimmee, take Hwy 192 west and follow the signs.

Disney Cruise Line

There are currently several choices of cruise offered by Disney. Firstly, there are the two seven-night Caribbean Disney cruises. **Western Caribbean** hits Key West, Grand Cayman, Cozumel and Castaway Cay, Disney's private island. **Eastern Caribbean** stops at St Maarten and St Thomas, with excursions to St John and a day at Castaway Cay.

The seven-night **Land & Sea Vacation** begins with a three- or four-night stay at WDW and then sets sail for the Bahamas and Castaway Cay. If you're not interested in the World aspect of that cruise, you can take either the three- or four-night **Bahamian** cruise.

All cruises feature wonderful Disney shows in a beautiful onboard theater, dancing, movie theaters, satellite-fed sports, fine food (you'll dine in a different restaurant each night), tons of kids' programs (even for older teens!) and health spas.

You'll depart from Port Canaveral, which is about a one-hour drive east of the Orlando airport.

Rates vary dramatically, but three-night cruises can go for as low as adult/child $399/199 a night, and remember, food is included in the price (although alcohol and tips are not). Call ☎ 800-370-0097 for a Disney agent or go to W www.disneycruise.com; but you'll get a better deal if you go with a non-Disney cruise agency. Like with resort stays, cruises are usually a better deal if you eschew packages and instead go à la carte.

Celebration

Walt never got to see his Experiment Prototype Community of Tomorrow in action. But chances are he would be very happy with the Disney town, Celebration. Celebration is just south of Walt Disney World; to get there, take exit 25A from Hwy 192.

There is a **hotel**, several **restaurants** and some decent high-end shopping, but many just come to Celebration to see this so-called utopia with their own eyes.

The whole community has a Pleasantville feel to it – not a single thing is out of place, not a piece of litter is in sight, not a blade of grass is too tall, and Disney music is piped in from the ground in many areas. Many find it blissful, and indeed, more and more are calling it home. On the other hand, some find it creepy, like the beginning of a David Lynch movie, and sense that there must be a very dark side to such a perfect place.

Using cutting-edge technology for better quality of life is an important aspect of living in Celebration. The town has its own local Intranet, and there are community bicycles and NEVs (Neighborhood Electric Vehicles). Best of all, many citizens own Segways, those awesome two-wheeled standing personal vehicles. If you don't see a Segway in Celebration, you can see one at Innoventions, at Epcot (see that section earlier in this chapter). The town's website is W www.celebrationfl.com.

Celebration has its own health-care system, its own education system and its own private cable channel. Homes range from small bungalows in the high $100,000s to estate homes in the mid $700,000s, but there are also townhomes (mid $200,000s) and condos (high $100,000s). Some say that anyone wanting to buy property in Celebration goes through a thorough background check, but that has not been confirmed.

If you have a car, take a drive through Celebration. The restaurants there are quite good, and there's a lovely lagoon in the downtown area that you can walk around or even sit by in large community rocking chairs and watch the Segways and NEVs go by. You've never seen anything like this, but who knows? If Disney keeps at it, such sights might not be so far away from your own home town.

Universal Orlando Resort

Universal Orlando Resort (☎ *407-363-8000;* ⓦ *www.universalorlando.com; 1000 Universal Studios Plaza; open 9am daily, closing times vary)* contains two theme parks: Universal Studios Florida, which is a combined working movie studio and theme park, and Islands of Adventure. Universal Studios Florida has a 'Ride the Movies' concept that inspires excellent 3-D shows, motion simulators and rides. For real thrills, however, head to Islands of Adventure. There's enough for small children to do here, no matter what their fear limitations are, but keep in mind that the two parks are more directed toward teens and adults than the Walt Disney World parks.

You can purchase discounted tickets at the Official Tourist Information Center on International Dr (see the Orlando chapter). Members of AAA – take advantage. You can get a 10% discount at many gift shops and restaurants in these parks.

Universal Studios Florida

ORIENTATION & INFORMATION
Call ☎ 407-363-8000 for an *Official Studio Guide* information packet or log onto ⓦ www.universalorlando.com for more thorough coverage. Be sure to take your time strolling the different 'cities' – Hollywood, San Francisco and New York. The architecture is downright remarkable and packed with neat storefronts (souvenir shops), bars and restaurants. The facades are so realistic that it can get frustrating when you're looking for a restaurant and you have to pass five fake ones before you find a real one!

Guest Services (☎ *407-224-6350)* is to the right of the entrance. It has foreign-language guides to the park, a lost-kids area, a **lost and found** (☎ *407-224-6355)*, a First Union bank where you can exchange most currencies, and the friendliest staff around. You can rent manual/electric wheelchairs ($8/35) and single/double strollers ($8/14) here, too. Most rides are wheelchair accessible.

You can find out what's currently in production during your visit by calling the **Studio Audience Center** (☎ *407-224-6355)*. There is also an office just right of the main turnstiles when entering Universal Studios Florida.

Highlights

- Plying tranquil night waters on a free, romantic boat ride to gorgeous Portofino Bay Hotel
- Nursing a cold drink outdoors on a warm night after a long day at Universal CityWalk
- Watching your kid get slimed at Nickelodeon Studios
- Admiring the truly wondrous Caro-Seuss-el while munching on green eggs and ham.
- Bragging to friends and family on braving some of the most thrilling rides in the world

Lockers are available ($5 per day), and there are free lockers outside rides that forbid bags and purses.

Buying Tickets
The price for Universal Studios and Islands of Adventure is the same: adult/child three to nine years $52/43. There are sometimes deals on two-park/two-day tickets, with, for example, a third day free; call for more information

Available online only is the **Bonus Pass**, a five-day ticket to both parks that must be used consecutively (adult/child three to nine years $90/77).

VIP tours take you to the front of long lines and backstage at the shows; call guest services Multigroup tours take up to 15 people ($120 per person, five hours); exclusive tours take one to 15 people ($1,700 total, eight hours) Both types of tour are available for both parks

UNIVERSAL ORLANDO RESORT

World Expo
San Francisco/Amity
Universal Studios Florida — Woody Woodpecker's Kidzone
New York — Hollywood
Production Central — Hard Rock Hotel
Islands of Adventure — CityWalk — Portofino Bay Hotel
Toon Lagoon — Jurassic Park
Marvel Super Hero Island — Royal Pacific Resort
Seuss Landing — The Lost Continent

0   0.5   1km
0   0.25   0.5mi

Discount tickets and package deals are available. You can often get a second day free (stop at the information desk on your way out) during low season.

PRODUCTION CENTRAL

This is the first area you'll hit when you enter the park. You're in Production Central if you're on Amblin Ave, 7th Ave or 8th Ave (and part of South St).

Nickelodeon Studios

Sadly, Nickelodeon is reducing the amount of programming actually filmed here, though kids will still go wild over the **Studio Tour** of, among other sets, *SlimeTime Live*. The **Green**

Slime Geyser out front erupts every few minutes (on a random schedule), spewing forth GAK onto anyone standing within the clearly marked SPLAT ZONE.

At the time of research, *SlimeTime Live* was being filmed Monday, Tuesday and Wednesday, but this changes often, so call the Studio Audience Center for up-to-date information (see Orientation & Information earlier). You have to get into the park and be right at the SlimeTime Geyser at 9am to get the free tickets to the filming; they'll be gone by 9:30am. Children must be at least eight years old, and only one adult per family is allowed – they really try to keep the audience as mostly kids. Generally speaking, the show is not filmed there during the summer.

SoundStage 54

This isn't so much an attraction as a display of various vehicles from recent films such as *The Mummy Returns* and *The Fast & the Furious.*

Jimmy Neutron's Nicktoon Blast (Universal Express)

The first part is a demonstration of Jimmy's newest rocket invention – one that lets the audience see what's happening elsewhere in the park. The second part is a motion simulator starring SpongeBob SquarePants, Rugrats, the Fairly OddParents and Arnold.

Shrek 4-D (Universal Express)

This new attraction picks up where the movie *Shrek* left off. It is a 4-D show because, in addition to the 3-D glasses, there is extra sensory stimulation (including smell) and lots of other special effects and surprises.

HOLLYWOOD
Universal Horror Make-Up Show (Universal Express)

This attraction – which used to be called the Gory, Gruesome & Grotesque Horror Make-Up Show – delivers, though if you're really

UNIVERSAL ORLANDO RESORT

Orlando FlexTicket

If you'd like to visit Wet 'n' Wild, Busch Gardens, both Universal Orlando parks and/or SeaWorld, it pays to get a five-park FlexTicket (adult/child three to nine years $203/165), which gets you *unlimited* entry to all of those places within a 14-day time period, plus a free express bus to Busch Gardens. If Busch Gardens is too far away and not on your agenda, there's a four-park FlexTicket (adult/child three to nine years $170/135) that excludes it.

Even if you visit each place only once, you will save significantly. The official tourist centers sell FlexTickets at a slight discount.

Don't Miss!

- Nickelodeon Studios
- Jimmy Neutron's Nicktoon Blast
- Shrek 4-D
- Terminator 2: 3-D Battle Across Time
- Twister
- Animal Planet Live!
- Curious George Goes to Town
- Back to the Future – The Ride

into horror makeup it may be a little too short. It's humorous (more for adults than children), full of silly antics and not really all that gross, although some optical illusions are performed that could freak out small children if they're not really clear from the get-go that *it's not real*. For example, most toddlers don't enjoy seeing mommy's arm cut off on stage, but if you're the mommy in question, just wave and smile and tell Junior that mommy's OK – 'It tickles!'

Terminator 2: 3-D Battle Across Time (Universal Express)

CyberDyne headquarters showcases the creepy future of technology here, including fully operational examples of their brand-new, heavily armed cybernetic soldiers. Watch their PowerPoint presentation – oh wait – the signal's been interrupted! Linda Hamilton and Arnold Schwarzenegger, in glorious 3-D, want you out of the building now! This is a favorite Orlando attraction, but it's very loud and overwhelming for small children. There's no gore, but there is lots of action.

Lucy – A Tribute

Fans of the famous redhead Lucille Ball will enjoy this biographical exhibit, but nonfans and children will quickly become bored. Clips, costumes, photos and Lucy's letters are displayed, and there is a tough trivia quiz at the end. The average, semi-interested person can spend about 10 minutes here.

NEW YORK

The New York area features 57th St, 42nd St, Park Ave, Delancey St, South St and Canal St. Apart from Twister, New York attractions are performances. In **Extreme Ghostbusters: The Great Fright Way**, Beetlejuice saves the Ghostbusters from being turned into an In-

Sync replica. In **The Blues Brothers**, Jake and Elwood pull out all the stops. Also, there's **Street Breaks**, which features a group of talented breakdancers strutting their stuff. Check the *Attractions & Show Times* guide (given to you at the park's entrance) for a schedule, and make sure to check out the amazing façade of the New York skyline, too.

Twister (Universal Express)

Despite the fact that this has the single most annoying preshow video in Orlando, this attraction rules! They create an 'actual' tornado – screaming wind, pouring rain, flying cows – right in front of you. Expect heat and mist, and hold on to your belongings.

WOODY WOODPECKER'S KIDZONE

Universal Studios has done a great job with this area. It's also the best place to spot and meet characters.

Animal Planet Live! (Universal Express)

Watch as Babe the pig, Beethoven the dog, Mr Ed, Benji, an alligator named Chompers, a sea lion, Holly the stunt chimp and even a skunk reprise their acclaimed cinematic performances with video backup.

A Day in the Park with Barney (Universal Express)

Floor seating and lots of singing, clapping and Barney-love make this show a must for kids who adore the purple dinosaur.

Curious George Goes to Town

The poor misguided monkey's footsteps are painted on the ground here, and you can fol-

Second-Wind Generator

If you're starting to get cranky and exhausted, if you don't know if you can make it to the end of the day, don't overlook the Woody's Automatic Foot Massage units, which are usually stationed around restrooms. Put a quarter in, place your feet in the designated spot, and let the machine make your tootsies brand new. It feels a little ticklish at first, but you'll quickly get used to it, and you'll be surprised how much better you feel and how much more energy you have when your quarter's run out.

Universal Express

Like Walt Disney World's FastPass, Universal Express is designed to improve flowthrough on attractions and to allow you to experience the most popular sites relatively quickly. Honestly, Universal Orlando Resort is a step ahead of Walt Disney World on this one. The passes are available for a higher percentage of attractions, and even on slow days, Express tickets are available. Even better, the preshow areas are often different with an Express ticket than they are if you just stand in line, so if you go twice, once with Express and once without, you'll see some different things. Walt Disney World seems to be more strict about the FastPass qualifying time too, whereas at Universal Orlando Resort, staff often don't mind if you slip in a couple of minutes early.

Get Express tickets when available! Even if there's not much of a line, the Express line will be even faster.

low them, and the story, as you go along. As Curious George gets into more and more trouble, you and the little ones get wetter and wetter. Both children and adults alike love the ball building, where soft foam balls can be shot or picked up and sucked into delightful pneumatic tubes by kids and their parents. Even children who have just learned to walk can spend a long time picking up the wonderfully colorful balls, putting them into a net bag, and then going with mommy or daddy to empty them into the big basin – they watch them fly up a clear tube toward the kid that's going to shoot them back down to the ground. Yay!

Woody Woodpecker's Nuthouse Coaster

This roller coaster is good for children and adults alike; it's not very fast or scary. Kids must be at least three years old and 36 inches tall.

Fievel's Playland

Universal Studios' answer to *Honey, I Shrunk the Kids*, this attraction was inspired by the cartoon *An American Tail,* about a family of Russian mice who immigrate to America. Kids can climb and slide all over giant 'garbage' that really does give you a mouse's-eye view.

ET Adventure (Universal Express)

Much like Peter Pan at Disney's Magic Kingdom, this charming ride lets you rescue ET in flying bicycle-like contraptions: skim the roof of a police car, then rise up over the city, past alien babies and other weird spacey stuff, to ET's home planet. There are a couple of slightly spooky spots here, but generally kids aren't upset by this one.

SAN FRANCISCO/AMITY
Beetlejuice's Rock 'n' Roll Graveyard Revue (Universal Express)

Beetlejuice, the Werewolf, Dracula, Frankenstein and his Bride rock out in this unbelievably corny show. This is one of those rare cases, however, when it's so corny that it's somehow enjoyable. The main theme song will stick in your head for days (or months, as was the case with your author). Beetlejuice makes lots of booger jokes – the kids find this uproarious. Despite the spooky characters, there's nothing scary about this to little ones, but it can be loud – if you go, try to sit away from the speakers.

Earthquake – The Big One (Universal Express)

After Charlton Heston demonstrates the now dated and creaky but once spectacular special effects from the movie *Earthquake,* you'll enter a really bitchin' replica of a San Francisco BART subway station. Suddenly, the Big One (8.3 on the Richter scale) hits: tracks buckle, the place crumbles and general mayhem ensues.

Jaws

You will probably get wet on this boat ride, which is like Disney's Jungle Safari only possibly a bit scary for kids. It's not scary for anyone else, although the suspense is pretty well done. The boat driver does his or her best to keep everyone safe with various weapons to stave off the great white beast.

The Wild, Wild, Wild West Stunt Show (Universal Express)

This is Universal Studios' parallel to the Indiana Jones show at Disney-MGM Studios. It's not as elaborate or explosion-heavy as

Indiana Jones Epic Stunt Spectacular, and volunteers don't participate, but it's a good show with some talented stunt people and fight choreographers.

WORLD EXPO
Men in Black Alien Attack
(Universal Express)
Can you qualify for the most elite law-enforcement agency in the galaxy? Well, you'll have to prove it. Aim your lasers at aliens of every size and description while your car swings and spins through a danger-laden downtown. Children must be at least 42 inches tall and must be accompanied by an adult if they're under 48 inches.

Back to the Future – The Ride
(Universal Express)
Hop in your DeLorean-shaped flight simula-tor and take off toward a seven-story, 60ft-high screening area filled with liquid-nitrogen fog…er, to the 1950s and prehistoric times. Second for second, this is said to be one of the most expensive films (almost $4 million per minute) ever made.

PLACES TO EAT
New York
Finnegan's Bar & Grill *(dishes $8-13)* is an Irish pub with Cornish pasties and shepherd's pie, but sadly, no Guinness. Other beer is available though.

Louie's Italian Restaurant *(dishes $8-16)* has table service and serves edible pastas and pizza.

San Francisco/Amity
Lombard's Seafood Grille offers steak and seafood; reservations are recommended.

San Francisco Pastry Co has sweet goodies and sandwiches.

Richter's Burger Co allows you to create your own sandwich or burger.

Captain Quint's has Fisherman's Wharf fare – seafood and chowder.

Midway Grill beefs things up with sausage hoagies, cheesesteaks and beer.

Boardwalk Funnel Cake Co and **Bordy's Ice Cream Shoppe** offer San Francisco–style treats.

World Expo
There's only one restaurant here – **International Food & Film Festival**. The food is hardly international, but you can watch Universal Studio films as you dine.

Hollywood
Café La Bamba has tasty rotisserie chicken, ribs, burgers and wraps.

Mel's Drive-In is a classic '50s diner with classic diner food.

Schwab's Pharmacy has, predictably, ice cream – but, predictably, no hand-carved meat sandwiches.

Beverly Hills Boulangerie offers soup and sandwiches and other small bites.

Islands of Adventure

Considered by some to be the best theme park in Orlando, Islands of Adventure has better characters than the Magic Kingdom, better rides than Universal Studios, better food than Holy Land and better architecture than Gaudí's cathedral in Spain. OK, maybe that's going a little overboard, but just wait until you get on that Spider-Man ride.

ORIENTATION & INFORMATION
Islands of Adventure is the sister park of Universal Studios Florida, and most information, including admission prices, is identical (see Orientation & Information in the Universal Studios Florida section earlier in this chapter). However, **Guest Services** (☎ 407-224-6350), disguised as the Open Arms Motel, does not exchange foreign currency. Lost & Found can be reached there or by calling ☎ 407-224-4245.

PORT OF ENTRY
This area is full of shops, eateries and fun architecture to get you in the mood for adventure.

Don't Miss!

- The Amazing Adventures of Spider-Man
- Incredible Hulk Coaster
- Dudley Do-Right's Ripsaw Falls
- Popeye & Bluto's Bilge-Rat Barges
- Jurassic Park River Adventure
- Pteranodon Flyers
- Poseidon's Fury
- The Mystic Fountain
- Dueling Dragons
- The Cat in the Hat

MARVEL SUPER HERO ISLAND

This is a thrill-lover's paradise, with two of the most unforgettable rides in Florida. Comic book heroes and characters patrol this area, so keep an eye out for your favorites.

The Amazing Adventures of Spider-Man (Universal Express)

After the space shuttle, this may be the coolest thing in Florida. Hop onto the combination roller coaster/motion simulator quickly – Spidey needs you! Supervillains rendered in state-of-the-art 3-D are on the loose (and jumping on your car, and chasing you around with giant electrical plugs), and it's up to you and your favorite webslinger to stop them. We don't want to give too much away, so just know that this is a spectacular experience. You must be at least 40 inches tall and children under 48 inches must be accompanied by an adult.

Doctor Doom's Fearfall (Universal Express)

This is less scary than it looks, which is great for timid folk but a bummer for adrenaline junkies. You'll be shot up in the air, which will take your breath away, and then dropped – but gently, and not very far. Riders must be at least 52 inches tall.

Incredible Hulk Coaster (Universal Express)

This is hands down the best roller coaster in Orlando – and watch that first hill, Dr Baxter! Riders must be at least 54 inches tall.

Storm Force Accelatron (Universal Express)

Another barf-o-rama, this one's on par with Walt Disney World's Mad Tea Party – only in the dark. Good luck with keeping down your last meal.

TOON LAGOON
Dudley Do-Right's Ripsaw Falls (Universal Express)

The confused Canadian Mountie has his hands full keeping logs packed with tourists from hurtling over the edge of – oh no – a huge waterfall! You will get soaked on this boat ride, which probably has the best design of anything like it. Kids under 48 inches must ride with an adult.

Me Ship, The Olive

Kids crawl, climb, squirm and squirt other kids on Popeye's playground ship.

More Fun Kid-Watching

Universal Orlando really has a great way of keeping kids interested and on their toes (see The Mystic Fountain later). In Jurassic Park, you may see staff members with what looks to be a small dinosaur or large lizard in their arms. It's a puppet, but children may not realize it. Grab a seat and watch the curious little ones come up to examine the creature more closely. Some are bold enough to stroke the reptile, others aren't, but staff do a great job of surprising the brave ones and encouraging and comforting the scared or shy ones. Bravo on this one, Universal.

Popeye & Bluto's Bilge-Rat Barges (Universal Express)

Ripsaw Falls not wet enough for you? Head across the way, where Popeye, Bluto and Olive Oyl operate a somewhat tamer (little kids can go), though no less drenching, raft ride. Kids must be at least 42 inches tall and must be accompanied by an adult if they're under 48 inches.

Toon Lagoon Beach Bash Show

Characters from all kinds of crazy cartoons dance and party in the streets here; check your *Attraction & Show Times* schedule to find out when to go.

JURASSIC PARK

The theme here is prehistoric, and Universal has done an excellent job surrounding you with that wild environment. **Camp Jurassic** and the **Discovery Center** are a kids' playground and an interactive natural-history exhibit, respectively.

Jurassic Park River Adventure (Universal Express)

If there's still a square inch of you that's dry after Toon Lagoon, perhaps you'd like to take the boat tour of the 'not-at-all-dangerous' velociraptor facilities here at the Jurassic Park Institute. It's a fun ride, like Jaws at Universal Studios but better and more visually convincing. Kids must be over 42 inches to ride and must be accompanied by an adult if under 48 inches tall.

Pteranodon Flyers

Parents finally find a use for their little ones: if you don't have a kid with you, you can't

UNIVERSAL ORLANDO RESORT

Free Money

If a young adult with a clipboard approaches you, don't be afraid! They are probably going to ask you if you'd like to participate in some market research. You're free to say no of course, but if you don't mind expressing your opinion to corporations for moolah, you might as well do it. It shouldn't take much more than 20 minutes total, and you won't have to eat any new products, just give information about the products you do buy and what you'd be likely to buy were it available. You'll probably earn about $3 in Universal money, which is good throughout the two parks. In many cases, participants must be over a certain age, often 18.

fly. And you really do fly, carried over the jungly Jurassic Park section and all its robotic dinosaurs in a quiet hang-glider assembly. Riders must be at least 36 inches tall and accompanied by an adult if under 48 inches tall.

THE LOST CONTINENT
Poseidon's Fury
(Universal Express)

More a show than a ride, this has a cheese factor of about 8.5 out of 10. You'll forgive them, though, when you see the most ingenious gimmick of entertainment technology in the park. Check the schedule in your guide for show times. Children under 48 inches must be accompanied by an adult.

The Mystic Fountain

Unless there's a crowd of screaming children around this fountain on The Lost Continent, you're sure to walk right by. But if you do see kids at the fountain, you can't miss it. Make a pit stop, find a seat in the shade and watch awhile – it's delightful. The fountain is controlled, possibly remotely, by a staff member (try to figure out where he actually is). He uses his voice to banter sassily with the kids, and his remote-controlled waterspouts soak them when they least expect it. It's very personalized, very improvisational and very funny – the people they hire for this role are talented indeed.

The Eighth Voyage of Sindbad
(Universal Express)

This is another stunt show and is missable if you've seen others; this one doesn't compare well. Check the schedule in your guide for show times.

Dueling Dragons
(Universal Express)

Get two roller coasters in one with these synchronized thrillers – sometimes you're so close to the other cars that you'll want to pull your dangling feet out of the way. The red coaster is

the Fire Coaster, the blue is the Ice Coaster, and each is a very different ride. The Fire Coaster is more death-defying, and coaster fans say the front car on Fire and the last car on Ice are the best. Riders must be at least 54 inches tall.

The Flying Unicorn
(Universal Express)

This wooden roller coaster, which is a good starter coaster for kids, compares well with Goofy's Barnstormer in the Magic Kingdom.

SEUSS LANDING

Audrey Geisel, widow of Dr Seuss (aka Ted Geisel), was heavily involved with the design and construction of this lyrical park, where the Lorax guards his trufula trees amid incredible architecture that makes Circus McGurkis real. And yes, you can eat real green eggs (and ham) here.

Caro-Seuss-El
(Universal Express)

Even if you don't want to ride this, check it out. This merry-go-round is so great looking that you might wonder if it will eventually end up in the Smithsonian – or Louvre. Little kids will no doubt insist on waiting in the (probably long) line for a ride. Kids under 48 inches must ride with an adult.

The Cat in the Hat
(Universal Express)

Grab a couch and watch as Thing One and Thing Two instigate all sorts of mayhem. Oh, that cat! This is very much like the Winnie the Pooh ride at Disney's Magic Kingdom, and every bit as wonderful – probably more so if you prefer the Cat to Pooh Bear. Kids under 48 inches must ride with an adult.

If I Ran the Zoo

Here's another interactive play area with squirty triggers and lots of color and climbing apparati.

One Fish, Two Fish, Red Fish, Blue Fish (Universal Express)

This is certainly going to suck your kid toward it like a moth to a candle. Much like Disney's Dumbo, and even more like the Aladdin ride, this midway attraction gives riders up and down controls so that they can avoid (or confront) the waterspouts streaming from those silly Seussian fish. Kids under 48 inches must ride with an adult.

PLACES TO EAT

All the usual fast-food suspects are sold at premium prices throughout the park, but with a commitment to theme that you don't see elsewhere.

Port of Entry

Arctic Express has hot funnel cakes and cold ice-cream sundaes and cones.

Confisco Grille & Backwater Bar is a full-service place with fajitas, burgers and salads. And guess what – it has a full bar (how do they get away with that?), and happy hour from 3pm to 5pm daily. Stay away from Storm Force Accelatron if you partake.

Pastries are good for a quick bite at either **Croissant Moon Bakery** or **Cinnabon**.

Seuss Landing

Hop on Pop Ice Cream Shop has refreshing ice cream and sodas, or you can head over to **Moose Juice Goose Juice** for smoothies, fruit, churros, pretzels and cookies.

Circus McGurkus Café Stoo-pendous is only open seasonally but has all the junk Americans love: pizza, fried chicken and theme-park pasta.

Green Eggs & Ham Café is the only place where you get the eponymous meal ($6).

The Lost Continent

Mythos Restaurant *(dishes $15-24)* is the only restaurant where you'll need to make reservations. The dining room is an ornate underwater grotto where you'll dine on acceptable pad Thai or vegetable gnocchi while imagining yourself among the merfolk.

Enchanted Oak Tavern sells good-smelling smoked meats. Like Confisco Grille (see under Port of Entry earlier), there is a full bar, and happy hour is also from 3pm to 5pm daily.

Fire-Eater's Grill has gyros, chicken tenders and hot dogs.

Frozen Desert is more than just a mirage and sells sundaes with fruity toppings.

Jurassic Park

You can sink your teeth into big burgers at **The Burger Digs**, or pizza at **Pizza Predattoria**, where beer is sold too. On that note, mixed fruity tropical drinks are ladled out at **The Watering Hole**, which has the earliest happy hour in the park (from 2pm to 4pm daily).

Toon Lagoon

Comic Strip Café, serving pseudoethnic (Mexican, Chinese and Italian) cuisines, **Cathy's Ice Cream** and **Blondie's** are all open seasonally. The latter sells American classics like meat-loaf sandwich and 'the Dagwood,' with ham, salami, turkey, bologna, Swiss and American cheeses and tomato ($7). An analogous veggie sandwich ($6) is almost as big.

Wimpy's is open year-round, and although his favorite food is the star here (we dare you to ask the cashier if you can pay her Tuesday), hot dogs are also on offer.

Marvel Super Hero Island

It's all junk food here, though fruit is available at the seasonally open, imaginatively named **Fruit** stand. Otherwise, it's all pizza, soda, ice cream, cotton candy and burgers.

CityWalk

Right by Universal Studios, this pedestrian mall is a little plastic but fun. It's a collection of restaurants and bars with great live music, and it's packed with tourists, buskers and Orlando teens looking for something to do. After 6pm parking is free, and you can get a pass which covers all the clubs for $10, a good deal considering cover is usually $5 to $10 per club after 9pm. There are often deals available for park ticketholders, where you can purchase all-club access with dinner and/or a movie. Check out Ⓦ www.citywalkorlando.com or call ☎ 407-363-8000 for more information.

Like at Downtown Disney, there are plenty of things to buy here – sports collectibles, cigars, novelties, movie-related schwag, produce and jewelry, to mention a few.

PLACES TO EAT

There's nothing here worth writing home about, apart from Emeril's, which can serve up some very good food.

Quick Food

There's a **Big Kahuna Pizza**, a **Cinnabon** and **Latin Quarter Express**, which sells Cuban sandwiches, nachos, tamales and other Latino fare. If you insist, there's a **Starbucks** too.

Table Service

In addition to the following places, there is a limited menu at **CityJazz** and **Pat O'Brien's** (see Entertainment later). All of the following are open for lunch and dinner.

Motown Café (☎ 407-224-2500; mains $12-20) has steaks and BBQ.

Bob Marley – A Tribute to Freedom doesn't serve Freedom Fries, but you can nibble on some Jamaican and Caribbean food here.

There's also a branch of Jimmy Buffet's **Margaritaville** (☎ 407-224-6916; W www.margaritaville.com; open 11am-2am daily; mains $8-15) which serves tamed Caribbean cuisine.

Pastamoré serves all the Ps: pastries, panini, pasta and pizza.

Emeril's has a branch here at CityWalk, in the rare case that you just haven't had enough of that man on the Food Network. Will someone kick him down a notch?

NBA City serves regular American food and has basketball-related games and memorabilia. Outside are the handprints of some of the NBA's greatest stars – Scottie Pippen, Kevin Garnett, Hakeem Olajuwon, Charles Barkley and others. You can compare your little paws to theirs – it's fun!

Nascar Café is the only officially sanctioned Nascar eatery in Florida, if that means anything to you.

Hard Rock Café Orlando is just like it is anywhere else in the world, but this one happens to be the biggest.

ENTERTAINMENT

Twenty state-of-the-art theaters grace **Universal Cineplex** – and you can get beer and wine at the concession stand!

Motown Café has a great collection of Motown memorabilia. DJs and dancing start at around 8pm.

Bob Marley – A Tribute to Freedom gets going around 8pm and features – you guessed it – reggae.

Pat O'Brien's looks just like the one in New Orleans, only super sanitized.

The Groove has three themed lounges and popular dance music. Some nights are for teens aged 13 to 19, and sodas are served.

Latin Quarter has salsa, merengue and all the other great Latin rhythms.

Margaritaville has live music nightly, usually classic rock but sometimes there's a steel drum player.

City Jazz (☎ 407-224-2189; cover $5; open 8pm-1am Sun-Thur, 7pm-2am Fri & Sat) has good live jazz, funk, soul or R&B every night.

Hard Rock Live Orlando (☎ 407-351-5483; tickets $20-30; box office open 10am-9pm daily) is that big coliseum you see across the water from the main strip of CityWalk. The 2800-seat auditorium draws some fairly big names.

Places to Stay

There are three resort hotels at Universal Orlando Resort, and all of them give Walt Disney World a good run for its money, offering the same sort of services. All three have a well-presented theme and are somewhat interesting to check out, even if you're not staying there. Especially easy on the eyes is the Portofino Bay, which can be reached by a wonderful boat ride. At night, the resort pops into vision after passing through a water tunnel, and you may really feel like you're about to dock at the Italian Riviera – very romantic. In fact, Universal Orlando Resort has honed its resorts into three distinct atmosphere categories: family (Royal Pacific), party (Hard Rock Hotel) and romance (Portofino Bay). Call ☎ 407-503-7000 or 800-837-2273 for updated rates and more details. And guess what? Present your room key to the line attendant at the parks, and you'll be ushered to the Express entrance (each guest must have a separate key). You can do the same for priority seating at the full-service restaurants at the two parks as well, except for Friday and Saturday nights. At the park's shows you'll also receive preferred seating.

You can get to each hotel via the free transport provided by Universal Orlando Resort (see Getting There & Around later). The rates provided are rack rates for double rooms from low season to high season, but call ahead to find out about better deals.

Royal Pacific (☎ 407-503-3000; 6300 Hollywood Way; low/high season $179/219), with its South Pacific theme, has about 1000 rooms and is the most family-oriented Universal Orlando Resort hotel. The pool has an interactive play area, real sand, volleyball, shuffleboard and ping pong. There are plenty of organized activities for children, too. Poolside cabanas are available to rent and feature TVs, phones, a fridge and a private patio. Every Saturday night, a luau (Hawaiian feast) is presented (adult/child under 13 $50/29).

Hard Rock Hotel (☎ 407-503-2000; 5800 Universal Blvd; low/high season $209/249) is based on the Hotel California and caters to the young party crowd – although many families enjoy it here. Keep in mind that a loud live band such as Loverboy could be playing in the lobby.

Portofino Bay (☎ 407-503-1000; 5601 Universal Blvd; low/high season $259/309) is sumptuous and romantic. Rooms are bigger, there are three pools instead of one, there are more restaurants (very good ones), and there is a health spa – all of which is well reflected in the room rates.

Getting There & Around

From the Orlando International Airport, take the Bee Line Expressway (Hwy 528; toll road) west and exit onto I-4 East. From there, take exit 75A and follow the signs.

From I-4, take exit 74B (west) or 75A (east) and follow the signs.

From International Dr, turn north onto Universal Blvd.

Parking costs $8/10 per car/recreational vehicle (RV). Do not forget to write down your parking location! Preferred parking, which puts you closer to the entrance, costs $11 (hardly worth it), and valet parking is $16.

Getting to and from the Universal Orlando Resort hotels and the two parks is made easy with the free shuttle buses and water taxis, which leave each point about every 20 minutes; service begins at 8:30am and ends at 2:30am. All resort hotels are also accessible by pedestrian walkways from CityWalk. There is also complimentary shuttle service to **SeaWorld** and **Wet 'n' Wild** for resort hotel guests.

Mears Shuttles can be arranged for transport to and from Walt Disney World for $13 round-trip, as well as to and from the airport. Contact your concierge desk for pick-up times.

Space Coast

The major attraction on the Space Coast is the Kennedy Space Center (KSC) – one of two places on Earth from which humans have been launched into space. But the area is also famed for its natural treasures: bird-watchers have a field day at Merritt Island National Wildlife Refuge, and whales have been spotted off Canaveral National Seashore. Some of Florida's finest sea turtle observation programs are also run here. And the strip between Sebastian Inlet and Cocoa Beach has the state's best surfing.

Despite its terrestrial attractions, the Space Coast is obsessed with celestial objectives, a theme you won't be able to escape: rock stations broadcast launch updates; shuttles adorn gas stations, banks and bakeries; even the area code is ☎ 321 (liftoff!).

KENNEDY SPACE CENTER

The KSC *(☎ 321-449-4444;* Ⓦ *www.kennedy spacecenter.com; adult/child 3-11 $33/23; open 9am-sundown)* is among the most popular attractions in Florida, drawing more than two million people a year. The KSC is also a working spaceport, with missions operating at all times. The robot- and rocket-packed complex is Walt Disney World for scientists and space junkies, albeit with only one ride (see the boxed text 'So You Wanna Be an Astronaut…', later in this chapter, for more information), and is a worthwhile diversion for anyone interested in the ultimate form of travel. Plan to spend a day seeing the massive launch apparatus, IMAX theater and absolutely stellar exhibits, including an enormous Saturn V rocket.

The price provided here is for **maximum access** and includes KSC admission, a bus tour to restricted areas, and admission to the Astronaut Hall of Fame (see that section, later in this chapter), which is not at the KSC, but further up the road. See Organized Tours & Programs, later in this chapter, for information on bonus features at additional cost.

Whichever kind of ticket you purchase, get to the KSC early. There's tons to see, and you'll want to get your money's worth before the center closes for the day.

History
Early Rocket Science In 1865 French science fiction author Jules Verne published *From Earth to the Moon,* in which three men

Highlights

- Watching space craft blast off for orbit
- Visiting the Kennedy Space Center and being awe inspired by the massive Saturn V rocket
- Attending Space Camp to learn rocket science – or offloading the kids for a week while you soak in the sun on nearby beaches
- Seeing an endangered American bald eagle in its nest and other wild birdlife at the Merritt Island National Wildlife Refuge, home to more endangered and protected species than any other refuge in the country
- Surfing the best breaks in Florida, between Cocoa Beach and Sebastian Inlet, dude

in a five-stage rocket are shot from Florida's 27° 7' north parallel to the lunar surface. In 1969 Neil Armstrong, Michael Collins and Buzz Aldrin would take the five-stage Saturn V rocket from the KSC (27° 27' north) to the Moon.

It wasn't prophecy, simply logical scientific conjecture (Verne felt the USA had the edge in technology, and the closer you are to the equator, the easier it is to get to the Moon). And in the 1890s, Verne fan and Russian scientist Konstantin Tsiolkovsky built on some of the book's other theories and designed a completely new rocket. It abandoned the use of solid fuel – that'd be gunpowder – in favor of multiple engines powered by liquid hydrogen and oxygen. Modern rocketry was born.

American scientist Robert Goddard launched the first successful guided rocket in 1926. Then, during WWII, Nazi Germany decided to explore the technology's potential. German scientists led by Wernher von Braun perfected the V2 rocket in 1942, which had a range of about 200 miles and could drop bombs from an altitude of 50 miles. After Germany surrendered, US war spoils included von Braun (who would become NASA's deputy chief) and about 100 V2s. The USSR acquired a somewhat less prestigious selection of scientists and equipment.

The Soviets, however, surprised everyone, launching the unmanned satellite *Sputnik* on October 4, 1957. *Vanguard* was launched from Cape Canaveral on March 17, 1958; Soviet premier Khrushchev reportedly called it 'Rearguard.' The race was on.

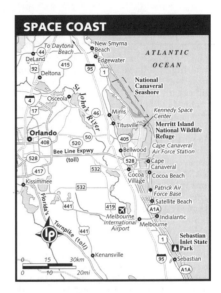

The Space Race The National Aeronautics & Space Administration (NASA) was established on October 1, 1958, at Cape Canaveral Air Force Station. It announced Project Mercury the following week. The mission: manned space flight. NASA put 110 American test pilots through an unprecedented battery of physical and psychological tests. Seven were chosen: Virgil 'Gus' Grissom, Deke Slayton, John Glenn, Wally Schirra, Alan Shepard, Scott Carpenter and

Was the Moon Landing a Hoax?

Some conspiracy theorists claim that the Moon landings were actually filmed right here on Earth. Well, this *is* the same government that – ahem – didn't have troops in Cambodia at the time, so let's take a quick look at the debate.

Conspiracy theorists: The flag rippled, but there's no wind on the Moon.
NASA: The Moon's gravity is a fraction of Earth's; thus, the flag continued to vibrate for longer than you'd expect after being planted.

Conspiracy theorists: There are no stars in any of the pictures.
NASA: Those photos were taken in full sunlight, requiring a narrow aperture that couldn't register faint daytime stars.

Conspiracy theorists: There were no flames during takeoff.
NASA: The lander used a mixture of hydrazine and dinitrogen tetroxide for fuel, which doesn't produce flames.

Conspiracy theorists: Some photos show objects in front of the lens crosshairs.
NASA: This effect is common in overexposed film.

Why would NASA paint giant crosshairs on the back of the set, anyway? Sheesh. The agency also points to its 1000lb (450kg) Moon rock collection as proof they were there, as well as the fact that the USSR and other less-than-friendly nations monitored, and verified, all communications.

Paige R Penland

Gordon Cooper. None would be the first person in space. Soviet cosmonaut Yury Gagarin took that honor on April 12, 1961. A month later, Shepard completed a 15-minute suborbital flight, followed by Glenn's successful orbit, but NASA – and the USA – was wiping egg off its face.

On May 25, 1961, President John F Kennedy announced that the US intended to land a man on the Moon by the end of the decade. As part of the ambitious initiative, a new facility on Merritt Island, just north of Cape Canaveral Air Force Station, opened in 1962: NASA's Launch Operations Center. After the forward-thinking president's assassination in 1963, the facility was renamed the John F Kennedy Space Center.

Soon after, NASA initiated Project Gemini, which would develop the skills and technology necessary for a Moon landing. Gemini used huge Titan II intercontinental ballistic missiles to achieve those goals: space walks, two-week endurance flights, serious piloting and the rendezvous of Gemini VI-A and Gemini VII. Gemini was declared successful in January 1967, and Project Apollo was announced. NASA was shooting for the Moon. It began tragically. During a test run for the Apollo I, astronauts Gus Grissom, Edward White and Roger Chaffee were killed when their capsule caught fire. Yet the horrible accident inspired upgrades that would culminate with the Apollo 11 flight: On July 20, 1969, the *Eagle* module landed on the Moon's surface. As the world watched, Neil Armstrong delivered one of the best lines ever: 'That's one small step for man, one giant leap for mankind.'

Moving Ahead A total of six Apollo expeditions had landed on the Moon by 1972. (Apollo 13 had suffered a debilitating explosion in one of its oxygen tanks and was unable to land; just making it home was an Odyssean ordeal dramatized in the excellent eponymous movie.) Despite these successes, the taxpaying public was losing interest in yet another (yawn) Moon landing, so NASA turned its attention to creating a space station. Skylab was completed in 1973 and, despite numerous technical difficulties, hosted three crews and 79 successful experiments before falling back to Earth in 1979.

The 1970s marked several historic moments for the space program. The Soviet *Soyuz 19* and *Apollo 18* rendezvous on July 17, 1975, witnessed the first international handshake in space. The Viking and Voyager probes, which have since collected data from Mars, Jupiter and Saturn, were launched. And NASA built its first reusable spacecraft, a delta-winged space plane called an orbiter, but better known as the space shuttle.

In 1981, space shuttle *Columbia* lifted off from the KSC for its maiden voyage. Designed as transport vehicles, shuttles carried everything from military and commercial satellites to scientific experiments into space. Shuttles also took the first female American, Sally Ride, and the first African American, Guion S Bluford Jr, into zero gravity.

The Challenger Orbiters could also carry civilians. In 1985 charismatic Christa McAuliffe was chosen from a field of 11,000 applicants to be the first 'teacher in space.' The world fell in love with McAuliffe and with the idea that regular people could fly. It was the public relations coup that NASA, reeling from budget cuts, desperately needed.

On January 28, 1986, about 73 seconds after liftoff, the space shuttle *Challenger* suffered an explosion in the external fuel tank; all aboard, including McAuliffe, were killed. The event, televised worldwide, was, at the time, the worst accident in NASA's history. And unfortunately, it was not the last.

The Columbia On February 1, 2003, the orbiter *Columbia* burst into flames and exploded, killing all seven crew members.

Unlike the *Challenger* tragedy, which occurred during liftoff, when millions were watching either on TV or in person, the *Columbia* disintegrated high in the sky over Texas, with few onlookers. Still, the accident pierced the hearts of people worldwide. See the boxed text '*Columbia's* Final Flight.'

The incident's cause is still under investigation, which, like that of the *Challenger,* is sure to be expensive. Most signs point toward deficient ceramic tiles on the wing of the orbiter. These seemingly insignificant tiles can withstand the thousands of degrees of heat that attack the craft during re-entry, and the slightest flaw in a single tile can result in a fatal fire.

It's likely that such a flaw would not have occurred if NASA had been receiving proper funding all along - which leads us to our next topic.

Space on a Shoestring Gravity is no longer our biggest obstacle to becoming a space-faring species. Today's hurdles are financial. During the Cold War, the US space

Incredible Hulk Coaster, Islands of Adventure

Astronaut Hall of Fame, Titusville

Apollo/Saturn V Center, Kennedy Space Center

Rocket Garden, Kennedy Space Center

program got 4% of the federal budget; today it receives only 0.7%, about $15 billion annually.

The loss of the *Challenger* in 1986 set the shuttle program back three years, as investigations and redesigns devoured the agency's resources, and as lucrative contracts with private companies and the Department of Defense were pulled. The drastic drop in funding led to massive layoffs, and NASA's once cutting-edge capabilities became compromised.

In 1995, hoping to stretch its resources, NASA announced the 'Faster, Cheaper, Better' program, launching two probes – the *Mars Observer* and *Mars Climate Orbiter* – on Delta II launch vehicles instead of the recommended Titans. The savings? Three hundred million dollars a shot. But the discount launches necessitated using an experimental aerobraking system upon entering Mars' atmosphere; neither probe made it. There are other explanations for the failures that can't be blamed on budget cuts, such as a fuel leak and engineering flaws (some scientists were using imperial measurements, others metric – d'oh!). Still, the adage 'you get what you pay for' had humans, hopeful for a permanent Mars colony in our lifetimes, sighing over opportunities lost.

But NASA finally learned how to play politics. By awarding International Space Station (ISS) contracts to companies in 20 different states, it managed to keep key members of Congress somewhat interested. Still, this strategy, not surprisingly, has produced a ridiculously expensive station with huge technical problems. And to top it off, the collapse of the Russian economy in the early 1990s stuck NASA with an extra $600 million bill.

Even though lobbyists for NASA's new private contractors are now responsible for keeping NASA in business, Congress has more generous donors to feed. And after the loss of the *Columbia* and an expensive war in Iraq, lawmakers may be less likely to approve funding for NASA programs. 'The conquest of space is worth the risk of life,' said astronaut Gus Grissom, who perished in *Apollo I*'s flames. But is it worth risking re-election? That's a tougher call. Funny how the government obviously has little problem with the idea that the conquest of oil is worth the risk of life, re-election or no. Ah, money.

Orientation

The KSC takes up about 46,000 acres on Merritt Island. Much of it is used for NASA facilities, but the northern third of the island is wilderness area, comprising Merritt Island National Wildlife Refuge and Canaveral National Seashore.

The Visitor Complex is located on the east side of the Intracoastal Waterway (called Indian River here), accessible from Titusville via Columbia Blvd (Hwy 405; NASA Pkwy) and from Cocoa Beach and Orlando via Hwy 528 (Bee Line Expressway). The Banana River separates the KSC from Cape Canaveral Air Force Station.

All commercial maps of the facility are distorted to protect sensitive areas, but colorful handouts at the information desk are helpful for finding your way around. Facilities outside the Visitor Complex are accessible by tour bus only.

Information

There's an **information desk** (☎ 321-449-4444; open 9am-sundown) at the Visitor Complex. In addition to pamphlets and a friendly, multilingual staff, it provides lockers and audio guides in several languages. Guests with disabilities can call ☎ 321-449-4364 (voice) or ☎ 321-454-4198 (TDD) to arrange special tours in advance.

There are **ATMs** at the Visitor Complex, Apollo/Saturn V Center and, of course, the Space Shop. The Space Shop also has an enormous selection of hard-to-find books on NASA and space travel. NASA broadcasts countdowns and other space news on 920 AM, available throughout the Space Coast. Television channel 15, also available throughout the Space Coast, has a constant video feed of NASA operations.

Note that security has increased dramatically since September 11, 2001. Backpacks and electronics will be checked.

Visitor Complex

The entryway to America's Spaceport is no longer free – you pay your admission, which covers all IMAX shows and a bus tour, at the Skylab-inspired ticket plaza before entering the facilities. Standard admission to the Visitor Complex (adult/child $28/18) does not include the Astronaut Hall of Fame (see that section, later in this chapter, for separate admission prices).

The Visitor Complex features excellent – nay, mind-blowing – exhibits accompanied by explanations geared for the average spaceaholic with a high school education; for more technical discussions of events and hardware, visit the Space Shop bookstore and prepare to be overwhelmed.

SPACE COAST

Overpriced eateries abound, including the Moon Rock Café at the Apollo/Saturn V Center, which enhances your dining experience with a chunk of Earth's oldest satellite. Buses to the LC-39 Observation Gantry, Apollo/Saturn V Center and International Space Station Center leave the Visitor Complex every 15 minutes from 10am to 2:45pm daily.

NASA for Kids Several exhibits at the Visitor Complex are designed to lure youngsters into the world of math and science, using the promise of potential space travel as bait. You can help by picking up an interplanetary passport at the gift shops. The kids can have the passports stamped throughout the KSC. The **Children's Play Dome** is for smaller children, who like the climbable versions of the space shuttle and ISS, and **Exploration in the New Millennium** will entertain older kids with interactive displays and the opportunity to touch a rock from Mars. Don't miss **Robot Scouts**, which introduces young people to talkative 'trailblazers for human exploration.'

Rockets & Spacecraft The Rocket Garden, visible from anywhere in the complex, is an inspiring collection of Redstone, Atlas and Titan rockets, originally developed by the military to blow people up but adapted by NASA to send them into outer space. The massive Apollo Saturn 1B rocket is the exception, designed specifically to carry astronauts up, up and away.

Inside the Visitor Complex are dozens more spacecraft and scale models, including the *Gemini 9* and a mockup of the Apollo-Soyuz rendezvous (the Apollo capsule is real, the Soyuz is a full-scale model). Some vessels are covered with transparent plastic, allowing you to peer inside and wonder just how astronauts could stand being cooped up in those things for so long.

The **Shuttle Plaza** features a full-size model of a space shuttle, dubbed *Explorer*. Walk through the cockpit and check out the cargo bay, which was recently refitted with a mock-up of the new Canadian-engineered payload arm. Don't miss the steering rockets or the custom-fitted heat tiles outside, which must be replaced after each reentry using an exacting process that would send Henry Ford into conniptions.

Next to the Shuttle Plaza is the moving **Astronaut Memorial**, its black granite expanse inscribed with the names of those who have heroically given their lives so that, one

Columbia's Final Flight

On January 16, 2003, the United States' first orbiter, space shuttle *Columbia*, filled the air with fire and noise as it left planet Earth behind. STS-107 was one of those rare missions devoted entirely to scientific research; rather than launching commercial satellites, the seven astronauts – William McCool, Rick Husband, Michael Anderson, Kalpana Chawla, David Brown, Laurel Clark and Ilan Ramon – would conduct a marathon 79 experiments.

Some studies were designed by students, including one from China that examined silkworms maturing in zero gravity. 'It was just starting to puff its wings up so that it would be able to fly,' remarked mission specialist Clark. 'Life is a magical thing.'

More ambitious were those experiments devised by Arab scientists and overseen by the first Israeli in space, Ilan Ramon. When he was originally selected for flight, NASA was concerned with developing space-friendly kosher food, while Israeli schoolchildren debated how Ramon would observe the weekly Sabbath while watching 17 sunsets every 24 hours.

To the untrained observer, *Columbia* seemed to have enjoyed a textbook takeoff. But while first-time astronaut and former circus performer Dave Brown was doing back flips for the cameras, engineers on the ground had begun to worry.

Large chunks of insulating foam, sprayed on the external fuel tanks before each mission, had come loose and smashed into the orbiter's left wing. Yet when NASA scientists suggested that a US military satellite photograph the damage, they were ignored.

If the astronauts were told of these concerns, they betrayed no fear. It was a sense of wonder that moved them. 'In the retina of my eye, the whole Earth and the sky could be seen reflected,' noted mission specialist Kalpana Chawla, a native of Karnal, India. 'I called all the crew members one by one, and they saw it, and everybody said, "Oh, wow!"'

day, our own planet might not feel quite so lonely.

IMAX Theater The five-story-high screens of the Complex's two IMAX theaters show films throughout the day. *The Dream Is Alive* includes footage taped during various missions, and *L5: First City in Space* features a truly awesome sequence depicting a space shuttle launch in 3D.

In the same building, the **NASA Art Gallery** has works commissioned by the agency to render data they've collected from other celestial bodies into images – landscapes, really – that nonscientists can comprehend. Many of the Hubble space telescope's best shots are also on display.

Astronaut Encounter Yes, the 'I Want to Be an Astronaut' song hurts, but it's just the introduction to a guaranteed highlight of your visit: a question-and-answer period with a real, live astronaut. Inevitable questions about bathroom breaks aside, it's interesting to hear tales of weightlessness and radiation from the people who've experienced them. Please, *please* don't ask if we really got to the Moon (see the boxed text 'Was the Moon Landing a Hoax?' earlier in this chapter).

You'll sound like a moron, and even if it was a hoax, it's not like they're going to tell you.

LC-39 Observation Gantry

The first stop on the bus tour into the real meat of the KSC facility is this 60ft observation tower, with great views of launch pads 39A and 39B, from which the space shuttle is hurled into space. A couple of films show simplified explanations of how shuttles are loaded and prepped for flight once they've made it to the launch pad. More interesting is the 14ft-long, 7000lb main engine from one of the shuttles.

Launch Facilities

The bus continues its tour through the launch facilities themselves. As you might imagine, there are plenty of superlatives involved. Our favorite factoid predates the shuttle: When Apollo 5 left the facility in 1967, it produced the loudest sound humans have ever made. Yes, even louder than a nuclear bomb.

The **Vehicle Assembly Building** (VAB), where Saturn rockets and later space shuttles have been assembled and stored, is among the largest in the world. The **Crawler Transporters**, which carry the shuttle at a blistering 1mph from the VAB to the launch pad, weigh

Columbia's Final Flight

There was little that could have been done, anyway. *Columbia* could not have reached the International Space Station; a space walk would have been dangerous and probably useless. On February 1, 2003, the astronauts re-entered Earth's atmosphere, flames licking the craft mercilessly.

'You definitely don't want to be outside now,' joked Commander Rick Husband.

'What, like we did before?' Clark replied. The other astronauts chuckled.

Over California, things began to go wrong. An amateur San Francisco photographer recorded an electrical discharge near the craft. Above Arizona, Husband was cut off mid-sentence. Other readings had gone haywire. And as *Columbia* streaked across the Texas sky, it broke into hundreds of fiery pieces that rained down upon a horrified nation.

The world grieved the loss of what was more than a single nation's pride; *Columbia* represented humanity's aspirations to touch the stars. Support came from all quarters; even Palestinian Authority president Yasser Arafat expressed his condolences to the grieving American and Israeli families. It was a tragedy that transcended politics.

At the time this book went to press, NASA could not confirm that foam had caused the accident; other theories included errant meteorites, cracked ball bearings and even lightning. Terrorism was ruled out almost immediately. The three remaining shuttles were grounded, but NASA administrator Sean O'Keefe had vowed to return to space within months, not years, as followed the loss of the *Challenger*.

The quest for space is not a tea party, as humanity has been too often reminded. These seven astronauts, like those who follow, knew what they risked – and why they risked it. The heavens they sought will one day be humanity's to explore, while the heavens they have found will reward them for bravery, displayed on behalf of us all.

Paige R Penland

So You Wanna Be an Astronaut...

Think you've got the right stuff? NASA picks new astronauts about every two years, and US citizens have first priority. You'll need at the very least a degree in biology, physics or mathematics and three years of related professional experience. Pilot astronaut applicants must have logged at least 1000 hours of pilot-in-command time on jet aircraft and must be able to pass a NASA class one space physical. Mission specialists must pass a class two space physical.

Wanna try? Download the appropriate forms at W www.nasajobs.nasa.gov/jobs/astronauts/aso/application.htm, fill them out and send them in to the Astronaut Selection Office, Mail Code AHX, Johnson Space Center, 2101 NASA Rd One, Houston, TX 77058.

May the force be with you.

6 million pounds (2.7 metric tons) apiece and are two of the world's heaviest vehicles. Even the runway where the space shuttle lands, at 15,000ft (4572m) long, is in the record books.

Apollo/Saturn V Center

The **Saturn V** rocket is still one of the most complex pieces of machinery we humans have ever come up with: it's big, it's bad, and it put us on the Moon. You can see one of the few remaining examples right here, in all of its lovingly restored glory. And that's just the beginning. The center contains some of the most important relics of the space race, including the **Lunar Module** and **Command Service Module** from the Apollo program.

Even better is the **Firing Room Theater**, where the main feature is a remarkable multimedia recreation of the frenetic Apollo 8 launch. For those too young to remember the Cold War, this feature is preceded by a movie that illustrates the drive those tensions inspired. It uses the original equipment from mission command as props, plus video footage on three huge screens and a sound-and-light show that approximates what technicians experienced at the moment of liftoff. Wow!

The **Lunar Theater** attempts to dramatize Neil Armstrong's riveting Moon landing with equal flair but ends up feeling a little too sticky sweet. Don't miss the preview footage, however, which has Walter Cronkite's classic coverage of the event.

International Space Station Center

This center is so cutting-edge that it was off-limits at the time of research because of new and hopefully temporary antiterrorism protocols. Drat. If it's open, you'll see the actual facility where NASA processes ISS components, as well as replicas of living quarters and work modules on the station.

Organized Tours & Programs

In addition to the bus tour included with your admission, the KSC offers several other special tours and programs, most costing a bit extra. You can order tickets by calling ☎ 321-449-2444 or logging on to W www.kschtickets.com. There's a free tour of the **Rocket Garden** at 11am and 3pm daily.

Maximum access (adult/child $33/23) includes regular admission plus a two-hour tour of 'restricted areas,' where the space shuttle is refitted after landing and is prepped for launch. Admission to the off-site Astronaut Hall of Fame is included as well (but transportation there isn't). The ticket is valid for two consecutive days. This is an excellent option, but note that just prior to a launch, this tour is cut short (no refunds).

NASA Up Close (adult/child $53/43) includes maximum access plus a 90-minute guided tour by a 'space expert.'

Cape Canaveral Then and Now (adult/child $53/43) tops off your visit with a two-hour tour of the sites where Alan Shepard and John Glenn blasted off on their historic Mercury missions. 'Hanger S,' where early astronauts lived and trained, and the Cape Canaveral Lighthouse are also included on this tour. Maximum access is also included in the price.

Lunch with an Astronaut (adult/child $60/40) is really fun, and great for kids. You'll get to watch a funny film showing astronauts goofing off in zero gravity, followed by a decent buffet meal (with butter in the shape of orbiters), then hear an astronaut talk. After the talk are Q&A and picture-taking sessions. Maximum access admission is included.

At the time this book went to print, there were no shuttle launches scheduled. However, when they resume, the best place to watch a **launch** is from the KSC. Car passes to the viewing site have been suspended

KENNEDY SPACE CENTER & AROUND

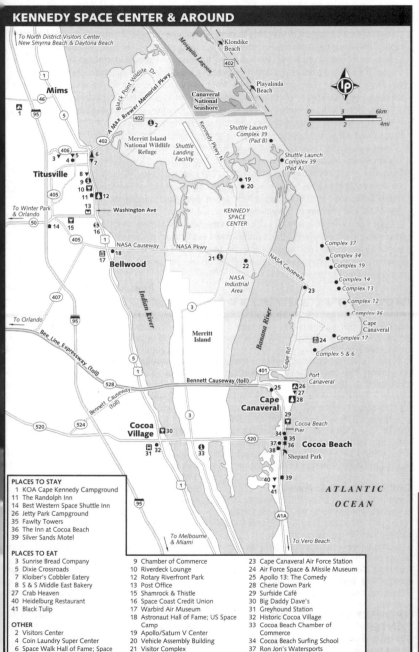

To North District Visitors Center,
New Smyrna Beach & Daytona Beach

Klondike
Beach

Mosquito Lagoon

402

Black Point Wildlife Dr.

A Max Brewer Memorial Pkwy

Canaveral
National
Seashore

Playalinda
Beach

Mims

46

1

95

5

402

402

2

Merritt Island
National Wildlife
Refuge

Shuttle
Landing
Facility

Kennedy Pkwy N

Shuttle Launch
Complex 39
(Pad B)

Shuttle Launch
Complex 39
(Pad A)

406

6

3   4   5

7

Titusville

8

9

405

10

11

12

19

20

13

Washington Ave

KENNEDY
SPACE
CENTER

To Winter Park
& Orlando

50

14   15

16

405

1

NASA Causeway   NASA Pkwy

21

Complex 37

Complex 34

Complex 19

Bellwood

18

17

22

NASA Causeway

NASA
Industrial
Area

Complex 14

Complex 13

Complex 12

23

Complex 36

407

Indian River

Cape
Canaveral

To Orlando

95

3

Merritt
Island

Complex 17

Banana River

24

Complex 5 & 6

Bee Line Expressway (toll)

5

1

Cape Rd

401

Port
Canaveral

528

Bennett Causeway (toll)

Bennett Causeway
(toll)

25

26

27

28

29

Cocoa Beach
Pier

520   524

Cocoa
Village

30

3

34

35

37   36   Cocoa Beach

31   32

33

520

38

Shepard Park

ATLANTIC
OCEAN

40   39

1

41

95

To Melbourne
& Miami

A1A

To Vero Beach

0   3   6km
0   2   4mi

PLACES TO STAY
1 KOA Cape Kennedy Campground
11 The Randolph Inn
14 Best Western Space Shuttle Inn
26 Jetty Park Campground
35 Fawlty Towers
36 The Inn at Cocoa Beach
39 Silver Sands Motel

PLACES TO EAT
3 Sunrise Bread Company
5 Dixie Crossroads
7 Kloiber's Cobbler Eatery
8 S & S Middle East Bakery
27 Crab Heaven
40 Heidelburg Restaurant
41 Black Tulip

OTHER
2 Visitors Center
4 Coin Laundry Super Center
6 Space Walk Hall of Fame; Space
View Park

9 Chamber of Commerce
10 Riverdeck Lounge
12 Rotary Riverfront Park
13 Post Office
15 Shamrock & Thistle
16 Space Coast Credit Union
17 Warbird Air Museum
18 Astronaut Hall of Fame; US Space
Camp
19 Apollo/Saturn V Center
20 Vehicle Assembly Building
21 Visitor Complex
22 International Space Station Center

23 Cape Canaveral Air Force Station
24 Air Force Space & Missile Museum
25 Apollo 13: The Comedy
28 Cherie Down Park
29 Surfside Café
30 Big Daddy Dave's
31 Greyhound Station
32 Historic Cocoa Village
33 Cocoa Beach Chamber of
Commerce
34 Cocoa Beach Surfing School
37 Ron Jon's Watersports
38 Luna Sea

Let's Do Launch

It's the modern equivalent of watching those first ambitious fish haul themselves up onto dry land, topped off with the explosive power of the world's most expensive firework. If you ever need a little inspiration, watching a launch will make you appreciate how remarkable human beings really are.

Since the *Columbia* tragedy, shuttle launches have been suspended indefinitely, but they could be set back into motion at any time. Also, remember that shuttles aren't the only things launched – there are always opportunities to watch unmanned craft (called 'expendable vehicles') soar into space.

For the latest update on what's sailing to the stars, and when, go to **W** www.ksc.nasa.gov or call ☎ 321-867-4636 for launch dates. For launch status during countdown, call ☎ 321-867-0600. Also, Space Coast news stations cover NASA operations obsessively: Weather broadcasts begin with 'There's a 40% chance of a successful launch,' rather than boring you with hurricane warnings.

You can also order tickets to view the launch; see Organized Tours & Programs in the Kennedy Space Center section of this chapter. But if you can't get tickets to KSC facilities, don't worry. There are plenty of great places to see a launch: Try the Astronaut Hall of Fame, Jetty Park Campground, Cherie Down Park, Rotary Riverfront Park, Space View Park, Cocoa Beach Pier, Bennet Causeway (Hwy 528) and the Brewer Pkwy bridge in Titusville.

Make hotel reservations early, and plan to stay for a while (there are often many delays). Get to your viewing site early, and bring binoculars and extra beer – it's an international tailgate party no matter where you end up. Vendors sell ice cream, soda and even mission-specific T-shirts ($10; they make great souvenirs). Tune into 920 AM for up-to-the-minute reports and, five minutes before the big event, the countdown.

Paige R Penland & Wendy Taylor

indefinitely, but you can still purchase bus tickets (order early) from NASA at **W** www.ksctickets.com/ltt.html.

Note that all launch tickets must be tracked for security reasons, and shipping within the USA costs at least $10, overseas $30. If a launch is delayed, your tickets may be used for subsequent attempts (same mission only) or exchanged for one movie at the IMAX theater. If you didn't get your tickets in time, there are still plenty of places outside the KSC with fine views (see the boxed text 'Let's Do Launch' earlier in this chapter).

Getting There & Away
From I-95, Hwy A1A or US Hwy 1, the KSC is almost impossible to miss. From Orlando, take Hwy 528 (the Bee Line Expressway) straight east to the entrance.

Getting here without a car is difficult. Greyhound only has service as close as Cocoa Village and Titusville; from Orlando it's $18, though that doesn't include the taxi (about $15) from Cocoa Village to the KSC.

AROUND KENNEDY SPACE CENTER
The area around the KSC is federally protected wilderness area and usually open to the public. Many of these areas are closed the day before a launch – days, if there are delays or terrorism alerts. Call ahead. Great information about the area is available on the web at **W** www.space-coast.com.

Note that policy changes are frequent in this time of shuttle explosions and terrorism, so call ahead to make sure these places are still open if you'd like to visit.

Merritt Island National Wildlife Refuge
NASA uses only about 5% of its total landholdings for making things that go boom. In 1963, NASA turned management of its unused land over to the US Fish & Wildlife Service (USFWS), which then established this refuge (☎ 321-861-0667; **W** www.nbbd.com /godo/minwr; admission free; open 8am-4:30pm Mon-Fri, 9am-5pm Sat & Sun, closed Sun Apr-Oct). The park may be closed around liftoff and landing dates.

The **visitors center**, 4 miles east of Titusville on SR 402 (exit 80 off I-95), has informative pamphlets, including a self-guided tour around the refuge's most popular and easily accessible attraction, **Black Point Wildlife Drive**, a 6-mile loop. **Boardwalk Trail** is a quarter-mile nature trail next to the center.

Three other hiking trails begin about a mile east of the main visitors center: the half-mile

Oak Hammock Trail; the 2-mile **Palm Hammock Trail**, which winds through hardwood forest and has boardwalks above the open marsh; and the 5-mile **Cruickshank Trail**, which begins at stop eight along the Black Point Wildlife Drive.

The refuge is notable because its mangrove swamps, marshes and hardwood hammocks are home to more endangered and threatened species than any other refuge in the continental USA. Along with Canaveral National Seashore, the area is also one of the best birding spots in the country. Located on the Atlantic Flyway, this is migration central, as birds head back and forth between North and South America. You can pick up a free bird-spotting guide at the visitors center.

The best time to visit is from October to May, as that's the height of migratory bird season and also when the climate is most comfortable. From March to September, thousands of wading birds can be seen in spectacular breeding plumage throughout the park.

Canaveral National Seashore

The 25 miles of windswept beaches along this seashore (☎ 321-267-1110; ⓦ www.nps .gov/cana; open 6am-6pm daily winter, 6am-8pm daily summer; pedestrian/car $1/5) are a favorite haunt of surfers, campers and nature lovers.

All of the park's visitor programs and information services are handled by the **North District Visitors Center** (☎ 321-267-1110), located 9 miles south of New Smyrna Beach on Hwy A1A. It shows an excellent 12-minute video of the park's facilities, campsites and trails, and has pamphlets and monthly activity schedules available. **Sea turtle watching** programs take small groups (a strict maximum of 20 people) along the beach between June and July starting at about 10:30pm. Call for reservations up to eleven months in advance.

The park also maintains a **South District Office** (☎ 321-867-4077), located 12 miles east of Titusville on SR 402. Note that the South District is closed for four days around shuttle launches.

The real reason you're here, however, is the seashore. **Apollo Beach**, to the north, is favored by families because of the calm surf (watch out for riptides, though). **Klondike Beach**, the 12-mile stretch between Apollo and Playalinda Beaches, is as pristine as it gets, with nary a nature trail to mar it. **Playalinda Beach**, at the southern end, is surfer central, with decent (for Florida) breaks and lots of guys named Dude.

You can canoe or kayak through Mosquito Lagoon, though winds can get strong. **Village Outfitters** (see Activities in the Cocoa Village & Cocoa Beach, later in this chapter) operates kayak tours through the area.

You can **camp** (☎ 386-428-3384; sites $10) at Apollo Beach from November to mid-April. If you've got a boat, there are 11 primitive campsites, open year-round and scattered throughout the islands. Make reservations early, and note that there is no camping during shuttle launches.

Air Force Space & Missile Museum

Located on the grounds of Space Launch Complex 5/6, where Alan Shepard took off to become the first American in space, this museum (☎ 321-853-3245; Complex 26 at Cape Canaveral Air Force Station; admission free; open 10am-2pm Mon-Fri, 10am-4pm Sat & Sun, closed on launch days) is amazing. It's got hardware from the early days of space travel, mementos from the Mercury missions, and Jupiter and Redstone rockets on display. Military launches still blast off nearby, so it's been closed since September 11, 2001, for security reasons. Give them a call to see if it's reopened.

TITUSVILLE

Titusville is the main gateway to both the KSC and the wildlife refuge, and it has excellent vantage points for watching a launch. NASA cutbacks (see the boxed text 'Space on a Shoestring,' earlier in this chapter) have been hard on the city, which now boasts some of the most affordable real estate on Florida's Atlantic Coast.

Information

The **Chamber of Commerce** (☎ 321-267-3036; ⓦ www.space-coast.com; 2000 S Washington Ave; open 9am-5pm Mon-Fri) is geared primarily toward businesspeople and residents but has some helpful information.

Banks are plentiful, but check out the **Space Coast Credit Union** (☎ 321-724-5730; 5445 S Washington Ave), with a logo remarkably similar to Lonely Planet's. There's a **post office** (686 Cheney Hwy) in the Winn-Dixie shopping plaza.

Florida Today (ⓦ www.floridatoday.com) is the major daily and publishes a map of shuttle-viewing sites the day of a launch. The *Star-Advocate* is a more in-depth weekly publication. *Brevard Live* has events listings for the entire county.

SPACE COAST

Tourists in Space

So you forgot to join the military and got your degree in art history. Now you'll never get to go up into space. Right? Don't be so sure. San Diego equity-fund manager Dennis Tito made history in 2001, spending a reported $20 million for eight days on the International Space Station (ISS) as a guest of the Russian space program. NASA fought against it, but eventually accepted that the Russians are just die-hard capitalists – they even let Pizza Hut advertise on a Proton rocket in 2000 – and so the era of space tourism began.

The Russians have since hosted the coincidentally named Mark Shuttleworth, a South African Internet millionaire (well, he *was* a millionaire) on Soyuz, making him the first African-born person in space. Up until late 2002, the Russians were training Lance Bass, member of boy band N'Sync, to fly, but his funding wasn't coming through, so he was eventually ousted from the program. Interestingly, NASA was waiting in the wings to sweep up Lance if the Russians dropped him, but once the *Columbia* disaster happened, this fell by the wayside.

If funding stays so low, NASA may in the future be resorting to celebrities and civilian multimillionaires to raise funds and interest.

The **Coin Laundry Super Center** (☎ 321-383-1358; 600 S Park Dr) actually is pretty super, especially if you like video games.

Astronaut Hall of Fame

This entertaining museum (☎ 321-269-6100; 6225 Vectorspace Blvd; adult/child $14/10; open 9am-5pm daily, until liftoff on launch days) is open for launches (unlike the KSC) and has one of the prime viewing spots in Titusville. Admission is included with maximum access admission to the KSC. You can contact the KSC (see that section, earlier in this chapter) for more information.

If NASA scrubs the flight, they'll even let you in with your old ticket for their next attempt(s). Launch days are packed, but you may get to see 'Mod' Maury Hersom's Space Shuttle Columbia – a rare 1942 Chevrolet that has a NASA paint job and (oh yes!) propane-fueled booster engines – parked outside.

Much of the museum is kid-oriented, but it's definitely of interest to any space junkie. Pass the mural painted by astronaut Alan Bean to enter the theater, where sitting through the smarmy film is worth what's waiting on the other side.

A room filled with spinning rides and motion simulators (obsolete for astronauts but still packing a 4G wallop) is the highlight of the show. Colorful and technologically impressive displays transform physics problems into video games. Exhibits include a life-sized model of the space shuttle, a tribute to the astronauts lost in the Apollo I disaster and the actual Apollo 14 module. All are accompanied by explanations that make no bones about

where this museum stands in the 'small probes versus human explorers' debate.

'Some came to believe the old fallacy that robots can explore space as well as people, but more cheaply,' they note, discussing early problems with the shuttle program. Newly appointed NASA chief Sean O'Keefe, a proponent of robot exploration, will (hopefully) have his hands full with folks who've experienced this fine attraction.

The **Hall of Fame** is very well done but oddly only includes American astronauts – Yury Gagarin, the first person in space, is not mentioned.

US Space Camp

One of the most innovative ideas in summer camp is this program (☎ 321-269-6100, 800-897-5798; ⋓ www.spacecamp.com; 6225 Vectorspace Blvd), on the grounds of the Astronaut Hall of Fame. Rocket pioneer Wernher von Braun came up with the idea as a way of encouraging kids to study math and science. The original Space Camp opened in Huntsville, Alabama, in 1982, and this one opened in 1988. Since then, more than 30,000 kids have attended programs here.

Courses teach space science and rocket propulsion, and require simulated shuttle missions and astronaut training from different eras of the space program. Participants also perform experiments in physics, chemistry and space science. You can see many of the facilities free with your admission to the Astronaut Hall of Fame; if you want a closer look, you'll need to enroll.

Four-day programs are $500, and five-day programs run $700 to $800, including room and board, but they're only for nine- to 11-year-olds. Jealous? Find a willing kid, age seven to 12, to accompany you for the three-day weekend parent/child program ($700); one or two extra family members bring the total to $900 and $1000, respectively. No kids in your life? There's a three-day Space Camp for adults ($400) in Huntsville, Alabama (same website).

Warbird Air Museum
In the TICO (pronounced after **Ti**-tus-ville **Co**-coa) Space Center Airport, this museum (☎ 321-268-1941; ⓦ www.nbbd.com/godo/vac; 6600 Tico Rd; adult/child $9/5; open 10am-6pm daily) offers exhibits of historic war aircraft. The star here is a functioning C-47, built in October 1942, that's a veteran of the Normandy invasion. Other highlights include an F-14 Tomcat, a supersonic Crusader that flies using the computer that originally operated Apollo I, and the last UH-1 to make it out of Vietnam after the fall of Saigon. You can also see planes in various stages of restoration; when we were there, they were working on a Wildcat that had spent 50 years underwater. Each year, the museum holds an air show as a fundraiser for itself and its aviation scholarship program; the show is held the second week of March, and more than 100 warbirds take part.

To get here from I-95, take exit 79 to Hwy 405 east and follow the signs; the airport's on the right.

Space Walk Hall of Fame
Located on the Indian River at Broad St, just south of SR 406 at Space View Park, this monument and museum (☎ 321-264-0434; ⓦ www.spacewalkoffame.com; admission free; open 10am-5pm Mon-Sat, noon-5pm Sun) celebrates the achievements of the Mercury and Gemini programs with stately monoliths. At the base of the monuments, topped with the astrological symbols for Mercury and Gemini, are the bronzed handprints of the astronauts of those programs. The small museum features the handprints of various Apollo astronauts (a monument is in the works), models on loan from the KSC and other space relics that various astronauts have donated from their private collections. The park, open 24/7, is a great place to view a shuttle launch.

Places to Stay
Accommodations here aren't cheap for what you get, and prices rise astronomically during the week of a shuttle launch. There's a cluster of chain places around exit 79 (Cheney Hwy) off I-95, and a string of older hotels along Washington Ave (Hwy 1), some with great views of liftoff.

KOA Cape Kennedy Campground (☎ 321-269-7361, 800-848-4562; 4513 W Main St; sites with/without hookups $23/20, Kamping Kabins $30-40) is up in the town of Mims, just north of Titusville.

The Randolph Inn (☎ 321-269-5945; 3810 S Washington Ave; rooms nonlaunch/launch $64/99) is nicer than the average Washington Ave hotel, with a pool and great Continental breakfast.

Days Inn KSC (☎ 321-269-4480; ⓦ www.daysinn.com; 3755 Hwy 50; rooms nonlaunch/launch $59/149) is tidy and reliable, and offers a fitness center and laundry facilities.

Best Western Space Shuttle Inn (☎ 321-269-1000, 800-523-7654; ⓦ www.spaceshuttleinn.com; 3455 Cheney Hwy; rooms nonlaunch/launch $75/112) has typically pleasant rooms – and a few strange ones. For a little extra cash, you can stay in the Evergreen Rooms, with filtered drinking systems and custom air cleaners, or the Space Shuttle Fantasy Room, where you get to sleep in your very own orbiter.

Places to Eat
Sunrise Bread Company (☎ 321-268-1009; 2825 Garden St; open 6am-6pm Mon-Sat) has great coffee to wash down cinnamon buns, scones and other breakfast treats, as well as loaves of excellent bread.

S&S Middle East Bakery (☎ 321-269-0702; 1309 S Washington Ave; sandwiches $2-4; open 8am-7pm Mon-Sat) is great for vegetarians. Falafel, homemade hummus and excellent tabouli are just some of the good stuff in the deli case; try a spinach pie.

Kloiber's Cobbler Eatery (☎ 321-383-0689; 337 S Washington Ave; dishes $3-7; open 8am-4pm Mon, 8am-8pm Tues-Sat) has more substantial breakfasts and an excellent chicken-salad sandwich. Delicious fresh-fruit cobbler is made from scratch daily.

Dixie Crossroads (☎ 321-268-5000; 1475 Garden St; mains $9-18; open 11am-10pm daily), 2 miles east of exit 80 off I-95, is always packed with tourists and locals. The specialty is rock shrimp ($9 dozen, $12 two dozen), but all sorts of seafood and steak dishes are on the menu.

Entertainment
Titusville is more an abandoned blue-collar burg than a thriving beach town, and most

evening options involve cheap beer at dive bars. There are a few exceptions, however.

Riverdeck Lounge *(☎ 321-383-1288; 1829 Riverside Dr; open noon-2am Mon-Sat, 1pm-midnight Sun)* has pool tables, a pleasant outdoor patio and karaoke Monday and Tuesday, as well as other special events.

Shamrock & Thistle *(☎ 321-385-9611; 2035 Cheney Hwy; open 11am-2am Mon-Sat, 1pm-midnight Sun)* is your basic traditional Irish pub with 19 brews on tap, darts and pub grub like fish-and-chips ($6) to soak up all that Guinness. It has live music on 'special nights.'

Getting There & Around
If driving from Central Florida, take SR 50 or 528 (Beeline Expressway) East. Those taking I-95 to Titusville should get off at exit 79 or 80. **Greyhound** *(☎ 321-267-8760; 100 S Hopkins Ave)* serves Titusville.

If in Titusville and carless, **SCAT** *(☎ 321-633-1878; W www.ridescat.com; tickets $1)* is an inconvenient public bus system that serves the entire Space Coast (but not the Kennedy Space Center). Bus No 2 operates along Cheney Hwy, Washington Ave (US Hwy 1) throughout downtown and Garden St; buses run Monday to Friday and come infrequently – about every 1½ hours, sometimes longer.

COCOA VILLAGE & COCOA BEACH
Snuggled between Cape Canaveral and Patrick Air Force Base is the optimistically named city of Cocoa Beach. As *I Dream of Jeannie* fans may already suspect, this is basically a service town for NASA and the air force bases, albeit with a hard-packed sand beach filled with partiers and surfers.

Historic Cocoa Village, due west across the causeway, has upscale restaurants, shops and lots of historic buildings; pick up a brochure with a self-guided tour at the Chamber of Commerce.

You will find Cocoa Beach's **Chamber of Commerce** *(☎ 231-459-2200; 400 Fortenberry Rd; open 9am-5pm Mon-Fri)* on Merritt Island.

Cocoa Beach Pier
This festive pier is 800ft long and often features live music on weekends. Parking is $5, and fishing is $4/3/0.50 per adult/child/spectator. You can rent a rod and reel for $10, which includes pier access, and buy bait for $3. Restaurants and bars pack the first (free)

half of the pier, and the **Tiki Bar** at the very tip may be the finest spot in Cocoa Beach to watch a launch.

Beaches
Cocoa has three public beaches. **Shepard Park**, at the end of Hwy 580, is more family oriented, while **Cocoa Beach**, by the pier, is by far the busiest and caters to space tourists and the surf crowd, the stretch at the intersection of Minuteman Causeway and Hwy A1A, is geared toward adults, with a collection of cool bars and upscale restaurants abutting the sand.

Activities
Village Outfitters *(☎ 321-633-7245; W www.villageoutfitters.com; 113 Brevard Ave; open 10am-6pm Mon-Fri, 10am-4pm Sat)*, in Cocoa Village, runs half-day kayak tours (single/double kayak $30/45) to Merritt Island Refuge, Pine Island and elsewhere, including tours of wild beaches with awesome views of the shuttle launch. It also operates more challenging trips throughout the area.

Ron Jon's Watersports *(☎ 321-799-8840; 4151 N Atlantic Ave; open 8am-8pm daily)*, next to the larger Ron Jon Surf Shop in Cocoa Beach, rents just about anything water-related you'd want: fat-tired beach bikes ($15 daily), kayaks (singles/doubles $30/35), wetsuits ($10), oxygen tanks ($6) and other diving equipment, surfboards ($30) and much, much more.

Don't know how to surf? Contact **Surfguy's Surfing School** *(☎ 321-956-3268; W www.surfguyssurf.com)*, and they'll teach you. Private classes run $35 per hour, three or more people $25 each per hour. The school also offers four-day 'camps' for $130. The **Cocoa Beach Surfing School** *(☎ 321-868-1980; W www.cocoabeachsurfingschool.com)* is a little more expensive, but boasts members of the US national surfing team as instructors.

Places to Stay
Cocoa Beach attracts surfers during spring break and space junkies during launches, so expect higher prices at those times.

Jetty Park Campground *(☎ 321-783-7111; 400 E Jetty Rd; with/without hookups $26/19)*, in the nearby city of Cape Canaveral, has some of the best shuttle-launch views in the area.

Luna Sea *(☎ 321-783-0500; W www.lunaseacocoabeach.com; 3185 N Atlantic Ave; rooms $49-150)* has a very friendly staff, a pool and a continental breakfast.

Silver Sands Motel (☎ 321-783-2415; 225 N Atlantic Ave; rooms nonlaunch/launch $65/90) has clean rooms, friendly service and a beachfront location.

Fawlty Towers (☎ 321-784-3870; 100 E Cocoa Beach Causeway; rooms nonlaunch/launch $60/140) is garishly overdressed in Pepto-Bismol pink but has really nice rooms and a tropical-themed pool fronted by the Tiki Bar.

The Inn at Cocoa Beach (☎ 321-799-3460; W www.theinnatcocoabeach.com; 4300 Ocean Beach Blvd; rooms nonlaunch/launch $135/295) isn't the quaintest B&B in the world, but it does have onsite spa treatments and a great beachside location.

Places to Eat

Mama D's Deli (☎ 321-638-1338; 109 Brevard Ave; mains $3-6; open 8am-5pm Mon-Sat) does salads, sandwiches and big breakfasts with Italian flair. Have yours with a Torani fizz and top it off with the homemade tiramisu.

Crab Heaven (☎ 321-783-5001; 6910 N Atlantic Ave; open 11am-10pm Mon-Sat, 11am-9pm Sun) is technically in Cape Canaveral and worth the trip for crab lovers. Huge, wonderful fish sandwiches ($6) and crab soup ($4) are perfect for lighter appetites, but it's the all-you-can-eat crab specials ($25 blue crab, $28 snow crab) that are the real draw.

Heidelberg Restaurant (☎ 321-783-6806; 7 N Orlando Ave; mains $15-20; kitchen open 10am-10pm Tues-Sat, 5pm-10pm Sun) serves authentic German cuisine, including Jaegerbratten and Wienerschnitzel, along with German wines and great jazz nightly.

The **Black Tulip** (☎ 321-631-1133; 207 Brevard Ave; mains $13-24; open 11:30am-2:30pm daily, 5pm-9:30pm Mon-Sat), across the street, serves New American cuisine: veal Oscar and roast duck are recommended, as is the Sunday jazz brunch ($13).

Café Margaux (☎ 321-639-8343; 222 Brevard Ave; lunch $9-12, dinner $18-26; open 11am-3pm & 5pm-9pm daily) is a French gourmet restaurant. Lunch – try the curried scallops – is affordable. At dinner, the prices and selection double; servers recommend the artichoke Asiago pasta.

Entertainment

Apollo 13: The Comedy (☎ 800-888-8388; 8701 Astronaut Blvd), at the Radisson at the Port, in Cape Canaveral, is a long-running dinner theater that involves guitar-playing astronauts and audience participation. Oh dear.

Murdock's Bistro & Char Bar (☎ 321-633-0600; 600 Brevard Ave; open 11am-10pm Mon-Thur, 11am-midnight Sat & Sun) has an outdoor patio where you can drink, dine on catfish tacos and listen to some great music. On Wednesday, the Phat Cats play the blues, and there are live oldies on Thursday and big bands on Friday and Saturday.

Big Daddy Dave's (☎ 321-633-7653; 401 Delannoy Ave; open 5pm-2am Tues-Sat), next to Riverfront Park, is the premier jazz venue on the Space Coast. Get dressed up in your snazzy best and listen to tunes while you get started on that two-drink minimum.

Surfside Café (☎ 321-799-3566; 211 E Cocoa Beach Blvd; open 11am-2pm daily) is the quintessential beach bar, with Budweiser on tap, live music nightly and the occasional bikini contest or DJ competition.

Getting There & Around

Melbourne International Airport is about 18 miles away (see the Melbourne & Indialantic section later in this chapter) and has plenty of car rental companies. The Beeline Expressway (SR 528) is the most efficient way to reach Cocoa Beach and Cocoa Village by car from Orlando and other cities west of the Space Coast. If you're coming from the north or south, I-95 could be the best bet; take exit 75 if going this route, and then go east on SR 520 for about 10 miles. You can take **Greyhound** (☎ 321-636-6531; 302 Main St) to the Cocoa area, but there are no public bus stops near the station, so you'll need a cab to your next destination from there.

Getting around without a car in this area will be troublesome. **SCAT** (☎ 321-633-1878; W www.ridescat.com; ticket $1) serves Cocoa Beach and other Space Coast spots; see the useful website for details. Be aware that buses come infrequently.

MELBOURNE & INDIALANTIC

Melbourne and Indialantic make a good base for turtle watchers and more affluent surfers sick of battling the crowds at Cocoa Beach. For the latter, it's well located between the breaks at Patrick Air Force Base and Sebastian Inlet. Most of the Melbourne area's life is focused along the beach – on the east side of the Intracoastal Waterway – and in the towns of Melbourne Beach, Indialantic and Melbourne.

SPACE COAST

Information

The helpful **Melbourne Chamber of Commerce** (☎ 321-724-5400; ⓦ www.melpbchamber.org; 1005 E Hwy 192; open 9am-5pm Mon-Fri) has the usual pamphlets.

Things to See & Do

The **Historic Downtown Melbourne** area, along E New Haven Ave right behind the chamber of commerce, is a pleasant enough street lined with antique shops. Nearby is the **Crane Creek Manatee Sanctuary**, just two blocks west of the chamber of commerce, where you'll definitely see lots of river turtles and catfish and, if you're lucky, manatees. The excellent if small **Brevard Zoo** (☎ 321-254-9453; ⓦ www.brevardzoo.org; 8225 N Wickham Rd, Melbourne; adult/senior/child $7/6/5), remodeled largely by volunteer labor, focuses on Latin American jungles and has good exhibits on sloths, spider monkeys and jaguars. It also has a few Florida panthers, North America's rarest mammal. Kids will love the aviary, where they can feed exotic birds by hand.

The **Andretti Thrill Park** (☎ 321-956-6706; ⓦ www.andrettithrillpark.com; 3960 S Babcock St, Melbourne; admission $5, with all rides $22) is sure to keep kids who are bored with all that space stuff happy. It'll hold them over until you get to Orlando, anyway. Three go-cart tracks, bumper boats, laser tag and an 18-hole miniature golf course are just a few of the attractions.

Beach & Boardwalk

The area's main public beach and boardwalk, at the end of Hwy 192 in Indialantic, isn't the world's largest, but it's got great surfing and white sand speckled with sunbathers. There are a few restaurants and bars that cater to the locals – not too many tourists make it down this far.

The **Longboard House** (☎ 321-951-0730; ⓦ www.longboardhouse.com; 101 5th Ave; open 9am-9pm Mon-Sat, 9am-6pm Sun), in Indialantic, sells a huge selection of new and used surfboards and rents longboards for $25 per day, bodyboards for $10 per day. It also runs a **surfing information hotline** (☎ 321-953-0392).

The best breaks in the area (arguably, in Florida) are 18 miles south of Indialantic at Sebastian Inlet, which has strong currents and, on good days (as in, when storms brew in the Atlantic), 10ft breaks. In Indialantic, surf is good behind the Comfort Suites Hotel; at Patrick Air Force Base (to the north), good waves can generally be found behind the Officers' Club.

Places to Stay

Oceanside Motel (☎ 321-727-2723; 745 Hwy A1A, Indialantic; rooms $55) is a good deal, with clean rooms, a pool and giant sea turtles nesting outside from June to September.

Melbourne Harbor Suites (☎ 800-242-4251; 1207 E 1st St; rooms summer/winter $48/58), in the 'heart of Historic Downtown Melbourne,' is a great option, close to some excellent restaurants and the Crane Creek Manatee Sanctuary.

Windemere Inn by the Sea (☎ 321-728-9334; 800-224-6853; ⓦ www.windemereinn.com; 815 Hwy A1A, Indialantic; rooms $95-195) is a highly recommended oceanfront B&B with all the trimmings: country English antiques, Jacuzzis in some rooms, afternoon sherry and a full breakfast.

Melbourne Quality Suites Hotel (☎ 321-723-4222, 800-876-4222; ⓦ www.qualitysuites.com; 1665 N Hwy A1A; suites summer/winter $99/129) has very comfortable two-room oceanfront (yes, all of them) suites with balconies.

Places to Eat

Community Harvest Café (☎ 321-242-2398; 1405 Highland Ave, Melbourne; dishes $3-5; open 9am-7:30pm Mon-Fri, 9am-4pm Sat), next to the library and art museum, serves unusual vegetarian and vegan fare – try the pita pizzas or tempuna (tempeh with kelp salad) sandwich.

Oceanview Diner (☎ 321-723-2270; 1 5th Ave; dishes $3-7; open 24/7) serves basic diner food on a great outdoor patio overlooking the beach anytime – unless you're an Indialantic city official, in which case you've been permanently banned from the premises.

Pop's Casbah (☎ 321-723-9811; 2005 S Waverly Place, Melbourne; dishes $4-7; open 6am-2:30pm Sat-Wed, 6am-8:30pm Thur & Fri), in the historic downtown, serves food just like grandma's (assuming your grandmother is an outstanding Southern cook) in a cool, low-ceilinged dining room decorated with Highwaymen art. Breakfasts are huge, and the meat-and-three plates ($7) come with truly divine cornbread.

Cantina Dos Amigos (☎ 321-724-2183; 990 N Hwy A1A, Indialantic; mains $8-15; open 4pm-10pm Sun-Thur, 4pm-11pm Fri & Sat) has a breezy patio, more than 50 different kinds of tequila, and magnificent, authentic

Mexican food. Try the *pollo borracho* (sautéed chicken with ham) or vegetables Acapulco for a real treat.

Djon's (☎ 321-722-2737; 522 Ocean Ave, Melbourne; mains $16-40; open 5pm-10pm daily) is a wonderful place to be treated to a three-star, dress-up, gourmet dinner. Start with yummy seafood crepes ($9) and continue with delectable sea bass with mussels in lobster broth ($22), both *highly* recommended. Don't miss the dramatic bananas Foster flambé ($9) for dessert.

For a little nighttime fun, try **Meg O'Malley's** (☎ 321-952-5510; W www.megomalleys.com; 810 E New Haven Ave, Melbourne), which has 20 brews on tap, including its own Irish cider, and live music – usually Irish bands or local jazz and blues groups – every night at around 8pm. This place gets packed.

Getting There & Around

Melbourne International Airport (☎ 321-723-6227; W www.mlbair.com) is a growing airport served by Delta, Continental, Atlantic Southeast and Comair, as well as a handful of car rental companies. The airport is also served by SCAT (see below) bus No 21 daily, and the **Greyhound** (☎ 321-723-4329; 460 S Harbor) bus station is at the airport as well. To drive to Melbourne and Indialantic from west of the Space Coast, take the Beeline Expressway (SR 528) East to I-95 South, then take the US 192 exit. If coming from north or south, take I-95 to US 192.

SCAT (☎ 321-633-1878; W www.ridescat.com; ticket $1) is the Space Coast's rather inconvenient bus system. However, SCAT bus No 26 (every couple of hours, Monday to Friday) serves Indialantic and the beaches. There are a few buses that have routes in Melbourne. See the useful website for details on stops, route maps and schedules.

SEBASTIAN INLET STATE PARK

About 20 miles south of Indialantic on Hwy A1A is Sebastian Inlet, which is known for its fishing, surfing and camping opportunities. The park (☎ 321-984-4852; 9700 S Hwy A1A; pedestrian/car $3.25/1; open 8am-sunset daily), on a narrow stretch of the barrier island chain, attracts folks who love the ocean. There's great surfing, and you can snorkel or scuba dive the remains of Spanish galleons (and perhaps find a doubloon of your very own). Regular visitors also say that this is a great place for fishing or clam-digging your own dinner.

The Indian River and Atlantic Ocean also provide ample opportunities for boating. Visit the **Inlet Marina** (☎ 321-724-5424; 9502 S Hwy A1A; open 8am-6pm daily) to rent canoes (half/full day $21/30), kayaks ($25/35 single, $29/39 double), catamaran sailboats ($75/119) or even a 10-passenger pontoon boat ($139/179). The concession stand also runs ranger-led, two-hour boat tours at 2pm daily (adult/child $16/10) and serves cheap meals ($3 to $6).

There's a **campground** (9700 S Hwy A1A; sites with/without hookups $24/19) right on the water. To make reservations call ☎ 800-326-3521 or visit W www.reserveusa.com.

North of Orlando

You don't have to travel far north before you'll say to yourself, 'We're not in Orlando anymore.' Orlando is Orlando; Florida is Florida – and just an hour or so from the city you can see land unblemished by flashy signs, a national forest, spiritualist colony, natural springs and lots more. Daytona Beach can be party central if you show up at the right time of year, and quaint and historic St Augustine, farther north, makes an excellent day or overnight trip.

If you're in search of the *real* Central Florida, with gingerbread Victorian townships populated with down-to-earth folks just a generation removed from subsistence farming, surrounded by palmetto wilderness where manatees and gators swim wild through clear, natural springs, you've found it. Saddle up your horse, car or bicycle and get ready for a little adventure, Central Florida style.

BLUE SPRING STATE PARK

Blue Spring State Park (☎ 386-775-3663; *2100 French Ave; pedestrian $1, car with 1/2-8 people $2/4; open 8am-sunset*) is the best place in the state to see manatees in their natural habitat. Visit between November and March, when the St John's River gets too cold and these peaceful mammals seek the relative warmth of Blue Spring's 72°F spring. During the peak season, an average of 25 to 50 manatees swim here daily. Swimming is prohibited when manatees are present, which is usually in the morning. There is a wheelchair-accessible walkway that leads from the parking lot to concessions and then along the springs for manatee viewing. For more information on these endangered creatures see the boxed text 'Mad about Manatees' in the Facts about Central Florida chapter.

Even if you're not here during manatee season, there are plenty of reasons to come by. This is one of the most singularly beautiful swimming holes in Florida. For certified divers (registration $5.33) there's a real treat: you can make your way underwater through the narrow fissure at the source of the spring, past railroad tracks, abandoned car parts and fossils, to 'cork rock,' a boulder suspended in the upwelling water.

The **concessions office** (☎ 386-775-6888; *open 9am-5pm Mon-Fri, 8am-5pm Sat & Sun, rentals closes 4:30pm daily*) rents snorkels

Highlights

- Seeing a manatee and her pup in the wild at Blue Spring State Park
- Peering into your future with one of the mediums in Cassadaga, a community of psychics
- Feeding the fish from a glass-bottom boat at Silver Springs, in Ocala
- Getting to the heart of Florida's history with a side trip to St Augustine, the USA's first European settlement
- Checking out the 31° bank at Daytona International Speedway, then driving on the hard-packed sands of the original track, Daytona Beach itself

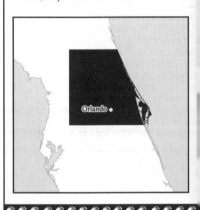

and masks, fins, volleyballs and innertubes (first hour/extra hours/per day $4/2/10) and canoes (3-person max $10/5/28). Manatee souvenirs and hot junk food such as burgers, hot dogs and pizza are also on offer at concessions ($2 to $3.50), and there are regular manatee programs (1:30pm, 2:30pm, 3:30pm Monday to Friday, 11am Saturday and Sunday), which consist of a 15-minute tear-jerking film about the plight of the mammal, followed by a question-and-answer session with a park ranger.

If you'd rather not paddle, **St John's River Cruises** (☎ 386-917-0724, 407-330-1612; W *www.sjrivercruises.com; adult/seniors 60+/child 3-12 yrs $16/14/10*) offers two-hour nature cruises through the park. The tours depart

NORTH OF ORLANDO

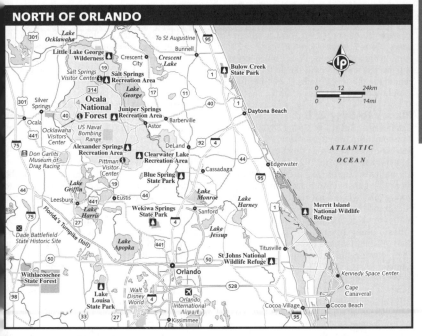

at 10am and 1pm daily from May to December and at 3:30pm only January to April.

There's also **camping** *(with/without hookups $17/15, cabins for 4/5/6 people $56/62/68)* in the developed campground. Primitive **campsites** *(adult/youth under 17 $3/2)* are at the end of a scenic 4-mile hike into the wilderness. You can make reservations up to a year in advance; the earlier the better.

The park is off E French Ave at the northern end of Orange City. To get there, take I-4 to exit 114 and follow the signs.

CASSADAGA

About 35 miles north of Orlando, on the I-4, this registered historic district is home to the Cassadaga (pronounced kassuh-**day**-guh) Spiritualist Camp, established in 1884 to further research into our elusive sixth sense. The camp houses a group of about 25 spiritualist-mediums who live and work here. The church, the **Southern Cassadaga Spiritualist Camp Meeting Association** *(SCSCMA;* ☎ *904-228-3171)*, believes in infinite intelligence, everlasting life on many planes of existence and the precepts of prophecy and healing.

For what it's worth, these folks genuinely believe in what they are doing. They don't

practice witchcraft or black magic; they don't condone hypnotism; and they don't call themselves psychics but rather mediums.

There's not much to see in town, and the main attraction is having your fortune told. SCSCMA-certified mediums do not use tarot or other tools to do their readings; while they aren't morally opposed to such things, they believe that cards and crystal balls tend to block or channel energy rather than allowing it to flow naturally.

There are dozens of tarot card readers in town, however, who will be more than happy to tell your future if you'll cross their palms with silver (usually about $50 for 30 minutes).

Orientation & Information

There's no public transportation to Cassadaga. By car, take I-4 to exit 54, head west, go north on County Rd (CR) 4101 for a quarter mile, then turn right onto CR 4139.

The camp is mainly south of CR 4139, bordered roughly by Horseshoe Park to the west, Lake St to the south and Marion St to the east.

You can arrange a reading in advance through the Cassadaga Hotel (see Places to Stay & Eat following), but there are plenty of walk-in places along CR 4139.

For more information visit the **Cassadaga Camp Bookstore** (☎ 386-228-2880; w www .cassadaga.org; cnr Steven St & Cassadaga Rd; open 10am-5:30pm Mon-Sat, noon-5:30pm Sun), which sells New Age books, crystals and incense and serves as the de facto visitors center for the town, with a community bulletin board and informative staff.

Places to Stay & Eat

Cassadaga Hotel (☎ 386-228-2323; 355 Cassadaga Rd; rooms Sun-Thur $50, Fri & Sat $60) is on the site of a convalescence home that burned down in 1925, killing most of the patients. So, as you'd expect, there are plenty of ghosts: Sarah and Caitlin are two young girls who enjoy playing with visiting children; Henry, who has a flair for the dramatic, tends to wander around in long dark robes looking mysterious; and Mary, who died of a heart attack, likes to sit in the green chair outside the gift shop and greet early risers.

Whether or not you're sensitive to these things, you will feel a bit creeped out – the hallways definitely have a *Shining* feel to them. The hotel offers **Spirit Tours** (adult/child $10/5; 7:30pm Fri, 3pm & 7:30pm Sat), so you can judge for yourself.

The hotel also hosts about ten **psychics and tarot card readers**, and you can make an appointment through the hotel reservations number. The cost is $50 for 30 minutes, and it's considered gracious to tip. There's also an on-site restaurant, **Lost in Time Café** (dishes $5-8; open 11am-3pm Mon-Fri, 11am-5pm Sat & Sun) that serves light lunches, as well as your continental breakfast if you stay overnight – but you'll be much happier if you self-cater at the grocery store.

Old Cassadaga Grocery (☎ 386-228-3797; 1083 Stevens St; dishes $3-6; open 11:05am-5pm Sun-Thur, 11:05am-7pm Fri & Sat), across the street, is the other place to eat in town. It's refreshingly Enya-free and serves decent sandwiches and vegetarian chili.

OCALA
pop 45,943

Ocala, in a region famed for its beautiful scenery and plethora of natural springs, has been continuously occupied for at least 4000 years, first by Timucuan Indians, who greeted explorer Hernando de Soto in the village of Ocali, probably located just east of the current city center. Fort King was erected here in 1827 as the base of military operations in the Seminole War, and in 1846 the town was incorporated as the seat of Marion County.

Today, this often overlooked city has plenty to offer: a couple of fine museums and a unique theme park, a thriving and compact downtown, and the best backyard in Florida – Ocala National Forest.

Orientation & Information

Ocala's main drag, which connects it with the neighboring resort town of Silver Springs and Ocala National Forest, both due east, is Silver Springs Blvd (Hwy 40). It's bisected by Pine Ave (Hwy 441), which runs between Gainesville to the north and Orlando to the south. The two roads divide addresses into north, south, east and west, and the downtown square is centered at their crossroads.

The **Chamber of Commerce** (☎ 352-629-8051; w www.ocalacc.com; 110 E Silver Springs Blvd; open 9am-5pm Mon-Fri) has useful free maps and lots of pamphlets, including a self-guided tour to the nearby Tuscawilla Historic District.

There's a **Bank of America** (☎ 352-620-1220; 35 SE 1st Ave) right downtown.

Silver Springs

Built around seven natural springs and the resultant stunningly clear Silver River, this unusual park attraction (☎ 352-236-2121, 800-234-7458; 5656 E Silver Springs Blvd; adult/child $32/23; open 9am-5:30pm daily) is allegedly where glass-bottomed boats were invented in 1878. If that's not enough of a claim, try this one: *Tarzan* movies and portions of *The Abyss* were shot here as well.

There aren't really any thrill rides here, as this park was built to show off the Florida wilderness – the **glass-bottom boat ride** is spectacular. As you slowly cruise over the eel grass, you'll pass six small spring formations before the grand finale: floating over Mammoth Spring, the world's largest artesian limestone spring.

There are other tours as well, including the **Lost River Voyage**, a boat ride through dense jungle; **Jeep Safari**, a trailer ride through 35 acres of African and Asian animals; Florida panther exhibits; and **Gator Lagoon**, with some very large alligators. There are also wildlife shows featuring birds, snakes, bears and creepy-crawlies like hissing cockroaches.

Twin Oaks Mansion is a concert venue that features both kinds of music: country *and* western. Concerts are included with the price of admission. Parking is an extra $5.

Daytona Beach

Main St during Bike Week, Daytona Beach

Daytona USA

Daytona International Speedway

Castillo de San Marcos, St Augustine

Reenactors, Castillo de San Marcos, St Augustine

Manatees

Wild Waters Water Park
Next door to Silver Springs, this good-sized water park (☎ 352-236-2121; W www.wild waterspark.com; 5656 E Silver Springs Blvd; adult/child $25/22; open 9am-5:30pm daily) has plenty to keep you cool. There are five huge water slides, a couple of smaller ones for little kids, a wave pool and a few small thrill rides. You can get a combination ticket (adult/child $35/26) to both Silver Springs and Wild Waters.

Appleton Museum of Art
Featuring a surprisingly impressive collection of fine art, the Appleton Museum of Art (☎ 352-236-7100; W www.appletonmuseum .org; 4333 NE Silver Springs Blvd; adult/child $12/5; open 10am-6pm daily) is worth a stop. In an imposing edifice between Ocala and Silver Springs, curators rotate permanent collections of American and European art (think Van Gogh, Matisse, Cezanne) with even better exhibits featuring Middle Eastern, North African and pre-Columbian American art and artefacts. The museum also offers free lectures and films throughout the year (with the cost of admission).

Don Garlits Museum of Drag Racing
This excellent automotive attraction (☎ 352-245-8661; W www.garlits.com; 13700 SW 16th Ave; adult/child $12/3; open 9am-5pm daily) features an absolutely outstanding collection of race cars, including the seminal dragster Swamp Rat I, 'Big Daddy' Don Garlits' own prize-winning speedster. The cluttered and comprehensive array of trophies and mementos from the sport's 50-year history is unparalleled. Also on-site is the Drag Racing Hall of Fame, a shrine to the fastest men and women around.

Garlits, a legend who designed and raced some of the sport's most impressive pieces of machinery, and his wife Pat, a trophy-winning racer herself, run this museum. Stock cars, long-nosed top fuel rides, and antique classics and customs, mostly pre-WWII Fords, are displayed alongside involved explanations of how they were bored and blown for maximum horsepower. Bonus: you may even get to meet Don's mom, who just hates the fact that her son has started hitting the raceways again in recent years.

The museum is located about 15 miles south of downtown Ocala on I-75; take exit 67 (CR 484) and follow the signs.

Organized Tours
Ocala Carriage & Tours (☎ 352-867-8717, 877-996-2252; W www.ocalacarriage.com) offers tours in carriages pulled by Clydesdales, visiting horse farms throughout the countryside, for $95 per carriage (four to six people). It also offers tours of Ocala's historic districts on weekends, by reservation only, for $50.

Many Marion County horse farms open their gates for private tours, some offering trail rides, others just letting you take a look at the more than 40 breeds of horses raised here. Try Double Diamond (☎ 352-237-3834), Paso Fino (☎ 352-867-5305; W www.paso beat.com/farms/youngs) or Ocala Foxtrotter Ranch (☎ 352-347-5551; W www.ocalafox trotter.com).

Places to Stay
There's a cluster of cheap lodgings just south of downtown Ocala on Hwy 441 (S Pine Ave) and more hotels within walking distance of Silver Springs. Camping opportunities in Ocala National Forest (see later in this chapter) are endless. Note that even out here, rooms are hard to come by during Bike Week (early March) and the Daytona 500 (February).

Sun Plaza (☎ 352-236-2343; W www.sun plazamotel.com; 5461 E Silver Springs Blvd; rooms $55-70) boasts that this is where country artists performing at nearby Silver Springs stay. It's got basic rooms with refrigerators and microwaves.

The Ritz Historic Inn (☎ 352-671-9300, 888-382-9390; W www.ritzhistoricinn.com; 1205 E Silver Springs Rd; rooms $70-125), in a striking Spanish colonial building, has theme rooms (African safari, floral gardens) arranged around gardens and a courtyard. There's also an on-site restaurant and bar.

Seven Sisters Inn B&B (☎ 352-867-1170; W www.7sistersinn.com; 820 SE Fort King St; rooms $119-269), in a very large, very pink Victorian mansion, has beautiful rooms, expansive flower gardens and gourmet candlelight breakfasts.

Places to Eat
The restaurant scene in Ocala runs primarily to steakhouses, greasy buffets and fast food, but there are some exceptions.

The Brass Rooster (☎ 352-402-0097; 30 S Magnolia St; dishes $3-6; open 8am-4pm Mon-Thur, 8am-9pm Fri, 11am-3pm Sat) is a classic soda fountain and café with salads, sandwiches and ice cream floats, right on the square downtown.

El Ranchito Mexican Restaurant (☎ 352-622-4808; 1655 S Pine Ave; dishes $6-15; open 11am-10pm Mon-Fri, noon-10pm Sat & Sun) serves huge portions of great Mexican grub, and there's a mariachi band on Wednesday night.

Tea with Lee (☎ 352-867-5530; 944 E Silver Springs Blvd; prices & hrs by arrangement) is different. Lee serves high teas with spectacular trimmings, including the single most beautiful pastry you will ever see (it's called a Napoleon, but that's like calling Don Garlits a commuter), in a frilly dining room decked out with about fifty shimmering portraits of Jesus.

Felix's Restaurant (☎ 352-629-0339; 917 E Silver Springs Blvd; lunch $7-13, dinner $12-24; open 11am-2:30pm Tues-Fri, 4:30pm-10pm Tues-Sat) has a beautiful, dark-wood dining room perfect for impressing your prom date. It's gourmet Southern cuisine, and at dinner you can order two 'petite entrées,' exactly half of a regular entrée, if you can't decide on just one.

Entertainment

The square in downtown Ocala has half a dozen different bars and clubs within easy hopping distance of one another.

O'Malley's Alley (☎ 352-690-2262; 24 S Magnolia Ave) is your basic Irish pub, with Guinness on tap and live music on weekends.

Harry's Seafood Bar & Grill (☎ 352-840-0900; W www.hookedonharrys.com; 24 SE 1st Ave) has a great happy hour.

OCALA NATIONAL FOREST

One of Florida's most important natural treasures is the 400,000-acre Ocala National Forest, a confederation of national, state and locally administered wilderness areas that work with private landowners to preserve and manage one of the most incredible ecosystems in the USA. There are 18 developed campgrounds, 219 miles of trails, 600 lakes (30 open for boating), and countless opportunities for biking, horse riding, canoeing, birdwatching or just meditating on how great it is that the government got here before the theme parks did.

Visitors unfamiliar with the concept of a national forest, as opposed to a national park, should be aware that this is a very different setup from, say, the Everglades. There's no single admission fee and no one number to call and reserve campsites. Some areas of the forest are extremely well developed, with

paved roads and easy-to-follow trails, while others may only be accessible by dirt roads or blazed trails. And you'll find lots of things here you won't see in a national park: logging trucks, biker bars, school buses, restaurants, car-repair shops, and signs that say 'Private Property.' You'll also find dozens of natural springs, several very different biomes – from sand pine scrub to palmetto wilderness to subtropical forest – and more species of endangered flora and fauna than you could take in over a two-week stay.

Orientation & Information

Two highways cross the park: Hwy 19 runs north–south and Hwy 40 runs east–west. You can pick up free maps at any of the visitors centers, or order them through **Ocklawaha Visitor Center** (3199 NE Hwy 315, Silver Springs, FL 34488). Topographical maps, hiking guides, wildlife guides and other books are also available at any of the visitors centers.

Of the many trails crisscrossing the park, the most popular are the 66-mile Florida National Scenic Trail (orange blazes), the 22-mile Paisley Woods Bicycle Trail (yellow blazes; off-road bikes highly recommended), and the 7-mile St Francis Trail (blue blazes), which leads to the abandoned 1880s town of St Francis. During hunting season (November to January), hikers should wear a bright orange vest or hat. Seriously. And if you're planning to do much trekking into the forest's vast interior, invest in a topographical map; there's a US naval bombing range here, too, and it just takes one little missile to ruin your whole vacation.

The following three visitors centers are open from 8am to 5pm daily:

Ocklawaha Visitor Center (☎ 352-236-0288; 3199 NE Hwy 315) is located in the park. It's your first stop if coming from Ocala and Silver Springs.

Pittman Visitor Center (☎ 352-669-7495; 45621 State Rd 19) is on the major throughway from Orlando and Mt Dora.

Salt Springs Visitor Center (☎ 352-685-3070; 14100 N Hwy 19), in Salt Springs, is accessible from Jacksonville and Palatka.

Rangers serve most of the forest, and all campgrounds have volunteers (usually chatty retirees) who live on-site year-round and are great sources of information. Sites at developed campgrounds cost between $4 and $25 per night, and day-use areas are generally open from 8am to 8pm daily. Note that the areas listed are just a few of the many here;

ick up a free park guide at the visitors cen-
er for many other camping, hiking, swim-
ning and wildlife-watching opportunities.

uniper Springs Recreation Area
This is the forest's most popular and easily ac-
essible area (☎ 352-625-3147; admission $3,
ampsites $13-15; open 8am-8pm daily), first
leveloped in the mid-1930s. Concessions sell
roceries and firewood and rent kayaks and
anoes ($20 per day) for making the 7-mile
un down Juniper Creek; there's a pick-up and
eturn shuttle at the bottom, which is free if
ou rent a canoe and $5 per person round-trip
f you don't. This area also has the most com-
rehensive wheelchair access in the forest.

The main attractions are two of the most
eautiful springs around: Juniper Spring,
vhere swimming is permitted, and Fern
Hammock Spring, which is the beginning of
an unbelievably lovely little nature trail. You
an also pick up the Florida National Scenic
Trail here.

Salt Springs Recreation Area
Rumored to have curative powers and home
o an interesting array of wildlife, Salt Springs
☎ 352-685-2048; admission $3; campsites
with/without hookups $17/13; open 8am-
8pm daily) is home to numerous black bears
and alligators, and is a favorite with the recreational vehicle (RV) set. There's a 2-mile nature trail, but the real attraction here is that, in
addition to canoes ($28 per day), you can rent
pontoon boats ($110 per day) and powerboats
($45 per day), perfect for making mischief on
enormous Lake Kerr.

Alexander Springs Recreation Area
This beautiful region (☎ 352-669-3522; admission $3, campsites $15; open 8am-8pm
daily) has one of the last untouched subtropical forests left in Florida, home to several endangered species. The area has suffered more
than the rest of the park during the drought of
the past several years. Still, the stunning freshwater spring attracts wildlife, swimmers,
scuba divers (extra $5 fee) and sunbathers, and
there's a 1.1-mile nature trail that accesses the
Florida National Scenic Trail and Paisley
Woods Bicycle Trail. Renting a canoe ($10 for
two hours, $26 per day) is an excellent idea.

Lake Eaton Recreation Area
Accessible by a well-maintained dirt road,
this isolated area (admission $2, campsites
$6-8; open 6am-10pm daily) has the excel-
lent Lake Eaton sinkhole, which is 80ft deep
and about 450ft in diameter. A 2.2-mile in-
terpretive walking trail leads past it, a boardwalk runs around it, and a staircase leads
down into it. Lake Eaton, nearby, doesn't rent
boats but does have a launch.

Clearwater Lake Recreation Area
Another relatively isolated area (☎ 352-669-
0078; admission $3, campsites $15; open
8am-8pm daily), this lovely little lake marks
the southern terminus of the Florida National
Scenic, Paisley Woods Bicycle and St Francis Trails. There's a 1-mile trail around the
lake, which you can also enjoy in a rental
canoe ($20 per day).

Getting There & Away
The only way for nonathletes to get around the
forest is by car. All public roads are well maintained; even dirt roads are fine for 2WD cars.
However, if you get lost, you may find yourself
on private dirt roads, which are not as firmly
packed: If the sand looks soft, don't stop, OK?

There are several different entries to the
park, all convenient to different urban areas.
From Orlando, take Hwy 441 north to the
Eustis turnoff and continue north on Hwy 19
(about 40 miles); from Daytona, take Hwy
92 west to DeLand, then head north on Hwy
17 to Barberville and west on State Route
(SR) 40 for about 30 miles; from Ocala, take
Silver Springs Blvd due west about 5 miles
to the forest's main entry.

DAYTONA BEACH
pop 65,000
Daytona's early history is typical of Florida:
Timucuan Indians had the run of the place
until the late 18th century, when Europeans
settlers moved in. Henry Flagler built a railroad, Matthias Day (hence Daytona) built a
hotel, and the city got a few tourists, though
not as many as St Augustine. Then in 1902
Daytona had a high-speed date with destiny.

Racecar drivers Ransom Olds and Alexander Winston realized that the unusually hard-
packed sands of Daytona Beach were good
for more than just sunbathing. They waged a
high-profile race along the water to prove it,
reaching an unheard-of 57mph. Suddenly, it
all became clear: God and Mother Nature had
created this beach for racing, an epiphany that
Daytona's public-relations machinery trum-
peted in every national forum they could find.

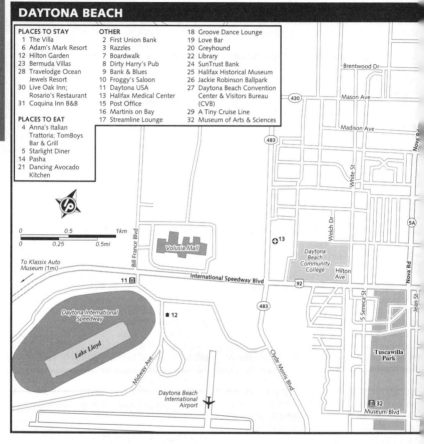

DAYTONA BEACH

PLACES TO STAY
1 The Villa
6 Adam's Mark Resort
12 Hilton Garden
23 Bermuda Villas
28 Travelodge Ocean
   Jewels Resort
30 Live Oak Inn;
   Rosario's Restaurant
31 Coquina Inn B&B

PLACES TO EAT
4 Anna's Italian
   Trattoria; TomBoys
   Bar & Grill
5 Starlight Diner
14 Pasha
21 Dancing Avocado
   Kitchen

OTHER
2 First Union Bank
3 Razzles
7 Boardwalk
8 Dirty Harry's Pub
9 Bank & Blues
10 Froggy's Saloon
11 Daytona USA
13 Halifax Medical Center
15 Post Office
16 Martinis on Bay
17 Streamline Lounge

18 Groove Dance Lounge
19 Love Bar
20 Greyhound
22 Library
24 SunTrust Bank
25 Halifax Historical Museum
26 Jackie Robinson Ballpark
27 Daytona Beach Convention
   Center & Visitors Bureau
   (CVB)
29 A Tiny Cruise Line
32 Museum of Arts & Sciences

The Florida East Coast Automobile Association was founded in 1903, the Winter Speed Carnival (predecessor to today's Daytona 500) began in 1904, and for the next 30 years Daytona Beach was where speed records were made and smashed.

Stock-car racing came into vogue during the late 1930s, and Race Weeks packed the beaches with fans. On December 14, 1947, at the Streamline Hotel, Bill France Sr founded National Association for Stock Car Auto Racing (Nascar) with the then-unbelievable statement, 'I believe stock-car racing can become a nationally recognized sport.' Civic leaders felt that this was a fine dream, and in 1959 they opened the Daytona Speedway.

Today, Daytona Beach thrives on racing- and party-based tourism. It has one of the last Atlantic Coast spring breaks (arrests, hookers, drunk kids, fire engines), and during Bike Week the town goes absolutely insane as hordes of Harleys – and their remarkably well-behaved owners – roar into town. But the heart and soul of Daytona remain committed to the pursuit of one thing: speed.

Orientation

Daytona lies near the intersection of I-95 and I-4 and consists of both a mainland area and a barrier island, which are separated by the Halifax River. The main east–west drag, International Speedway Blvd (US Hwy 92) connects the beaches with the Daytona Speedway, Daytona International Airport and I-95.

I-95 is the quickest way to Jacksonville (about 70 miles) and Miami (200 miles), though Hwy A1A and US Hwy 1 are more scenic. Beville Rd, an east–west thoroughfare

DAYTONA BEACH

To Rumors (0.25mi)

To St Augustine (53mi)
& Jacksonville (95mi)

Nova Rd

Riverside Dr

Riverview Blvd

A1A

2nd St

Glenview Blvd

N Halifax Ave

Seabreeze
Bridge

Mason Ave

Seabreeze Blvd

N Atlantic Ave

Ridgewood Ave N

Oakridge Blvd

Madison Ave

Madison Ave

Ballough Rd

Pier

Halifax River

Ora St

Earl St

North St

Fairview Ave

N Beach St

Auditorium Blvd

Main St Bridge

Main St

S Wild Olive Ave

Harvey Ave

S Ocean Ave

Main St
Pier

George W Engram Blvd

Manatee
Island
Park

Dr Mary Bethune Blvd

Second Ave

Carlton Blank
Bridge

15

16

Bay St

18

19

Intl Speedway Blvd

17

Vermont Ave

Goodall Ave

14 International Speedway Blvd

20

21

City Island
Recreation
Area

22

Lenox Ave

Peninsula Ave

Grandview Ave

Revilo Blvd

23

ATLANTIC OCEAN

S Keech St

S Adams St

Lockhart St

Magnolia Ave

E Magnolia Ave

24

25

26

Memorial
Bridge

Eastwood Ln

A1A

Orange Ave

27

Silver Beach Ave

28

Loomis Ave

S Segrave St

Ridgewood Ave

Palmetto Ave

S Beach St

Basin St

Hillside Ave

S Atlantic Ave

29

Cedar St

31 30

South St

To Aunt Catfish's
on the River (5.4mi)
& Space Coast (47mi)

To Little Chapel by the Sea (8.6mi)
Dream Inn (9mi), Lighthouse Landing (15mi) &
Ponce de León Inlet Lighthouse Museum (15.3mi)

south of Daytona proper, becomes I-4 after crossing I-95; it's the fastest route south to Orlando and Tampa.

The main north–south road on the barrier island is Atlantic Ave (Hwy A1A), while US Hwy 1, on the mainland, is called Ridgewood Ave. Beach St runs parallel and is the main north–south road through downtown. Main St is the north–south divider. Mason Ave, Main St, International Speedway Blvd and Orange Ave, as well as Dunlawton Ave to the south, all have bridges connecting the mainland with the beaches.

Parking is free and easy in most places, but watch out for meter agents downtown – use store-provided lots when you can. During major events, the speed limits in this speed capital are steady-as-she-goes or she-goes-to-jail.

Information

The **Daytona Beach Convention Center & Visitors Bureau** (CVB; ☎ 386-255-0415, 800-544-0415; W www.daytonabeach.com; 126 E Orange Ave; open 9am-5pm Mon-Fri) is excellent. There's another visitors center at the Daytona International Speedway.

If your wallet's feeling light, head to **SunTrust Bank** (☎ 386-258-2306; 120 S Ridgewood Ave) or **First Union Bank** (☎ 386-323-1475; 441 Seabreeze Blvd). The **post office** (220 N Beach St) is convenient to downtown.

Daytona International Speedway & Daytona USA

The most famous raceway in the USA, **Daytona International Speedway** (☎ 386-947-6782, box office ☎ 386-253-7223; W www.daytonaintlspeedway.com) is a pilgrimage-worthy

Special Events

When planning your trip to Daytona, keep in mind that several large, annual events can quadruple your costs, even if you don't participate. Of course, they can also double your fun.

Speed Weeks (February) With the Rolex 24 Hour Race and Daytona 500, there's a lot of partying to be done.
Bike Week (early March) Ten days of motorcycle-racing, leather-wearing, breast-baring fun.
Spring Break (March) College kids on a mission to drink more than they have ever drunk before. Some will succeed, others will fail. All will wake up confused and dehydrated.
Black College Reunion (second week in April) See spring break above.
Easter & Memorial Day Even more of the same for a broader age group.
Pepsi 400 Meet (4th of July weekend) Nascar fans fly the checkered flag.
Biketoberfest (mid-October) Raise a glass because it's finally cool enough (by Florida standards) to wear leather again!
Turkey Run (late November) The custom car crowd enjoys a weekend in the sun.
World Karting Racing (last week in December) What else are you going to do until New Year's Eve?

destination for auto aficionados – and worth seeing even if you're not. Event tickets (see the boxed text 'Special Events' for a partial list of events) range from $30 to $220, though scalpers get three times that for the big races. If nothing's on, the complex is designed to make you think that you need to enter the excellent but pricey **Daytona USA** (☎ 386-947-6800; Ⓦ www.daytonausa.com; adult/child $20/14; open 9am-7pm daily) just to see the track. This is an illusion. Just go through the gift shop, located to the right of the ticket counter, and wander into the grandstands for free.

If you're a car person, however, you'll happily fork over the cash to see Daytona USA, a very flashy shrine to a very flashy sport. Stock cars driven by Nascar's biggest names are the stars of the show, but there's much, much more. See how sneaky teams try to circumvent Winston Cup weight regulations with lead goggles and helmets (every ounce counts in Nascar). Try to change a tire in 16 seconds at the **Pit-Stop Challenge** or drive your own virtual vehicle in **Acceleration Alley**. It's well worth the extra $7 to tour the Speedway and see the 31° bank negotiated three cars wide by the best drivers in the nation.

If you're so inspired, you could even try the **Richard Petty Experience** (☎ 800-237-3889; Ⓦ www.1800bepetty.com), where you'll drive a 600-horsepower Winston Cup–style car ($350 to $2500, depending on the program) or ride shotgun for only $106, including admission to Daytona USA. There's another one of these outlets at Walt Disney World (see that chapter).

Klassix Auto Museum
This wonderful museum (☎ 386-252-0940; Ⓦ www.klassixauto.com; 2909 W International Speedway Blvd; adult/child $9/4; open 9am-6pm daily), just west of the Speedway, has a rotating collection of classic cars with an emphasis on mouthwatering muscle, including every Corvette from 1953 to 1994 (and an explanation of why there was no '83 'Vette).

The tastiest treat, however, is the selection of masterworks by (arguably) the greatest automotive artisan of all time, George Barris. They include the Batmobile, Drag-u-la, Greased Lightning and the Flintstones car, as well as a few of his seamlessly chopped and dropped Mercs and a hybrid that splits into two motorcycles. If you're not an automobile enthusiast, understand that this is comparable to walking into a small-town museum and finding a handful of Louvre-quality Leonardo da Vincis.

Other delectables include vintage Winston Cup pace cars, the Blues Brother's Crown Victoria and a Harley Davidson powered by a Chevy 350 small block engine. If you're only going to see one car museum while you're here, this one is better than Daytona USA (though you should still check out the Speedway itself).

Museum of Arts & Sciences
You normally don't think of Daytona as a cultural center, but this museum (☎ 386-255-0285; 1040 Museum Blvd; adult/student or child $7/2; open 9am-4pm Tues-Fri, noon-5pm Sat & Sun), off Nova Rd, is an incredible surprise.

The museum is heavy on arts: the **Cuban Museum** alone, with an amazing variety of paintings by Cuban artists, is worth the entry fee, and there are separate galleries exhibiting stunning artefacts from Africa and China, as well as the **Dow Gallery of American Art**, with noteworthy paintings and examples of antique furniture and silver.

Root Hall, sponsored by the family that bottled Coca-Cola from 1916 to 1982, has a surreal assortment of relics from the soda's history, from ancient vending machines to 1920s delivery vans. Oh, and this is Daytona, where no museum would be complete without autos: experimental speedsters have been restored to perfection.

The **Science Center** has a giant sloth skeleton unearthed only a few miles from here, as well as other exhibits on Florida's natural history. Its 96-seat **planetarium** *(admission $3; programs 2pm Tues-Fri)* does astronomy pre-sentations and also offers free films every Saturday.

The Beach & Boardwalk

Beautiful **Daytona Beach** *(☎ 386-239-7873)* is great for sunbathing, swimming, spring breaking and a host of other outdoor activities, but that's not what made this 18-mile stretch of sand world famous. The beach itself was once the raceway where, in 1935, Sir Malcolm Campbell reached a blistering 276mph. Today, *you* can drive these hallowed sands for $5, or $3 after 3pm, though the (strictly enforced) top speed is only 10mph. Oh well. There are six well-marked entries onto the beach between Granada Blvd and Beach St, but the area between Seabreeze Blvd and International Speedway Blvd is traffic-free.

If you don't have a car you can rent all-terrain vehicles (ATVs), some painted like

Nascar

To understand the American South, one must first understand stock-car racing (well, that and college football, fried okra and rocking chairs, but you've got to start somewhere). The National Association for Stock Car Auto Racing (Nascar) was founded in Daytona Beach back in 1947, but that's not where this story begins.

During Prohibition in the 1920's, moonshine (a potent corn liquor) production was an important segment of the rural Southern economy, and young people with cars fast enough to outrun local cops handled distribution. On their off-time, they tried to outrun each other. When alcohol was relegalized the races continued, and the most glamorous venue was the Beach St track in Daytona. There, an entrepreneurial driver named Bill France began promoting 'Race Weeks,' which brought fans to Daytona by the thousands.

The popularity of the sport spread like wildfire, though it was often dismissed by other automotive enthusiasts as upstart rednecks racing cars that any mechanic could build in their own garage. France knew better, however, and organized Nascar with the aim of transforming his obsession into a world-class sport. He succeeded beyond his wildest dreams.

Today, despite the acronym, these cars aren't even close to stock. Beneath the myriad product endorsements covering each colorful contender, the bodies are still recognizably Mustangs and Monte Carlos, but the similarity ends there. Each auto (teams typically have several) is stripped to the frame, with only the required safety and speed equipment remaining. Each conforms to strict regulations that guarantee the driver and pit crew, *not* the car, are being tested. Sanctioned races take place at tracks large and small throughout the country, and the granddaddy of them all is the Winston Series.

Just finishing a Winston Cup race (heck, just qualifying for one) is an impressive feat, and the winner isn't really determined by who gets there first. Points, which accumulate throughout the season, are doled out for a variety of reasons, such as for how many laps the driver led during the race. It's not unusual for a third-place team to 'win.'

The real appeal for many fans, however, is less the competition than the fact that this is a quintessentially Southern family affair. The kids of female Nascar star Shawna Robinson come down to the track and cheer her on, while racing dynasties like the Pettys, Jaretts and Earnhardts are legendary. More than that, it's a down-to-earth sport – none of your polo snobs around here – with open arms for anyone who wants to join the Nascar family – even Yankees.

Paige R Penland

your favorite Nascar, from half a dozen vendors on the beach for around $35 to $45 per hour (you must have a driver's license to rent these). You can also rent boogie boards (usually $5/10 per hour/day), fat-wheeled pedal trikes (tricycle; $10/25 per hour/day) and umbrellas and chairs ($8 to $10 per day) from various stands.

If you're feeling extra adventurous, contact **Daytona Beach Parasail** (☎ *386-547-6067;* W *www.daytonaparasailing.com; $55-100)*. The price, which depends on height (800 to 2000ft; the higher, the more expensive), includes a free shuttle to and from your hotel. Flights last about 8 minutes for single riders, 15 for double riders.

Most beachside vendors are open daily from 8am to 5pm, and later during special events when prices rise according to demand.

The **boardwalk** has just what you want in a boardwalk – thrill rides, go-carts and beachside patios where you sip beer from plastic cups. It's good family fun with just a hint of sleaze to keep things interesting.

Jackie Robinson Ballpark

Off Beach St on City Island, opposite the CVB, Jackie Robinson Ballpark is where black American Robinson broke the color barrier in professional sports, playing his first MLB spring training game in 1946. The Class A **Daytona Cubs** (☎ *386-257-3172)*, a farm team of the Chicago Cubs, play here April through September.

Halifax Historical Museum

Visit this museum (☎ *386-255-6976;* W *www.halifaxhistorical.org; 252 S Beach St; adult/child $4/1)* just to see the great model of Daytona Beach Pier, circa 1938. There's lots of other stuff housed in this old bank building, including a comprehensive exhibit of local black history. Check out the old-school vault.

Ponce de León Inlet Lighthouse Museum

This lighthouse museum (☎ *386-761-1821; 4931 S Peninsula Dr; adult/child $7/1; open 10am-7pm daily)*, about 5 miles south of Daytona, is an interesting place to spend an afternoon, and climbing the 203 steps to the top makes for a splendid view. Also on display are rickety Cuban rafts that were found on Ormond Beach, nautical navigation tools and photos of lighthouses from all over the USA. You'll also learn to appreciate the difference between various Fresnel lens orders!

Little Chapel by the Sea

Check out this photo opportunity: the chapel (☎ *386-767-8716; 3140 S Atlantic Ave; admission free)* is a drive-in Christian church! Attach a speaker to your car (tourists love this) or be like the locals and tune in to 680 AM or 88.5 FM to hear Reverend Larry G Deitch do his thing. He and the choir hold service on a balcony overlooking the autos at 8:30am and 10am Sunday. There's free coffee and donuts between services.

This used to be the Neptune Drive-In Theater, but when that closed down, local church leaders felt that the venue would appeal to car-crazy Christians visiting Daytona to see the races. They opened in 1954 and have been preaching to a packed parking lot ever since.

Places to Stay

Daytona has more hotels than you can shake a crankshaft at, and they're fairly predictable. For $35 you'll get a basic, cleanish room with laundry and a pool; for $55, a newer room and perhaps some wacky amenity, like miniature golf or a water slide; and for $80, a relatively luxurious chain hotel. For events like Speed Week, prices double and rooms fill weeks in advance.

The following are just a few of Daytona's more than 400 hotels. For more choices contact the CVB about its *Superior Small Lodging* booklet, or log onto W www.daytonalodging.com. And pay attention to the architecture and neon along the Atlantic Ave strip: Daytona is a living museum of 1950s pop culture.

Travelodge Ocean Jewels Resort (☎ *386-252-2581; 935 S Atlantic Ave; rooms year-round/special events $49/99)* has two pools and nice rooms with coffeemakers.

Dream Inn (☎ *386-767-2821;* W *www.dreaminn.com; 3217 S Atlantic Ave; rooms year-round $50-110, special events $120-190)* is a bit off the main strip but worth the drive for its flowery courtyard and big pool.

Bermuda Villas (☎ *386-255-2438; 505 S Atlantic Ave; rooms year-round/special events $55/125)* has airy rooms and a much better location.

Coquina Inn B&B (☎ *386-254-4969;* W *www.coquinainndaytonabeach.com; 544 S Palmetto Ave; rooms $90-140)* has fireplaces in some rooms, and there's a lush garden patio and a Jacuzzi. Free bicycle rental is available.

Live Oak Inn (☎ *386-252-4667; 444-448 S Beach St; rooms with/without Jacuzzi $120/90, special events $150/110)*, in a sprawling 1881

Victorian building close to the marina, has relaxing rooms and lots of regulars.

Hilton Garden (☎ 386-944-4000; W www .hiltongardeninn.com; 189 Midway Ave; rooms $94, special events $300-450), convenient to the airport and International Speedway, has all the amenities you'd expect, including an airport shuttle.

The Villa (☎ 386-248-2020; W www.the villabb.com; 801 N Peninsula Dr; rooms $100-150) is one of the nicest B&Bs around. It's in a Spanish colonial–style mansion with stained glass windows, shady gardens, lots of antiques, two cats and Andy the dog. It's gay-owned and a grand place for anyone.

Adam's Mark Resort (☎ 386-254-8200, 800-444-2326; W www.adamsmark.com; 100 N Atlantic Ave; rooms from $135, special events $385) is a fabulously luxurious resort, with heaps of amenities and a traffic-free beach that, with its patrols and activities, is all but private.

Places to Eat

Pasha (☎ 386-257-7753; 919 W International Speedway Blvd; dishes $4-6; open 10am-7:30pm Mon-Sat, noon-6pm Sun) has unusually authentic Middle Eastern food. *Fatoush*, *foulemudammas* and *labriah* join standards like hummus and tabouli on a combination plate of your design. It's also a deli.

Starlight Diner (☎ 386-255-9555; 401 N Atlantic Ave; dishes $4-8; open 7am-9pm daily) looks like an Airstream trailer and has a great jukebox, huge burgers and real malts.

Dancing Avocado Kitchen (☎ 386-947-2022; 110 S Beach St; mains $5-8; open 8am-4pm Mon-Sat) has absolutely stellar vegetarian dishes, including five different meatless burgers and the recommended dancing avocado melt sandwich.

Lighthouse Landing (☎ 386-761-9271; 4940 S Peninsula Dr; mains $5-15; open 11:30am-10pm daily), near the Ponce de León Inlet Lighthouse, has a pleasant outdoor patio overlooking the water and kitsch to spare. Good fish sandwiches and seafood entrées come with fries. Spend the extra 50¢ for onion rings.

Aunt Catfish's on the River (☎ 386-767-4768; 4009 Halifax Dr; mains $8-16; open 11:30am-9pm daily) serves fried, grilled and Cajun-style catfish (Cajun-style is the best); all meals include a great salad bar. A huge Sunday brunch ($11) is served from 9am to 2pm.

Anna's Italian Trattoria (☎ 386-239-9624; 304 Seabreeze Blvd; mains $13-20; open 5pm-10pm Tues-Sun) is a great place to splurge on veal marsala or fettuccini Alfredo, unless they have the shrimp cognac on special – it's the chef's favorite.

Rosario's Restaurant (☎ 386-258-6066; 444 S Beach St; mains $16-28; open 5pm-10pm Tues-Sat) has a 175-item wine list and dishes like filet mignon in whiskey sauce and veal shank, though the chef recommends the specials. It's in the same building as Live Oak Inn.

Entertainment

There are almost as many bars as hotels in this town, and that's saying something.

Dirty Harry's Pub (☎ 386-252-9877; 705 Main St) provides the perfect excuse to wear leather, with live music Wednesday and Saturday night and an impressive collection of automatic weapons on the wall.

Froggy's Saloon (☎ 386-254-8808; 800 Main St), down the street, also caters to the biker crowd. Shirts are required after 7pm.

Razzles (☎ 386-257-6236; 611 Seabreeze Blvd; admission $5-10; open 8pm-3am daily) is a high-energy dance club. Ladies drink free Wednesday and Friday till midnight.

Lovo Bar (☎ 386-252-7600; 116 N Beach St; open 10pm-3am Fri & Sat) is a Gothic-kitsch, couch-laden meat market with a groovy dance lounge.

Groove Dance Lounge (☎ 386-252-7600; 124 N Beach St) is in the same complex, and has a shag (the material, not the British verb) bar.

Martinis on Bay (☎ 386-258-1212; 101 Bay St; open 11am-1am Mon-Thur, 5pm-3am Fri & Sat) attracts an upscale crowd with classic movies on Tuesday, DJs on weekends, and ladies night on Thursday, complete with complimentary chair massages from 8pm to 1am.

Streamline Lounge (☎ 386-258-6937; 140 S Atlantic Ave; open 11am-3am daily) is a threadbare gay bar that attracts an older male crowd. Patrons here also recommend **Tom-Boys Bar & Grill** (☎ 386-257-6464; 322 Seabreeze Blvd) and **Rumors Nite Club & Bar** (☎ 386-252-3776; 1376 N Nova Rd).

Bank & Blues (☎ 386-257-9272; 701 Main St) has lots of good blues events throughout the year and an open jam on Wednesday night.

Getting There & Around

Daytona Beach International Airport (☎ 386-248-8030), just east of the Speedway, is served by Continental, Northwest and Delta airlines and all major car-rental companies.

NORTH OF ORLANDO

Excursion to St Augustine

The oldest European settlement in the USA, St Augustine was founded by the Spanish in 1565. It's Europe without Disney and without the admission fees: an American city with, at least in the downtown area, more cobblestone than asphalt, more coquina than cement, and more time and patience for the pleasures of living. Spanish-colonial architecture combined with many workers' period costumes render the downtown one huge, permanent Renaissance fair.

Horse-drawn carriages clop through the 144-block National Historic Landmark District, and throngs of pedestrians gawk at the architecture and fill sidewalks lined with crafts shops, cafés, restaurants and pubs. It all adds up to a living time capsule (and tourist trap, but of the very highest quality) that's a real pleasure to visit. See History under Facts about Central Florida for more information.

The main **visitor information center** (☎ 904-825-1000; Ⓦ www.visitoldcity.com; 10 Castillo Dr; open 8:30am-5:30pm daily) displays an overwhelming number of pamphlets and sells tickets for sightseeing trains, trolleys, horse-drawn carriages and other **organized tours**. There are smaller visitor information booths all over town.

Walking Tour

Most visitors spend time walking the pedestrian mall of St George St and visiting the fascinating Castillo de San Marcos. This walking tour will lead you to only some of the numerous sites, so if you want to know more, consult a visitors center or the Lonely Planet *Florida* guide for more extensive information. Keep in mind that parking is difficult to find in the historic area.

Start at **Casa del Hidalgo** (cnr St George St & Hypolita), which was reconstructed by the Spanish government and is representative of a typical Spanish gentleman's abode. From there walk north up St George St and on your left you'll see the **Casa de Nicolas de Ortega**, a fine example of an Anglicized Spanish home – the chimneys are a British influence. Across Cuna St, on the right, you'll see the **Peso de Burgo-Pellicer Houses**, an old-style duplex built in 1785. It now houses a Minorcan exhibit (many British settlers hailed from Minorca, which was at the time owned by Great Britain).

A little farther north you'll see the **Casa Avero,** home to a somewhat out-of-place but gorgeous Greek Orthodox Shrine – definitely take a look; it's free. Across the street is the balconied **Casa Arrivas**, which features Spanish, English and American architectural characteristics of the 18th and 19th century. Nearby, up a short alley, is the **Spanish Bakery** (☎ 904-471-3046; 47½ St George St; dishes $1-3; open 9:30am-3pm daily). This reconstructed historic building serves Spanish stews and fresh-baked, melt-in-your-mouth rolls (50¢).

Back on St George St on your left is the **Casa Josef Salcedo**, a classic example of an 18th-century St Augustine building. Moving along, cross St George St once again to find the entrance to the **Spanish Quarter Village & Museum Store** (☎ 904-825-6830; St George St; adult/child $6.50/4; open 9am-5pm daily), which performs blacksmithing, woodwork and cooking demos à la 18th century.

Next door is the **Casa Gomez**, which looks like a wooden shack; it was once the home of Spanish foot soldier Lorenzo Gomez. Towards the end of St George St, on your left is the **Oldest Wooden Schoolhouse** (☎ 904-824-0192, 800-653-7245; 14 St George St; adult/child $3/2; open 9am-5pm daily). Inside are an old classroom, animatronic teachers and students, and rare old school supplies. Now you're ready to pass through the **Old City Gate** (1739), marked by coquina pillars built in 1808.

For the grand finale, cross the busy Ave Menendez to the unmistakable, unmissable **Castillo de San Marcos** (☎ 904-829-6506; adult/child $5/2; open 8:45am-4:45pm daily). There, pick up a map and guide, and be prepared to be impressed – especially if you're an American – by the antiquity and history. This coquina fort, built in 1695, is the oldest masonary fort in the continental US! Reenactments, complete with pirate ships, firefights and villagers running amok, take place here occasionally, and the cannons are fired every Sunday – you can hear the ancient iron beasts all over town.

Places to Stay

There are *at least* 25 registered B&Bs in town, all with outstanding reputations. For more options you can contact **Historic Inns of St Augustine** (Ⓦ www.visitoldcity.com).

Excursion to St Augustine

Pirate Haus (☎ 904-808-1999; W www.pir atehaus.com; 32 Treasury St; dorm beds $15, rooms $36-56) is a truly fine place with a fantastic location: two blocks north of King St downtown (though parking is limited, which can be a hassle). What more could you want? Well, how about an all-you-can-eat breakfast featuring 'pirate pancakes'?

St George Inn (☎ 904-827-5740; W www .stgeorge-inn.com; 2-6 St George St; rooms $79-159) is smack in the middle of the sights. Rooms are only superficially elegant (indoor/outdoor carpeting), but you'll probably be overlooking a lovely plaza.

Casablanca Inn (☎ 904-826-1892, 800-826-2626; W www.casablancainn.com; 24 Av Menendez; rooms Sun-Thur $90-200, Fri & Sat $130-225) has lovely rooms and offers a big breakfast on the expansive veranda overlooking the water.

Secret Garden Inn (☎ 904-829-3678; W www .secretgardeninn.com; 56½ Charlotte St; rooms Sun-Thur from $105, Fri & Sat $150), tucked way back in the alley, is shady and romantic. With only three suites, you won't have to worry about finding quiet time in the gardens.

Casa Monica (☎ 904-827-1888, 800-648-1888; W www.casamonica.com; rooms in winter $199-239, summer $219-259), in the former Cordova Hotel (circa 1880), is a grand restoration project done right. It's got amenity-packed rooms, a spectacular lobby and a grand swimming pool, as well as gourmet restaurants, art galleries, clothing shops, jewelry stores…need we go on?

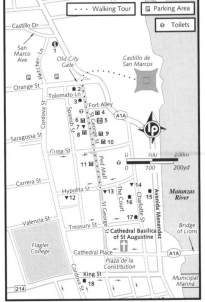

Downtown St Augustine

PLACES TO STAY
2 St George Inn
15 Casablanca Inn
16 Secret Garden Inn
17 Pirate Haus
18 Casa Monica

PLACES TO EAT
7 Spanish Bakery
12 Schmagel's Bagels
13 Bunnery Café;
   Casa del Hidalgo
14 Bistro Hypolita

OTHER
1 Visitor Information Center
3 Oldest Wooden Schoolhouse
4 Casa Gomez
5 Spanish Quarter Village &
   Museum Store
6 Casa Josef Salcedo
8 Casa Arrivas
9 Casa Avero; Greek Orthodox
   Shrine
10 Peso de Burgo-Pellicer
   Houses
11 Casa de Nicholas de Ortega

Places to Eat

The number of good eateries just in the historic area is too great to go into – don't forget the Spanish Bakery (see the 'Walking Tour' section earlier).

Schmagel's Bagels (☎ 904-824-4444; 69 Hypolita St; dishes $2-5; open 7am-3pm daily, 7am-2pm summer) has delicious bagels and bagel sandwiches – try the hummus!

Bunnery Café (☎ 904-829-6166; 121 St George St; dishes $7-9; open 8am-6pm daily) serves healthy salads and sandwiches, then sabotages any good intentions with its surreally delectable sticky pecan buns and cinnamon rolls.

Bistro Hypolita (☎ 904-808-8395; 15 Hypolita St; entrées $8-10) is small, cute and even romantic, with very good fresh salads, quiche, croque moniers and other French favorites.

Getting There & Away

Take the Hwy 16 exit off I-95 and head east past US Hwy 1 to San Marcos Ave. Turn right and you'll end up at the Old City Gate, just past the fort, Castillo de San Marcos. Alternately, you can take Hwy A1A along the beach, which intersects with San Marco Ave, or US Hwy 1 south from Jacksonville.

The **Greyhound bus station** (☎ 386-255-7076, 800-231-2222; 138 S Ridgewood Ave) has four buses daily to DeLand, seven to Miami and others to just about anywhere you'd like to go on the seaboard.

Votran (☎ 386-761-7700; Ⓦ http://velusia .org/votran; adult/child $1/50¢) runs buses and trolleys throughout the city. Exact change is required. Ask for a free transfer when you get on the bus. Buses run 6am to 7:30pm daily, trolleys noon to midnight Monday through Saturday from January through Labor Day. The CVB and most hotels have schedules and system maps. Bus No 10 connects the airport with downtown and the beaches, while bus No 11 will get you to the International Speedway. Take bus No 17AB to the lighthouse. The trolley runs along Atlantic Ave (Hwy A1A) from Granada Blvd in Ormond to Dunlawton Ave in Daytona Beach Shores. For information about car travel and parking see Orientation earlier in this chapter.

South of Orlando

TAMPA
pop 303,400

Tampa is a city that's no longer on the rise – it's newly risen and it likes its newfound status, thank you very much. At the center of its revitalization is Ybor City, the national historic landmark district built within the heart of the old cigar industry, which once dominated this town. But Busch Gardens is undeniably a strong draw, as it combines an excellent zoo with some of the best roller coasters you'll ever encounter. Tampa also offers a great hands-on science museum, a wonderful aquarium, several high-quality art museums, a large performing arts center and the elegant but haunted Tampa Theatre. And it all sits on a nice bay and is sliced in half by the tranquil, lazy Hillsborough River.

History

An Indian fishing village when Hernando de Soto arrived in 1539, Tampa wasn't really settled by Europeans (who drove off or killed – by war or disease – most of the natives) until the late 18th century, and it didn't become a city of consequence until 1855, when Fort Brooke was established here.

Towards the end of the 19th century, Cuban cigar makers moved into the area en masse, and over the next 50 years, the city would be known as the Cigar Capital of America. Vicénte Martínez Ybor and Ignacio Haya put Tampa on the cigar-making map. In 1885, they moved their considerable cigar factories – Principe de Gales (Prince of Wales) and La Flor de la Sanchez y Haya, respectively – to present-day Ybor City. Haya's factory opened first, in February 1886, and Ybor's soon after. (Ybor's opening had been delayed due to a strike by factory workers.) The move from Key West – which had until then been the cigar-making capital of the USA due to its proximity to Cuba – was precipitated by the strong organization of workers there: the cigar barons decided that moving was the only way to break the union's grip on their factories.

Workers were imported to the new (and non-unionized) factories from Key West and directly from Havana. And as if to send a message to Key West that its cigar-making days were over, a fire broke out there on April 1, 1886, that destroyed several cigar factories, including Ybor's Principe de Gales Key West branch. Ybor City became the largest func-

Highlights

- Sipping strong coffee over a Cuban sandwich in the late morning, then partying in Tampa's historic and unique Ybor City
- Screaming for mercy on Montu and watching a cluster of giraffes from a distance over a beer at Busch Gardens
- Seeing some of the best of Dalí and other renowned artists in cultural St Petersburg
- Sifting through the powdery white sand at beautiful Clearwater Beach
- Dipping into Greek-American culture at Tarpon Springs

tioning production facility, and the cigar business never looked back.

As the factories drew thousands and thousands of workers – such as cutters and support staff like packers and shipping personnel – Ybor City grew to have the largest concentration of Cubans outside Cuba. These Cubans began organizing themselves into leagues and clubs – notably El Liceo Cubano (the Cuban Lyceum) and La Liga Patriotica Cubana (the Cuban Patriotic League). These organizations, and later others like the Ignacio Agramonte Cuban Revolutionary Club, formed the backbone of revolutionary organization through fund-raising and propaganda.

José Martí became a member of the Cuban Patriotic League (there is a statue of him across the street from the Ybor Cigar Factory building

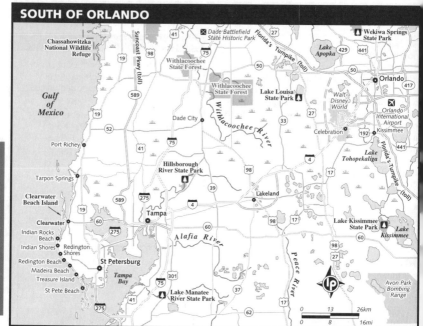

SOUTH OF ORLANDO

today) and stayed in Tampa when not traveling around Florida. In mid-November 1892, agents of the Spanish government attempted to assassinate Martí by poisoning him.

The prosperity of the area made it attractive to other immigrant groups, Italians chief among them. Blacklisted from working in the Cuban factories, the Italians founded their own 'buckeye' factories, in which they manufactured cheap cigars known as cheroots (see any Clint Eastwood film made prior to 1976 for more information).

These Italians, along with Cubans and Spaniards, created mutual aid societies to provide health care for the workers. In the earliest example of cooperative social health care in the USA, several societies – among them El Porvenir, El Circulo Cubano and L'unione Italiana – provided medicine and hospitalization to their members.

Spaniards, Germans and Jews from various countries also migrated to the area.

During the Spanish-American War and the Cuban Revolution, Tampa was an important staging area for revolutionaries and troops to Havana, since it had the most developed communication with the island (established ship routes supplied the area with Cuban tobacco).

Ybor City remained America's cigar-making capital until the 1959 Castro Revolution and the resulting US embargo of Cuban products. Over the next three decades, Ybor City and the entire city of Tampa hit the skids; crime increased and the abandoned factories and housing became dangerous and dilapidated.

Tampa's resurgence of late is due in large part to the renovation, rehabilitation and gentrification of historic Ybor City, which was named a National Historic Landmark District in 1990 and is the center of Tampa nightlife. Tampa's excellent museums and Busch Gardens, and the popularity of nearby beaches along the Gulf, have turned southwest Florida's oldest city into a prime tourist destination once again. Its economy also thrives on a revitalized seaport and a well-developed banking industry; and although it's not the economic engine it once was, over a half billion cigars are produced here annually.

Orientation

Tampa is crisscrossed by major highways and interstates. US Hwy 41 (the Tamiami Trail) cuts straight north through the center of the city. The Hillsborough River runs roughly north–south through the western side of downtown before turning eastward. The Lee Roy Selmon Expressway (SR 618) is a 15-mile toll road that runs southwest–northeast and cuts diagonally through Tampa.

I-75 runs north–south and skirts the eastern edge of Tampa. I-275 also runs north–south and cuts through downtown before it heads west across the Howard Frankland Bridge over Tampa Bay, south through St Petersburg and on to Sarasota.

Northeast of downtown, I-275 breaks off from I-75 as it goes south into downtown, until it meets up with I-4 – this intersection is lovingly referred to by local motorists as Malfunction Junction. I-4 runs east and then northeast to Orlando and on to meet I-95 on Florida's east coast.

Downtown Tampa is bordered by I-275 at the north, the Hillsborough River at the west, Garrison Channel at the south and Meridian Ave at the east. Franklin St, in the center of downtown, is a pedestrian zone. Between 6am and 7pm, Marion St is closed to all vehicular traffic except buses. Ybor City is just northeast of downtown; Channelside and the Port of Tampa are due east, just beyond the railroad tracks.

Davis Island and Harbour Island are situated in Hillsborough Bay, on the southern edge of downtown.

South Tampa is really old Tampa, the peninsula southwest of downtown (south of Kennedy Blvd), reached via the northeast–southwest Bayshore Blvd and the north–south S Dale Mabry Hwy. MacDill Air Force Base, where the Joint Chiefs of Staff's Central Command is located ('CenCom' covers the Middle East, so ostensibly the US war on terrorism is headquartered here), occupies the southern tip of this peninsula; Bay-to-Bay Blvd and Gandy Blvd (which heads over the bridge to St Petersburg) run east–west across it. North Tampa feels like the set of *The Truman Show*.

Information

The **Tampa Bay Convention & Visitors Bureau** (☎ 813-223-1111, 800-448-2672; W *www .visittampabay.com; 615 Channelside Dr; open 9:30am-5:30pm Mon-Sat, 11am-5pm Sun*) maintains a very good visitors' center near the Florida Aquarium. Their free map shows how all the neighborhoods and interstates fit together. The **Centro Ybor Museum & Visitor Information Center** (☎ 813-248-3712; W *www .ybor.org; 1600 E 8th Ave; open 10am-6pm Mon-Sat, noon-6pm Sun*) has tons of informa-

tion on this National Historic Landmark District and very good historical displays on the cigar connection. Pick up their excellent historic walking tour brochure, which illuminates Ybor City's former cultural and working heritage.

There's a **Bank of America** (☎ 800-299-2265; 101 E Kennedy Blvd) – call for other Tampa branches. There's a BofA ATM on La Setima in Ybor City, between 18th and 19th Sts. Also on La Setima, at the corner of 21st St, is a branch of Southern Exchange Bank, with an ATM. Change money at **American Express** (☎ 813-273-0310; One Tampa City Center).

The **post office** (925 N Florida Ave; 1900 E 12th Ave, Ybor City) has a number of branches.

The **Old Tampa Book Co** (☎ 813-209-2151; 507 N Tampa St), downtown, has a huge selection of used books and some remainders. **Inkwood Books** (☎ 813-253-2638; 216 S Armenia Ave; open 10am-7pm Mon-Wed & Fri, 10am-9pm Thur, 10am-6pm Sat, 1-5pm Sun) has a great selection of literature and Lonely Planet books to top it off.

Downtown Tampa hosts the **main library** (☎ 813-273-3652; 900 N Ashley Dr), while Ybor City gets a **branch library** (☎ 813-272-5747; 1505 Nebraska Ave); both have free web surfing.

The major daily newspaper is the *Tampa Tribune* (W www.tampatrib.com), though the *St Petersburg Times* (W www.sptimes.com) and the *Miami Herald* are available everywhere. In the hotel, tune into Bay News 9, the nation's first all-Spanish cable station. In the car, tune into National Public Radio (NPR) at 89.7 FM.

Laundromat Express (☎ 813-837-9100; Phar Mor Plaza, 4306 S Dale Mabry Hwy) has pool tables, snacks and beer.

Tampa General Hospital (☎ 813-251-7000), south of downtown on Davis Island, is the biggest area hospital.

The gay and lesbian scene is big but hard to pin down: things are always in a state of flux. Look around the city for the biweekly *Watermark* (W www.watermarkonline.com), with up-to-date listings of gay, lesbian and bisexual community groups and resource centers.

The **Center of Tampa Bay** (☎ 813-875-8116; W www.tampacenter.org; 3708 W Swann Ave) has helpful information on the Tampa Film Festival.

Museum of Science & Industry

MOSI (☎ 813-987-6000; W www.mosi.org; 4801 E Fowler Ave; adult/child 2-12 including one IMAX film $15/11; open 9am-5pm

DOWNTOWN TAMPA

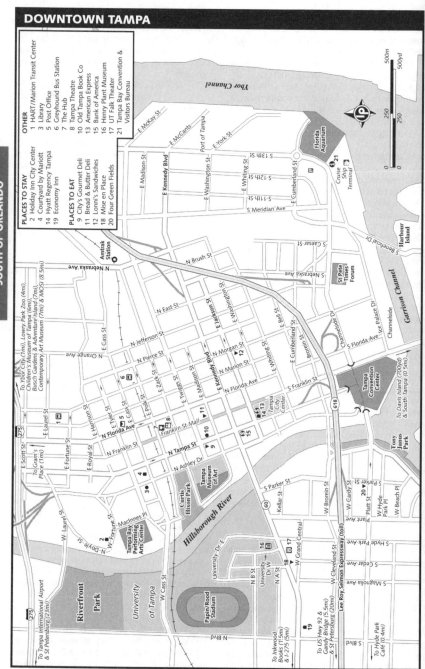

PLACES TO STAY
2   Holiday Inn City Center
4   Courtyard by Marriott
14 Hyatt Regency Tampa
19 Economy Inn

PLACES TO EAT
9   City's Gourmet Deli
11 Bread & Butter Deli
12 Lonni's Sandwiches
18 Mise en Place
20 Four Green Fields

OTHER
1   HART/Marion Transit Center
3   Library
5   Post Office
6   Greyhound Bus Station
7   The Hub
8   Tampa Theatre
10 Old Tampa Book Co
13 American Express
15 Bank of America
16 Henry Plant Museum
17 UT Falk Theater
21 Tampa Bay Convention &
    Visitors Bureau

Mon-Fri, 9am-7pm Sat & Sun) is deservedly one of the biggest draws around, and it's definitely in contention for Florida's best hands-on science museum. With upwards of 450 'minds-on' activities, hyperactive kids will think they're in heaven. Look for varied traveling exhibits and a (permanent) cool hot-air balloon exhibit, as well as ones on the human body, Florida, and the amount of garbage the average American generates annually. Enter a flight avionics simulator or a Gulf Coast hurricane before taking to a one-mile trail within the on-site wetland preserve.

Tampa Museum of Art

This modern-looking museum *(☎ 813-274-8130; W www.tampamuseum.com; 600 N Ashley Dr; adult/child 6 & older $7/3, admission by donation 5pm-8pm third Thur & 10am-noon Sat; open 10am-5pm Tues-Sat, 11am-5pm Sun, 10am-8pm 3rd Thur)* belies an impressive abundance of classical Greek and Roman antiquities. It also features a wide range of rotating exhibitions – from avant-garde to old masters, and from sculpture and photography to works by emerging Florida artists. Overlooking the Hillsborough River, the glassed-in Terrace Gallery provides a great backdrop for sculptures. The grounds make a nice place for a picnic.

Channelside

This huge entertainment megaplex *(☎ 813-223-4250; W www.channelside.com; Channelside Dr)*, directly on Ybor Channel, boasts a fun sports bar (Newk's Cafe), an IMAX theater, an upscale billiards hall (Pop City), a movie theater, lots of eateries, some clubs and open-air shops. You'll also find cruise ships pulling into the Port of Tampa here, as well as the Florida Aquarium (see below).

Channelside Dr is southeast of downtown and southwest of Ybor City. From I-4, get off at exit 1 and follow the signs.

Florida Aquarium

This great fish bowl *(☎ 813-273-4000; W www .flaquarium.net; 701 Channelside Dr; adult/ child 3-12 $15/10; open 9:30am-5pm daily)*, with exhibits on three floors, traces how water travels from its freshwater source to the open sea. Take the elevator to the top to start at the beginning, Florida Wetlands, where you'll find itty-bitty fish, a limestone cavern, a mangrove forest and alligator hatchlings. In Bays & Beaches, the indoor beach is complete with dunes, waves, sea oats and live seabirds. The

Coral Reef Gallery is the best, though. Its 500,000-gallon tank teems with colorful coral and thousands of fish. Divers jump into the coral reef and shark tank and speak to crowds via intercom several times daily (11am to 3pm), providing a window onto the undersea world. It's interactive: the audience asks questions of the diver, who swims around pointing out the answers.

The aquarium also has a 64ft catamaran, the *Dolphin Quest Eco Tour,* that heads out into Tampa Bay looking for the 400 or so bottle-nosed dolphins that live here. Along the way you'll also see manatees and a bird island. Tickets cost $18/17/13 for an adult/ senior/child, but there are combo tickets with the aquarium that will save you about $3 per person. Adjacent parking is $4. An average visit takes 2½ hours.

Ybor City

Once a dangerous and scary place because of muggers and car thieves, the renaissance of Ybor City (pronounced **ee**-bore) almost matches that of Miami Beach. For power-drinkers and 20-somethings, the area is a must-see for its energy and drink-till-you-barf potential; there are 60-plus bars and clubs within a small area, plus a few tattoo parlors. Indeed, you might want to visit twice: it's G-rated during the day with conventioneers and business lunches; PG-rated with middle-aged folks during the dinner hour; and often X-rated late at night when E 7th Ave is closed to vehicular traffic. For everyone else, it's a must-see for its history (see History earlier in this section) and sheer success at recreating itself. You'll find palm-lined and brick-paved streets, wrought iron balconies à la New Orleans' Bourbon St, and handsome former cigar factories and social clubs. Note that parking is difficult and expensive at night, but a breeze during the day.

Ybor City is in the northeast section of Tampa. The main drag, 7th Ave (La Setima), is closed to vehicles on Fridays and Saturdays from about 9pm to 4am. The area is roughly bordered by 23rd St at the east, 13th St at the west, Palm Ave (between 9th and 11th Aves) at the north and the railroad tracks along 6th Ave at the south. Fourteenth St is also called Avenida República de Cuba.

An Ybor City **market** *(☎ 813-241-2442)* takes place every Saturday from 9am to 3pm at Centennial Park, at the corner of 8th Ave and 18th St, offering arts and crafts, fruits and veggies.

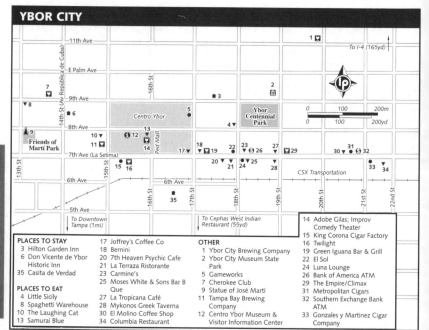

YBOR CITY

To I-4 (165yd)

CSX Transportation

To Downtown Tampa (1mi)

To Cephas West Indian Restaurant (55yd)

PLACES TO STAY
3   Hilton Garden Inn
6   Don Vicente de Ybor Historic Inn
35 Casita de Verdad

PLACES TO EAT
4   Little Sicily
8   Spaghetti Warehouse
10 The Laughing Cat
13 Samurai Blue

17 Joffrey's Coffee Co
18 Bernini
20 7th Heaven Psychic Cafe
21 La Terraza Ristorante
23 Carmine's
25 Moses White & Sons Bar B Que
27 La Tropicana Café
28 Mykonos Greek Taverna
30 El Molino Coffee Shop
34 Columbia Restaurant

OTHER
1   Ybor City Brewing Company
2   Ybor City Museum State Park
5   Gameworks
7   Cherokee Club
9   Statue of José Martí
11 Tampa Bay Brewing Company
12 Centro Ybor Museum & Visitor Information Center
14 Adobe Gilas; Improv Comedy Theater
15 King Corona Cigar Factory
16 Twilight
19 Green Iguana Bar & Grill
22 El Sol
24 Luna Lounge
26 Bank of America ATM
29 The Empire/Climax
31 Metropolitan Cigars
32 Southern Exchange Bank ATM
33 Gonzales y Martinez Cigar Company

Ybor City Museum State Park Covering about half a city block, this park (☎ 813-247-6323; 1818 9th Ave; admission $2; open 9am-5pm daily) includes La Casita (guided tours only; it's a typical but reconstructed 'shotgun'-style abode that housed immigrant cigar workers), the Ferlita Bakery (with its original brick ovens and exhibits on the bakery and cigar industry), cigar-rolling demonstrations (9:30am to 1:30pm Friday to Sunday) and fascinating photographs of the cigar factories and late-19th-century Ybor City. Informative walking tours ($4) are offered on Saturdays at 10:30am.

Centro Ybor Converted in 1999, this dominating upscale shopping, dining and entertainment emporium runs along 8th Ave between 15th and 17th Sts, but it also cuts through what would have been 16th St down to 7th Ave.

Friends of Martí Park The Parque Amigos de José Martí (cnr 13th St & 8th Ave) contains a not-very-good but life-size monument to Martí that was dedicated by Martí's son, actor Cesar Romero. The park is sited at Paulina Pedroso's house, where Martí stayed after the Spanish government attempted to assassinate him in 1892.

Cigar Shops To listen in on a thoroughly fascinating discussion of the merits of particular cigars and the paraphernalia that's necessary for their enjoyment, tune into **The Cigar General**, a radio talk show on Saturdays from noon to 2pm on 970 AM. But if someone lights up and you can't see, taste or smell it, does that make a radio sound? Somehow this metaphysical question is answered through passionate commentary and your ability to close your eyes and imagine. Perhaps afterwards you'll be able to answer this compelling variation of the ancient Zen riddle: what is the sound of one man smoking?

Metropolitan Cigars (☎ 813-248-3304; 2014 E 7th Ave) is the best cigar shop in this former cigar capital of America. It is one of the country's only shops to be set up as a humidor. They sell Arturo Fuente and Cuesta Rey cigars.

The largest is **King Corona Cigar Factory** (☎ 813-241-9109; 1523 E 7th Ave; open 9:30am-9pm Mon-Fri, 10:30am-5:30pm Sat), complete with an old-fashioned cigar bar and live entertainment. They carry Honduran- and Dominican-made cigars.

El Sol (☎ 813-248-5905; 1728 E 7th Ave; open 9:30am-5pm Mon-Thur, 9:30am-10pm

Fri, 10am-10pm Sat, noon-4pm Sun), established in 1929, is the oldest cigar store in Ybor City. They sell mainly Dominican cigars.

The **Gonzales y Martinez Cigar Company** *(☎ 813-247-2469; 2025 E 7th Ave)* has entertaining cigar-rolling demonstrations Monday through Saturday.

The most well known of the Tampa brands is Havatampa, whose mass-marketed Tampa Sweets are available in supermarkets and tobacco shops throughout the state and the country.

Ybor City Brewing Company Within the former cigar factory of Seidenberg & Co (1894), this microbrewery *(☎ 813-242-9222; 2205 N 20th St)* produces 8000 barrels of beer annually, including their Hurricane Reef products, Key West Sunset Ale and Lager, Ybor Gold, Ybor Calusa Wheat, Ybor Brown Ale and Gaspar's Ale. Brews are available throughout Ybor City and Florida. Thirty-minute brewery tours are given daily at 11am, noon and 1pm (call for the off-season schedule from May through August). Tours ($3) include a look at the brewing and bottling process, a history of the building and a beer tasting (it's not enough to get you drunk).

Tampa Theatre

This atmospheric movie palace *(☎ 813-274-8286; W www.tampatheatre.org; 711 N Franklin St; adult/senior, student or child $7/5)*, on the National Register of Historic Places, was built in 1926 by John Eberson. These days it screens independent and classic films and hosts concerts and other special events. Come early to hear the mighty Wurlitzer organ played before every movie; it features sirens, boat horns, cymbals, sleigh bells and other wacky sounds. The interior is special; stars (though no star formations), some of which twinkle, are painted onto the ceiling. All of the furniture (like the old Broadway seats) in the 1446-seat theater is original, and, oh yes, the place is haunted by one Hank Fink, a projectionist here for 25 years who died in the late 1960s. Stories abound: some claim to have seen apparitions; a projectionist apparently quit because he heard strange noises in the booth; other staff members have heard keys rattling.

Lowry Park Zoo

The lush zoo's *(☎ 813-932-0245; W www.lowryparkzoo.com; 7530 North Blvd; adult/senior/child $9.50/8.50/6; open 9:30am-5pm daily)* best feature is the manatee encounter and aquatic center, but there are also good exhibits on panthers, alligators, Komodo dragons, pandas, primates and bison. The Asian domain highlights a rare Indian rhinoceros, while families love the Wallaroo Station, an Australian theme area with kangaroos and wallabies that kids can pet. They can also pet and feed stingrays elsewhere in the park. Don't miss the 18,000-sq-ft free-flight aviary. To reach the zoo from downtown, take I-275 north to Sligh Ave (exit 48). You'll be going west on Sligh Ave, and the zoo will be on the right.

Henry B Plant Museum

Railroad magnate Henry Plant's Tampa Bay Hotel, which opened in 1891, was one of the most luxurious places imaginable in the early days of the city, when Tampa was about as remote as Miami at the southern tip of the state. All 500 guest rooms had private bathrooms and electricity, and the extravagant hotel contained all the furniture, sculptures and mirrors Plant's wife had collected during their European and Oriental travels.

After the hotel failed in the early 20th century, the city of Tampa took it over and today the National Historic Landmark is a museum *(☎ 813-254-1891; W www.plantmuseum.com; 401 W Kennedy Blvd; adult/child $5/1; open 10am-4pm Tues-Sat, noon-4pm Sun)*, across the river from downtown on the University of Tampa campus. You can gawk at the luxury and tour the hotel's grand salon, guest room, solarium and lobby, among others. Even if you don't go in, look for the dramatic Moorish revival architecture and silver minarets. The annual Victoria Christmas Stroll takes place from December 1 to 21, and includes dramatizations of fairy tales by actors in period costume in different rooms of the museum. Tickets are $6 for adults, $3 for children.

Children's Museum of Tampa

Also known as Kid City *(☎ 813-935-8441; 7550 North Blvd; admission over age 2 $4; open 9am-5:30pm Mon-Fri, 10am-5:30pm Sat, noon-5:30pm Sun)*, this place has rotating, hands-on interactive displays and a permanent, 45,000-sq-ft outdoor exhibition that kids love: child-size replicas of 13 municipal buildings, each with activities. Care to try your hand as a judge in the courthouse or a reporter at a TV station? Follow directions to the Lowry Park Zoo, above.

South Tampa

The world's longest contiguous **boardwalk**, measuring a whopping six miles, is a great place to bike, walk or run along the water. While you're in the area, you can drive or walk around the **Old Hyde Park** neighborhood, a residential area with brick streets, gas lanterns and renovated Victorian-style architecture. Head up Rome, Dakota or Oregon Ave from Bayshore Blvd. You'll also find an upscale, outdoor retail and dining complex where these three roads intersect with Swann Ave. Look for the old-time fruit stands in South Tampa, too.

Davis Island

The only reason to pop over here for a few minutes is to get a glimpse of real Tampa, and the little village straddling the roadside will provide just such a window. Take Davis Island Blvd off Bayshore Blvd and then at the split, take E Davis Blvd. Grab a coffee and hang around a bit; or settle in with some chips and salsa at **Estela's Mexican Restaurant** (☎ 813-251-0558; 209 E Davis Blvd; open daily for lunch & dinner; dishes up to $12), with sidewalk seating. Portions are big, but stick with the basics.

Contemporary Art Museum

The University of South Florida's museum (CAM; ☎ 813-974-2849; ⓦ www.usfcam.usf.edu; USF campus, 4202 E Fowler Ave; admission free; open 10am-5pm Mon-Fri, 1pm-4pm Sat) mounts six to eight exhibitions by university students and alumni. Weekday parking costs $2.

Busch Gardens

Sprawling over 300 acres, the area's biggest theme park (☎ 813-987-5082, 866-353-8622; ⓦ www.buschgardens.com; 10000 McKinley Dr; adult/child 3-9 $52/43; hrs vary but usually open 9:30am-7pm daily) draws crowds with the state's best roller coasters and one of the state's best zoos. Despite the woolly mammoth–sized admission price, a trip to Busch Gardens is worth it, although you should probably cough up $11 more per person, which will entitle you to a return visit the following day. Also consider getting a combination ticket to Busch Gardens/Adventure Island (see later in this section). And add another $7 for parking. Several rides have height restrictions, which vary from 42 to 56 inches. In general, lines at Busch Gardens are far shorter than their Orlando counterparts; on a

high-season day, you'll probably have to wait only about 10 minutes for a ride. Themed shows, performances and craft demonstrations occur several times daily and change often; check at the ticket window for the day's shows and activities. The same goes for animal acts starring alligators, elephants, tortoises, orangutans, warthogs and tigers; they occur at various villages around the park.

Additionally, Busch Gardens, in an attempt to stay ahead of the curve, is always inventing new rides and theme areas. Check at the gate. Also check for details on two tours once you're inside: the Animal Adventure Tour and the Serengeti Safari Tour.

Busch Gardens is about 7 miles north of downtown and accessible from both I-75 and I-275, both of which have Busch Blvd exits. From I-75 head west at the exit; from I-275 head east. The entrance to the park is on McKinley Dr, which juts north from Busch Blvd.

Crown Colony You can catch the monorail and Skyride here, to use as an orientation tour or for transportation. The Crown Colony House Restaurant overlooking the Serengeti Plain has a welcoming Hospitality Center, where you can get a 10oz cup of Anheuser-Busch beer (limit two per person per day, 21 and older). The Clydesdale Hamlet features trademark Budweiser Clydesdale horses.

Egypt The star of Egypt, **Montu**, claims to be the southeastern USA's largest inverted steel roller coaster. The three-minute killer ride features an inverse loop – a 104ft vertical loop that is the world's largest on an inverted coaster. As if that wasn't enough, there are two more vertical loops at a 45¼-degree angle. These coasters don't coast; speeds reach 60mph, and the G-force hits a maximum of 3.85 (minimum height 54 inches).

Other attractions include a replica of King Tutankhamen's tomb, a gigantic wall inscribed with hieroglyphics, and a Sand Dig area, where children can discover Egyptian antiquities in the sand. There are, of course, shopping bazaars and Egyptian-costumed characters roaming around.

Serengeti Plain The most authentic area, this 80-acre habitat is populated by about 500 animals that are best seen from the monorail (a bumpy 15- to 20-minute ride) and reasonably well seen from the Skyride (more peaceful) and steam locomotive. Although giving animals free range makes it harder to see them, the zebras, giraffes, kudus, hippos, lions, camels and buffalo are in a more natural setting. Hip-hip, hooray. Take the Skyride so you can hear the wind and animal sounds; it's much more relaxing.

Edge of Africa You can get close up with big animals here, sometimes getting nose-to-nose with lions, hyenas, ostriches, zebras, hippos and giraffes. The viewing is similar to that of Myombe Reserve, with glass between the visitor and the animal habitat. Inquire about wildlife tours led by park zoologists.

Myombe Reserve The 3-acre reserve resembles the western lowlands of Africa, complete with gorillas and chimpanzees. It all feels very tropical and rainforesty, complete with waterfalls and piped-in tropical fog. From here you can participate in a Rhino Rally, cruising around the 'plains' in 4WD vehicles like you see on safaris and then racing other 4WDs.

Nairobi This is where you'll find the Animal Nursery, a petting zoo and the kid-fave Nocturnal Mountain, where nocturnal creatures are exposed (so to speak). Other exhibits include the Show Jumping Hall of Fame and feature reptiles, tortoises and elephants.

Timbuktu This area draws 'em in with **Scorpion** – a 50mph ride with a 360-degree loop and 62ft drop (minimum height 42 inches) – and **Phoenix**, a boat-swing ride (minimum height 48 inches). There are also kiddie rides and a video-game arcade. The Dolphin Theater stages live entertainment.

Congo Everyone is trying to get to the northwest corner of Busch Gardens for one reason: **Kumba**, one of the best roller coasters anywhere. It's a crazy ride, featuring a diving loop that plunges from a height of 110ft, a camelback loop (spiraling 360 degrees and creating three seconds of weightlessness) and a 108ft vertical loop. In addition, there are ducks, dips and swirls around pedestrian walkways and a generally terrifying vibe (minimum height 54 inches).

The other roller coaster ride here is the relatively tame (ha!) **Python**, a double-spiral corkscrew that hits speeds of 50mph (minimum height 48 inches). Rafts take you down the **Congo River Rapids** (minimum height 39 inches, or at least two years old), but note you *will* get wet – if not from the current splashing against the raft, then from the water cannons that line the route. People actually *pay* to shoot water at innocent rafters as they float by.

Claw Island is home to heartbreakingly beautiful Bengal tigers. Feeding times are posted near the fence, and it's gruesomely fascinating to watch these fluffy, elegant creatures ripping into lunch. There are more kiddie rides here, including the Ubanga-Banga Bumper Cars.

Stanleyville Prepare to get wet, since this African village features the **Tanganyika Tidal Wave** – a boat ride that plunges over a 55ft waterfall (minimum height 48 inches). Stanley Falls is a log-flume ride with a 40ft drop (minimum height 46 inches, or with guardian). Catch a kid-friendly show at the Zambezi Pavilion or Stanleyville Theater. Or walk through the Orchid Canyon, where there are orangutans and warthogs.

Bird Gardens & Land of the Dragons Busch Gardens originated at the ever-so-humble Bird Gardens, which was merely a minor detour from the main action at the Anheuser-Busch Brewery tour: you'd guzzle some free beer and walk outside to see the birds. These days the site of the old brewery and Bird Gardens features **Gwazi**, a double wooden roller coaster (the largest in the southeastern USA). Standing at a mere 90ft tall, this may be just the coaster to ride if you're normally queasy about these topsy-turvy machines. You'll also want to check out the interactive Land of the Dragons, an enchanted forest filled with colorful dragons. Or climb around a three-story tree house, hop on the Ferris wheel, climb aboard a flume ride or a waterfall and dragon carousel (minimum height 56 inches for all). Other draws include exotic birds and birds of prey, which are seen in the lush, walk-through aviary. Flamingos and pelicans abound. A koala habitat features all manner of Australian animals, including Queensland koalas.

Adventure Island

This 25-acre water park (☎ 813-987-5600; Ⓦ www.adventureisland.com; 10001 McKinley Dr; adult/child 3-9 $30/28, combination Busch Gardens & Adventure Island for 2/3 days $59/70; open seasonally, hours vary), also run by Anheuser-Busch, has 16 different areas, including **Key West Rapids**, on which rafters go down a six-story twist, ending in a 60ft-long pool. Other slide rides include the **Aruba Tuba** (portions are in total darkness, others in daylight) and **Rambling Bayou**, where you go through weather 'effect' areas (parts are foggy, others have heavy rain). There's also a 9000-sq-ft swimming pool with waterfalls, diving platforms and translucent tube slides. And don't forget the 76ft, free-fall body slide, **Tampa Typhoon**. Parking is $5.

Activities

Ice-Skating There are afternoon and evening sessions at **Town and Country Skateworld** (☎ 813-884-7688; 7510 Paula Dr; open year-round), one block north of Hillsborough Ave (call for specific opening times). Fees are $4.50 for afternoon sessions and $7 to $8 for evening sessions. Rental is included, unless you want in-line or speed skates ($3 and $2.50, respectively). From downtown, take I-275 south to the Veteran's Expressway (Tampa International Airport exit off the interstate) to Hillsborough Ave. Then head about two miles west to Hanley Rd and turn right.

Cruises From the Port of Tampa's cruise ship terminal, **Carnival Cruise Lines** (☎ 800-438-6744; Ⓦ www.carnival.com) operates the *Sensation*; the seven-night trip heads to New Orleans, Grand Cayman and Cozumel, Mexico, and departs every Sunday. It also sails on similar four- and five-day cruises, perhaps adding a stop in Key West.

Holland America Cruise Line (☎ 206-281-3535, 800-426-0327; Ⓦ www.hollandamerica.com) operates the *Noordam* (February through April), a 14-day sailing with stops in San Juan, St Thomas, Dominica, St Lucia, Bonaire and Georgetown.

Organized Tours

Ybor City Ghostwalk (☎ 813-242-4660) runs scheduled tours hosted by an actor in period costume telling tales of Ybor City past. They depart at 4pm Thursdays and Saturdays. Reservations are highly recommended (the tours can be canceled for lack of interest and besides, you have to know where to meet). Tickets are $10 for adults and $8 for children (it's not recommended for children under seven).

Narrated **Duck Tours** (☎ 813-310-3825; Ⓦ www.ducktoursoftampabay.com; 514 Channelside Dr at Newk's Cafe), which take place within authentic WWII army amphibious vehicles, waddle around Ybor City and downtown sites, and then plunge into the Hillsborough River for a view of Tampa from the water. The 80-minute tours cost $18.50 for adults, $16.50 for seniors and $10 for children. At the time of writing, the company had suspended operations but check the website to see if everything's ducky again for them.

Places to Stay

Both full-facility and primitive camping are possible at the appealing **Hillsborough River State Park** (☎ 813-987-6771, reservations 800-326-3521; Ⓦ www.reserveamerica.com; 15402 US 301 North, Thonotosassa; sites $8-20). Otherwise, you'll be stuck at mega sites. Like the others in the area, **Sunburst Super Park Tampa East** and **Encore RV Park Tampa East** (☎ 813-659-0002, 877-917-2757; 12720 Hwy 92; sites summer $25-33, winter $33-41) cater to tourists traveling along I-4 and winter snowbirds. These superstore RV parks have hundreds of sites, amenities galore and a pool that's open 24/7. From I-75, take the I-4 exit east three miles to exit 9 (McIntosh Rd), turn right (south) and drive 220 yards, or continue south to Hwy 92, turn right and drive for about a quarter-mile.

Downtown About as fun and funky as it gets, **Gram's Place** (☎ 813-221-0596; Ⓦ www.grams-inn-tampa.com; 3109 N Ola Ave; 'train' dorm room $15-25, rooms with shared bath $65-80, private bath $80-95) has private rooms, each with a musical theme (jazz, rock & roll etc), and the dorm room is made to look like a sleeper car on a train. There are few places like it in Tampa.

Economy Inn (☎ 813-253-0851; 830 W Kennedy Blvd; rooms summer $45-50, winter $50-55), near the University of Tampa, has 50 decent rooms; HBO is free.

In the immediate downtown area, you'll find **Holiday Inn City Center** (☎ 813-223-1351; 111 W Fortune St; rooms summer $89-129, winter $109-153), a three-story place with 312 units behind the Tampa Bay Performing Arts Center; **Courtyard by Marriott** (☎ 813-229-1100, 800-321-2211; Ⓦ www.marriott.com; 102 E Cass St; rooms summer/winter from $99/159), with 141 typically good rooms; and the 521-room **Hyatt Regency Tampa** (☎ 813-225-1234, 800-233-1234; Ⓦ www.hyatt.com; 211 N Tampa St; rooms $125-294), which is geared toward business travelers.

Ybor City There are cute places to stay in Ybor – just remember that it can get crazy at night.

Hilton Garden Inn (☎ 813-769-9267, 877-367-4458; Ⓦ www.hiltonybor.com; 1700 E 9th Ave; rooms & suites summer/winter from $89/149), with 95 rooms and suites in a four-story building, has more of a homey feel than you might expect.

Don Vicente de Ybor Historic Inn (☎ 813-241-4545; Ⓦ www.donvicenteinn.com; 1915 14th St; rooms summer $99-129, winter $129-159), with 16 boutique-style rooms, was built in 1895 by the founder of Ybor City. It's a good choice.

Casita de Verdad (☎ 813-654-6087; Ⓦ www .yborguesthouse.com; 1609 E 6th Ave; whole house weekday/weekend $180/250), a lovingly restored 1908 cigar maker's house, has just two period rooms, with either an antique sleigh bed or a four-poster bed and a claw-foot bathtub. Features include a courtyard deck, multinight discounts, a plethora of packages (perhaps including a flamenco show at Columbia Restaurant) and full breakfast.

Busch Gardens Chains here include **Economy Inn** (☎ 813-933-7831; 11414 N Central Ave; rooms $31), with 48 rooms; a nicely renovated **Motel 6** (☎ 813-932-4948, 800-466-8356; 333 E Fowler Ave; rooms $44), with 150 rooms; **Red Roof Inn** (☎ 813-932-0073, 800-733-7663; 2307 E Busch Blvd; rooms summer $39-55, winter $49-70), with 108 rooms, a pool and free local phone calls; **Holiday Inn** (☎ 813-971-4710, 800-465-4329; 2701 E Fowler Ave; rooms $75-80), with 408 rooms; and **Howard Johnson Maingate** (☎ 813-988-9191, 800-446-4656; 4139 E Busch Blvd; rooms summer $69-79, winter $89-99), with 100 rooms and a pool.

Less than a mile from Busch Gardens, the excellent 150-room **Best Western All Suites** (☎ 813-971-8930, 800-786-7446; Ⓦ www .thatparrotplace.com; 3001 University Center Dr; rooms summer/winter $109/119) has a nice heated pool and spa, friendly staff and enough perks to satisfy most everyone. Look for two TVs, a refrigerator, a microwave, a VCR, a boom box, and a bedroom and living room. Breakfast is an all-you-can-eat hot buffet. They also have a 99¢ happy hour from 4:30pm to 6:30pm daily.

South Tampa Neither here nor there, South Tampa may split the difference nicely for you. The prices are decent at **EconoLodge Midtown** (☎ 813-254-3005, 800-553-2666; 1020 S Dale Mabry Hwy; rooms summer $50-70, winter $60-80), with 74 rooms and a pool.

Tahitian Inn (☎ 813-877-6721, 800-876-1397; Ⓦ www.tahitianinn.com; 601 S Dale Mabry Hwy; rooms summer $69-99, winter $89-119), with 62 rooms and suites, also has a nice heated pool and workout room.

Places to Eat
Downtown If you're downtown, you'll find standard lunch places.

Broad & Butter Deli (☎ 813-301-0505; 507 N Franklin St; dishes $4-7; open 6am-4pm Mon-Fri), a Greek-run deli with a lot more than the name implies, has good homemade soups, upwards of 20 salads, sandwiches from 'A to Z,' and Greek and Lebanese specials.

City's Gourmet Deli (☎ 813-229-7400; 514 N Tampa St; sandwiches $5-6; open 10:30am-3pm Mon-Sat), with homemade everything, is an excellent choice. From salads and soups to wraps and sandwiches heaped with good stuff, this is not your average deli. For instance, they roast their own meats and use French chocolate in their brownies.

Lonni's Sandwiches (☎ 813-223-2333; 513 E Jackson St; dishes $5-8; open 9am-4pm Mon-Fri) swarms with county workers who flock here for enormous, cheap and sometimes creative sandwiches, with Cuban, American and sometimes Asian blends.

Four Green Fields (☎ 813-254-4444; 205 W Platt St; dishes $10-12; open 11am-3am Mon-Sat, noon-3am Sun) looks like a traditional Irish cottage (with, yes, a thatched roof). Sure enough, it features traditional Irish cooking, thick brogues, Irish music, 30-weight Guinness, pints that pack a punch and friendly folk.

Ybor City Head to Ybor City if you want an interesting meal.

El Molino Coffee Shop (☎ 813-248-2521; 2012 E 7th Ave; open 8am-noon & 12:30pm-4pm Mon-Fri) boasts serious Cuban coffee, not that wimpy American stuff.

La Tropicana Café (☎ 813-247-4040; 1822 E 7th Ave; dishes $2-5; open 8am-4pm Mon-Sat) features traditional Ybor breakfasts (toast and café con leche), Cuban dishes and desserts (like guava pastries), and *papas rellenas* (fried potato cakes). Best of all, it has a drive-thru window.

7th Heaven Psychic Cafe (☎ 813-242-0400; 1725 E 7th Ave; meals $5-8; open 5-11pm Tues, 11:30am-11pm Wed, 11:30-midnight Thur, 11:30am-1:30am Fri & Sat, 1-7pm Sun) couldn't psychically determine why we wanted their prices, but that doesn't mean their readings ($25 for 15 minutes) aren't up and up. You can get coffee and snacks here.

Little Sicily (☎ 813-248-2940; 1724 E 8th Ave; dishes $3-6; open 8am-5pm Mon-Sat), a good Italian-style deli with a few small outside tables, has huge sandwiches, good calzones, pasta dishes and very friendly service.

Joffrey's Coffee Co (☎ 813-248-5282; 1616 E 7th Ave; sandwiches $5; open 7:30am-6pm Mon & Tues, 7:30am-midnight Wed & Thur, 7:30am-3am Fri & Sat) has croissant and bagel sandwiches, pastries and lots of coffee and tea. Or better yet, how about some pure oxygen ($8 for 10 minutes)?

The Laughing Cat (☎ 813-241-2998; 1820 N 15th St; dishes $6-12; open 11am-3pm Mon, 11am-9pm Tues & Wed, 11am-11pm Thur-Sat) has a truly huge selection of affordable Italian dishes and a bargain lunch buffet for $7.95 (11am to 2:30pm Monday to Friday).

The friendly **Cephas West Indian Restaurant** (☎ 813-247-9022; 1701 E 4th Ave; dishes $5-11; open 11:30am-9pm Tues-Thur, 11:30am-3:30am Fri & Sat), a little piece of Jamaica in Ybor City, is run by Cephas Gilbert, who showed up in America in 1982 with only $37 in his pocket. If you're a fan of enormous plates of jerked chicken wings, curried goat or chicken and brown stew, start jumping up and down.

Moses White & Sons Bar B Que (☎ 813-247-7544; 1815 E 7th Ave; platters $7-10; open 11am-6pm Mon-Thur, 11am-3am Fri & Sat), with a real oak-fired pit and some of Florida's best barbecue sauce, has platters (half a chicken or ribs) with two side dishes and a half slab o' ribs.

Carmine's (☎ 813-248-3834; 1802 E 7th Ave; lunch $4-7, dinner $7-14) has both

Cuban and American food, as well as a decent bar.

La Terraza Ristorante (☎ 813-248-1326; 1727 E 7th Ave; lunch $8-10, dinner $12-20; open 11:30am-2pm & 6pm-closing Tues-Fri, 6pm-closing Sat) has great authentic Italian pastas and seafood dishes.

Mykonos Greek Taverna (☎ 813-242-4545; 1833 E 7th Ave; entrees $9-19; open 11am-11pm Sun-Thur, 11am-3am Fri & Sat) is new in town and making an impression with its fine Greek food, late hours and Greek dancing. They get crazy in here, breaking plates and what not.

Spaghetti Warehouse (☎ 813-248-1720; 1911 N 13th St; dishes under $10; open noon-10pm daily) doles out serviceable Italian food in a renovated warehouse behind Ybor Square. The atmosphere is cool enough, regardless of whether you've got an indoor or outdoor table.

Samurai Blue (☎ 813-242-6688; 1600 E 8th Ave; lunch $10-13, dinner mains $15-22; open 11am-2pm Mon-Sat, 5pm-11pm Sun-Thur, 5pm-2am Fri & Sat), with cool architecture, boasts a remarkable 30ft sushi bar, an unusual sake bar and a creative Asian fusion menu for the less adventurous.

Bernini (☎ 813-248-0099; 1702 E 7th Ave; mains $10-15; open 5pm-10pm Sun, 11:30am-10pm Mon-Thur, 11:30am-11pm Fri, 4pm-11pm Sat), housed in the old Bank of Ybor City building, serves delicious wood-fired pizzas and flavorful fresh salads.

Columbia Restaurant (☎ 813-248-4961; 2117 E 7th Ave; set lunch $9-22, dinner mains $15-22; open 11am-10pm Mon-Sat, noon-9pm Sun), family-owned since it opened in 1920, is the oldest restaurant in Florida and a legitimate historical place. It's a gaudy, glitzy place that many people write off as a tourist trap. You should go; just make sure you're in a fun mood. The interior is gorgeous, with 11 dining rooms decorated lavishly with tiled scenes from *Don Quixote* and a fountain. Salads and the black bean appetizers are excellent (especially the '1905' salad), paella à la Valenciana is a specialty and dinner is better than lunch. Consider catching the hot flamenco show (twice nightly except Sunday) for an extra $6. Or pop into the Cigar Bar for some tapas, smokes and jazz (Thursday to Saturday).

Busch Gardens The mainstay of the classic **Mel's Hot Dogs** (☎ 813-985-8000; 4136 E Busch Blvd; open 11am-8pm Sun-Thur, 11am-9pm Fri & Sat), made by the Chicago

Vienna Beef Company, is the Mighty Mel Hot Dog ($3), a flabbergastingly large dog with relish, mustard and pickles on a poppy-seed bun. For wiener-haters who travel with wiener-devotees, there are veggie burgers.

Taj *(☎ 813-971-8483; 2734-B E Fowler Ave; lunch buffet $8, dinner mains $8-16; open 11:30am-2:30pm & 5pm-10pm Tues-Sun)*, which can get very crowded, serves good Indian food and has an all-you-can-eat lunch buffet. Try the chicken tandoori and chicken curry.

South Tampa Referred to by locals as SoHo (ie, South Howard Ave), this burgeoning dining area offers a number of varied choices.

Bean There Traveler's Coffee House *(☎ 813-837-7022; 3203 Bay-to-Bay Blvd; dishes $3-6; open 7am-3pm Mon-Fri, 8am-3pm Sat, 8am-2pm Sun)* serves breakfast (all day), sandwiches and coffee alongside their maps, globes and the big 'Where You Bean' bulletin board where patrons put up photos, postcards and other travel mementos. Take Bayshore Blvd from downtown to Bay-to-Bay Blvd and turn right; it's on the right side of the road, past MacDill Ave.

The Yellow Door *(☎ 813-258-3074; 311 S Howard Ave; dishes $7-13; open 6pm-11pm Mon-Sat)* serves Southeast Asian–style tapas dishes bursting with flavor (shrimp rolls, Mongolian sea bass) in low-key, minimalist surroundings. This is a very good choice.

Mise en Place *(☎ 813-254-5373; 442 W Kennedy Blvd; mains $16-27; open 5:30pm-10pm Tues-Thur, 5:30pm-11pm Fri & Sat)*, a longtime chef-owned bistro across from the University, is arguably Tampa's brightest culinary shooting star. The creative and seasonal menu, with Floribbean twists, is decidedly eclectic and always a treat. Always. Put on some trendy black and saunter over; you won't be disappointed. Or head next door (in that same black garb) for some appetizers and jazz at their adjacent **442** club. Or settle for takeout at their **Mise en Place Market** *(2616 S MacDill Ave)*.

Side Bern's *(☎ 813-258-2233; 1002 S Howard Ave; mains $24-26; open 6pm-10pm Tues-Sun)*, the Bern's Steak House spin-off, is nothing like its parent. What, you never thought that could happen? You'll find contemporary fusion cuisine here, which utilizes spices from around the world to enliven the mostly seafood dishes. Ostrich or lamb devotees need not worry, though; you'll find those on the menu.

Bern's Steak House *(☎ 813-251-2421; 1208 S Howard Ave; steaks from $27, desserts from $4; open 5pm-10:30pm daily)*, Tampa's landmark restaurant, serves some of the best steaks east of the west. Perhaps you're in the mood to share a 60oz slab with five of your closest friends? No problem, if you have $225. Downstairs the slick atmosphere is heavy on red velvet, gold leaf and statuary; upstairs, where patrons head for sweets in the cigar-friendly dessert room, the tables are made from redwood wine casks. Reservations are a must. Not widely known, you can always just order a steak sandwich at the bar. Or you can just come for one of a hundred desserts (a scoop of ice cream, flaming cherries jubilee or bananas Foster served in paneled booths) to get a sneak peek at the place, but they don't take reservations for just dessert, and you may find yourself waiting for the privilege. Bern's wine list boasts more than 7000 labels and 1800 dessert wines, but the cellars stash over a million bottles. Take Bayshore Blvd from downtown to Howard Ave, and then turn right on Howard.

Entertainment

For up to the minute Tampa Bay cultural events, call the **arts line** *(☎ 813-229-2787)* operated by the Arts Council of Hillsborough County. There's no shortage of printed information, either: get local news and entertainment listings in the free Wednesday *Weekly Planet* (🖳 www.weeklyplanet.com); the pullout Thursday *Weekend* section of the *St Petersburg Times*; and the pullout Friday 'Extra' section of the *Tampa Tribune*.

Gameworks *(☎ 813-241-9675; 1600 E 8th Ave; open 11am-midnight Sun-Wed, 11am-2am Thur-Sat)*, a high-tech play place with virtual-reality free-falling simulators and the like, has plenty of eateries and bars to keep you spending money.

Seminole Indian Casino *(☎ 813-621-1302, 800-282-7016; 🖳 www.casino-tampa.com; 5223 N Orient Rd; open 24/7)* is about 15 minutes from downtown Tampa off I-4 (head east to Orient Rd and then head left). This casino sucks in those who love the thrill of winning big time, instantly. But don't bet on it. Like a spider spinning a web with high-stakes bingo and stud poker, this place has it all and plans on keeping it.

Performing Arts Beautifully sited on a river park, the **Tampa Bay Performing Arts Center** *(☎ 813-229-7827, 800-955-1045; 1010 N MacInnes Place; tickets $10-50)* is the largest performing arts center south of the Kennedy Center in Washington, DC. It's home to major concerts, touring Broadway productions, plays, the Tampa Ballet and special events. There are four theaters in the complex: Festival Hall (a 2500-seat venue where touring Broadway shows and headliners perform), Ferguson Hall (with 1000 seats), the Jaeb (a three-floor cabaret) and the 100-seat Shimberg Playhouse, a 'black box' venue that's home to cutting-edge performances by local and national artists and groups. Free backstage guided tours are offered Wednesdays and Saturdays at 10am; call ☎ 813-222-1000 to make a reservation.

UT Falk Theater (☎ 813-253-3333; 428 W Kennedy Blvd), a 900-seat theater, is operated by the University of Tampa.

The **Florida Orchestra** (☎ 813-286-2403, 800-662-7286; tickets $20-42), a 90-piece orchestra, plays at the Performing Arts Center as well as venues in St Petersburg and Clearwater and at free park concerts.

USF School of Music (☎ 813-974-2311; USF campus, Fowler Ave; tickets $2-4; season Sept-Mar), where the USF Theater also performs, is accessible from Fowler Ave exits on I-275 and I-75. They stage a variety of concerts and recitals open to the entire community.

Sun Dome (☎ 813-974-3111; W www.sun dome.org; 4202 E Fowler Ave), also on the USF campus, hosts rock, jazz, pop and other concerts – from Jimmy Buffet to *NSYNC, from Luciano Pavarotti to the World Wrestling Federation (now there's some 'performing arts' for you!).

Raymond James Stadium (☎ 813-350-6500; W www.tampasportsauthority.com; 4201 N Dale Mabry Hwy) often presents concerts, too.

Ticketmaster (☎ 813-287-8844) sells tickets to most events and tacks on a surcharge for its trouble.

Bars & Clubs If the words 'party central', 'meat market' and 'bouncers' show up regularly in your conversations, Ybor City is your kind of place. Intense weekend crowds and partyers revel into the wee hours. Locals suggest showing up early, getting your hand stamped and coming back later to push through the crowds like you're a celebrity. Check flyers on walls and lampposts – they're the most reliable source of up-to-date party, concert and nightclub information. Nightly drink specials and cover charges change more quickly than a leopard changes spots, so it's pointless to include them here

(for the most part). Cruise E 7th Ave between 15th and 20th Sts on Friday and Saturday nights between 9pm and 3am and you might not be able to control yourself.

Adobe Gilas (☎ 813-241-8588; 1600 E 8th Ave; open 11am-3am Mon-Sat, 1pm-3am Sun) mixes margaritas. The 2nd-floor balconies are also a very good vantage point from which to take in the street scene below.

Improv Comedy Theater (☎ 813-864-4000; W www.tampaimprov.com; 1600 E 8th Ave; tickets $10-22) puts on good doses of nightly comedic schtick. Some national acts come to town.

Tampa Bay Brewing Company (☎ 813-247-1422; 1812 N 15th St; pub food $8-16; open 11:30am-midnight Mon & Tues, 11:30am-2am Wed-Sat, 1pm-midnight Sun) is a fun place with microbrews, $4 liters on Wednesdays and weekday happy hours (4pm to 7pm).

Green Iguana Bar & Grill (☎ 813-248-9555; W www.greeniguana.net; 1708 E 7th Ave; open 11am-2am nightly) is a cool but laid-back bar and restaurant by day (with Floribbean food, sandwiches and burgers). By night, it's really two clubs in one – deal with either high-energy cover bands or high-energy, DJ-driven dance music – and has $1 drinks on Wednesdays.

Twilight (☎ 813-247-4225; 1507 E 7th Ave; open 9pm-3am Wed-Sat) reels 'em in with college nights, live music, hot DJs and hotter dancing on two floors. Soul and funk, anyone?

The Empire/Climax (☎ 813-247-2582; 1902 E 7th Ave; open from 9pm Fri & Sat) attracts a diverse crowd with techno, hip-hop and booty. Downstairs is ruled by a DJ and color laser lights; head upstairs to Climax with R&B and reggae.

Cherokee Club (☎ 813-247-9966; 1320 E 9th Ave; open 8pm-3am Fri & Sat), with dancing and infrequent live music, is a predominantly lesbian (but gay as well) club. Exuding a satisfying irony, this former 'gentlemen only' club was frequented by such luminaries as José Martí, Winston Churchill and Teddy Roosevelt. Bully, ladies!

So you've decided to forgo Ybor City to see what the rest of Tampa has to offer? Here are two dependable choices.

The Hub (☎ 813-229-1553; 701 N Florida Ave), a fun local hangout with a jukebox and cheap drinks, looks like a hole in the wall. But the bar gets packed on weekends with a Jack-Daniels-and-Coke drinking crowd. Be prepared to call a cab after ordering a few too many.

The all-around scene at **Hyde Park Cafe** (☎ 813-254-2233; W www.thehydeparkcafe .com; 1806 W Platt St; open from 8pm Tues-Sat), a late-night pizza place ($10 to $15), indoor-outdoor cafe and VIP club, gets really packed on Tuesday nights with eclectic music. Other nights see a good DJ spinning tunes behind the rack; happy hour (and no cover) dominates from 8pm to 10pm. Silicone implants and South Beach–slick attire dominate the club. See also Four Green Fields, under Downtown Places to Eat earlier in this chapter.

Spectator Sports

Football The NFL's **Tampa Bay Buccaneers** (☎ 813-870-2700; W www.buccaneers.com) play at Raymond James Stadium. Games are played from August (pre-season) to December, but you'll probably have to catch them on TV since season ticket holders grab all the seats.

On every New Year's Day, **the Outback Bowl** (☎ 813-874-2695; W www.outbackbowl .com), an NCAA (National College Athletic Association) football game, is played at Raymond James Stadium. If you've never seen an American college football game, this should not be missed (but at $50 per ticket it may have to be!).

The **USF Bulls** (☎ 813-974-2125, 800-462-8557; W www.gousfbulls.com), a Division I-AA football team, play at Tampa Stadium; tickets are about $20.

Baseball The **New York Yankees** (☎ 813-875-7753; W www.legendsfieldtampa.com; 3802 ML King Jr Blvd at Dale Mabry Hwy) play spring-training games at Legends Field in March. Tickets cost $10 to $14. The 10,000-seat stadium is modeled after the House that Ruth Built, or Yankee Stadium, which is in the Bronx, New York. The Yankees' minor-league team, the Tampa Yankees, plays at Legends Field from April to September. Tickets cost $3 to $5; parking is free.

Hockey The **Tampa Bay Lightning** (☎ 813-301-6600; W www.tampabaylightning.com) play at the Ice Palace in the Channel District from October through March. Tickets cost $15 to $60. The entertainment complex also hosts NHL hockey games, basketball games, concerts and ice shows.

Shopping

Oversized flea markets are a Florida fixture, but this one north of downtown is extra special. **Big Top Flea Market** (☎ 813-986-4004;

Tampa Bay's First Super Bowl Success

Thanks to a defense stronger than an army of Arnold Schwarzeneggers, Tampa Bay blasted the Oakland Raiders 48–21 in Super Bowl XXXVII on January 26, 2003, capping the best year in franchise history.

In the Super Bowl, the Bucs' league-leading defense threw a plastic bag over the Raiders, suffocating quarterback Rich Gannon, the National Football League's regular-season MVP (most valuable player), into a clueless five-interception performance, easily his worst showing of the season. How impenetrable was the Bucs' defense?

'I'm not saying it's the best defense I've ever seen,' Oakland receiver Tim Brown, a 15-year NFL veteran, was quoted as saying. 'But it's very good defense.'

Much of the season's credit went to the Bucs' first-year coach, Jon Gruden, 39, who ironically led Oakland for four years before joining Tampa in February 2002. The fiery, emotional coach, nicknamed Chucky after the horror-movie character in the Child's Play series, became the youngest to win a Super Bowl.

The Super Bowl season felt like it was a thousand years in the making for Tampa fans; some of them are old-timers who saw their franchise drop the first 26 games in their premiere season, 1976–77. That ignominious beginning, coupled with their then puke-orange uniforms, made the Bucs the NFL's laughingstock. No-one is laughing now.

Will opponents gain revenge when Tampa's players are released from their contracts and are free to play elsewhere, a fate that befell many past champions? Only time will tell, but the Bucs will be a contender in 2003.

And Chucky? He, too, will return in 2003, although Tampa fans hope his second season will be superior to Child's Play II.

Barry Sollenberger

W www.bigtopfleamarket.com; 9250 E Fowler Ave; open 9am-4:30pm Sat & Sun) redefines 'bargain' with a capital 'B.' Forget retail when these 1000 enclosed and covered stalls can provide every essential and nonessential item ever produced. You gotta love it…or hate it.

Getting There & Away

Air The **Tampa International Airport** (TPA; ☎ 813-870-8700; W www.tampaairport.com) is about 5 miles west of downtown, off Hwy 589. From I-275, it's off exit 39 or 39B. Since it's the major regional airport, most flights to the Tampa area land here – as opposed to at St Petersburg-Clearwater International Airport.

Bus Tampa's **Greyhound bus station** (☎ 813-229-2112, 800-231-2222; 610 Polk St) serves the region. The trip from Tampa to Miami takes seven to nine hours ($36/65 one way/round-trip); to Orlando takes two to three hours ($16/28); to Sarasota takes two hours ($11/21); and to Gainesville takes three to 3½ hours ($18/36).

Train Several times daily **Amtrak** (☎ 813-221-7600; W www.amtrak.com; 601 N Nebraska Ave) has shuttle buses running between Tampa and Orlando. The ticket office is open from 5:45am to 9:50pm daily, except from 10:30am to 11:30am and from 7:30pm to 8:30pm. Now that you know, don't get caught empty-handed. The Silver Service/Palmetto line (New York to Miami) stops here as well.

Car & Motorcycle Tampa is 245 miles northwest of Miami, 135 miles southwest of the Space Coast and 85 miles south of Orlando. Between Tampa and Orlando, take I-4. Between Tampa and Miami, the fastest way is to take I-75 south to Fort Lauderdale and then I-95 south, though the more scenic route is US Hwy 41 (Tamiami Trail) south to Everglades City and due east to Calle Ocho in Miami. Major car rental agencies are located at the airport.

Getting Around

To/From the Airport The No 30 HART bus picks up and drops off at the Red Arrival Desk on the lower level; exact change is required. From the airport, buses run to the downtown terminal (see Bus below) about every half-hour from 6am to 8:30pm. The trip takes about 40 minutes. From downtown to the airport, buses run about every half-hour from 5:45am to 7pm.

Super Shuttle (☎ 800-282-6817; W www.supershuttle.com) plies the road outside the arrival areas; it generally costs from $15 to $19 to downtown Tampa.

All major car agencies have desks at the airport. By car, take I-275 to N Ashley Dr, turn right and you're in downtown.

Bus The **Uptown-Downtown Connector** (☎ 813-254-4278) is free and runs up and down Florida Ave, Tampa St and Franklin St every 10 minutes from 6am to 6pm Monday through Friday.

Hillsborough Area Regional Transit (HART; ☎ 813-254-4278; W www.hartline.org) buses converge on the Morgan St terminal. Buses cost $1.25 one way or $3 for an all-day pass. To take your bike on the bus, you'll need to go to the terminal and buy a photo ID permit ($2); from then on, there's no extra charge. Check out these popular destinations by bus (all leave from the main terminal):

destination	bus no	departs
Ybor City	8, 46	half-hourly
Busch Gardens & USF	5	half-hourly
Lowry Park Zoo	7	half-hourly
Henry Plant Museum	10	half-hourly
MOSI	6 to University Transit Center*	hourly

*Note: there are two routes on bus No 6, so check the destination.

Express rush-hour buses ply the route between Tampa and the coast: bus No 10 goes to St Petersburg and bus No 20 to Clearwater.

Trolley Darling electric streetcars (☎ 813-242-5491; W www.hartline.org; $1.25) tootle around Ybor City from Channelside on a 2.3-mile route.

ST PETERSBURG
pop 248,000

Rejuvenated St Petersburg, a lovely city set on a peninsula, boasts a collection of museums that together form what may be the state's cultural powerhouse. The Salvador Dalí Museum is the largest collection of that artist's works outside Spain; the St Petersburg Fine Arts Museum has one of the finest collections in the state; and the Florida International Museum's blockbuster rotating exhibitions have brought national attention with groundbreaking international shows. And, to boot, they're all connected by a convenient trolley and intermingled with fine bistros and cafés. Throw in about seven miles of accessible waterfront and you've got yourself one serious destination.

Orientation

St Petersburg is a typically sprawling southwest Florida town. For instance, it's a good 25 minutes to the beach in the best of traffic. Downtown is about 10 miles northeast of St Pete Beach and about 20 miles southwest of Tampa across Old Tampa Bay.

The city is oriented on the ever-familiar grid: avenues run east–west and streets and boulevards run north–south. The north–south dividing line is Central Ave, and 34th St (Hwy 19) is the east–west divider, though people usually ignore the east–west designation. The directional indicator is placed after the street. Avenues count upward away from Central Ave, so 1st Ave N is one block north of Central, and 1st Ave S is one block south.

Downtown is the area roughly bordered by the bay at the east, Martin Luther King Jr Blvd (9th St) at the west, 10th Ave N at the north and 17th Ave S at the south.

Information

Contact the **St Petersburg/Clearwater Area Convention & Visitors Bureau** (☎ 727-464-7200, 800-345-6710; ⓦ www.floridasbeach .com; 14450 46th St N) for advance information; its location across from the airport is inconvenient for drop-ins.

Once in town, head to the **St Petersburg Area Chamber of Commerce** (☎ 727-821-4715; ⓦ www.stpete.org; 100 2nd Ave N; open 9am-5pm Mon-Fri, 10am-4pm Sat, noon-4pm Sun) for brochures, pamphlets and maps. It produces a good downtown arts guide as well as a general map with pullouts of different neighborhoods. The Chamber also has an information booth at The Pier (see later in this section) and at 2001 Ulmerton Rd (exit 18 off I-275 south, just beyond the Howard Frankland Bridge).

Bank of America has many branches downtown.

The main post office (3135 1st Ave N) is less convenient than the open-air downtown **post office** (76 4th St N). This branch, within a Mediterranean Revival building, was the nation's first open-air post office, and it's a glorious thing, with a keystone-arched open front. It contains an itty-bitty display case in the rear with postal paraphernalia such as

stamps, inkwells and a numbering device. Mailing letters has never been so educational!

The incredible **Haslam's Book Store** (☎ 727-822-8616; 2025 Central Ave) could be designated an attraction without raising any eyebrows. Founded in 1933, the shop needs a half block to house its 300,000 titles (who's counting?), all arranged with a surprising degree of organization. To no-one's surprise, it has a good Florida section, new and remaindered books and a core of used books. **Lighthouse Books** (☎ 727-822-3278; 1735 1st Ave N) has Florida and Caribbean sections as well as rare books, maps and prints. **The Age of Reason** (☎ 727-821-0892; 621 Central Ave) offers used books with friendly service. **Bayboro Books** (☎ 727-821-5477; 121 7th Ave S) has great staff and a good travel section.

Visit the main **library** (☎ 727-893-7724; 3745 9th Ave N; open 9am-9pm Mon-Thur, 9am-5:30pm Fri & Sat, 10am-6pm Sun) or the downtown branch, the **Mirror Lake Library** (☎ 727-893-7268; cnr 5th St & 2nd Ave N; open 9am-6pm Mon-Fri, 9am-5pm Sat) for Web surfing. Call ahead to make an appointment, or take your chances with a couple of walk-in computers.

The good *St Petersburg Times* has great up-to-date information on its website ⓦ www.sp times.com. Tune into NPR at 89.7 FM.

For medical emergencies, the area's largest hospital is **All Children's Hospital** (☎ 727-898-7451; 6th St S), between 8th and 9th Aves S; otherwise, there's **Bayfront Medical Center** (☎ 727-823-1234; 701 6th St S).

Check out the biweekly publication *Watermark* (ⓦ www.watermarkonline.com) for coverage of gay, lesbian and bisexual matters.

Salvador Dalí Museum

Boasting the largest collection of Dalí's work outside Spain, this must-see treasure trove (☎ 727-823-3767; ⓦ www.salvadordalimus eum.org; 1000 3rd St S; adult/student 10 & over/child 5-9 $12.50/6/3, half price after 5pm on Thur; open 9:30am-5:30pm Mon-Sat, noon-5:30pm Sun) is easily one of St Petersburg's star attractions. While Dalí is best known for surrealist work, this $125 million collection covers the entire range of the artist's work: from early impressionism, cubism, still lifes and landscapes (1914–27), through his transitional period (1928), onto surrealism (1929–40) and back to classical works (1943–89)…not to mention the collection of masterworks – 18 major oil paintings produced between 1948 and 1970. Of these, don't miss

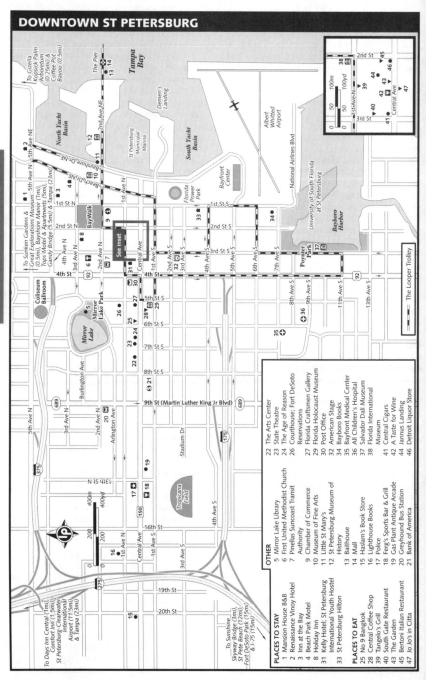

DOWNTOWN ST PETERSBURG

PLACES TO STAY
1 Mansion House B&B
2 Renaissance Vinoy Hotel
3 Inn at the Bay
4 Beach Park Motel
8 Holiday Inn
31 Kelly Hotel; St Petersburg International Youth Hostel
33 St Petersburg Hilton

PLACES TO EAT
25 No 9 Bangkok
28 Central Coffee Shop
39 Tangelo's Grill
40 South Gate Restaurant
43 The Garden
45 Bertoni Italian Restaurant
47 Jo Jo's in Citta

OTHER
5 Mirror Lake Library
6 First United Methodist Church
7 Pinellas Suncoast Transit Authority
9 Chamber of Commerce
10 Little St Mary's
11 Museum of Fine Arts
12 St Petersburg Museum of History
13 Bathouse
14 Mall
15 Haslam's Book Store
16 Lighthouse Books
17 Police
18 Ferg's Sports Bar & Grill
19 Gas Plant Antique Arcade
20 Greyhound Bus Station
21 Bank of America
22 The Arts Center
23 State Theatre
24 The Age of Reason
26 Courthouse; Fort DeSoto Reservations
27 Florida Craftsmen Gallery
29 Florida Holocaust Museum
30 Post Office
32 American Stage
34 Bayboro Books
35 Bayfront Medical Center
36 All Children's Hospital
37 Salvador Dali Museum
38 Florida International Museum
41 Central Cigars
42 A Taste for Wine
44 Jannus Landing
46 Detroit Liquor Store

The Discovery of America by Christopher Columbus (1958–59); *The Ecumenical Council* (1960); *Galacidalacidesoxiribunucleicacid* (1962–63); and *The Hallucinogenic Toreador* (1969–70). How the heck did all these paintings end up in little old St Petersburg? Industrialist A Reynolds Morse began collecting Dalí in the 1940s and when he was searching for a location that would be suitable, the town had the common sense to woo him. Free, illuminating guided tours are offered throughout the day; be sure to take one or be prepared to be even more bewildered and bemused by the artist's work.

Florida International Museum

Ensconced in a former department store, this enormous space (☎ 727-822-3693, 800-777-9882; W *www.floridamuseum.org; 100 2nd St N; adult/youth 6-18 $12/6; open 10am-5pm Mon-Sat, noon-5pm Sun, box office closes 4pm)*, a Smithsonian Institute Affiliate, hosts some of the country's most spectacular temporary exhibits. All those international blockbusters that you read about in the London *Times* make a stop here. Shows that have traveled here in recent years include Norman Rockwell's Saturday Evening Post Covers, Treasures of the Tzars, Splendors of Ancient Egypt, Alexander the Great and Treasures of the Titanic. The only two permanent exhibits – on the Cuban Missile Crisis and the Kennedy Collection (with a scale replica of the Oval Office, Rose Garden and Dallas motorcade) – are excellent and alone worth the price of admission.

Museum of Fine Arts

This is one of the state's best fine arts museums (☎ 727-896-2667; W *www.fine-arts.org; 255 Beach Dr NE; adult/youth 6-18 $8/4, suggested donation on Sunday $3; open 10am-5pm Tues-Sat, 1-5pm Sun)*, with an enormous permanent collection that constitutes a very diverse and well-rounded history of art. Look for Asian, Indian and African art, pre-Columbian sculpture, photographic works, Cycladic sculpture from the 3rd century BC, and American and European paintings and sculpture. Perhaps non-Americans will get lucky and see some O'Keefe, Stella, Lichtenstein and Rauschenberg. Americans would be fortunate to admire fine European impressionists. Free regular tours and special events like concerts, plays and films are often scheduled; check with the front desk on arrival. The waterfront location is appealing, as are the courtyards.

St Petersburg Museum of History

This museum (☎ 727-894-1052; W *www.st petemuseumofhistory.org; 335 2nd Ave NE; adult/youth 7-17 $5/3; open 10am-5pm Mon-Sat, 1pm-5pm Sun)* features upwards of 60 permanent and rotating exhibits celebrating the town's long history. Check out a dog-powered butter churn, million-year-old fossils, a 400-year-old carved cypress canoe and a pioneer-era general store, not to mention taking a trip back in time to St Petersburg's Victorian influences. It also has a great display on the early days of aviation – St Petersburg was the takeoff site for America's first scheduled airline flight on January 1, 1914. The plane used for that flight, the *Benoist Airboat* (restored in 1984), now hangs in the First Flight Gallery, which also has some interesting early aviation artifacts.

Florida Holocaust Museum

This memorial (☎ 727-820-0100; W *www .flholocaustmuseum.org; 55 5th St S; adult/ youth under 19 $8/3; open 10am-5pm Mon-Fri, noon-5pm Sat & Sun)*, the fourth largest in the USA, is worth a visit not just for its Holocaust exhibits but for those of Jewish life around the world. It also exhibits one of three boxcars in the USA used to transport prisoners to death camps in Poland. Visit the quiet meditation court before leaving and vow to make the museum's mission your own: promote tolerance today.

Coffee Pot Bayou

This old northeast neighborhood, the heart of which is between 19th and 30th Aves NE (but it's also very sweet around 9th Ave NE), east of 4th St, was developed in the 1920s and is lined with brick streets and authentic architecture. A 30-minute drive will reward you with an insider's view of St Petersburg beyond the museums and marinas. While you're in the area, drive over the Venetian-style Snell Island Bridge (at Coffee Pot Blvd and 21st Ave NE) to appreciate some Mediterranean-style architecture. To reach Coffee Pot, follow the waterfront north of downtown; take Bayshore Dr to North Shore Dr to Coffee Pot Blvd.

BayWalk

The downtown revitalization continues with this upscale shopping mall, bounded by 2nd and 3rd Aves N and 1st and 2nd Sts. The open-air emporium has lots of shops, eateries and the 20-screen **Muvico Theater** (☎ 727-502-9573), complete with stadium seating.

The Pier

Formerly a railroad pier (☎ 727-821-6164; W www.stpete-pier.com; 800 2nd Ave NE; open 10am-9pm Mon-Sat, 11am-9pm Sun), this dominating inverted pyramid is something of a tourist trap. It's, well, a long pier with a fishing platform at the end. And it's been converted to hold a five-story shopping mall with three restaurants and a free 2nd-floor **aquarium** (open 11am-7:30pm Mon-Sat, noon-6pm Sun). Pier parking (including valet) costs $3, and there's a shuttle that runs between the parking lots and the action.

You can feed resident pelicans (which are standing around waiting for you) with fish food from the **baithouse** (☎ 727-821-3750); 10 fish cost $5. Or you can rent a fishing rod for $10 a day; the price includes bait.

The story of **Little St Mary's** begins with Henry Taylor, who was never paid for his design work at St Mary's Church, located at 515 4th St S. Out of spite he then built this Romanesque-revival miniature church and dubbed it Little St Mary's. The only rub: it's a toilet. This is perhaps the only toilet in Florida that is also a historic landmark.

South of the pier, **Demen's Landing** waterfront park (Bayshore Dr SE at 1st Ave S), with picnic facilities, hosts **American Stage in the Park** (☎ 727-822-8814), a Shakespeare festival that takes place from mid-April to mid-May. The park was named for a Russian-born railroad developer who brought passengers to the area in the late 1880s.

Great Explorations Museum

'Hands-on' reaches new heights at this fun science museum (☎ 727-821-8992; W www.greatexplorations.org; 1925 4th St N; adult/child 3-18 $8/7; open 10am-4:30pm Mon-Sat, noon-4:30pm Sun). It really lets kids get down and dirty with a Touch Tunnel, an 8ft-long, pitch-black maze and a dino dig (where kids dig for fossils in the sand and try to reconstruct the creature). Fire up the imagination with interactive computer games, a reptile room (snakes, scorpions and spiders, anyone?) and a floor maze.

First United Methodist Church

This 1925 Gothic Revival church (☎ 727-894-4661; 212 3rd St N), listed on the National Register of Historic Places, has some pretty stunning Tiffany-style stained-glass windows. Sunday services are held at 8am and 11am.

Gizella Kopsick Palm Arboretum

This two-acre arboretum (☎ 727-893-7335; cnr North Shore Dr & 10th Ave NE; admission free; open dawn to dusk daily) contains upwards of 300 different exotic and rare palms and cycads, representing about 75 worldwide species. Follow the brick walkways to inspect the wildly diverse jelly palm, windmill palm and triangle palm, but don't overlook the garden-variety gru gru palm.

Sunken Gardens

Opened in 1935, this garden (☎ 727-551-3100; 1825 4th St N; adult/child $7/3; open 10am-4:30pm Mon-Sat, noon-4:30pm Sun), with lots of water features, consists of four tropical acres and a walk-through butterfly aviary. The city of St Petersburg took over the site recently and plans to revamp it.

Biking

The **Friendship Trail Bridge** (☎ 727-549-6099), aka the old Gandy Bridge and US 92, is basically a 2.6-mile-long dedicated biking, walking and in-line skating path that runs alongside the Gandy Bridge, which connects St Petersburg and Tampa. Look for the trailhead on 34th St S near 8th Ave.

See also Pinellas Trail under Around Clearwater Beach, later in this chapter.

Organized Tours

Biplane Rides (☎ 727-895-6266), at Albert Whitted Airport near Bayfront Center, offer downtown tours in a 1933 WACO biplane originally owned by William Randolph Hearst. Tours start at $90 for up to three people, for 15 to 20 minutes; they're best taken in the morning.

Narrated **Duck Tours** (☎ 727-432-3825; W www.ducktoursoftampabay.com; 200 2nd Ave NE at The Pier), which take place within authentic WWII army amphibious vehicles, waddle by downtown attractions and then plunge into the bay near Demen's Landing for a view of St Petersburg from the water. At the time of writing, the company had suspended operations but check the website to see if everything's ducky again for them.

Places to Stay

Camping Fort DeSoto Park Campground (☎ 727-582-2267; 3500 Pinellas Bayway S; sites summer/winter $23/33) has 235 shaded

Tampa skyline

Ybor City Museum State Park

Museum of Science & Industry, Tampa

Harmonica player, 7th Ave, Ybor City, Tampa

Giraffe, Serengeti Safari Tour, Busch Gardens

Sunset, Clearwater Beach Pier

Children's sand art, Clearwater Beach

tent and RV sites, many of which are water-side. Only cash payments are accepted, and reservations must be made in person and within 30 days of your planned stay. You can make reservations at the camp address above *(8am-9pm daily)*, in Clearwater at 631 Chestnut St *(8am-5pm Mon-Fri)* or in St Petersburg at the courthouse *(501 1st Ave N, Room A116; 8am-4:30pm Mon-Fri)*. To get there from downtown, take I-275 south to the 54th Ave S/Sr 682 W exit, then take the Pinellas Bayway/St Petersburg Beach exit (No. 17). Turn right onto 54th Ave S and continue onto Pinellas Bayway S until you reach the park.

Hotels & Motels The **Kelly Hotel** *(☎ 727-822-4141; 326 1st Ave N; dorm beds $20, singles/doubles daily $39/49, weekly $145/165)*, on the National Register of Historic Places, has a nice staff, 65 spartan rooms and hostel-style dorms. Rooms on higher floors are cheerier, but all are basically clean, and many have a view of adjacent brick walls. One hostel-style floor has eight rooms, some of which have four bunks and some of which are semiprivate rooms. Dorm rooms, while clean enough and air-conditioned, are not the cheeriest in the world.

Beach Park Motel *(☎ 727-898-6325, 800-657-7687; 300 Beach Dr NE; rooms $74)* has 26 older but good rooms with fridges and a great location.

St Petersburg Hilton *(☎ 727-894-5000, 800-774-1500; W www.stpetehilton.com; 333 1st St S; rooms summer/winter from $89/139)* has 333 Hilton-ish rooms with a fine downtown location, restaurants, bars and a pool and fitness center.

Holiday Inn *(☎ 727-822-4814, 800-283-7829; W www.holiday-inn.com; 234 3rd Ave N; rooms summer/winter $109/139)*, a great choice with 70 rooms, is *almost* more like a B&B than a motel, since it's partially housed in a 1926 Victorian-style building, complete with a wraparound porch and some antiques.

There are a bunch of cheap motels of varying quality on 4th St N (which runs right into downtown) and 34th St N (which is just west of I-275). Here are the best of the bunch: **Tops Motel & Apartments** *(☎ 727-526-9071; 7141 4th St N; units summer $35-40, winter $40-50)*, with 16 rooms and apartments; **Days Inn Central** *(☎ 727-321-2958, 800-325-2525; 650 34th St N; rooms $60-66)*, with 28 rooms, a third of which have kitchens; and **Comfort Inn** *(☎ 727-323-3100, 800-228-5150; 1400 34th St N; rooms summer $59-79,* *winter $69-89)*, with 75 rooms, half of which are efficiency apartments.

Resorts A large, pink and flashy grande dame on the bay, **Renaissance Vinoy Resort** *(☎ 727-894-1000, 800-468-3571; W www.renaissancehotels.com; 501 5th Ave NE; rooms summer/winter from $179/199)* is reminiscent of a bygone era. Built in 1925, the National Historic Landmark boasts 360 richly furnished guest rooms (many with bay views), a day spa, huge fitness center, excellent golf and tennis, and opulent dining and entertainment areas.

B&Bs One of St Petersburg's least expensive B&Bs, **Bay Shore Manor** *(☎ 727-822-3438; W www.bayshoremanor.com; 635 12th Ave NE; rooms $69-84)* includes a German-style breakfast with coffee, milk, juice, breads, cold cuts, cheese, eggs and cereal. Each of the seven rooms has a TV, coffeemaker, microwave and mini-refrigerator.

Inn at the Bay *(☎ 727-822-1700, 888-873-2122; W www.innatthebay.com; 126 4th Ave NE; rooms & suites $109-250)*, with 12 guest rooms in an old northeast neighborhood house that dates to 1910, offers a full breakfast, feather beds, data ports and robes. Most bathrooms have two-person whirlpool tubs.

Mansion House B&B *(☎ 727-821-9391, 800-274-7520; W www.mansionbandb.com; 105 5th Ave N; rooms summer $99-165, winter $149-220)*, with a tranquil pool and courtyard garden, has 12 rooms and a suite in two wonderful old houses. Other pluses include gracious hosts, complimentary afternoon wine, full breakfast and a great location.

Bayboro House B&B *(☎ 727-823-4955, 877-823-4955; W www.bayborohousebandb.com; 1719 Beach Dr SE; rooms summer $129, winter $149-229)*, a waterfront B&B built in 1907 in a quiet neighborhood on Tampa Bay, has lots of Victorian charm (read: lace and antiques) and a wraparound veranda. Each of the eight rooms and suites has a private bath and a VCR/TV. You'll also appreciate beach chairs, beach towels and a pool and spa. Call for directions.

Places to Eat
Central Coffee Shop *(☎ 727-821-1125; 530 Central Ave; dishes $2-6; open 6:30am-1pm Mon-Fri)* is the place for no-frills meals.

South Gate Restaurant *(☎ 727-823-7071; 29 3rd St N; dishes $3-7; open 7am-5:30pm daily)* serves cheap breakfasts all day, cheap sandwiches and burgers at lunch, and good Greek salads and chicken *gyros*.

Tangelo's Grill (☎ 727-894-1695; 226 1st Ave N; dishes $4-10; open 11am-6pm Mon, 11am-8pm Tues-Thur, 11am-9pm Fri & Sat) serves Cuban-style sandwiches like roast pork on grilled Cuban bread, Spanish grouper and some Caribbean dishes.

The Garden (☎ 727-896-3800; 217 Central Ave; lunch $5-8, dinner mains $9-15; open 11:30am-2am daily), the oldest restaurant in town, makes a good lunchtime pesto pasta and Lebanese sampler plate. Mediterranean-influenced dinner dishes might include grilled lamb chops or wild mushroom pasta. Otherwise, just choose a few dishes from the tapas menu. The Garden also hosts live jazz (see Entertainment following).

Number 9 Bangkok (☎ 727-894-5990; 571 Central Ave; dishes $7-11; open 11am-3pm & 5-10pm Mon-Thur, Fri & Sat 5pm-10pm) has decent Thai food like *pad thai* and yellow curry with beef or shrimp, as well as Japanese food, including sushi. It's smoke-free, too.

Jo Jo's in Citta (☎ 727-894-0075; 200 Central Ave; lunch specials $6, dinner mains $9-15; open 11am-10pm Sun-Thur, 11am-11pm Fri & Sat) has decent Italian dishes like baked pasta and veal *piccata*. Midday subs and pizza are cheaper.

Bertoni Italian Restaurant (☎ 727-822-5503; 16 2nd St N; mains $12-20; open 5-10pm Mon-Sat) offers fancier Italian dishes along with fine service, a nice bar and comfortable surroundings.

Entertainment

The local entertainment scene is less than dynamic. For recorded information on upcoming events, call the **Hotline** (☎ 727-892-5700).

Theater The area's oldest professional theater ensemble, **American Stage** (☎ 727-822-8814; W www.americanstage.org; 211 3rd St S) stages American classics and Broadway shows.

The **Bayfront Center** (☎ 727-892-5767; 400 1st St S) houses the 8400-seat Times Bayfront Arena and the 2000-seat Mahaffey Theater as well as hosting Broadway shows, concerts and some sporting events.

Live Music Also called the Palace of Pleasure, the **Coliseum Ballroom** (☎ 727-892-5202; 535 4th Ave N) opened in 1924 and, over the years, big bands, classical orchestras and rock bands have all played here. It also hosts tennis matches, and in 1985, it made its film debut in *Cocoon* in that incredible ballroom scene. The red oak dance floor is classic. If you're here on a Wednesday, definitely hit the big band Tea Dance sessions, which run from 1pm to 3:30pm. Most events are BYOB.

State Theatre (☎ 727-895-3045; W www .statemedia.com; 687 Central Ave), a restored art deco theater (1927), has live music regularly – from the acoustic stylings of unplugged women to 'old wave' and new bands. Buy your tickets at the bar ($5 to $10) and head upstairs.

Ticketmaster (☎ 813-287-8844) sells tickets with a surcharge to most events.

Bars & Clubs There are several weekly concerts by local and national bands at **Jannus Landing** (☎ 727-896-1244; W www.jannus landing.net; 200 1st Ave N), an outdoor courtyard behind the Bertoni Italian Restaurant (see Places to Eat earlier). It's very casual – shorts, T-shirts and jeans. There is a full cash bar, and all ages are admitted – but you'll be carded if you look under 30 and try to buy alcohol. They also serve burgers, hot dogs and such, catered by Harvey's 4th St Grill. Tickets are generally about $15, and you can get them from the nearby **Detroit Liquor Store** (☎ 727-821-7466; 201 Central Ave).

The 2nd-floor **A Taste for Wine** (☎ 727-895-1623; 241 Central Ave; open 1pm-9pm Tues-Thur, 2pm-midnight Fri & Sat, 2pm-6pm Sun), with a New Orleans–style balcony, is a fun place with wine tastings, wines by the glass, appetizers (unless you *want* to drink on an empty stomach) and a very nice atmosphere.

The Garden, with indoor and outdoor seating and a martini bar, also has live jazz outdoors with the Buster Cooper Jazz Trio every Friday and Saturday from 9pm to 1:30am. On some Thursdays, they have a DJ or live music. See Places to Eat earlier.

Ferg's Sports Bar & Grill (☎ 727-822-4562; 1320 Central Ave; open 11am-2am Mon-Sat, noon-10pm Sun), a friendly neighborhood place with an outdoor bar, really gets hopping before and after gametime.

Central Cigars (☎ 727-898-2442; 273 Central Ave; open 10am-10pm Sun-Thur, 10am-midnight Fri & Sat) carries an enormous selection of cigars (Arturo Fuente, Ous X, Padron, Partagas) as well as a full line of humidors and accessories. Stop into their cigar bar, where you can sink into an overstuffed leather chair, sample smokes, sip port and catch up on all your cigar-related reading.

Spectator Sports

From April through September, **Tropicana Field** (☎ 727-825-3333; **W** www.devilrays .com; 1 Stadium Dr; tickets $2-19) is home to the Tampa Bay Devil Rays, one of major-league baseball's newest expansion teams and also, sadly, one of its worst. But the games are fun anyway. You'll find parking (about $5) all over the place around 10th St and 4th Ave S. The Devil Rays play spring training games at **Florida Power Park** (☎ 727-822-3384; 230 1st St S) in March.

You can take a behind-the-scenes tour of Tropicana Field (adults $5, seniors and children $3) and check out the dugouts, press box, batting tunnels, weight room and field. On nongame days, the 45- to 90-minute tours are given from 10am to 4pm Monday through Friday; on game days, they run from 10am to noon Monday through Friday.

Shopping

Antique stores litter downtown, especially on the north side of Central Ave between 6th and 11th Sts (it's a street waiting to happen, really), and along 4th St. If you're really interested, pick up a good brochure at the Chamber of Commerce. Specifically check out the **Gas Plant Antique Arcade** (☎ 727-895-0368; 1246 Central Ave), with 150 dealers on four floors.

Florida Craftsmen Gallery (☎ 727-821-7391; **W** www.floridacraftsmen.net; 501 Central Ave) is a retail and exhibition space featuring more than 150 statewide artists and craftspeople.

The Arts Center (☎ 727-822-7872; **W** www .theartscenter.org; 719 Central Ave; open 10am-5pm Mon-Sat, noon-4pm Sun), with five galleries, shows paintings, ceramics, printmaking, drawing and mixed media art.

Tyrone Square (☎ 727-345-0126; 66th St & 22nd Ave N), the area's big shopping mall, has 150 retail stores, including a Burdines, Dillard's, Sears, Gap, Borders, Disney Store and Sunglass Hut.

Getting There & Away

Air Although St Petersburg-Clearwater International Airport (☎ 727-453-7800; **W** www .fly2pie.com; Roosevelt Blvd & Hwy 686 in Clearwater) is served by several major carriers, if you're flying into the region, you'll probably land in Tampa; see the Tampa Getting There & Away section earlier in this chapter. If you're in the mood for a quick jaunt to Key West, check flights out of here.

Bus Regular services to and from all over Florida operate from the **Greyhound bus station** (☎ 727-898-1496; 180 9th St N). The trip from St Petersburg to Miami takes six to 10 hours ($35.50/64.50 one way/round-trip); to Orlando takes three to four hours ($15.25/27.25); to Tampa takes a half-hour to 1½ hours ($7.25/11.25).

Pinellas Suncoast Transit Authority (PSTA; ☎ 727-530-9911; **W** www.psta.net; 340 2nd Ave N; open 7am-5:45pm Mon-Sat, 8am-11:30am & 12:30pm-4pm Sun) serves Clearwater and Tarpon Springs from St Petersburg; consult the very good system map available from most Chambers of Commerce. Hourly departures from St Petersburg to St Pete Beach take about an hour on trolley No 35 (fare $1, bills accepted).

Train A continuing rail shuttle-bus link between Tampa and St Petersburg is provided by **Amtrak** (☎ 800-872-7245); it'll drop you at the inconvenient Parkside Mall at the intersection of Hwy 19 and Park Blvd. From there take PSTA bus No 75 (hourly departures) to Madeira Beach, where you catch the Suncoast Beach Trolley north to Sand Key and change to PSTA bus No 80 for Clearwater Beach, or you take the Suncoast Beach Trolley south to St Pete Beach.

Car & Motorcycle Several **car rental** companies have offices at the airport. St Petersburg is 289 miles from Miami and 84 miles from Orlando. From Tampa, the best route is I-275 south, which runs right through downtown St Petersburg and continues across the Sunshine Skyway Bridge; it connects with I-75 and US Hwy 41 (Tamiami Trail) on the south side of Tampa Bay. From Sarasota, take I-75 north to I-275 across the Sunshine Skyway. From Orlando, take I-4 south to I-75, then on to I-275.

To get to Clearwater, take Roosevelt Blvd north to the Bayside (49th St) Bridge and go west on Causeway Blvd.

To get to St Pete Beach, take I-275 to Hwy 682, which connects to the Pinellas County Pkwy and west to the beach, or take Central Ave due west to either the Treasure Island Causeway or turn south on 66th St to the Corey Causeway.

Getting Around

To/From the Airport PSTA bus No 79 connects the airport to downtown. By car to downtown, take Roosevelt Blvd (Hwy 686) south, across the jig on Ulmerton Rd, to I-275 south.

Bus PSTA has a convenient downtown bus station at Williams Park, between 3rd and 4th Sts. They sell daily/weekly/monthly unlimited-ride Go Cards ($3/12/40) and give transit information.

Trolley The excellent **Looper** (☎ 727-821-5166), which you can use as a 30-minute orientation tour since there is narration, is a bargain because it stops at a dozen popular museums, hotels and shops (including The Pier) around downtown. Tickets cost only $1 per ride (50¢ for seniors). The service operates 10am to 5pm Monday through Friday and 11am to 5pm Saturdays and Sundays.

Car & Motorcycle Getting around and parking here is a cinch. Just be sure to have a lot of quarters since you'll be feeding the hungry meters. Consider parking at The Pier and taking the Looper trolley.

ST PETE BEACH
pop 9000

With a great white-sand beach and clear, blue water, St Pete Beach (they officially changed the name from St Petersburg Beach in the early 1990s) makes a great day or overnight trip from St Petersburg. Pass-a-Grille, a more quiet and residential neighborhood with sandy streets and little houses, is at the southernmost tip of St Pete Beach.

See the St Petersburg Getting There & Away section for information on how to get here by bus and car. Excellent PSTA Suncoast Beach Trolleys frequently ply Gulf Blvd, from Pass-a-Grille north to Sand Key, where you can connect with the Clearwater Beach Jolley Trolley.

Orientation & Information
Part of a 30-mile-long string of barrier islands west of St Petersburg, St Pete Beach is on Long Key, about 10 miles west of downtown St Petersburg across the Corey Causeway or the Pinellas County Bayway. The island is long and narrow, and the main (and only) artery is Gulf Blvd (Hwy 699).

The **St Pete Beach Chamber of Commerce** (☎ 727-360-6957; W www.tampabaybeaches .com; 6990 Gulf Blvd; open 9am-5pm Mon-Fri) has tons of pamphlets and coupons and an excellent (free) area beach map.

Change money at **Bank of America** (4105 Gulf Blvd & 7500 Gulf Blvd).

Wash clothes at the **Washboard Laundry** (☎ 727-360-0674; 6350 Gulf Blvd).

Potential bikers should head to **Beach Cyclist** (☎ 727-367-5001; 7517 Blind Pass Blvd), where rentals cost $5 hourly, $20 daily and $50 weekly.

Don CeSar Beach Resort & Spa
This 275-room landmark resort (☎ 727-360-1883, 800-282-1116; W www.doncesar.com; 3400 Gulf Blvd; rooms from summer/winter $209/244) occupies a strategic stretch of prime beachfront – it will probably be the first thing you notice when you pull into St Pete Beach. Built in 1928, this monster of a hotel was a hot spot for F Scott Fitzgerald, Clarence Darrow, Lou Gehrig and Al Capone. In 1942 the enormous pink palace was bought by the US Army and turned into a hospital and convalescent center for army personnel. Stripped of all its splendor, the building was abandoned in 1967 by the Veterans Administration, which had taken it over after the war. It was reopened in 1973, and from 1985 to 1989 it was completely restored. Today, the luxurious resort hotel is complete with a European-style spa, fine dining and an extensive kids' program. They don't make 'em like this anymore. If you want an excuse to loiter, have a drink at the lovely poolside Beachcomber Bar, or rent chairs for $10 in front of the hotel on the beach.

Gulf Beaches Historical Museum
This museum (☎ 727-552-1610; 115 10th Ave at Pass-a-Grille Beach; admission free; open 10am-4pm Thur &-Sat, 1-4pm Sun), about 2 miles south of the Don CeSar hotel, is located in the former Pass-a-Grille Church (1917) – the first to be built on a west coast barrier island. In addition to a large collection of beach photographs and artifacts dating from the early 1800s, the museum has a good selection of old postcards and church memorabilia. Take Gulf Blvd south past the Don CeSar; the road becomes Pass-a-Grille Blvd, which runs into 10th Ave.

Organized Tours
Dolphin Landings Charter Boat Center (☎ 727-367-4488; W www.dolphinlandings .com; 4737 Gulf Blvd) offers several tours, including two-hour daily dolphin-watching excursions ($25 for adults, $15 for kids), four-hour shelling excursions ($35/25) and sunset sails ($25 per person). Prices include free soft drinks (and a cooler, so you can BYO beer); reservations are required.

Places to Stay

KOA St Petersburg/Madeira Beach (☎ 727-392-2233, 800-562-7714; 5400 95th St N; sites without/with hookups $30/39 summer, $40/49 winter, kamping kabins $58-68), set on the Pinellas bike trail north of St Pete Beach, is about 2 miles from Madeira Beach and has a whopping 350 shaded and grassy sites, 60 'kamping kabins,' canoe rentals and a nice pool. From downtown St Petersburg, take I-275 north to 38th Ave N and go west for 5½ miles; take a left onto 66th St, then a right onto Tyrone Blvd, and go 1½ miles to 95th St. Turn right and it's about a half-mile ahead.

Lamara Motel Apartments (☎ 727-360-7521, 800-211-5108; W www.lamara.com; 520 73rd Ave; units summer $44-49, winter $65-75), with a pool and 16 units featuring kitchens, is just west of Gulf Blvd.

Palm Crest Motel (☎ 727-360-9327, 888-558-1247; W www.palmcrest.com; 3848 Gulf Blvd; rooms summer $57-76, winter $85-103) has 18 units with kitchens and a pool.

Travel Lodge of St Pete Beach (☎ 727-367-2711, 800-237-8918; 6300 Gulf Blvd; rooms summer/winter from $80/104) has 200 very nice rooms and an Olympic-sized heated pool. Sound familiar?

The best motel beachside chain is **Howard Johnson** (☎ 727-360-7041, 800-231-1419; 6100 Gulf Blvd; rooms summer/winter $90/115), with 130 contemporary rooms and a large pool on a quiet stretch of beach.

The lovely **Pasa Tiempo B&B** (☎ 727-367-9907; W www.pasa-tiempo.com; 7141 Bay St; rooms & suites $110-150) has eight units (one with a kitchen, one with a private terrace) facing east toward the Intracoastal Waterway. Afternoon wine and cheese are included and the lush, brick-paved courtyard makes a nice respite.

Alden Beach Resort (☎ 727-360-7081, 800-237-2530; W www.aldenbeachresort.com; 5900 Gulf Blvd; units summer $97-179, winter $125-254), a step up from its neighbors, has two pools, tennis courts, a Jacuzzi, bar, barbecue area and good service. The six-story family-owned resort has 143 waterfront rooms and one-bedroom suites.

Places to Eat

Aunt Heidi's Italian Restaurant (☎ 727-367-3448; 6340 Gulf Blvd; lunch $4-7, dinner mains $9-11; open 11am-10pm Mon-Sat, 2pm-10pm Sun) is fine for a quick bite. Hoagies, pizza or baked ziti, anyone?

Ted Peter's Famous Smoked Fish (☎ 727-381-7931; 1350 Pasadena Ave; dishes $10-15; open 11:30am-7:30pm Wed-Mon), on the way to St Pete Beach from St Petersburg, has been smoking fish since the 1950s. It's an institution. Its smoked salmon, mackerel and mullet, straight from the little smokehouse, are succulently fresh. Get takeout for the beach, or head next door where they serve more smoked seafood specialties and patrons drink lots of beer by the fireplace.

Bruno's (☎ 727-367-4420; 432 75th Ave; mains $10-17; open 4pm-10pm Mon-Sat), a decent Northern Italian place, dishes up fettuccine primavera, veal rollatini and chicken cacciatore.

Hurricane's Seafood Restaurant (☎ 727-360-9558; 807 Gulf Way; lunch $8-10, dinner mains $14-20; open 8am-1am daily), in the Pass-a-Grille neighborhood, has been a popular seafood eatery and hangout for locals and visitors since forever. Even though the food's sometimes inconsistent, you can't beat the sunset views. It offers live entertainment Wednesday through Sunday and a happenin' rooftop deck-cum-bar. Gulf Way is on the opposite side of the peninsula from Gulf Blvd and runs parallel to it.

Crabby Bill's (☎ 727-360-8858; 5100 Gulf Blvd; dishes $10-29; open 11:30am-10pm daily), a casual place with picnic tables (or inside dining) and water views, serves all kinds of fried seafood but obviously specializes in crab.

Maritana Grille (☎ 727-360-1882; 3400 Gulf Blvd; mains $27-32; open 5:30pm-10pm daily), serving creative American cuisine with slight Caribbean overtones, is one of the area's better restaurants. Try the pan-seared sea scallops with a lemongrass and ginger risotto.

CLEARWATER BEACH

Despite being overdeveloped and lined with beachfront cookie-cutter hotels, Clearwater Beach draws visitors because of incredible white-sand beaches, a large fishing fleet (read: fresh fish dinners) and its proximity to Tampa and St Petersburg. It also has a great HI/AYH-member hostel and is a prime area for kayaking, shelling, bicycling and broiling yourself on the beach – which just about sums up the local 'tourist attractions.'

Backpackers will appreciate the scale of the island; unlike many Florida towns, it's only 3½ miles long, and it's easy to get around by foot or bicycle.

Orientation & Information

This northernmost barrier island is about 22 miles north of St Pete Beach and 2 miles west of downtown Clearwater (a separate city on the mainland) over the Memorial Causeway (Hwy 60), which to the east becomes Causeway Blvd. From here the road south is S Gulfview Blvd and north is Mandalay Ave, Clearwater Beach's main drag. Pier 60 is right at the roundabout where these three roads meet. From St Petersburg, it's about a half-hour drive or a 1½-hour bus ride.

The **Clearwater Beach Welcome Center** (☎ 727-461-0011; W www.beachchamber.com; open 9am-1 hr before sunset daily) is located at Pier 60. This and the youth hostel (see Places to Stay) are the best sources of local information.

Internet access at the **Clearwater Beach Public Library** (☎ 727-462-6890; 483 Mandalay Ave; open 9am-5pm Mon-Fri) is free, but it's limited to 30 minutes daily.

Wash clothes 24/7 at **Beach Coin** (575 Mandalay Ave), north of the rotary.

Clearwater Marine Aquarium

This nonprofit aquarium (☎ 727-447-0980, 888-239-9414; W www.cmaquarium.org; 249 Windward Passage; adult/child $8.75/6.25; open 9am-5pm Mon-Fri, 9am-4pm Sat, 11am-4pm Sun) is a very nice place dedicated to educating the public and to rescuing and rehabilitating marine animals like dolphins, fish, sea otters and threatened loggerhead and endangered Kemp's ridley turtles. Informative presentations run throughout the day. Inquire about their two-hour Sea Life Safari with an onboard biologist; their dolphin-trainer-for-a-day program; and their trips to monitor loggerhead nests (May through October). Between Clearwater and Clearwater Beach, off Memorial Causeway (Hwy 60), it's conveniently located since the Jolley Trolley stops here.

Pier 60

Sunset celebrations at Pier 60 are equivalent to those at Key West's Mallory Square. Jugglers and magicians perform, musicians play, and craftspeople and artists hawk their wares. Head down to the pier nightly, two hours before and after sunset. The pier is also a good spot for fishing and the beach is popular with college students and watersports concessionaires.

Activities

The bay side of the beach, filled with mangrove islands, is prime for **canoeing**. The calm Gulf waters also promote easy paddling up to the beautiful retreat of Caladesi Island (see Around Clearwater Beach later in this chapter). The hostel has free canoes for its guests (see Places to Stay later).

Just south of the rotary on Coronado Dr and across from the pier, activity booths hawk their services, including **Parasail City** (☎ 727-449-0566), which will get you up for $40 to $60, depending on how high you want to go.

You can **bike** along the beach or the Pinellas Trail, a 47-mile bicycle path (see Around Clearwater Beach later in this chapter); the hostel rents bicycles ($5 daily). Otherwise, head to **Transportation Station** (☎ 727-443-3188; 652 Gulfview Blvd), which rents them for $5 to $8 hourly, or $20 to $26 daily; the higher prices are for mountain bikes and bikes with more gears.

Organized Tours

See Resorts, later, for the historical tour of the Belleview Biltmore hotel.

Located opposite Pier 60, **Dolphin Encounter** (☎ 727-442-7433; W www.dolphin encounter.org) runs very good, frequent, daily, 80-minute dolphin-watching cruises into the Gulf of Mexico ($13 for adults, $7.50 for kids). They also have daily sunset cruises for the same price.

Captain Memo's Pirate Cruise (☎ 727-446-2587; W www.captainmemo.com), opposite Pier 60, operates daily two-hour cruises aboard a replica pirate ship ($28 for adults, $18 for kids). Mom and Dad get blurry eyed with free beer and wine, while the kids go treasure hunting and take home swashbuckler fantasies.

Places to Stay

Hostels A resort-style hostel, **Clearwater Beach International Youth Hostel** (☎ 727-443-1211; W www.clearwaterbeachhostel .com; 606 Bay Esplanade; dorms HI/AYH members/nonmembers nightly $12/13, weekly $75/84, private rooms summer $39-43, winter $47-51) has 38 beds, a swimming pool surrounded by lush gardens, a picnic area and tiki huts. Best of all, it's only a three-minute walk to the beautiful beach. In addition to having kitchen and laundry facilities, the air-conditioned hostel rents linen and offers free canoes (as long as you fork over a $50 deposit). For diversion, there is table tennis, shuffleboard and a barbecue; a nearby recreation center has tennis, basketball and volleyball.

Motels & Hotels The **Patio Motel** (☎ 727-442-1862; W www.patiomotel.com; 15 Somerset St; rooms summer/winter $45/55, apartments summer $46-74, winter $55-88), about a mile north of Pier 60 (at the quiet end of town), has 14 clean units, many of which look right out to the Gulf. There is no pool, but the motel is on the water and has a private beach.

Koli-Bree Motel (☎ 727-461-6223; 440 E Shore Dr; units summer/winter $56/82), with only 10 apartments, is a clean and tidy choice northeast of the rotary. It doesn't have a pool, but it's only three blocks from the beach.

Across from the beach, **Palm Pavilion Inn** (☎ 727-446-6777; W www.palmpavilioninn.com; 18 Bay Esplanade; rooms summer $59-89, winter $87-125) has a pool and 29 units, only a few of which have a kitchen. It's adjacent Grill and Bar is on the beach and has live music most nights. Light sleepers need not apply.

There's a denser concentration of louder, more action-oriented hotels south of the rotary. Chains along the beach include the ultra-pricey **Hilton Clearwater Beach Resort** (☎ 727-461-3222, 800-753-3854; 400 Mandalay Ave; rooms $159-299), with 425 rooms; the more medium-pricey **Holiday Inn Sunspree Resort** (☎ 727-447-9566, 800-465-4329; 715 S Gulfview Blvd; rooms $139-199), with 216 rooms; and the cheaper **Days Inn** (☎ 727-447-8444, 800-329-7466; 100 Coronado Dr; rooms summer/winter $69/110), with 80 rooms.

Resorts The 21-acre **Belleview Biltmore Resort & Spa** (☎ 727-373-3000, 800-237-8947; W www.belleviewbiltmore.com; 25 Belleview Blvd; rooms from $99), off Hwy 60 and Fort Harrison Ave, in Belleair on the mainland, was built in the 1890s by railroad magnate Henry Plant as a retreat for wealthy northeasterners. In the 1950s, the Duke of Windsor, his dogs and possibly Mrs Simpson stayed here. The Duke even wrote part of his memoirs here while dancing with the bandleader's wife and the staff; he was apparently a hit at costume balls. As was, we assume, Lady Thatcher, who also stayed here. It's not exactly a backpacker's hangout: while the pool and opulent spa are certainly charming, the atmosphere is akin to a swanky golf retreat. The best rates are bed and breakfast packages.

If these 300 or so rooms and suites are too rich for your blood, take a tour; there's one daily at 11am for $5. For a mere $10 more,

it'll include a buffet lunch at the hotel restaurant. You'll get to see the tunnels underneath the hotel, a museum and a section devoted to the Army Air Corps, which was stationed here during WWII. Still not striking the right chord? You could always just soak away your troubles at the spa.

Places to Eat
There are plenty of places, but Frenchy's really has a lock on the market; in fact, there are even more Frenchy's outlets than mentioned here.

Computer Port Cafe (☎ 727-441-2667; 432 Poinsettia Ave; open 9am-6pm Sun-Thur, 9am-10pm Fri & Sat) has smoothies, sweets, fast Internet connections, coffee and an open mike night on Saturday (7pm to 10pm). It's a block north of the roundabout.

Frenchy's Original Cafe (☎ 727-446-3607; 41 Baymont St; dishes $5-10; open 11:30am-11pm Sun-Thur, 11:30am-midnight Fri & Sat), 'the original hole in the wall' dating way back to 1981, is a tiny local hangout with picnic benches. Specials include seafood gumbo, smoked fish spread, grouper sandwiches and crabby shrimp sandwiches. It's off Mandalay Ave north of the rotary.

Frenchy's Rockaway Grill on the Beach (☎ 727-446-4844; 7 Rockaway St; dishes $8-14; open 11am-midnight daily), off Mandalay Ave north of the center of town, serves salads, excellent she-crab soup, burgers, seafood and a few Mexican and Jamaican dishes. Alternatively, check out the live music on most nights, pool tables and happy hour (4pm to 7pm).

Entertainment
The beachfront tiki bar at **Shephards** (☎ 727-441-6875; 601 S Gulfview Blvd) has reggae on Saturday and Sunday afternoons. Let's get together and feel alright.

Storman's (☎ 727-571-2202; 2675 Ulmerton Rd), in Largo just south of Clearwater, hosts a Friday night party (5pm to 8pm) with two-for-one drinks, cheap draft beers and a free buffet.

Singles mingle at **Old New York New York** (☎ 727-539-7441; 18573 US Hwy 19) on Friday and Saturday nights.

Getting There & Away
A **Greyhound bus station** (☎ 727-796-7315; 2811 Gulf-to-Bay Blvd) services six buses daily that make the half-hour trip from Tampa to Clearwater ($7/14 one way/round-trip).

From Clearwater, take **PSTA** (☎ 727-530-9911) bus No 60 from the stop across Causeway Blvd westbound to the Park St Bus Depot, and change there to bus No 80 to Clearwater Beach. Buses run every 30 to 60 minutes. For the hostel, get off at the tennis courts at the corner of Mandalay Ave and Bay Esplanade; it's a two-minute walk to the hostel.

From Tampa, take Hwy 60 (Courtney Campbell Causeway) through Clearwater and west out to the beach. From St Petersburg, take Hwy 19 (34th St N) north to Hwy 60 and go west. From St Pete Beach, take Gulf Blvd north.

Getting Around
The red **Jolley Trolley** (☎ 727-445-1200; adult/child or senior $1/50¢) runs around Clearwater Beach and onward to Sand Key. The beach route runs 10am to 10pm daily; pick up maps at the trolley office (483 Mandalay Ave). A second Jolley Trolley runs between the beach and Clearwater's Park St Station during the same time frame.

AROUND CLEARWATER BEACH
Ready for some excellent beaches and great biking?

Heritage Village
Just south of Clearwater in Largo, this 21-acre historical park and open-air museum (☎ 727-582-2123; 11909 125th St; admission free; open 10am-4pm Tues-Sat, 1pm-4pm Sun) has period craft demonstrations and 22 structures. You can visit the county's oldest house, two Victorian houses, a one-room schoolhouse, mercantile store, doctor's office, mill, barn and church. By car or bike (it's about 10 miles), take Alt Hwy 19 south to Ulmerton Rd, turn right, then left on 125th St. From Clearwater Beach, take bus No 80 to Park St Station and then change for bus No 52 or 61 to the stop at Walsingham and 125th St; the entrance is very close by.

Pinellas Trail
This 47-mile paved bicycle trail, built on the abandoned CSX railway bed, runs from St Petersburg to Tarpon Springs. To date, it's the longest urban trail in the country. It's also very smooth – smooth enough for in-line skates or roller skates as well as bicycles. There are lots of stops along the way, with cafés, pubs, bike shops, skate shops, and fast-food places. As it's on the route of the old railway, the corridor cuts through widely var-ied terrain: sometimes you're in the middle of downtown (as in Dunedin), sometimes along waterways, sometimes among orange groves (near Pinellas Park) and sometimes you're riding practically through people's backyards in bedroom communities.

From the Clearwater Beach International Youth Hostel, which rents bikes (see the Clearwater Beach section, earlier in this chapter), head over the causeway and ride north on Fort Harrison Ave then east on Jones St for about three blocks. You'll pick up the southern end of the Clearwater to Tarpon Springs section of the path. It's 13.2 miles from Jones St to Tarpon Ave.

Contact the **Pinellas County Planning Department** (☎ 727-464-4751; W www.co.pinellas.fl.us/mpo) for their free guidebook to the Pinellas Trail, which lists rest stops and local attractions and has a mileage chart.

Sand Key Park & Beach
This 65-acre beach park (☎ 727-464-3347), at the southern end of Clearwater Beach just south of the Clearwater Pass Bridge, is often voted one of the top 20 beaches in the country. The half-mile-long beach is the widest in the area. It's also a great spot for dolphin watching, especially on the channel side, and a pretty good spot for shelling (best at low tide, especially during new and full moons and after storms). The Jolley Trolley (see Getting Around under Clearwater Beach earlier) passes by; otherwise, it's an easy bicycle ride. Be prepared to feed quarters to the parking meters.

Founded in 1971, the **Suncoast Seabird Sanctuary** (☎ 727-391-6211; W www.seabirdsanctuary.org; 18328 Gulf Blvd; admission free; open 9am-sunset daily), south of Indian Shores, is the largest wild-bird hospital in North America (1½ acres). About 40 species of injured birds have found a home here, and at any given time there are usually between 400 to 600 sea and land birds being treated and recuperating. Whenever possible, the birds are released back into the wild. When it's not, their offspring are released. Tours take place at 2pm Wednesdays and Sundays.

Honeymoon & Caladesi Islands
Honeymoon Island State Recreation Area (☎ 727-469-5942; 1 Dunedin Causeway; admission $4 per carload; open 8am-sunset daily) began life as a grand prize in a 1940s contest. Paramount newsreels and *Life* magazine were giving away all-expenses-paid

honeymoons here to newlyweds, who would stay in the 50 or so thatched huts lining the beach. During the war, Honeymoon Island served as a prime R&R site for exhausted war factory workers, and after that the place was never a honeymoon spot again. After a road connecting the island to the mainland was built in 1964, the state bought the land in the early 1970s.

Today the park offers diverse birding, good swimming and great shelling. Coastal plants include mangrove swamps, rare virgin slash pine, strand and salt marshes. There are also nature trails and bird observation areas, as well as a ferry to Caladesi Island. Take Alt Hwy 19 north to the city of Dunedin (pronounced dun-**eden**) and go west on Curlew Rd (Hwy 586) and the Dunedin Causeway, which leads to the island.

Just south of Honeymoon Island, **Caladesi Island State Park** (☎ 727-469-5918; admission free; open 8am-sunset daily) always ranks at the top of national surveys for best natural beaches. It can actually be reached on foot from Clearwater Beach, although it's a 3-mile beach walk – a 1921 hurricane and a 1985 storm filled in the gap between north Clearwater Beach and the island. Perhaps better yet, you can canoe there or take a ferry from Honeymoon Island. In addition to nature trails and an unspoiled, palm-lined 3-mile beach (with rental umbrellas and chairs available), it's nice for picnicking beneath shaded pavilions, swimming and shelling. You'll probably see armadillos, threatened gopher tortoises, raccoons, snakes, turtles, pelicans, ibis, ospreys, cormorants and others. Keep your eyes open and stay light on your feet.

Caladesi Connection (☎ 727-734-5263), at the western end of Curlew Rd (Hwy 586) in Honeymoon Island State Recreation Area, operates hourly weekday ferries to Caladesi. On weekends the 30-minute ferries run on the half-hour, starting at 10am; the last departure from Caladesi is around 4:30pm. The round-trip fare is $7 for adults, $3.50 for children. One note: to manage passengers coming and going, you'll get a card stamped with your return-trip departure time (no more than four hours later). If you want to stay longer, you can, but other folks with that time will be taken first. It's rather like an airline standby.

It's Our Nature (☎ 727-441-2599, 888-535-7448; 🖳 www.itsournature.com) runs guided eco-heritage and bird-watching trips in Caladesi Island State Park and Honeymoon Island State Recreation Area. Fees are $15 to $25, plus the cost of the park fee or boat ride.

TARPON SPRINGS

About 15 miles north of Clearwater, this tidy little tourist trap is touted as an authentic Greek sponging village. But it's more akin to a collection of tourist attractions and touristy restaurants. If you've never been to Crete or don't have a passport, though, you might find it ever-so-slightly appealing. Regardless, after seeing the rest of southwest Florida, Tarpon Springs *is* a fish out of water.

Once upon a time, the city was indeed a sponging center, and attracted the Greek immigrants who made up much of the town's culture from the early 1900s until the sponge died off in the 1940s. After new sponge beds were discovered in the 1980s, the sponge docks are again bustling, though you may find items overpriced and shopkeepers cynical. If you've never tried Greek appetizers, it may be interesting to sample some at the dozens of Greek restaurants and bakeries around the docks. If you've had *baklava* on Rhodes, though, you probably won't hang around long.

The seven-block Tarpon Springs Downtown Historic District, however, is a charming 19th-century area, with brick streets, lots of antique stores and the fabulous **St Nicholas Church**. This Greek Orthodox church, built with 60 tons of Greek marble and featuring Czech stained glass, is the focal point of the annual Epiphany Day celebration on January 6. Before leaving, take a little drive along the riverfront Spring Bayou (off Tarpon Ave west of downtown), where manatees linger and big Victorian estates line the road.

The **Chamber of Commerce** (☎ 727-937-6109; 🖳 www.tarponsprings.com; on the sponge docks; open 8am-5pm Mon-Fri) has more details than you'll ever need. Speaking of which, if you can't get enough, pop in to the free **Spongeorama** museum on the main drag, Dodecanese Blvd.

From Clearwater, Alt Hwy 19 heads straight north to Tarpon Springs.

LONELY PLANET

You already know that Lonely Planet produces more than this one guidebook, but you might not be aware of the other products we have on this region. Here is a selection of titles that you may want to check out as well:

USA
ISBN 1 86450 308 4
US$24.99 • UK£14.99

USA Phrasebook
ISBN 1 86450 182 0
US$6.99 • UK£4.50

Florida
ISBN 1 74059 136 4
US$19.99 • UK£12.99

Miami & the Keys
ISBN 1 74059 183 6
US$16.99 • UK£10.99

New Orleans Condensed
ISBN 1 74059 455 X
US$12.99 • UK£6.99

World Food New Orleans
ISBN 1 86450 110 3
US$13.99 • UK£8.99

Travel Journal
ISBN 1 86450 343 2
US$12.99 • UK£7.99

Available wherever books are sold

Index

Text

Boxed Text

LEGEND

ROUTES

City **Regional**

............Freeway
............Tollway
............Primary Road
............Secondary Road
............Tertiary Road
............Dirt Road

............Pedestrian Mall
............Steps
)=====(............Tunnel
............Trail
●●●●●●● ....Route, Tour
............Path

ROUTE SHIELDS

(80) Interstate Freeway

(2) State Highway

AREAS

↗ ....Beach
............Building
............Campus

............Cemetery
............Forest
⚽ 🏛 ....Garden; Zoo

🏌 ....Golf Course
............Park
............Plaza

TRANSPORTATION

├─┼─●............Train
├─Ⓜ............Metro

┄┄Ɑ┄┄............Bus Route
─ ─ Ɑ ─ ....Ferry

HYDROGRAPHY

............River; Creek
............Canal
............Lake

⊙~.....Spring; Rapids
◐~≈~............Waterfalls
◯ ◯ .... Dry; Salt Lake

BOUNDARIES

■─ ·─·■·─·............International
■─ ·· ─·· ·............State

── ─ ─ ─............County
── ─ ─ ─............Disputed

............Reservation
............Sports Field
⊥ ≈ ...Swamp; Mangrove

POPULATION SYMBOLS

✪ **NATIONAL CAPITAL** ..National Capital
◉ **STATE CAPITAL**............State Capital

● **Large City** ....Large City
● **Medium City** ....Medium City

● **Small City** ....Small City
● **Town; Village** ....Town; Village

MAP SYMBOLS

■............Place to Stay
▼............Place to Eat
●............Point of Interest

🏕............Airfield
✈............Airport
🏛.....Archeological Site; Ruin
💲............Bank
⬛.....Baseball Diamond
↗............Beach
🚴............Bike Trail
🦅............Bird Sanctuary
●............Border Crossing
🚌.........Bus Station; Terminal
🚏............Bus Stop
🏠............Cabin
⛺............Camping
🛶............Canoeing, Kayaking
⬛............Cave

🏢............Church
🎬............Cinema
🏛............Embassy
⛴............Ferry Terminal
🎣............Fishing, Fish Hatchery
⤫............Footbridge
⊛............Garden
⛽............Gas Station
●............Golf Course
✚............Hospital
ℹ............Information
🔲............Internet Access
🔆............Lighthouse
☀............Lookout
⬛............Mine

🏃............Monument
▲............Mountain
🏛............Museum
⬛............Observatory
⬛............Park
🅿............Parking
)(............Pass
⊕............Picnic Area
⬛............Police Station
🅿............Pool
✉............Post Office
⬛............Pub; Bar
⬛............RV Park
⬛............Shelter
⬛............Shopping Mall

⛷............Skiing
✛............Spot Height
⊙............Spring
🏛............Stately Home
⊥............Swamp
🚕............Taxis
☎............Telephone
🎭............Theater
🚻............Toilet - Public
🏃............Trailhead
●............Train Station
🚌............Transportation
●............Waterfall
🍷............Winery
🐾............Zoo

Note: Not all symbols displayed above appear in this book.

LONELY PLANET OFFICES

Australia

Locked Bag 1, Footscray, Victoria 3011
☎ 03 8379 8000 fax 03 8379 8111
email: talk2us@lonelyplanet.com.au

USA

150 Linden St, Oakland, CA 94607
☎ 510 893 8555 TOLL FREE: 800 275 8555
fax 510 893 8572
email: info@lonelyplanet.com

UK

72-82 Rosebery Ave, London, EC1R 4RW
☎ 020 7841 9000 fax 020 7841 9001
email: go@lonelyplanet.co.uk

France

1 rue du Dahomey, 75011 Paris
☎ 01 55 25 33 00 fax 01 55 25 33 01
email: bip@lonelyplanet.fr
www.lonelyplanet.fr

World Wide Web: www.lonelyplanet.com *or* AOL keyword: lp
Lonely Planet Images: www.lonelyplanetimages.com